MICROECONOMICS OF BANKING

MICROECONOMICS OF BANKING

Xavier Freixas

Jean-Charles Rochet

The MIT Press
Cambridge, Massachusetts
London, England

Third printing, 1998

© 1997 Massachusetts Institute of Technology

This book was set in Times Roman by Windfall Software using ZzTEX and was printed and bound in the United States of America.

Library of Congress Cataloging-in-Publication Data

Freixas, Xavier.
    Microeconomics of banking / Xavier Freixas and Jean-Charles
    Rochet.
        p.   cm.
    Includes bibliographical references and index.
    ISBN 0-262-06193-7
    1. Banks and banking.   2. Finance—Mathematical models.
    3. Microeconomics.   4. Information theory in finance.   I. Title.
    HG1601.F74   1997
    332.1—dc21   97-20047
                                                                    CIP

A la Glòria, la Laia i en Pau
 X. F.

A Brigitte pour son courage et son amour
 J. C. R.

Contents

Figures

During the last two decades, the economic theory of banking has entered a process of change that has overturned economists' traditional vision of the banking sector. Before that, banking courses of most doctoral programs in Economics, Business, or Finance focused either on management aspects (with a special emphasis on risk) or on monetary aspects (modeling the whole banking sector as a passive aggregate) and their macroeconomic consequences. Twenty years ago, there was no such thing as a "Microeconomic Theory of Banking," for the simple reason that the Arrow-Debreu general equilibrium model (the standard reference for Microeconomics at that time) was unable to explain the role of banks in the economy.[1]

Since then, a new paradigm has emerged (the "asymmetric information paradigm"), centered around the assumption that different economic agents possess different pieces of information on relevant economic variables, and that agents will use this information for their own profit. This paradigm has proved extremely powerful in many areas of economic analysis. Regarding banking theory, it has been useful in both explaining the role of banks in the economy and pointing out the structural weaknesses of the banking sector (exposition to runs and panics, persistence of rationing on the credit market, solvency problems) that may justify public intervention.

This book provides a guide to this new microeconomic theory of banking. Rather than seek exhaustivity, we have focused on the main issues, providing the necessary tools to understand how they have been modeled. We have selected contributions that we found to be both important and accessible to second-year doctoral students in Economics, Business, or Finance. Unfortunately, our selection also reflects the incomplete state of the art of a fast-growing and fascinating area of literature.

Prerequisites

This book focuses on the theoretical aspects of banking. A preliminary knowledge of the institutional aspects of banking, taught for instance in undergraduate courses on Money and Banking, is therefore useful. Good references are the textbooks of Mishkin (1993) or Garber and Weisbrod (1992). An excellent transition between these textbooks and the theoretical material developed here can be found in Greenbaum and Thakor (1995).

A good knowledge of microeconomic theory (at the level of a first-year graduate course) is also needed: decision theory, general equilibrium theory and its extensions to uncertainty (complete contingent markets) and dynamic contexts, game theory, incentives theory. An excellent reference that covers substantially more material than is needed here is Mas Colell, Whinston, and Green (1995). More specialized knowledge on contract theory (Salanié 1996) or game theory (Fudenberg and Tirole 1991, Gibbons 1992, Kreps 1990, or Myerson 1991) is not needed but can be useful. Similarly, a good knowledge of the basic concepts of modern finance (Capital Asset Pricing Model [CAPM], Option Pricing) is recommended (see, for instance, Huang and Litzenberger 1988 or Ingersoll 1987). Finally, the mathematical tools needed in this book are to be found in undergraduate courses in differential calculus and probability theory. Some knowledge of diffusion processes (in connection with Black-Scholes's option pricing formula) is also useful.

Acknowledgments

Our main debt is the intellectual influence of the principal contributors to the *Microeconomic Theory of Banking,* especially Benjamin Bernanke, Patrick Bolton, Doug Diamond, Douglas Gale, Martin Hellwig, David Pyle, Joe Stiglitz, Jean Tirole, Robert Townsend, and several of their co-authors. We were also influenced by the ideas of Franklin Allen, Ernst Baltensperger, Sudipto Bhattacharya, Arnoud Boot, John Boyd, Pierre André Chiappori, Mathias Dewatripont, Phil Dybvig, Gérard Gennotte, Charles Goodhart, Gary Gorton, Ed Green, Stuart Greenbaum, André Grimaud, Oliver Hart, Bengt Holmström, Jack Kareken, Nobu Kiyotaki, Hayne Leland, Carmen Matutes, Robert Merton, Loretta Mester, John Moore, Rafael Repullo, Tony Santomero, Elu Von Thadden, Anjan Thakor, Xavier Vives, Neil Wallace, David Webb, Oved Yosha, and Marie-Odile Yannelle. Some of them have been very helpful through their remarks and encouragement. We are also grateful to Franklin Allen, Arnoud Boot, Vittoria Cerasi, Gabriella Chiesa, Gerhard Clemenz, Hans Degryse, Antoine Faure-Grimaud, Denis Gromb, Loretta Mester, Bruno Parigi, François Salanié, Elu Von Thadden, and Jean Tirole, who carefully read preliminary versions of this book and helped us with criticism and advice.

The material of this book has been repeatedly taught in Paris (ENSAE), Toulouse (DEA "Marchés et Intermédiaires Financiers"), Barcelona (Universitat Pompeu Fabra), and Philadelphia (Wharton School). We benefited a lot from the remarks of our students. The encouragement and intellectual support of our colleagues in Toulouse (especially Bruno Biais, André Grimaud, Jean-Jacques Laffont, François Salanié, and Jean Tirole) and Barcelona (Thierry Foucault and José Marin) have also been very useful. Finally, we are extremely indebted to Claudine Moisan, who competently typed the (too many) different versions of this book without ever complaining about the sometimes contradictory instructions of the two co-authors.

Outline of the Book

Because of the discouraging fact that banks are useless in the Arrow-Debreu world (see Section 1.2 for a formal proof), our first objective (after providing a general introduction in Chapter 1) will be to understand why financial intermediaries exist. In other words, what are the important features of reality that are overlooked in the Arrow-Debreu model of complete contingent markets? In Chapter 2, we explore the different theories of financial intermediation: transaction costs, liquidity insurance, coalitions of borrowers, and delegated monitoring. The second important aspect that is neglected in the complete contingent market approach is the notion that banks provide costly services to the public (essentially management of loans and deposits), which makes them compete in a context of product differentiation. This is the basis of the Industrial Organization approach to banking, studied in Chapter 3.

Chapter 4 is dedicated to optimal contracting between a lender and a borrower. In Chapter 5 we study the equilibrium of the credit market, with particular attention to the possibility of rationing at equilibrium, a phenomenon that has provoked important discussions among economists.

Chapter 6 is concerned with the macroeconomic consequences of financial imperfections. In Chapter 7 we study individual bank runs and systemic risk, and Chapter 8 is dedicated to the management of risks inside the banking firm. Finally, Chapter 9 is concerned with bank regulation and its economic justifications.

Teaching the Book

According to our experience, the most convenient way to teach the material contained in this book is to split it into two nine-week courses. The first of these courses covers the most accessible material of Chapters 1 through 5. The second course is more advanced and covers Chapters 6 through 9. At the end of most chapters we have provided a set of problems, together with their solutions. These problems not only will allow the students to test their understanding of the material contained in each chapter, but also will introduce students to some advanced material recently published in academic journals.

Notes

1. This disappointing property of the Arrow-Debreu model is explained in Chapter 1.

References

Fudenberg, D., and J. Tirole. 1991. *Game theory.* Cambridge: MIT Press.

Garber, P., and S. Weisbrod. 1992. *The economics of banking, liquidity and money.* Lexington, Mass.: D. C. Heath.

Gibbons, R. 1992. *A primer on game theory.* New York: Wheatsheaf.

Greenbaum, S., and A. Thakor. 1995. *Contemporary financial intermediation.* Fort Worth: Dryden Press.

Huang, C. F., and D. Litzenberger. 1988. *Foundations for financial economics.* Amsterdam: North-Holland.

Ingersoll, J. E. 1987. *Theory of financial decision making.* Savage, Md.: Rowman and Littlefield.

Kreps, D. 1990. *Game theory and economic modelling.* Oxford: Clarendon Press.

Mas Colell, A., M. Whinston, and J. Green. 1995. *Microeconomic theory.* Oxford: Oxford University Press.

Mishkin, F. S. 1993. *The economics of money, banking and financial markets.* New York: Harper Collins.

Myerson, R. 1991. *Game theory, analysis of conflicts.* Cambridge, Mass.: Harvard University Press.

Salanié, B. 1996. *The theory of contracts.* Cambridge, Mass.: MIT Press.

1.1   What Is a Bank, and What Do Banks Do?

As this book will discuss throughout, banking operations may be varied and complex, but a simple, operational definition of a bank is available: *a bank is an institution whose current operations consist in granting loans and receiving deposits from the public.* This is the definition regulators use when they decide whether a financial intermediary (this term will be defined in Chapter 2) has to submit to the prevailing prudential regulations for banks. This legal definition has the merit of insisting on the core activities of banks, namely deposits and loans. Note that every word of it is important :

• The word "current" is important because most industrial or commercial firms occasionally lend money to their customers (or borrow from their suppliers).[1]

• The fact that both loans *and* deposits are offered is important because it is the combination of lending and borrowing that is typical of commercial banks. Banks finance a significant fraction of their loans through the deposits of the public. As will be discussed later, this is the main explanation for the fragility of the banking sector and the justification for banking regulation. Some economists predict that commercial banks offering both loans and deposits will someday disappear in favor of two types of specialized institutions,[2] on the one hand "narrow" banks or mutual funds, which invest the deposits of the public in traded securities, and on the other hand finance companies or credit institutions, which finance loans by issuing debt or equity.

• Finally, the term "public" emphasizes that banks provide unique services (liquidity and means of payment) to the general public. However, the public is not, in contrast with professional investors, armed to assess the safety and soundness of financial institutions (i.e., to assess whether individuals' interests are well preserved by banks). Moreover, in the current situation, a public good (access to a safe and efficient payment system) is provided by private institutions (commercial banks). These two reasons (protection of depositors and the safety and efficiency of the payment system) have traditionally justified public intervention in banking activities.

As is true with any other institution, the existence of banks is justified by the role they play in the process of resource allocation, and more specifically in the allocation of capital. As Merton (1993, 20) states, "A well developed smoothly functioning financial system facilitates the efficient life-cycle allocation of household consumption and the efficient allocation of physical capital to its most productive use in the business sector." For centuries, the economic functions of the financial system were essentially performed by banks alone. These functions are sufficiently stable to apply generically to any financial system, from Italy's Renaissance to today's world. Nevertheless, financial markets have evolved, and financial innovations have emerged at a spectacular rate in recent years. In addition, the development of security markets has led to a functional differentiation, with financial markets providing some of the services financial intermediaries used to offer exclusively. Thus, for example, it is as simple today for a firm involved in international trade to hedge exchange rate risk through a futures market as through a bank contract. Prior to the development of futures markets, one would have tended to think that this was a function characteristic of banks' activity.

In order to provide a better understanding of how financial intermediation improves resource allocation, it is necessary to examine what functions banks perform. Whereas twenty years ago these functions would have been grouped under the general heading of "lowering transaction costs," today this type of activity would be identified with only a fraction of what banks are supposed to do. Contemporary banking theory classifies banking functions into four main categories:

1. Offering access to a payment system

2. Transforming assets

3. Managing risk

4. Processing information and monitoring borrowers

This, of course, does not mean that every bank has to perform each of these functions. Universal banks will do this, but specialized banks need not. In view of this classification, the definition of banks as the institutions whose current operations consist in making loans and supplying deposits may seem oversimplified. Therefore, to illustrate the proposed classification, the following subsections will examine how banks perform each of these functions.

1.1.1 Liquidity and Payment Services

In a world without transaction costs, like in the standard Arrow-Debreu paradigm, there would be no need for money. However, as soon as one takes into account the existence of frictions in trading operations, it becomes more efficient to exchange goods and services for money, rather than for other goods and services, like in barter operations.[3] The form taken by money quickly evolved from commodity money (a system in which the medium of exchange is itself a useful commodity) to fiat money (a system in which the medium of exchange is intrinsically useless, but its value is guaranteed by some institution, and therefore it is accepted as a means of payment).[4] Historically, banks played two different parts in the management of fiat money: money change (i.e., exchange between different currencies issued by distinct institutions) and provision of payment services. These payment services cover both the management of clients' accounts and the "finality" of payments, i.e., the guarantee by the bank that the debt of the "payor" (who has received the goods or services involved in the transaction) has been settled to the "payee" through a transfer of money.

Money Changing

Historically, the first activity of banks was money changing. This is illustrated by the etymology of the word: the Greek word for bank (*trapeza*) designates the balance that early money changers used to weigh coins in order to determine the exact quantity of precious metal the coins contained.[5] The Italian word for bank (*banco*) designates the bench on which the money changers placed their precious coins. Clearly, the difference in liquidity between currencies (for instance, national and foreign) was so important that banks had an obvious role to play in the supply of money-changing services.

The second historical activity of banks, namely management of deposits, is related to money changing. Early deposit banks were fairly primitive because of the necessity for both the payee (i.e., the deposit bank) and the payor to meet with a notary.[6] Most of the time these deposits had a negative return because they were kept in vaults, rather than invested in productive activities. If depositors considered it advantageous to exchange coins for a less liquid form of money it was mainly because of the advantages of safekeeping, which reduced the risk of loss or robbery. For safekeeping to develop, two conditions had to be fulfilled: increasing returns to scale in the safekeeping technology and incentives for the agent in charge of the deposit (either through the contract offered or simply through monitoring) not to invest it unduly in some risky venture.

Thus, initially, these deposits were not supposed to be lent. Therefore deposit banks were not supposed to be lending banks, and presumably the confidence of depositors depended on this information being public and credible. This means that deposit banks tried to build a reputation of being riskless.[7]

Apart from safekeeping services, the quality of coins was also an issue, because coins differed in their composition of precious metals and the governments required the banks to make payments in good money (regulation already). This issue had implications on the return paid on deposits. As Kindleberger (1993, 48) puts it, "The convenience of a deposit at a bank—safety of the money and the assurance that one will receive money of satisfactory quality—meant that bank money went to a premium over currency, which varied from zero, or even small negative amounts when the safety of the Bank was in question, to 9 to 10 percent. . . . " Still, once the coins themselves became of homogeneous quality, deposits lost this attractive feature of being convertible into "good money." However, because deposits were uninsured, the improvement in efficiency obtained by having a uniform value for coins (supposedly a decrease in transaction costs), with coins and bills exchanging at their nominal value, did not necessarily apply to deposits. This point was later considered of critical importance during the free banking episodes discussed in Chapter 9.

Payment Services

Species proved to be inadequate for making large payments, especially at a distance, because of the costs and risks involved in their transportation. Large cash imbalances between merchants were frequent during commercial fairs, and banks played an important part in clearing merchants' positions. Clearing activities became especially important in the United States and Europe at the end of the nineteenth century, creating the notion of payment systems, which are networks that facilitate the transfer of funds between the bank accounts of economic agents. The safety and efficiency of these payment systems has become a fundamental concern for governments and central banks, especially since the deregulation and internationalization of financial markets, which have entailed a large increase in interbank payments, both nationally and internationally.[8]

1.1.2 Asset Transformation

There are three types of asset transformation: convenience of denomination, quality transformation, and maturity transformation. *Convenience of denomination* means that the bank chooses the unit size (denomination) of its products (deposits and loans) in a way that is convenient for its clients. It is usually seen as one of the main justifications of financial intermediation. A typical example is that of small depositors facing large investors willing to borrow indivisible amounts. More generally, as Gurley and Shaw (1960) argued in their early contribution, financial intermediaries are justified as providing the missing link between the financial products that firms want to issue and the ones desired by the investors. Banks then simply play the role of intermediaries by collecting the small deposits and investing the proceeds into large loans, which, in this context, could even be riskless.

Quality transformation occurs when by issuing a claim in its own name, a bank is offering better risk-return characteristics than by selling (or securitizing) a portfolio of loans. This may occur when there are indivisibilities in the investment, in which case a small investor cannot diversify its portfolio. It may also occur in an asymmetric information situation, when banks have better information than depositors. In such a situation, quality transformation would be on the border between asset transformation and the fourth function of banks, that is, information processing.

Finally, modern banks can be seen as providing the transformation of securities with short maturities, offered to depositors, into the securities with long maturities that borrowers desire. This *maturity transformation* function necessarily implies a risk, since the banks' assets will be illiquid, given the depositors' claims. Nevertheless, interbank lending and derivative financial instruments (swaps, futures) offer possibilities to limit this risk.

To clarify the distinction between the different functions exerted by banks, it may be worth emphasizing that the three types of asset transformation that we are considering occur even in the absence of credit risk on the loans granted by the bank. A pawnbroker, a bank investing only in repos,[9] and a bank making only loans to the government already perform the three transformation functions we have mentioned: convenience of denomination and quality and maturity transformation.

1.1.3 Managing Risk

Usually, bank management textbooks define three sources of risks affecting banks: credit risk, interest rate risk, and liquidity risk. This is a helpful distinction from an operational viewpoint, but from this book's perspective it is worth mentioning also the risks of off-balance-sheet operations which have been soaring during the last two decades.[10] The following subsections briefly sketch a historical perspective of the management of these different risks by banks. Chapter 8 offers a formal analysis of risk management in banks.

Estimating Risk on Bank Loans

When the first bank loans spread in Florence, Siena, and Lucca, and later in Venice and Genoa, lending was limited to financing the harvest that could be seen in the fields and appraised. However, financing wars soon became primary banking activities.[11] Still, bankers tried to make their loans secure, either through collateral (jewels), through the assignment of rights (excise tax), or generally through a city (which could be sued in case of default, whereas kings could not be).

The riskiness of these loans seems to have increased through time. When a bank arranges a fully collateralized loan, its activity is not intrinsically different from that of a pawnbroker. On the contrary, when the loans made by a bank are risky, the necessary contracts will be much more elaborate, since issues related to risk aversion and moral hazard come into play.

The change in the acceptable riskiness of bank loans can be traced back to the origins of investment banking. Investment banking was both a different type of institution and a different concept from traditional credit activity. In continental Europe, the practice developed in the nineteenth century, with the Société Générale de Belgique or the Caisse Générale du Commerce et de l'Industrie (founded by Laffite in France). It introduced a different philosophy of banking, since it involved advancing money to industry rather than being a simple lender and getting good guarantees. This implied making more risky investments and, in particular, buying stocks.[12] This appraisal of risk and correlative estimation of the risk return on a bank loan is one of the main functions of modern banking.

Managing Interest Rate and Liquidity Risk

The asset transformation function of banks also has implications in their management of risks. Indeed, when transforming maturities or when issuing liquid deposits guaranteed by illiquid—even if riskless—loans, a bank takes a risk. This is because the cost of funds—which depends on the short-term interest rates—may rise above the interest income, determined by the (fixed) interest rates of the loans granted by the bank. Even if no interest is paid on deposits, the bank may face unexpected withdrawals, which will force it to seek more expensive sources of funds. As a consequence the bank will have to manage the total risk of its portfolio, both interest rate risk (due to the difference in maturity) and liquidity risk (due to the difference in the marketability of the claims issued and that of the claims held). It is interesting to note that although interest rate risk has always existed, the management of interest rate risks has been introduced only recently in standard bank management practice. The reason for this change could presumably be the increase in the volatility of interest rates after the end of the Bretton-Woods fixed exchange system.

Off-Balance-Sheet Operations

In the 1980s, competition from financial markets made it necessary for banks to shift to more value-added products, which were better adapted to the needs of customers. To do so, banks offered more sophisticated liquidity management techniques, such as loan commitments, credit lines, and guarantees.[13] They also developed swaps and hedging transactions, and underwrote securities. From an accounting viewpoint, none of these operations corresponds to a genuine liability (or asset) for the bank, but only to a random cash flow. This is why they have been classified as "off-balance-sheet operations."

The factors that have fostered the growth of off-balance-sheet operations have different natures. Some are related to the banks' desire to increase their fee income and to decrease their leverage; others are aimed at escaping regulation and taxes. Still, the very development of these services shows that firms have a demand for more sophisticated, custom-made financial engineering.

Clearly, if banks have developed a know-how in managing risks, it is only natural that they buy and sell risky assets, whether or not they hold these assets on their balance sheets. Depending on the risk–return trade-off observed for these assets, banks may want to hedge their risk (that is, behave as someone who buys insurance) or, on the contrary, they may be willing to take a risk (and take the position of someone who sells insurance). Given the fact that a bank's failure may have important externalities (see Chapters 7 and 9), banking regulators must carefully monitor off-balance-sheet operations.

1.1.4   Monitoring and Information Processing

As will be discussed later, it is reasonable to assume that banks have a specific part to play in managing some of the problems resulting from imperfect information on borrowers. Banks may invest in an informational technology that allows them to screen the different demands for loans they are confronted with and to monitor the projects, thus limiting the risk that the borrower may implement a project different from the one agreed upon initially.[14] According to Mayer (1988), this monitoring activity implies that firms and financial intermediaries develop long-term relationships, thus mitigating the effects of moral hazard.

This is clearly one of the main differences between bank lending and issuing securities in the financial markets. It implies that whereas bond prices reflect market information, the value of a bank loan results from this long-term relationship and is a priori unknown, both to the market and to the regulator.[15] In this sense we may say that bank loans are "opaque" (Merton 1992).

1.1.5   The Role of Banks in the Resource Allocation Process

Banks exert a fundamental influence on capital allocation, risk sharing, and economic growth (see Hellwig 1991). Gerschenkron (1962), in one of the most important theses on economic history, holds this influence to have been of capital importance. Gerschenkron's position regarding the role of banks in economic growth and development has led to a continuing debate (Edwards and Ogilvie 1995). The importance of the historical impact of financial institutions on economic performance is still far from being well established. From a theoretical standpoint, the idea of "scarcity of funds" (which is difficult to capture in a general equilibrium model) could be useful in the study of economic development: underdeveloped economies with a low level of financial intermediation and small, illiquid financial markets may be unable to channel savings efficiently. Indeed, "large projects" that are essential to development, such as infrastructure financing, could be seen as unprofitable because of the associated risk premia. This role of financial markets in economic development has now begun to be studied from a theoretical point of view, following the contribution of Greenwood and Jovanovic (1990).

Simultaneously, the fact that more bank-oriented countries such as Japan and Germany have experienced higher rates of growth has motivated additional research on the economic role of banks (Mayer 1988; Allen and Gale 1995a).

For instance, Allen and Gale (1995b) closely examine the differences between the financial markets in Germany and in the United States.[16] They draw from this examination an innovative and stimulating view: although the existence of more sophisticated financial instruments contributes to financial welfare (because it allows the agents to hedge their risks), the existence of financial intermediaries smoothes the shocks affecting consumption. Germany's financial system would therefore have the advantage of allowing for better intertemporal risk sharing. In addition, Germany's intermediation has the advantage of reducing the volatility of the returns that consumers obtain on their investments. Finally, the fact that the market for corporate control collapses when stock markets are thin could be made up for by the role of banks as delegated monitors holding equity and exercising their voting rights. Allen and Gale (1995) present a theoretical example of an economy in which the incompleteness of financial markets leads to underinvestment in reserves, whereas optimality requires the holding of large reserves in order to smooth asset returns over time. They show that a long-lived intermediary may be able to implement the optimum. Hence the choice between financial institutions is not straightforward and the functions of financial intermediaries must be examined with caution.

To summarize, *banks have an important function in the economy because of the demand for different monies; for divisible, low-risk, short-term liabilities; for indivisible, risky, long-term capital; and for project monitoring.* These issues are, of course, central to this book: the book will study in detail the different theoretical contributions that have addressed these questions. But first a preliminary issue must be discussed: why a model of banking cannot be developed that builds on standard microeconomic theory, as, for instance, Fama (1980) does.

1.2   Banking in General Equilibrium Theory

In order to explain the earlier statement that a microeconomic theory of banks could not exist before the foundations of the economics of information were laid (in the early 1970s), this section will present a simple general equilibrium model à la Arrow-Debreu, which will include a banking sector. To put things as simply as possible, the model will use a deterministic framework, although uncertainty could be introduced without any substantial change in the results, under the assumption of complete financial markets (Arrow 1953).

The financial decisions of economic agents in this simple model are represented by the following familiar diagram in which notations are introduced. Each type of agent is denoted by a particular subscript: f for firms, h for households, and b for banks. For simplicity, the public sector (government and central bank) will not be introduced. A more complete diagram is presented in Chapter 3.

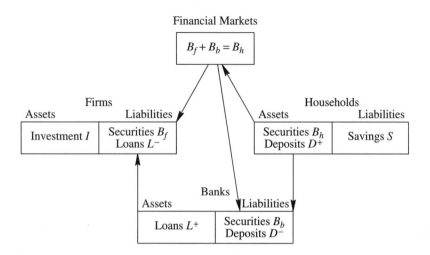

For simplicity again, consider a two period model ($t = 1, 2$) with a unique physical good, initially owned by the consumers. Some of it will be consumed at date 1, the rest being invested by the firms to produce consumption at date 2. All agents behave competitively. To simplify notations, the model assumes a representative firm, a representative consumer, and a representative bank. The superscript $+$ represents a supply, and the superscript $-$ a demand.

1.2.1   The Consumer

The consumer chooses her consumption profile (C_1, C_2), and the allocation of her savings S between bank deposits D^+ and securities B_h, in a way that maximize her utility function u under her budget constraints:

$$\max u(C_1, C_2)$$

$$\mathcal{P}_h \quad C_1 + B_h + D^+ = \omega_1, \tag{1.1}$$

$$C_2 = \pi_f + \pi_b + (1 + r)B_h + (1 + r_D)D^+ \tag{1.2}$$

where ω_1 denotes her initial endowment of the consumption good, π_f and π_b represent respectively the profits of the firm and of the bank (distributed to the consumer-stockholder at $t = 2$), and r and r_D are the interest rates paid by securities and deposits. Since in this simplistic world securities and bank deposits are perfect substitutes, it is clear that the consumer's program ($\mathcal{P}_h$) has an interior solution only when these interest rates are equal:

$$r = r_D. \tag{1.3}$$

1.2.2   The Firm

The firm chooses its investment level I and its financing (through bank credit L and issuance of securities B_f) in a way that maximizes its profit:

$$\max \pi_f$$

$$\mathscr{P}_f \quad \pi_f = f(I) - (1+r)B_f - (1+r_L)L^- \tag{1.4}$$

$$I = B_f + L^- \tag{1.5}$$

where f denotes the production function of the representative firm and r_L is the interest rate on bank loans. Again, since bank loans and securities are here perfect substitutes, $\mathscr{P}_f$ has an interior solution only when

$$r = r_L. \tag{1.6}$$

1.2.3   The Bank

The bank chooses its supply of loans L^+, its demand for deposits D^-, and the issuance of securities B_b in a way that maximizes its profit:[17]

$$\max \pi_b$$

$$\mathscr{P}_b \quad \pi_b = r_L L^+ - r B_b - r_D D^- \tag{1.7}$$

$$L^+ = B_b + D^-. \tag{1.8}$$

1.2.4   General Equilibrium

General equilibrium is characterized by a vector of interest rates (r, r_L, r_D) and three vectors of demand and supply levels—(C_1, C_2, B_h, D^+) for the consumer, (I, B_f, L^-) for the firm, and (L^+, B_b, D^-) for the bank—such that

• each agent behaves optimally (i.e., his or her decisions solve $\mathscr{P}_h$, $\mathscr{P}_f$, or $\mathscr{P}_b$ respectively).

• each market clears

$I = S$ (good market)

$D^+ = D^-$ (deposit market)

$L^+ = L^-$ (credit market)

$B_h = B_f + B_b$ (financial market).

From previous remarks (relations 1.3 and 1.6), it is clear that the only possible equilibrium is such that all interest rates are equal:

$$r = r_L = r_D. \tag{1.9}$$

In that case, it is obvious from $\mathscr{P}_b$ that banks necessarily make a zero profit at equilibrium. Moreover, their decisions have no impact on other agents, since households are completely indifferent as to the distinctions between deposits and securities, and similarly firms are completely indifferent as to bank credit versus securities. This is the analogue of the Modigliani-Miller theorem (see, for instance, Hagen 1976).

Result 1.1   If firms and households have unrestricted access to perfect financial markets, then at the competitive equilibrium

- banks make a zero profit.

- the size and composition of banks' balance sheet have no impact on other economic agents.

This rather disappointing result extends easily to the case of uncertainty, provided financial markets are complete. Indeed, for each future state of the world s ($s \in \Omega$) one can determine the price p_s of the contingent claim that pays one unit of account in state s and nothing otherwise. Now suppose a bank issues (or buys) a security j (interpreted as a deposit or a loan) characterized by the array x_s^j ($s \in \Omega$) of its payoffs in all future states of the world. By the absence of arbitrage opportunities, the price of security j has to be

$$Z^j = \sum_{s \in \Omega} p_s x_s^j.$$

An immediate consequence is that all banks still make a zero profit, independently of the volume and characteristics of the securities they buy and sell. This explains why the general equilibrium model with complete financial markets *cannot* be used for studying the banking sector.

Consequently, the Arrow-Debreu paradigm leads to a world in which banks are redundant institutions and does not account for the complexities of the banking industry. There are basically two (complementary) ways out of this disappointing result:

- The incomplete information paradigm, which explains why financial markets *cannot* be complete and shows why banks (and more generally financial intermediaries) exist. This is the topic of Chapter 2.

- The industrial organization approach to banking, which considers that banks essentially offer *services* to their customers (depositors and borrowers), and that financial transactions are only the visible counterpart to these services. As a consequence, the cost of providing these services has to be introduced, as well as some degree of product differentiation. This approach is studied in Chapter 3.

Notes

1. Even if it is recurrent, this lending activity, called "trade credit," is only complementary to the core activity of these firms. For recent theoretical analyses of trade credit, see Biais and Gollier (1996) and Kiyotaki and Moore (1996).

2. Consider for example the title of a recent article by Gorton and Pennacchi (1993): "Money market funds and finance companies: Are they the banks of the future?"

3. The main reason is the famous argument of "double coincidence of wants" between traders.

4. For a theoretical analysis of commodity money, see Kiyotaki and Wright (1989, 1991).

5. Actually, a recent book by Cohen (1992) shows that in ancient Greece, banks were already performing complex operations, such as transformation of deposits into loans. We thank Elu Von Thadden for indicating this reference to us.

6. There is a strong tendency to locate the origins of banking in the deposit activities of goldsmiths in England in the seventeenth century. Their capacity to deal with goldware and silverware made them develop into bankers. This view clearly identified banking with deposit banking. Still, as Kindleberger puts it, "the scriveners seem to have preceded the goldsmith as ones who accepted deposits. Needed to write out letters and contracts in a time of illiteracy, the scrivener became a skilled adviser, middleman, broker, and then lender who accepted deposits" (Kindleberger, 1993, 51).

7. Nevertheless, the need for the cities or the government to obtain cash could be such that the deposit bank could be forced to give credit to the city or to the king, as happened for the Taula de Canvi in Valencia and the Bank of Amsterdam. Also, Charles I confiscated the gold and silver that had been deposited in the Tower of London in 1640, and returned it only after obtaining a loan.

8. For an economic analysis of the risks involved in large payment interbank systems, see Rochet and Tirole (1996).

9. A repurchase agreement (repo) is a financial contract very similar to a fully collateralized short-term loan, the principal of which is fully guaranteed by a portfolio of securities (100 percent collateralization). For legal and accounting reasons, it is presented as if the borrower had sold its securities to the lender, with a promise to buy them back later under specified conditions.

10. Note however that these risks could be traced back to the three classical forms of banking risks.

11. This type of activity resulted in bankruptcy for some Italian bankers, such as the Bardi, the Peruzzi, and the Ricciardi (see, for instance, Kindleberger 1993).

12. It is interesting to note that, theoretically, an estimate of the risk return characteristics of an investment could be made not only for bank loans but also for any other type of investment, and particularly for stocks. Some countries have imposed regulations, such as the Glass-Steagall Act in the United States, that draw a dividing line between the type of assets a bank is allowed to hold and those it is not.

13. Since this book will not go into the details of these operations, the reader is referred to Greenbaum and Thakor (1995) for definitions and an analysis.

14. Screening and monitoring of projects can be traced back to the origins of banking, when bill traders identified the signature of merchants, and gave credit knowing the bills' quality, or even bought the bills directly (as in today's factoring activities).

15. Recent empirical contributions (e.g., James 1987) have emphasized this specific role of banks.

16. For another theoretical analysis of different banking systems, see Hauswald (1995).

17. Notice that, as for the firm, B_b and B_f are considered as bonds (with a given rate of return r) rather than equity. Additional profit (net of financial expenses) is assumed to remunerate the property rights on technology.

References

Allen, F., and D. Gale. 1994. *Financial innovation and risk sharing.* Cambridge: MIT Press.

———. 1995a. Financial markets, intermediaries and intertemporal smoothing. Discussion paper 5-95, Rodney L. White Center for Financial Research, Wharton School. Philadelphia.

———. 1995b. A welfare comparison of intermediaries in Germany and the US. *European Economic Review.* 39(2):179–209.

Arrow, K. 1953. Le rôle des valeurs boursières pour la répartition la meilleure des risques. In *Cahiers du Séminaire d'Econométrie.* Paris.

Biais, B., and C. Gollier. 1996. Why do firms use trade credit: A signaling approach. Discussion paper, GREMAQ-IDEI, Toulouse University.

Cohen, D. 1992. *Athenian economy and society: A banking perspective.* Princeton, N.J.: Princeton University Press.

Debreu, G. 1987. *Theory of value: An axiomatic analysis of economic equilibrium.* Cowles Foundation Monograph, no. 17. New Haven.

Edwards, J., and S. Ogilvie. 1995. Universal banks and German industrialization: A reappraisal. Working paper no. 1171, Centre for Economic Policy Research, London.

Fama, E. 1980. Banking in the theory of finance. *Journal of Monetary Economics* 6(1):39–57.

Gerschenkron, A. 1962. *Economic backwardness in theoretical perspective.* Cambridge: Harvard University Press.

Gorton, G., and G. Pennacchi. 1993. Money market funds and finance companies: Are they the banks of the future? In *Structural change in banking*, edited by M. Klausner and L. White. New York: Irwin.

Greenbaum, S., and A. V. Thakor. 1995. *Contemporary financial intermediation.* Fort Worth: Dryden Press.

Greenwood, J., and B. Jovanovic. 1990. Financial development, growth and the distribution of income. *Journal of Political Economy* 98(5):1076–107.

Gurley, J., and E. Shaw. 1960. *Money in the theory of finance.* Washington: Brookings Institution.

Hagen, K. P. 1976. Default risk, homemade leverage, and the Modigliani-Miller theorem: A note. *American Economic Review* 66(1):199–203.

Hauswald, R. 1995. Financial contracting, reorganization and mixed finance: A theory of banking systems. University of Maryland, College Park. Mimeograph.

Hellwig, M. 1991. Banking, financial intermediation and corporate finance. In *European financial integration,* edited by A. Giovannini and C. Mayer. Cambridge: Cambridge University Press.

James, C. 1987. Some evidence on the uniqueness of bank loans. *Journal of Financial Economics* 19(2):217–35.

Kindleberger, C. P. 1993. *A financial history of Western Europe.* Oxford: Oxford University Press.

Kiyotaki, N., and J. Moore. 1996. Credit-cycles. FMG discussion paper, London School of Economics.

Kiyotaki, N., and R. Wright. 1989. On money as a medium of exchange. *Journal of Political Economy* 97:927–54.

———. 1991. A contribution to the pure theory of money. *Journal of Economic Theory* 53(2):215–35.

Mayer, C. 1988. New issues in corporate finance. *European Economic Review* 32(5):1167–83.

Merton, R. C. 1993. Operation and regulation in financial intermediation: A functional perspective. In *Operation and regulation of financial markets,* edited by P. Englund. Stockholm: Economic Council.

Rochet, J. C., and J. Tirole. 1996. Interbank lending and systemic risk. *Journal of Money, Credit, and Banking* 28(4):733–62.

Although this book is specifically focused on banks, this chapter will adopt a broader perspective and study *financial intermediaries* (FIs) in general. Even if this term is widely used (both inside and outside the academic world), the chapter will first establish a precise definition of an FI.

The first definition of an FI that may come to mind is that of *an economic agent who specializes in the activities of buying and selling (at the same time) financial contracts and securities.* This is analogous to the notion of *intermediary* (or retailer) in the theory of Industrial Organization as an agent who buys certain goods or services from producers and sells them to final consumers. The justification given by the theory of Industrial Organization to the existence of such intermediaries is the presence of *frictions* in transaction technologies (for instance, transportation costs). *Brokers* and *dealers,* operating on financial markets, are a clear example of such intermediaries in the financial sector. As will be discussed later, this paradigm can also provide a (simplistic) description of banking activities. Roughly speaking, banks can be seen as retailers of financial securities: they buy the securities issued by borrowers (i.e., they grant loans) and they sell them to lenders (i.e., they collect deposits).

However, banking activities are in general more complex, for at least two reasons:

1. Banks usually deal (at least partially) with financial *contracts* (loans and deposits), which cannot be easily resold (marketed), as opposed to financial *securities* (stocks and bonds), which are *anonymous* (in the sense that the identity of their holder is irrelevant) and thus easily *marketable.* Therefore, banks typically must *hold* these contracts in their balance sheets until the contracts expire.[1] (This is also true to some extent for insurance companies.)

2. The characteristics of the contracts or securities issued by firms (borrowers) are usually different from those of the contracts or securities desired by investors (depositors).

Therefore, as first argued by Gurley and Shaw (1960), and more recently by Benston and Smith (1976) and Fama (1980), banks (and also mutual funds and insurance companies) are there to *transform* financial contracts and securities. Of course, in the ideal world of frictionless and complete financial markets, both investors and borrowers would be able to diversify perfectly and obtain optimal risk sharing. But as soon as one introduces even small indivisibilities and nonconvexities in transaction technologies, this perfect diversification is no longer feasible and FIs are needed. This transaction costs approach (presented in Section 2.1) does not in fact contradict the assumption of (approximately) complete markets. For instance, as argued by Hellwig (1991), the vision offered by Malinvaud (1972, 1973) of the activity of insurance companies is that of mutualizing idiosyncratic risks so that insured persons obtain approximately the same diversification as they would under complete markets.[2] A similar description could be given of mutual funds' activity. FIs can therefore be seen as *coalitions* (mutuals) of individual lenders or borrowers who exploit economies of scale or economies of scope in the transaction technology. As a result of the activities of FIs, individuals obtain almost perfect diversification. The ownership structure of real FIs is another problem: the distinction between "genuine" mutuals owned and managed by their customers and stockholder-owned FIs can be analyzed within the general context of corporate governance (see Bhattacharya and Thakor 1993 and the references therein for a discussion of this issue in the specific context of FIs).

Of course this approach is not completely satisfactory, since these transaction costs are given exogenously. The nature of these costs must be explored. Even if physical and technological costs may have played a historical role in the emergence of FIs, the progress experienced recently in telecommunications and computers, as well as the related development of sophisticated financial instruments, implies that FIs would be bound to disappear if another, more fundamental, form of transaction costs were not present. Therefore, the subject of *informational asymmetries*—whether ex-ante (adverse selection), interim (moral hazard), or ex-post (costly state verification)—is further explored in several sections of this book. These asymmetries generate market imperfections that can be seen as specific forms of transaction costs. These costs can be partially overcome by institutions that this discussion will interpret as FIs.

Section 2.2 will study how the role of banks in providing liquidity insurance is related to these informational asymmetries. Following Diamond and Dybvig (1983), the discussion will consider banks as "pools of liquidity" or "coalitions of depositors" that provide households with insurance against idiosyncratic liquidity shocks, supposed to be privately observed.[3]

Section 2.3 will explore another interpretation of FIs as information sharing coalitions. For example, when individual borrowers (firms) have private information on the characteristics of the projects they wish to finance, the competitive equilibrium can be inefficient (as discussed in Akerlof 1970). As shown by Leland and Pyle (1977), this problem can be partially overcome if firms can use their level of retained equity as a *signal* to investors (an adaptation to the theory developed by Spence 1973 for the job market). However, this signal has a cost, since firms cannot obtain perfect risk sharing.[4] This cost—the informational cost of capital—can be seen as an *informational transaction cost*. Elaborating on Leland and Pyle (1977), Diamond (1984) and Ramakrishnan and Thakor (1984) were able to show that, under certain conditions, economies of scale were present. In other words, if firms are able to form coalitions (without internal communication problems) then the cost of capital per firm is a decreasing function of the number of firms in the coalition (size of the intermediary). Still in the context of adverse selection, coalitions of heterogenous borrowers can also improve the market outcome by providing cross-subsidiation inside the coalitions. An example is studied in Boyd and Prescott (1986). Another example of economies of scope due to adverse selection is that of screening activities (Broecker 1990).

Section 2.4 discusses the *delegated monitoring* theory of intermediation, first explored by Diamond (1984). The section will use the term more broadly than Diamond did, to refer to any activity aimed at preventing opportunistic behavior of the borrower, both interim (moral hazard) or ex-post (auditing).

Monitoring typically involves increasing returns to scale, which implies that it is more efficiently performed by specialized firms. Therefore, individual lenders tend to *delegate* the monitoring activity, instead of performing it themselves. This introduces a new problem: the information that the monitor provides may not be reliable (as first established in Campbell and Kracaw 1980). Thus, the monitor has to be given incentives to do the job properly. FIs can be seen as providing solutions to this incentive problem.[5] Several theories have been put forward:

• Diamond (1984) suggests that, if investors can impose nonpecuniary penalties on a monitor who does not perform well, the optimal arrangement will look like a deposit contract. Moreover, by diversifying the loan portfolio, the monitor (interpreted as a banker) can make the cost of delegation as small as possible, getting close to offering riskless deposits.

• Calomiris and Kahn (1991) argue that demand deposits provide the adequate instrument for disciplining bank managers: if anything goes wrong, investors withdraw their deposits.

• Holmström and Tirole (1993) invoke the personal involvement of the monitor in the project: outside investors require that the monitor participate in the financing. This gives rise to informational economies of scope between monitoring and lending activities, and explains the role of banking capital.

Section 2.5 will discuss the choice between direct and intermediate finance (public debt versus a unique lender) and will study the relationship between banks and customers. Direct finance is usually considered to dominate intermediate finance, in particular because direct finance is less expensive. Therefore, the firms that apply for bank loans are assumed to be the ones that cannot obtain direct finance. This can be because their reputation is insufficient (as in Diamond's 1991 model, presented in subsection 2.5.1) or because they do not have enough capital or collateral (as in the model of Holmström and Tirole 1993 studied in subsection 2.5.2). Subsection 2.5.3 offers a quick presentation of some related contributions.

2.1   Transaction Costs

The simplest way to justify the existence of FIs is to emphasize the difference between their inputs and their outputs and view their main activity as transformation of financial securities. Indeed, FIs do have a role in transforming particular types of assets into others. Specifically, they transform deposits of convenient maturity, such as demand deposits (without any restriction on the minimal amount and with a low risk), into nonmarketed loans (with a longer maturity and in larger amounts, and with credit risk). FIs may thus be viewed as providing services of divisibility, term, and risk transformation. Attractive as it may be, *this explanation fails to explain why this asset transformation is not done by the borrowers themselves.* A consistent model must include the assumption of economies of scale and/or economies of scope that make it profitable for separate units to specialize in transforming the financial assets issued by the borrowers. The origin of these economies of scale and/or of scope may lie in the existence of transaction costs. Thus, as Benston and Smith (1976) state, "the raison d'être for this industry is the existence of transaction costs" (p. 215). This concept of transaction costs that appears even in the early banking literature is more elaborate than a narrow interpretation might suggest. In fact, in addition to monetary transaction costs, it includes search costs[6] as well as monitoring and auditing costs (discussed in Sections 2.3 and 2.4).

The following subsections classify some of the classical transaction cost justifications of FIs by stating the implicit assumptions that each type of cost requires.

2.1.1   Economies of Scope

As mentioned in Chapter 1, a primitive form of banking involved money changers who decided to offer deposit services because they had a comparative advantage in storing valuables. Having already a need for safekeeping places for their own inventories of coins and metals, they could easily offer analogous services to merchants and traders. Our modern vocabulary would say that economies of scope existed between money-changing and safekeeping activities. Similarly, international traders who had counters in several countries could easily offer international payment services to other merchants. Another example is that of English goldsmiths who issued deposit certificates, guaranteed by their gold inventories.

However, this explanation does not apply to all financial intermediaries (like universal banks), since the economies of scope mentioned concern essentially payment and deposit services. To explain the existence of universal banks, economies of scope must exist between deposit and credit activities. Although frequently alluded to, these economies of scope are not easy to pinpoint, either at the empirical or the theoretical level.[7] It is true that in a location model, in which agents are geographically dispersed and face transportation costs, it is efficient for the same firm or the same branch to offer deposit and credit services in a single place. Similarly, the same clerk is more efficiently employed if he or she takes care simultaneously of customers' checking accounts and loan repayments. However, the same argument would also hold for any kind of services or activities: it is the "central place" story, which explains the existence of department stores or trade centers.

Something deeper must be involved in the economies of scope explanation of financial intermediation. A first possible explanation is given by portfolio theory. As Chapter 8 will discuss, if some investors are much less risk averse than the others, these investors will in equilibrium short sell (i.e., borrow) the riskless asset and invest more than their own wealth in the risky market portfolio. In a sense these investors have a comparative advantage in holding risky assets. Another possible explanation, also given by portfolio theory, is *diversification.* If a positive correlation exists between the returns of two categories of securities, one having a positive expected excess return (over the riskless asset) and the other a negative expected excess return, the typical investor will hold a long position in the first one and a short position in the second one. If we call these investors *banks,* the first security *loans,* and the second one *deposits,* we have a diversification theory of financial intermediation. This theory, advanced by Pyle (1971), is explained in detail in Chapter 8.

However, these portfolio theories of financial intermediation are not completely satisfactory: because of limited liability it is not possible to assimilate a deposit offered by an FI and a short position in a riskless asset (unless deposits are fully insured, as discussed in Chapter 9). Similarly, the specificity of banks and insurance companies (as opposed to mutual funds) is that they deal essentially with nonmarketable securities: loans and insurance contracts. Therefore, another approach is needed for explaining economies of scope between, say, credit and deposit activities. This is where information asymmetries come in: if lenders have doubts on the credit worthiness of borrowers, they will trust more those borrowers that they know better (for instance, because they manage the borrowers' checking accounts and security portfolios).[8] Similarly, if depositors are uncertain about the true value of risky projects, they may agree to participate in the financing of these projects if they know that their banker has a personal stake in them. These issues will be discussed in detail in the rest of Chapter 2.

2.1.2 Economies of Scale

Of course, an obvious justification for intermediation is the presence of fixed transaction costs, or more generally increasing returns in the transaction technology. For instance, if a fixed fee is associated with any financial transaction, depositors (or borrowers) will tend to form coalitions and will buy (or sell) together in order to divide the transaction costs. (This argument does not work with proportional transaction costs.) Similarly, because of indivisibilities, a coalition of investors will be able to hold a more diversified (and thus less risky) portfolio than the ones individual investors would hold on their own.

Another type of scale economy is related to liquidity insurance à la Diamond and Dybvig (see Section 2.2 and Chapter 7). By the law of large numbers, a large coalition of investors will be able to invest in illiquid but more profitable securities, while preserving enough liquidity to satisfy the needs of individual investors. Once more this argument is not specific to the banking industry: it is also valid for insurance activities and more generally for inventory management. To have a genuine specificity of banks (as opposed to other intermediaries) informational asymmetries must again be introduced. This will be done in Section 2.3 in the discussion of the signaling approach, originally advanced by Leland and Pyle (1977). These informational asymmetries are also crucial for explaining the superiority of banks over financial markets in the provision of liquidity insurance.

2.2   Liquidity Insurance

A very natural idea for justifying the existence of depository institutions is to consider them as "pools of liquidity" that provide households with insurance against idiosyncratic shocks that affect their consumption needs. As long as these shocks are not perfectly correlated, the total cash reserve needed by a bank of size N (interpreted as a coalition of N depositors) increases less than proportionally with N. This is the basis for the "fractional reserve system," in which some fraction of the deposits can be used to finance profitable but illiquid investments. However, this is also the source of a potential fragility of banks, in the event that a high number of depositors decide to withdraw their funds for reasons other than liquidity needs. An interesting modeling of these issues, put forth by Diamond and Dybvig (1983), will be presented in detail in Chapter 7. For the moment, a simplified version of this model will be presented in order to capture the notion of liquidity insurance that was initially modeled by Bryant (1980).

2.2.1   The Model

Consider a one-good, three-period economy in which a continuum of ex-ante identical agents is each endowed with one unit of good at period $t = 0$, and this good is to be consumed at periods $t = 1$ and $t = 2$. The simplest way to model "liquidity shocks" is to consider that consumers learn at $t = 1$ whether they will have to consume *early* (i.e., at $t = 1$), in which case their utility function is $u(C_1)$, or *late* (at $t = 2$), in which case their utility function is $\rho u(C_2)$ (where $\rho < 1$ is a discount factor). In ex-ante terms the expected utility of a depositor is

$$U = \pi_1 u(C_1^1) + \pi_2 \rho u(C_2^2), \tag{2.1}$$

where π_1 (resp. π_2) is the probability of being of "type 1" (resp. type 2) that is having to consume early (resp.late), and C_t^i denotes the consumption of an agent of type i at date t.[9]

u is assumed to be increasing and concave. Notice that preferences are state contingent and do not fit the standard Von Neumann–Morgenstern representation (they would if ρ were equal to one).

The good can be stored from one period to the next or can be invested at $t = 0$ in a long-run technology, which returns $R > 1$ units at $t = 2$, but only $L < 1$ units if it has to be liquidated at $t = 1$. The following discussion will compare different institutional arrangements and will show that a depository institution can improve the efficiency of the economy.

2.2.2 Autarky

The simplest case, in which there is no trade between agents, is called "autarky." Each agent chooses independently the quantity I that will be invested in the illiquid technology, assumed to be perfectly divisible. If he has to consume early, then this investment will be liquidated at $t = 1$, yielding

$$C_1 = 1 - I + LI = 1 - I(1 - L) \leq 1, \tag{2.2}$$

with equality only when $I = 0$. On the contrary, if he has to consume late, he obtains

$$C_2 = 1 - I + RI = 1 + I(R - 1) \leq R, \tag{2.3}$$

with equality only when $I = 1$.

In autarky, each consumer will select the consumption profile that maximizes his ex-ante utility U (given by 2.1) under the constraints 2.2 and 2.3.

2.2.3 Market Economy

If agents are allowed to trade, welfare improves. In this simple context, it is enough to open at $t = 1$ a financial market (for, say, a bond) in which agents can trade the good at $t = 1$ against a riskless bond (that is, a promise to receive some quantity of the consumption good at $t = 2$). Let p denote the price at $t = 1$ of the bond which, by convention, yields one unit of good at $t = 2$. Clearly $p \leq 1$; otherwise people would prefer to store. By investing I at $t = 0$, an agent can now obtain

$$C_1 = 1 - I + pRI, \tag{2.4}$$

if she needs to consume early (in which case she will sell RI bonds). If, on the contrary, she needs to consume late, she will obtain

$$C_2 = \frac{1-I}{p} + RI = \frac{1}{p}[1 - I + pRI], \tag{2.5}$$

since she can then buy $\frac{1-I}{p}$ bonds at $t = 1$. Since I can be freely chosen by agents, the only possible equilibrium price is $p = \frac{1}{R}$. Otherwise either an excess supply or an excess demand of bonds will occur ($I = +\infty$ if $p > \frac{1}{R}$, $I = 0$ if $p < \frac{1}{R}$). The equilibrium allocation of the market economy is therefore $C_1^M = 1$, $C_2^M = R$ and the corresponding investment level is $I^M = \pi_2$. Notice that this market allocation Pareto dominates the autarky allocation (see 2.2 and 2.3) since there is no liquidation. However as the next subsection will show, it is not ex-ante Pareto optimal.

2.2.4 Optimal Allocation

From an ex-ante viewpoint, there is a unique symmetric Pareto optimal allocation (C_1^*, C_2^*) obtained by solving

$$\max \pi_1 u(C_1) + \rho\pi_2 u(C_2) \tag{2.6}$$

$$\pi_1 C_1 + \pi_2 \frac{C_2}{R} = 1. \tag{2.7}$$

This optimal allocation satisfies in particular the first-order condition:

$$u'(C_1^*) = \rho R u'(C_2^*). \tag{2.8}$$

Therefore, except in the very peculiar case in which

$$u'(1) = \rho R u'(R),$$

the market allocation ($C_1^M = 1$, $C_2^M = R$) is not Pareto optimal. In particular, Diamond and Dybvig (1983) assume that $C \to Cu'(C)$ is decreasing.[10] In that case, since $R > 1$,

$$\rho R u'(R) < \rho u'(1) < u'(1), \tag{2.9}$$

and the market allocation can be Pareto improved by increasing C_1^M and decreasing C_2^M:

$$C_1^M = 1 < C_1^*\ ;\ C_2^M = R > C_2^*. \tag{2.10}$$

In other words, the market economy does not provide perfect insurance against liquidity shocks, and therefore does not lead to an efficient allocation of resources. The following discussion will show how a financial intermediary can solve this problem.

2.2.5   Financial Intermediation

Provided the possibility of strategic behavior of depositors is ruled out (this issue will be studied in Chapter 7), the Pareto optimal allocation (C_1^*, C_2^*) can be implemented very easily by a financial intermediary who offers a demand deposit contract stipulated as follows: in exchange for a deposit of one unit at $t = 0$, individuals can get either C_1^* at $t = 1$ or C_2^* at $t = 2$. In order to fulfill its obligations, the FI stores $\pi_1 C_1^*$ and invests the rest in the illiquid technology. Thus we have established the following:

Result 2.1   In an economy in which agents are individually subject to independent liquidity shocks, the market allocation can be improved by a deposit contract offered by a financial intermediary.

The reason why the market allocation is not Pareto optimal is that complete contingent markets cannot exist: the state of the economy (i.e., the complete list of the consumers who need to consume early) is not observable by anyone. The only (noncontingent) financial market that can be opened (namely the bond market) is not sufficient to obtain efficient risk sharing.

Notice that a crucial assumption is that no individual withdraws at $t = 1$ if he or she does not have to. Provided $\rho R > 1$, this assumption is not unreasonable, since it corresponds to a Nash equilibrium behavior. Indeed 2.8 implies (since $\rho R > 1$) that $C_1^* < C_2^*$: in other words, a deviation by a single late consumer (withdraw at $t = 1$ and store the good until $t = 2$) is never in that consumer's own interest. However, Chapter 7 will show that another Pareto-dominated Nash equilibrium exists in which deviations of all late consumers occur simultaneously. Notice also that an FI cannot coexist (in this simple setup) with a financial market. Indeed, if there is a bond market at $t = 1$, the equilibrium price is necessarily $p = \frac{1}{R}$. Then the optimal allocation (C_1^*, C_2^*) is not a Nash equilibrium anymore: indeed 2.10 implies that

$$RC_1^* > R > C_2^*,$$

which means that late consumers are better off withdrawing early and buying bonds. This is of course a serious weakness of the model. Von Thadden (1994, 1996, 1997) has studied this question in a more general formulation that will be discussed in Chapter 7.

2.3   Information Sharing Coalitions

The common assumption for all the models presented in this section is that entrepreneurs are better informed than investors about the "quality" of the projects they want to develop. This "hidden information," or "adverse selection," paradigm will be explored in detail in several chapters of this book. The current discussion will show that this adverse selection paradigm can generate scale economies in the borrowing–lending activity, allowing interpretation of FIs as information sharing coalitions. After introducing (in subsection 2.3.1) a basic model of capital markets with adverse selection (that will be repeatedly used, under many variants, in several sections of this book), the seminal contribution of Leland and Pyle (1977) will be discussed in subsection 2.3.2. Leland and Pyle consider that entrepreneurs can "signal" the quality of their projects by investing more or less of their own wealth into these projects. In this way, they can partially overcome the adverse selection problem, since "good" projects can be separated from "bad" projects by their level of self-financing. However, if entrepreneurs are risk averse, this "signaling" is costly, since "good" entrepreneurs are obliged to retain a substantial fraction of the risk of their project. Leland and Pyle then study coalitions of borrowers and show that the "signaling cost" increases less rapidly than the size of the coalition. In other words, if borrowers form "partnerships," which Leland and Pyle interpret as FIs, they are able to obtain better financing conditions than by borrowing individually. This property is explained in subsection 2.3.3, and then several related contributions are summarized in subsection 2.3.4.

2.3.1   A Basic Model of Capital Markets with Adverse Selection

The following model of competitive capital markets with adverse selection will be used in several sections of this book. Consider a large number of entrepreneurs, each endowed with a risky project, requiring a fixed investment of a size normalized to one. The net returns $\tilde{R}(\theta)$ of these investments follow a normal distribution of mean θ and variance σ^2. Whereas σ^2 is the same for all projects, θ differs across projects and is the private information of each entrepreneur. However, the statistical distribution of θ in the population of entrepreneurs is common knowledge. The investors are risk neutral and have access to a costless storage technology. The entrepreneurs have enough initial wealth W_0 to finance their projects ($W_0 > 1$), but they would prefer to sell these projects because they are risk adverse. They have an exponential Von Neumann–Morgenstern utility function $u(w) = -e^{-\rho w}$, where w denotes their final wealth and $\rho > 0$ is their (constant) absolute index of risk aversion. If θ were observable, each entrepreneur would sell its project to the market at a price $P(\theta) = E[\tilde{R}(\theta)] = \theta$[11] and would be perfectly insured.[12] The final wealth of an entrepreneur of type θ would be $W_0 + \theta$.

Suppose now that θ is private information and that entrepreneurs are indistinguishable by investors. As in Akerlof (1970), the price P of equity will be the same for all firms, and in general only entrepreneurs with a lower expected return will sell their project. Indeed, by self-financing its project, entrepreneur θ obtains[13]

$$Eu(W_0 + \tilde{R}(\theta)) = u(W_0 + \theta - \frac{1}{2}\rho\sigma^2),$$

whereas by selling it to the market, he obtains $u(W_0 + P)$. Therefore entrepreneur θ will go to the financial market if and only if

$$\theta < \hat{\theta} = P + \frac{1}{2}\rho\sigma^2. \tag{2.11}$$

This means that only those entrepreneurs with a relatively low expected return ($\theta < \hat{\theta}$) will issue equity: this is exactly the adverse selection problem.

At equilibrium, the average return on equity will be equal to P (because of the investors' risk neutrality):

$$P = E[\theta|\theta < \hat{\theta}]. \tag{2.12}$$

The equilibrium of the capital market with adverse selection is thus characterized by a price of equity P and a cutoff level $\hat{\theta}$ such that relations 2.11 and 2.12 are satisfied. In general, the equilibrium outcome is inefficient. Assume, for instance, that the distribution of θ is binomial.[14] In other words, θ can take only two values: a low value θ_1 with probability π_1, and a high value θ_2 with probability π_2. Since the investors are risk neutral and the entrepreneurs are risk averse, efficiency requires that all entrepreneurs obtain 100 percent outside finance. By definition of the cutoff level, this means that $\hat{\theta} \geq \theta_2$. In that case, the price of equity equals

$$P = E[\theta] = \pi_1\theta_1 + \pi_2\theta_2.$$

Using 2.11 we obtain that this is only possible when

$$\pi_1\theta_1 + \pi_2\theta_2 + \frac{1}{2}\rho\sigma^2 \geq \theta_2,$$

or

$$\pi_1(\theta_2 - \theta_1) \leq \frac{1}{2}\rho\sigma^2. \tag{2.13}$$

In other words, the risk premium has to outweigh the adverse selection effect. If 2.13 is not satisfied, some entrepreneurs will prefer to self-finance, and the equilibrium outcome will be inefficient.[15]

2.3.2   Signaling Through Self-Financing

When 2.13 is not satisfied, the entrepreneurs who are endowed with good-quality projects ($\theta = \theta_2$) prefer to self-finance rather than to sell the entirety of their projects at a low price $P = E[\theta]$. In fact, they can limit themselves with partial self-finance if they can convince investors that the other entrepreneurs (who are endowed with low-quality projects, $\theta = \theta_1$) have no interest in doing the same (to "mimic" them, in the terminology of adverse selection models). In other words, deciding to self-finance a fraction α of the project will in that case "signal" to outside investors that this project is good. Intuitively, this is true when α is large enough. The "no mimicking" condition is:

$$u(W_0 + \theta_1) \geq Eu(W_0 + (1 - \alpha)\theta_2 + \alpha \tilde{R}(\theta_1)). \qquad (2.14)$$

The left side of 2.14 is the utility of a type θ_1 entrepreneur who sells all his project at a low price $P_1 = \theta_1$. The right side represents his expected utility when he mimics type θ_2, that is, sells only a fraction $(1 - \alpha)$ of his project at a high unit price $P_2 = \theta_2$, but retains the risk on the remaining fraction α. With this model's assumption this expected utility equals $u(W_0 + (1 - \alpha)\theta_2 + \alpha\theta_1 - \frac{1}{2}\rho\sigma^2\alpha^2)$, which gives a simplified version of 2.14:

$$\theta_1 \geq (1 - \alpha)\theta_2 + \alpha\theta_1 - \frac{1}{2}\rho\sigma^2\alpha^2,$$

or

$$\frac{\alpha^2}{1 - \alpha} \geq \frac{2(\theta_2 - \theta_1)}{\rho\sigma^2}. \qquad (2.15)$$

Result 2.2 *(Leland and Pyle 1977)* When the level of projects' self-financing is observable, there is a continuum of signaling equilibria, parameterized by a number α fulfilling 2.15, and characterized by a low price of equity $P_1 = \theta_1$ for entrepreneurs who do not self-finance and a high price of equity $P_2 = \theta_2$ for entrepreneurs who self-finance a fraction α of their projects.

As is usual in signaling models (see Spence 1973), there is a continuum of equilibria, parameterized for the level α of self-financing by good-quality entrepreneurs. These equilibria can be Pareto ranked, since all lenders break even and θ_1 entrepreneurs get the same outcome as in the full-information case. As for θ_2 entrepreneurs, they obtain a utility level of $u(W_0 + \theta_2 - \frac{1}{2}\rho\sigma^2\alpha^2)$, instead of $u(W_0 + \theta_2)$ in the full-information case. Expressed in terms of lost income, their "informational cost of capital" is therefore

$$C = \frac{1}{2}\rho\sigma^2\alpha^2, \qquad (2.16)$$

which is increasing in the level α of self-financing. The Pareto-dominating signaling equilibrium corresponds to the minimum possible value of α, which is defined implicitly by transforming 2.15 into an equality:

$$\frac{\alpha^2}{1 - \alpha} = \frac{2(\theta_2 - \theta_1)}{\rho\sigma^2}. \qquad (2.17)$$

It is natural to focus on this Pareto-dominating equilibrium, which allows definition of the (minimum) cost of capital

$$C(\sigma) = \frac{1}{2}\rho\sigma^2\alpha^2(\sigma) \tag{2.18}$$

where $\alpha(\sigma)$ is defined implicitly by 2.17.

2.3.3   Coalitions of Borrowers

This subsection will illustrate the main idea of this section, namely that in the presence of adverse selection, coalitions of borrowers can do better than individual borrowers. Suppose that N identical entrepreneurs of type θ_2 form a partnership and collectively issue securities in order to finance their N projects. If the individual returns of each project are independently distributed, and if the N entrepreneurs share equally both the proceeds of security issuing and the final returns, the situation is formally the same as before: the expected return per project is still θ_2, but (and this is the only difference) the variance per project is now $\frac{\sigma^2}{N}$ (because of diversification). Since one can prove that the function $\sigma \to C(\sigma)$ defined by 2.18 is increasing, the following result is obtained:

Result 2.3   (Diamond 1984) In the Leland-Pyle model (1977), the unit cost of capital decreases with the size of the coalition of borrowers (partnership or intermediary).

Proof   It is necessary only to prove that $\sigma \to C(\sigma)$ is increasing. But relation 2.17 implies both that $\sigma \to \alpha(\sigma)$ is decreasing (since $\alpha \to \frac{\alpha^2}{1-\alpha}$ is increasing on $[0, 1]$) and that

$$\frac{1}{2}\rho\sigma^2\alpha^2(\sigma) = (\theta_2 - \theta_1)(1 - \alpha(\sigma)).$$

Therefore, 2.18 shows that $\sigma \to C(\sigma)$ is increasing, which was to be proved.

∎

2.3.4   Related Justifications of FIs with Asymmetric Information

The Leland and Pyle (1977) model justifies FIs by considering the benefits obtained by borrowers when they form coalitions, provided they are able to communicate truthfully the quality of their projects within the coalition. But the framework of adverse selection (where the quality of projects is observable only by some investors) is sufficiently rich to study other possible justifications of FIs by coalition formation.

An agent endowed with private information faces two types of problems in order to benefit from this information. First, if she tries to sell her information directly she will be confronted with a classic credibility problem: the potential buyers may not be convinced that the information is true. Second, the profits she might obtain through trading on her information might be too small with respect to the cost of obtaining this information. These profits might even be zero if prices are fully revealing, leading to the well-known paradox of Grossman and Stiglitz (1980). Campbell and Kracaw (1980), and more recently Allen (1990), have studied the incentive issues associated with this problem and how they could be solved by the creation of FIs.

Ramakrishnan and Thakor (1984) have discovered another form of scale economies caused by asymmetric information, similar to the one already discussed. They study the case of security analysts who produce some information that is valuable to a risk neutral principal (investor). This principal observes a signal that is positively correlated to the effort spent by the analyst in producing the information. Ramakrishnan and Thakor (see problem 2.6.1) compute the optimal contract (incentive scheme) between the principal and the analyst (who is risk averse). Their crucial result is that, if the analysts are able to collude (i.e., form coalitions), sign separate contracts with different principals, and mutualize their remunerations, then they increase their total expected surplus. Millon and Thakor (1985) consider a variant of this model, with two additional elements: *information reusability* (i.e., the fact that gathering information about one project provides some information about similar projects) and *internal communication problems* (which tend to limit the optimal size of FIs).

Boyd and Prescott (1986) consider an economy with two types of agents (entrepreneurs) endowed with either a good or a bad project. Each entrepreneur knows the quality of his project. In a perfect information setting it would be optimal to implement all the good projects, implement some of the bad projects, and have the rest of the agents endowed with bad projects invest in the good projects. The stock market cannot implement the optimum, because agents who have bad projects and want them to be profitable have no incentive to reveal their type. Nevertheless, a coalition of agents (an FI) could do better, because the group could allow for cross-subsidization, decreasing the returns for good types and increasing the returns for bad types in such a way that each agent has an incentive to reveal truthfully the characteristic of his project. In this way, coalitions of heterogenous agents can improve the market equilibrium outcome. This is a standard phenomenon in economies with adverse selection, because the equilibrium outcome can be inefficient, even in a second best sense, when incentive compatibility constraints are introduced (see, for instance, Rothschild and Stiglitz 1976).

Finally, Gorton and Pennacchi (1990) emphasize the qualitative asset transformation activity of banks, which typically finance risky investments through riskless deposits. In an adverse selection world, where some agents have private information on these risky investments, riskless deposits (which are not sensitive to this private information) may be particularly suited for uninformed agents. Notice however that, as the authors point out, FIs are not a necessary ingredient of that story: riskless bonds, directly issued by firms, could do the same job as riskless deposits.

2.4   Financial Intermediation as Delegated Monitoring

In a context of asymmetric information, monitoring could clearly be a way to improve efficiency. Following Hellwig (1991), this discussion uses the term "monitoring" in a broad sense to mean:

- *screening* projects (a priori) in a context of adverse selection, as in Broecker 1990;
- *preventing* opportunistic behavior of the borrower during the realization of the project (moral hazard), as in Holmström and Tirole (1993); or
- *punishing* (as in Diamond 1984) or *auditing* (as in Townsend 1979, Gale and Hellwig 1985, and Krasa and Villamil 1992) a borrower who fails to meet contractual obligations; this is the context of "costly state verification."

Whereas these monitoring activities clearly improve the efficiency of lender–borrower contracts with asymmetric information, they can very well be performed by the individual lenders themselves or more accurately by specialized firms: rating agencies, security analysts, or auditors. The delegated monitoring theory of financial intermediation (originally advanced by Diamond 1984) suggests that banks have a comparative advantage in these monitoring activities. For this theory to work, several ingredients are needed:

- Scale economies in monitoring, which implies that a typical bank finances many projects.
- Small capacity of investors (as compared to the size of investment projects), which implies that each project needs the funds of several investors.
- Low costs of delegation: the cost of monitoring or controlling the FI itself has to be less than the surplus gained from exploiting scale economies in monitoring or controlling investment projects.

Following Diamond (1984), consider a framework in which n identical firms seek to finance projects, each firm requires an investment of one unit of account, and the returns of each firm are identically independently distributed. The cash flow $\tilde{y}$ that a firm obtains from its investment is a priori unobservable to lenders. This gives rise to a moral hazard problem that can be solved either by monitoring the firm (at a cost K) or by designing a debt contract characterized by a nonpecuniary cost C. This framework will be developed in more detail in Chapter 4; for the moment, take C as exogenously given.[16] Assume that $K < C$, which means that if the firm had a unique financier, it would be efficient to choose the monitoring technique. However, assume that each investor owns only $\frac{1}{m}$, so that m of them are needed for financing one project.

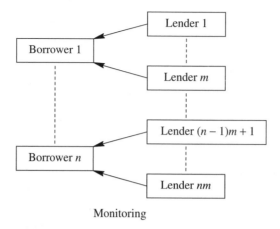

Monitoring

Figure 2.1
Direct Finance: Each Lender Monitors Its Borrower
Total Cost: nmK

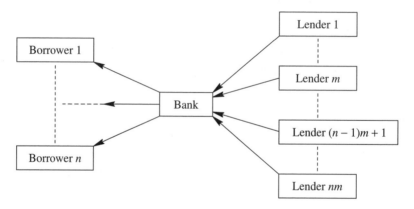

Figure 2.2
Intermediated Finance as Delegated Monitoring
Total Cost: $nK + C_n$

For simplicity, assume that the total number of investors is at least mn, so that all projects can be financed. Direct lending would then imply that each of the m investors monitors the firm she has financed: the total cost would be nmK (see Figure 2.1).

If a bank (FI) emerges, it can choose to monitor each firm (total cost nK) or to sign a debt contract with each of them (total cost nC). Since $K < C$, the first solution is preferable: the bank is therefore a delegated monitor, which monitors borrowers on behalf of lenders (see Figure 2.2). Now comes the question of monitoring the monitor. Direct monitoring of the bank by each investor would clearly be inefficient, so the only solution is that the bank offers a "debt" contract (more accurately termed a "deposit contract") under which each investor is promised a nominal amount $\frac{R_D}{m}$ (in exchange for a deposit $\frac{1}{m}$), and the bank is liquidated if its announced cash flow $\tilde{z}$ is less then nR_D, the total sum promised to depositors. Using nonpecuniary penalties, this contract can be made incentive compatible,[17] in the sense that the bank has an interest in sending a truthful declaration, so that $\tilde{z}$ equals the realized cash flow ($\sum_{i=1}^{n} \tilde{y}_i - nK$). The equilibrium level of R_D^n (which represents the nominal rate of return on deposits) and the cost of delegation will depend on n. Assume that depositors are risk neutral and have access to an outside investment technology yielding a gross expected return of R. The equilibrium repayment on deposits, R_D^n, is determined by

$$E[\min(\sum_{i=1}^{n} \tilde{y}_i - nK, nR_D^n)] = nR, \tag{2.19}$$

which expresses that the expected unit return on (risky) deposits equals R.

As Chapter 4 will explain, the total cost of delegation (denoted C_n, since it has the same nature as C) is equal to the expectation of the nonpecuniary penalty in case of bankruptcy:[18]

$$C_n = E[\max(nR_D^n + nK - \sum_{i=1}^{n} \tilde{y}_i, 0)]. \tag{2.20}$$

Now delegated monitoring will be more efficient than direct lending if and only if

$$nK + C_n < nmK. \tag{2.21}$$

Result 2.4 (Diamond 1984)   If monitoring is efficient ($K < C$), investors are small ($m > 1$), and investment is profitable ($E(\tilde{y}) > K + R$), financial intermediation (delegated monitoring) dominates direct lending as soon as n is large enough (diversification).

Proof   Condition 2.21 must be proved. Dividing it by n yields an equivalent form:

$$K + \frac{C_n}{n} < mK.$$

Since $m > 1$, it is enough to prove that $\frac{C_n}{n}$ tends toward 0 as n tends toward infinity. Dividing equations 2.19 and 2.20 by n yields

$$E[\min(\frac{1}{n} \sum_{i=1}^{n} \tilde{y}_i - K, R_D^n)] = R, \tag{2.22}$$

and

$$\frac{C_n}{n} = E[\max(R_D^n + K - \frac{1}{n}\sum_{i=1}^{n}\tilde{y}_i, 0)]. \tag{2.23}$$

The strong law of large numbers dictates that $\frac{1}{n}\sum_{i=1}^{n}\tilde{y}_i$ converges almost surely to $E(\tilde{y})$. Since $E(\tilde{y}) > K + R$, relation 2.22 shows that $\lim_n R_D^n = R$ (i.e., deposits are asymptotically riskless). Therefore, by 2.23

$$\lim_n \frac{C_n}{n} = \max(R + K - E(\tilde{y}), 0) = 0. \qquad \blacksquare$$

Several criticisms have been expressed regarding Diamond's theory. For instance, the use of nonpecuniary penalties that have to be modulated according to the cash flow reported by the borrower is not realistic: real-world nonpecuniary penalties (such as jail or the loss of reputation associated with failure) are more lump-sum. However, the delegated monitoring approach can also work in a context of costly state verification à la Townsend-Gale-Hellwig, in which the optimal contract is also a standard debt contract[19] but the deadweight loss C comes from auditing in case of low realizations of the cash flow.

Krasa and Villamil (1992) construct a model in which only monitoring ("auditing" in the terminology of Gale and Hellwig) is available, so that the problem of monitoring the monitors has to be solved. But if there are enough independent projects, the probability of the bank's insolvency goes to zero, and so does the cost of monitoring the bank. Duplication of monitoring costs is avoided, since only the bank will have to monitor the firms.

Another interesting contribution that builds on Diamond's (1984) model of delegated monitoring is the article by Cerasi and Daltung (1994), who introduce considerations on the internal organization of banks as a possible explanation for the fact that scale economies in the banking sector seem to be rapidly exhausted (see the appendix to Chapter 3), whereas Diamond's model predicts that banking should be a natural monopoly. The idea is that, in reality, monitoring is not performed by the "banker," but by loan officers, who in turn have to be monitored by the banker. This additional delegation becomes more and more costly as the size of the bank increases, since more and more officers have to be hired. Therefore a trade-off exists between the benefits of diversification (which, as in Diamond [1984] improve the incentives of the banker) and the costs of internal delegation (which increase with the size of the bank).

2.5   Coexistence of Direct and Intermediated Lending

So far, the discussion has centered on why FIs exist, and it has therefore focused on the "uniqueness of bank loans" (to recall the title of the important

1987 article by James, who shows in particular that financial markets tend to react positively when they learn that a quoted firm has obtained a bank loan). However, direct finance has experienced strong development in recent years (as part of the so-called disintermediation process), especially among large firms. Therefore, to be complete, this section will analyze the choice between direct and intermediate finance. Since in practice direct debt is less expensive than bank loans, it is usually considered that loan applicants are only those agents that cannot issue direct debt on financial markets. This discussion will study two models that explain the coexistence of the two types of finance. Both are based on moral hazard, which prevents firms without enough assets from obtaining direct finance. These assets can be monetary, as in the Holmström-Tirole (1993) model (covered in subsection 2.5.3), or reputational, as in the Diamond (1991) model, (presented in subsection 2.5.2). Subsection 2.5.4 will give a brief account of several related contributions. Subsection 2.5.1 will present a simple model of the credit market with moral hazard that will be used in several chapters of this book.

2.5.1   A Simple Model of the Credit Market with Moral Hazard

Consider a model in which firms seek to finance investment projects of a size normalized to one. The riskless rate of interest is normalized to zero. Firms have a choice between a "good" technology, which produces G with probability π_G (and zero otherwise), and a "bad" technology, which produces B with probability π_B. Assume that only good projects have a positive Net (expected) Present Value (NPV), $\pi_G G > 1 > \pi_B B$, but that $B > G$, which implies $\pi_G > \pi_B$. Assume also that the success of the investment is verifiable by outsiders, but not the firm's choice of technology or the return. Therefore the firm can promise to repay some fixed amount R (its nominal debt) only in case of success. The firm has no other source of cash, so the repayment is zero if the investment fails. The crucial element of this model is that the value R of the nominal indebtedness of the firm determines its choice of technology. Indeed, in the absence of monitoring, the firm will choose the "good" technology if and only if this gives it a higher expected profit:

$$\pi_G(G - R) > \pi_B(B - R). \tag{2.24}$$

Since $\pi_G > \pi_B$, 2.24 is equivalent to

$$R < R_C = \frac{\pi_G G - \pi_B B}{\pi_G - \pi_B}, \tag{2.25}$$

where R_C denotes the critical value of nominal debt above which the firm chooses the bad technology. Notice that $R_C < G < B$. From the lender's viewpoint, the probability p of repayment therefore depends on R:

$$p(R) = \begin{cases} \pi_G & \text{if } R \leq R_C, \\ \pi_B & \text{if } R > R_C. \end{cases}$$

In the absence of monitoring, a competitive equilibrium of the credit market is obtained for R such that

$$p(R)R = 1. \tag{2.26}$$

Because of the assumptions that have been made, this is only possible when $\pi_G R_C > 1$, which means that moral hazard is not too important. If $\pi_G R_C < 1$, the equilibrium involves no trade, and the credit market collapses (this is because bad projects have a negative NPV).

Now a monitoring technology is introduced: at a cost C, banks can prevent borrowers from using the bad technology. Assuming perfect competition between banks, the nominal value of bank loans at equilibrium (denoted R_m, where m stands for monitor) is determined by the break-even condition

$$\pi_G R_m = 1 + C. \tag{2.27}$$

For bank lending to appear at equilibrium, two conditions are needed:

1. The nominal value R_m of bank loans at equilibrium has to be less than the return G of successful firms. Given condition 2.27, which determines R_m, this is equivalent to

$$\pi_G G - 1 > C. \tag{2.28}$$

In other words, the monitoring cost has to be less than the NPV of the good project. This is a very natural condition.

2. Direct lending, which is less costly, has to be impossible:

$$\pi_G R_C > 1. \tag{2.29}$$

Therefore, bank lending appears at equilibrium for intermediate values of the probability $\pi_G (\pi_G \in \left[\frac{1+C}{G}, \frac{1}{R_C}\right])$ provided this interval is not empty. Thus we have established the following:

Result 2.5   Assume that the monitoring cost C is small enough so that $\frac{1}{R_C} > \frac{1+C}{G}$. There are three possible regimes of the credit market at equilibrium:

1. If $\pi_G > \frac{1}{R_C}$ (high probability of success), firms issue direct debt at a rate $R_1 = \frac{1}{\pi_G}$.

2. If $\pi_G \in [\frac{1+C}{G}, \frac{1}{R_C}]$ (intermediate probability of success), firms borrow from banks at a rate $R_2 = \frac{1+C}{\pi_G}$.

3. If $\pi_G < \frac{1+C}{G}$ (small probability of success), the credit market collapses (no trade equilibrium).

2.5.2   Monitoring and Reputation (Adapted from Diamond 1991)

The objective will be to show, in a dynamic version of the previous model (with two dates, $t = 0, 1$), that successful firms can build a reputation that allows them to issue direct debt, instead of using bank loans, which are more expensive. In order to capture this notion of reputation, assume that firms are heterogenous: only some fraction f of them strategically choose between the two technologies. The rest have access only to a given technology (for example, the bad one). This discussion will show that under some conditions of the parameters, the equilibrium of the credit market will be such that

- at $t = 0$, all firms borrow from banks.

- at $t = 1$, the firms that have been successful at $t = 0$ issue direct debt, while the rest still borrow from banks.

This example starts with the case of successful firms. Because of result 2.5, they will be able to issue direct debt if and only if

$$\pi_S > \frac{1}{R_C}, \tag{2.30}$$

where π_S is the probability of repayment at date 2, conditionally on success at date 0 (and given that all firms have been monitored at $t = 0$). Bayes's formula gives the following:

$$\pi_S = \frac{P \text{ (success at } t = 0 \text{ and } t = 1)}{P \text{ (success at } t = 0)} = \frac{f\pi_G^2 + (1 - f)\pi_B^2}{f\pi_G + (1 - f)\pi_B}. \tag{2.31}$$

If 2.30 is satisfied, successful firms will be able to issue direct debt at a rate $R_S = \frac{1}{\pi_S}$. On the other hand, the probability of success at $t = 1$ of the firms that have been unsuccessful at $t = 0$ is

$$\pi_U = \frac{f\pi_G(1 - \pi_G) + (1 - f)\pi_B(1 - \pi_B)}{f(1 - \pi_G) + (1 - f)(1 - \pi_B)}. \tag{2.32}$$

Result 2.5 implies that if $\frac{1+C}{G} < \pi_U < \frac{1}{R_C}$, these unsuccessful firms will borrow from banks, at a rate $R_U = \frac{1+C}{\pi_U}$. In order to complete the picture, it is necessary only to establish that, at $t = 0$, for the adequate values of the different parameters all firms (which are then indistinguishable) also choose bank lending.

The symbol π_0 denotes the unconditional probability of success at $t = 0$ (when strategic firms choose the good technology):

$$\pi_0 = f\pi_G + (1 - f)\pi_B.$$

The notion of reputation building comes from the fact that $\pi_U < \pi_0 < \pi_S$, i.e., the probability of repayment of the bank loan by the firm is initially π_0, but increases if the firm is successful (π_S) and decreases in the other case (π_U). Because of that, the critical level of debt (above which moral hazard appears) at $t = 0$ is higher than in the static case. Indeed, firms know that if they are successful at $t = 0$, they will obtain cheaper finance (R_S instead of R_U) at date 1. If $\delta < 1$ denotes the discount factor, the critical level of debt above which strategic firms choose the bad project at $t = 0$ (denoted by R_C^0) is now defined by

$$\pi_B(B - R) + \delta\pi_G[G - \pi_B R_S - (1 - \pi_B)R_U]$$
$$= \pi_G(G - R) + \delta\pi_G[G - \pi_G R_S - (1 - \pi_G)R_U],$$

which gives

$$R_C^0 = R_C + \delta\pi_G(R_U - R_S).$$

The following is the complete result:

Result 2.6 Under the following assumptions:

$$\pi_0 \le \frac{1}{R_C^0}, \quad \pi_S > \frac{1}{R_C}, \quad \text{and} \quad \pi_U > \frac{1 + C}{G},$$

the equilibrium of the two-period version of Diamond's model is characterized as follows:

1. At $t = 0$, all firms borrow from banks at rate $R_0 = \frac{1+C}{\pi_0}$.

2. At $t = 1$, successful firms issue direct debt at rate $R_S = \frac{1}{\pi_S}$, whereas the rest borrow from banks at rate $R_u = \frac{1+C}{\pi_U}$.

Although this model is very simple, it captures several important features of credit markets:

- Firms with a good reputation can issue direct debt.[20]

- Unsuccessful firms pay a higher rate than new firms ($R_U > R_0$).

- Moral hazard is partially alleviated by reputation effects ($R_C^0 > R_C$).

Proof It is necessary only to apply repeatedly result 2.5, after adjusting the parameters for the different cases:

Part 1 in result 2.6 comes from part 2 of result 2.5, since by assumption $\frac{1+C}{G} < \pi_U < \pi_0 \le \frac{1}{R_C^0}$. Part 2 comes from parts 1 and 2 of result 2.5, since by assumption $\pi_G^S > \frac{1}{R_C}$ and $\frac{1+C}{G} < \pi_U < \pi_0 \le \frac{1}{R_C^0} < \frac{1}{R_C}$. ∎

2.5.3   Monitoring and Capital (Adapted from Holmström and Tirole 1993)

Holmström and Tirole (1993) consider a simple model that elegantly captures the notion of a substitutability between capital and monitoring, both at the level of the firms and the level of banks. They obtain delegated monitoring without the complete diversification assumption of Diamond (1984): the moral hazard issue at the level of the bank is solved by bank capital. In a sense, their assumption is the opposite of that of Diamond (1984): they assume perfect correlation between the projects financed by banks, whereas Diamond assumes project independence.

More specifically, Holmström and Tirole's model considers three types of agents: (1) firms (borrowers) represented by the index f; (2) monitors (i.e., banks), represented by the index m; and (3) uninformed investors (depositors), represented by the index u. Each industrial project (owned by firms) costs I and returns R (which is verifiable) in case of success (and nothing in case of failure). There are two types of projects: a good project with a high probability of success p_H, and a bad project with a low probability of success p_L ($p_H - p_L$ is denoted by Δp). Bad projects give a private benefit to the borrower: this is the source of moral hazard.[21] Monitoring the firm (which costs C) implies a reduction of this benefit from B (without monitoring) to b (with monitoring). Investors are risk neutral, are uninformed (i.e., they are not able to monitor firms), and have access to an alternative investment of gross expected return γ. It is assumed that only the good project has a positive Net Expected Present Value, even if the private benefit of the firm is included:

$$p_H R - \gamma I > 0 > p_L R - \gamma I + B.$$

Firms differ only in their capital A (assumed to be publicly observable). The distribution of capital among the (continuum) population of firms is represented by the cumulative function $G(\cdot)$. Finally, the capital of banks is exogenous. Since it is assumed that bank asset returns are perfectly correlated, the only relevant parameter is total banking capital K_m, which will determine the total lending capacity of the banking industry. The following paragraphs examine the different possibilities through which a firm can find outside finance.

Direct lending: A firm can borrow directly from uninformed investors by promising a return R_u (in case of success) in exchange for an initial investment I_u. As usual, the incentive compatibility constraint gives an upper bound on R_u:

$$p_H(R - R_u) \geq p_L(R - R_u) + B \Leftrightarrow R_u \leq R - \frac{B}{\Delta p}. \qquad (2.33)$$

Now the individual rationality constraint of uninformed investors implies an upper bound on I_u:

$$p_H R_u \geq \gamma I_u \Rightarrow I_u \leq \frac{p_H R_u}{\gamma} \leq \frac{p_H}{\gamma} \left[R - \frac{B}{\Delta p} \right]. \tag{2.34}$$

Therefore, the project can be financed only if the firm has enough capital:

$$A + I_u \geq I \Rightarrow A \geq \bar{A} \stackrel{\text{def}}{=} I - \frac{p_H}{\gamma} \left(R - \frac{B}{\Delta p} \right). \tag{2.35}$$

Intermediated lending: If the firm does not have enough capital for issuing direct debt, it can try to borrow I_m from a bank (in exchange for a return R_m in case of success), together with a direct borrowing of I_u from uninformed investors (in exchange for a return R_u in case of success). The incentive compatibility constraint of the firm becomes

$$p_H [R - R_u - R_m] \geq p_L [R - R_u - R_m] + b \Leftrightarrow R_u + R_m \leq R - \frac{b}{\Delta p}. \tag{2.36}$$

The bank also must be given incentives to monitor the firm:

$$p_H R_m - C \geq p_L R_m \Leftrightarrow R_m \geq \frac{C}{\Delta p}. \tag{2.37}$$

Because banking finance is always more expensive than direct finance, the firm will borrow the least amount possible from the bank ($I_m = I_m(\beta) \stackrel{\text{def}}{=} \frac{p_H R_m}{\beta} = \frac{p_H C}{\beta \Delta p}$, where β denotes the expected rate of return that is demanded by the bank) and will obtain the rest ($I_u = \frac{p_H R_u}{\gamma}$) from uninformed investors. Therefore, constraint 2.37 is binding. Now, as a result of 2.36 and 2.37,

$$R_u \leq R - \frac{b+C}{\Delta p}, \text{ which implies } I_u \leq \frac{p_H}{\gamma} \left[R - \frac{b+C}{\Delta p} \right].$$

Therefore, the project will be financed if and only if

$$A + I_u + I_m \geq I \Rightarrow A \geq \underline{A}(\beta) \stackrel{\text{def}}{=} I - I_m(\beta) - \frac{p_H}{\gamma} \left[R - \frac{b+C}{\Delta p} \right]. \tag{2.38}$$

Finally, the rate of return β is determined by the equality between supply and demand of bank capital:

$$K_m = [G(\bar{A}) - G(\underline{A}(\beta))] I_m(\beta), \tag{2.39}$$

where K_m denotes the total capital of the banking industry (taken to be exogenous), $G(\bar{A}) - G(\underline{A}(\beta))$ represents the number ("proportion") of firms that obtain loans, and $I_m(\beta)$ represents the size of each loan (the quantity lent by the bank). The right side of 2.37 being a decreasing function of β, there is a unique equilibrium.

Result 2.7   At equilibrium, only well-capitalized firms ($A \geq \bar{A}$) can issue direct debt. Reasonably capitalized firms ($\underline{A}(\beta) \leq A < \bar{A}$) borrow from banks, and undercapitalized firms ($A \leq \underline{A}(\beta)$) cannot invest.

Chapter 6 describes the macroeconomic implications of the model of Holmström and Tirole.

2.5.4   Related Contributions

Sharpe (1990) and Rajan (1992) study bank–borrower relationships in dynamic models that are close to the spirit of the Diamond (1991) contribution. The key idea of Sharpe is that banks try to establish "customer relationships" with borrowers in order to gather information about them. As in Diamond (1991), firms that have been successful in the past are able to obtain better credit terms, since they are more likely to be successful in the future. However, Sharpe assumes that this information is known only to the bank that has initially lent to the firm (other banks have to use imperfect audit to assess the future profitability of the firms they do not know). As a consequence, successful firms face a switching cost if they decide to change banks.[22] A similar model is studied by Greenbaum, Kanatas, and Venezia (1989).

Padilla and Pagano (1993) address an issue related to the ex-post informational monopoly of the lender as studied by Sharpe (1990) and Rajan (1992). Since this effect distorts the borrowers' incentives (because they know that some fraction of their profit will be appropriated by the monopolistic lender), banks may commit to share their information, as occurs in countries where credit bureaus are important (Pagano and Jappelli 1993). In that case information sharing between banks has two opposite effects on their profits: borrowers' incentives raise the current profits, but the fiercer competition lowers future profits.

The coexistence of public debt and bank loans is also justified by Diamond (1997), who assumes a *limited participation* in the financial markets, so that some consumers do not trade. This possibility implies that assets offered for sale in the market will not attract bids from all possible buyers, and that a low resale price will be anticipated. As a consequence, the investment in long-term assets will tend to be depressed. Even so, banks will emerge endogenously to solve the liquidity problem generated by limited participation. Indeed, since banks have a large number of deposits, the liquidity needs of depositors are predictable, and limited participation is not an issue. An interesting outcome of this model is that it yields some predictions on financial development: as market participation increases, the market becomes more efficient, and the banking sector shrinks.

Another interesting paper explaining the coexistence of public debt and bank loans is Besanko and Kanatas (1993), which develops an attractive model sharing some of the main features of Holmström and Tirole's. Indeed, the former model also includes moral hazard on behalf of the firms, partially solved by monitoring services performed by the banks. But a bank must be provided with the correct incentives to monitor its borrowers, and this occurs only when the bank has a sufficient stake in the firm. (As in Holmström and Tirole, the monitoring activity is nonobservable, which creates a second moral hazard problem.) Also, once the bank lends to a firm and has incentives to monitor it, the firm can borrow from the security market, so security markets can get a free ride on the bank's monitoring services.

Yafeh and Yosha (1995) use data on Japanese manufacturing firms to investigate the nature of monitoring: they show that shareholders tend to monitor firms continuously, whereas banks intervene only when the firm is in financial distress.

The probability of success of the investments depends on the effort of entrepreneurs, which is not directly observable: this is the source of the moral hazard problem. However, banks can influence the entrepreneurs' effort through monitoring activities, the cost of which increases with the effort level that is required from the entrepreneurs. The equilibrium that is obtained is characterized by the fact that each firm combines direct lending and intermediated lending. Also, there is always a positive amount of monitoring, since it is not possible to reach the first best effort level. Finally, substituting bank financing for direct financing increases the firms' stock price, a fact that is in accordance with the main empirical findings. This model differs from that of Holmström and Tirole (1993) in two ways: collateral plays no role in Besanko and Kanatas (1993), and banks are not restricted in the amount of capital they are able to raise. As a consequence, a credit crunch cannot occur.

Also in the same vein as Holmström and Tirole, Repullo and Suarez (1995) develop a model of financial intermediation with a more general specification of the moral hazard problem and use it to explore the choice of the structure of short-term credit (commercial paper versus bank loans) over the business cycle. Boot and Thakor (1995) study a model that also explains the coexistence of FIs and securities markets by giving a different role to each institution. As before, banks arise in order to resolve post-lending or interim moral hazard. But the role of financial markets is to facilitate trades by informed agents and hence transmit information, a feature previously ignored in the related theoretical literature.

Bhattacharya and Chiesa (1995) study the problem of proprietary information disclosure by financiers. The word "proprietary" refers to the fact that the borrowing firms can be hurt if their competitors on the product market obtain this information. On the other hand, the lender is likely to gather this information in the monitoring process. This question may be particularly important in the context of Research and Development financing. Bhattacharya and Chiesa argue that, in such a context, bilateral bank–borrower relationships may be superior to multilateral lending. Similar arguments are modeled along the same lines by Yosha (1995a, b).

2.6   Problems

2.6.1   Economies of Scale in Information Production

The following example is inspired by Ramakrishnan and Thakor (1984). Consider an agent (for instance, a security analyst) who is able to produce some information that is valuable to a risk neutral principal (investor). The principal observes a signal β positively correlated with the effort e spent by the agent in producing the information. For simplicity, assume that both β and e are binomial:

Proba $(\beta = 1|e = 1) = p >$ Proba $(\beta = 1|e = 0) = q$

Proba $(\beta = 0|e = 1) = 1 - p <$ Proba $(\beta = 0|e = 0) = 1 - q$

The contract between the principal and the agent specifies the agent's wage Z as a function of β. The utility of the agent is

$$V(Z, e) = u(Z) - Ce,$$

where u is concave and increasing, and C denotes the cost of effort.

1. Compute the expected cost for the principal of inducing information production by the agent. It is defined as the minimum expected value wage schedule $\beta \rightarrow Z(\beta)$ such that

  • the agent makes an effort (incentive compatibility constraint).

  • the agent accepts the contract (individual rationality constraint). The reservation utility of the agent (i.e., the utility level the agent can obtain outside) is denoted by R.

2. Consider now the case of two agents (with no communication problems between them) who are able to sign separate contracts with the principal and equally share their total receipts. Show that they are better off in the coalition.

2.6.2   Monitoring as a Public Good and Gresham's Law

The following model formalizes the idea that an economy using several risky means of payment (monies) issued by competing banks is confronted with free rider and lemon problems, associated with Gresham's law: "Bad money drives away good money." Consider a model with N identical banks ($n = 1, \ldots, N$), each having M identical depositors with a unit deposit. The depositors of bank n are indexed by the couple (m, n) where $m = 1, \ldots, M$. Each bank issues bank notes that can be used as a store of value and/or circulated as a means of payment. The "quality" q_n of the notes issued by bank n (related to its probability of failure) increases according to the monitoring efforts spent by each of the bank's depositors. Assume the following simple specification:

$$q_n = \sum_{m=1}^{M} e(m, n) + \theta,$$

where $e(m, n)$ represents the effort spent by depositor (m, n) in monitoring his bank's management, and θ represents the intrinsic quality of the bank. It is assumed that q_n is known only to the depositors of bank n. The utility of depositor (m, n) is thus

$$U(m, n) = \begin{cases} q_n - \frac{1}{2}\gamma e^2(m, n) & \text{when he stores his bank notes,} \\ P - \frac{1}{2}\gamma e^2(m, n) & \text{when he circulates them,} \end{cases}$$

where $C(e) = \frac{1}{2}\gamma e^2$ represents the cost of effort, and P is the market price for money in circulation. As in Akerlof's (1970) market for lemons, this price is identical for all circulating monies: $P = k\bar{q}$, where $\bar{q}$ is the average quality of circulating monies, and $k > 1$ represents the utility gained from using money as a means of payment. Therefore, money n circulates if and only if $P \geq q_n$.

1. Show that in any symmetric situation $(e(m, n) \equiv e, q_n \equiv q)$ all monies circulate, and the utility of each depositor is

$$U = kq - \frac{1}{2}\gamma e^2, \quad \text{where } q = Me + \theta.$$

2. Show that in a first best situation all monies circulate and $e(m, n) \equiv e^* = \frac{kM}{\gamma}$; $q_n \equiv q^* = \frac{k}{\gamma}M^2 + \theta$.

3. Show that in a symmetric Nash equilibrium all monies circulate but $e(m, n) \equiv e^{**} = \frac{k}{\gamma}$; $q_n \equiv q^{**} = \frac{kM}{\gamma} + \theta$. Therefore the quality of money is dramatically insufficient (free rider effect).

4. Suppose now that banks have different intrinsic qualities $\theta_1 < \theta_2 < \ldots < \theta_N$.

   a. Show that if circulating monies were distinguishable, the first best effort levels would be the same as in question 2.

   b. Determine the characteristics of a Nash equilibrium and show that the free rider effect is aggravated by a lemon problem.

   c. Assume that k is less than the number N^* of monies in circulation. Is Gresham's law satisfied ?

   d. In the particular case in which $N = 2$, find conditions under which only money 1 circulates at equilibrium.

2.6.3   Intermediation and Search Costs (Adapted from Gehrig 1993)

Consider an economy with a continuum of potential buyers and sellers, characterized by their valuations b and s for a given good. b and s are uniformly distributed on the interval $[0, 1]$ and are publicly observed.

1. If there is a central marketplace, show that the (Walrasian) equilibrium involves the upper half of the buyers ($b \geq 1/2$) trading with the lower half of the sellers ($s \leq 1/2$) at a price $p^* = 1/2$. Compute the total surplus.

2. Assume now that traders meet only individually: when buyer b meets seller s, they trade at price $\frac{b+s}{2}$ (provided $b \geq s$). For simplicity, rule out other bargaining solutions and more complex search strategies. Compute the expected total surplus.

3. Introduce an intermediary who buys at an ask price $\hat{b}$ and sells at a bid price $\hat{s}$. Show that the upper part of the distribution of buyers ($b \geq b^*$) and the lower part of the distribution of sellers ($s \leq s^*$) trade with the intermediary (whereas the rest still search for a direct trade). Compute b^* and s^* as functions of $\hat{b}$ and $\hat{s}$.

4. Compute the bid and ask prices that maximize the profit of the intermediary (monopoly situation). Show that some traders are better off than in the competitive situation (question 1).

2.7 Solutions

2.7.1 Economies of Scale in Information Production

1. Let $Z(\beta)$ denote the agent's wage schedule in the optimal contract, and set

$$W_0 = u(Z(0)), \quad W_1 = u(Z(1)).$$

The agent will make an effort if and only if the incentive compatibility constraint is satisfied, namely

$$pW_1 + (1 - p)W_0 - C \geq qW_1 + (1 - q)W_0,$$

or equivalently

$$W_1 - W_0 \geq \frac{C}{p - q}.$$

The agent will accept the contract if and only if the individual rationality constraint is satisfied, namely

$$pW_1 + (1 - p)W_0 - C \geq R.$$

The optimal contract will be such that both constraints are binding, which gives

$$\begin{cases} W_0 &= R - \frac{q}{p-q}C \\ W_1 &= R + \frac{1-q}{p-q}C. \end{cases}$$

2. Suppose that each of the two agents separately signs the above contract with the principal, and that they decide to equalize their wages (mutual insurance). Denote the individual signals received by the principal on the performance of each agent as β_1 and β_2. Then if $\beta_1 = \beta_2$ the agents gain nothing by pooling their wages. However, if $\beta_1 \neq \beta_2$, each of them gets $\frac{Z(0)+Z(1)}{2}$. Since they are risk averse, they are better off in the coalition. In fact, their expected utility gain is exactly

$$\Delta U = \underbrace{2p(1-p)}_{\substack{\text{probability} \\ \text{that } \beta_1 \neq \beta_2}} \left[\underbrace{u\left(\frac{Z(0)+Z(1)}{2}\right)}_{\substack{\text{average wage} \\ \text{in the coalition}}} \underbrace{-\tfrac{1}{2}u(Z(0)) - \tfrac{1}{2}u(Z(1))}_{\substack{\text{risky wage} \\ \text{outside the coalition}}} \right].$$

2.7.2 Monitoring as a Public Good and Gresham's Law

1. In a symmetric situation,

$$q_n \equiv q < P = kq \quad (\text{since } k > 1).$$

Therefore all monies circulate, and the utility of any depositor is

$$U = kq - \frac{1}{2}\gamma e^2, \quad \text{with } q = Me + \theta.$$

2. The first best is symmetric (since utilities are concave and costs are convex); therefore all monies circulate and e is chosen to maximize U:

$$U = k(Me + \theta) - \frac{1}{2}\gamma e^2.$$

Thus,

$$e = e^* = \frac{kM}{\gamma}; \quad q = q^* = Me^* + \theta = \frac{kM^2}{\gamma} + \theta$$

3. In a symmetric Nash equilibrium all monies circulate but each depositor takes the efforts of others as given. Therefore e is chosen so as to maximize

$$U(e) = k((M-1)e^{**} + \theta + e) - \frac{1}{2}\gamma e^2.$$

Thus,

$$e = e^{**} = \frac{k}{\gamma}; \quad q = q^{**} = \frac{kM}{\gamma} + \theta.$$

Obviously $e^{**} << e^*$ and $q^{**} << q^*$.

4a. Since θ_i does not affect the marginal impact of effort on quality, the first best level of effort is the same as in question 2.

b. In a Nash equilibrium, the marginal utility of effort for a depositor varies according to whether his money circulates. In the first case it is equal to $\frac{k}{N^*}$ (where N^* denotes the number of monies in circulation), and in the second case it is equal to 1. Therefore, the Nash equilibrium level of effort equals

$$e_1^* = \frac{k}{N^* \gamma} \quad \text{in the first case, and}$$

$$e_2^* = \frac{1}{\gamma} \quad \text{in the second.}$$

c. If $N^* > k$ (which is assumed), then $e_1^* < e_2^*$. Money n circulates if and only if $P \geq q_n = \theta_n + M e_1^*$, and therefore Gresham's law is satisfied: "good-quality" monies are driven out of the market.

d. When $N = 2$, the conditions for money 1 to be the only circulating money at equilibrium are $P = kq_1 < q_2$, with $q_1 = \theta_1 + \frac{Mk}{\gamma}$, and $q_2 = \theta_2 + \frac{M}{\gamma}$. This is summarized by $k\theta_1 + \frac{Mk^2}{\gamma} < \theta_2 + \frac{M}{\gamma}$.

2.7.3　Intermediation and Search Costs

1. If there is a central marketplace, all trades take place at the same price p. The demand and supply functions are

$$D(p) = \int_p^1 db = 1 - p,$$

$$S(p) = \int_0^p ds = p.$$

Therefore the equilibrium price is $p^* = \frac{1}{2}$, and trade takes place between the upper half of buyers ($b \geq p^*$) and the lower half of sellers ($s \leq p^*$). The total surplus is

$$\int_{\frac{1}{2}}^1 b\,db - \int_0^{\frac{1}{2}} s\,ds = \frac{1}{4}.$$

2. If traders meet only individually, the expected surplus becomes

$$\int_0^1 \int_0^1 (b - s)_+ db\,ds = \frac{1}{6}.$$

3. A buyer of type b has to compare her surplus $(b - \hat{b})$ if she buys from the intermediary to her expected surplus $E\left[\frac{(b-s)_+}{2}\right]$ where for any value y we denote by $y_+ \equiv \max(y, 0)$ if she trades at random. The difference between these two expressions is clearly increasing in b, since the marginal surplus is 1 in the case of a transaction with the intermediary and less than $1/2$ in the case of direct trade. Therefore, for b larger than some cutoff level b^*, the buyer

will buy from the intermediary. By symmetry, a seller of type s will sell to the intermediary if and only if $s \leq s^*$. The cutoff levels b^* are s^* are jointly determined by the following two equations:

$$\begin{cases} b^* - \hat{b} & = & E\left[\frac{(b^*-s)_+}{2} \,\middle|\, \tilde{s} \geq s^*\right] \\ \hat{s} - s^* & = & E\left[\frac{(b-s^*)_+}{2} \,\middle|\, \tilde{b} \leq b^*\right], \end{cases}$$

where the two expectations are conditioned by the fact that the other part of the transaction (the seller in the first equation, the buyer in the second) does not trade with the intermediary. Easy computations lead to a transformation of these conditions into

$$\begin{cases} b^* - \hat{b} & = & \frac{1}{4}\frac{(b^*-s^*)^2}{1-s^*} \\ \hat{s} - s^* & = & \frac{1}{4}\frac{(b^*-s^*)^2}{b^*}. \end{cases}$$

Feasibility for the intermediary implies

$$b^* = 1 - s^*,$$

which, because of the earlier equations, gives

$$\hat{b} = 1 - \hat{s},$$

which could be expected from the symmetry of the problem. Now everything can be expressed in terms of $\hat{s}$:

$$\hat{s} - 1 + b^* = \frac{1}{4}\frac{(2b^* - 1)^2}{b^*},$$

which gives

$$b^* = \frac{1}{4\hat{s}}, \quad s^* = 1 - \frac{1}{4\hat{s}}.$$

4. The profit of the intermediary is

$$\pi = (\hat{b} - \hat{s})s^*$$

or

$$\pi = (1 - 2\hat{s})\left(1 - \frac{1}{4\hat{s}}\right),$$

$$= \frac{3}{2} - 2\hat{s} - \frac{1}{4\hat{s}}.$$

This is maximum for $\hat{s} = \frac{1}{2\sqrt{2}}$, which gives

$$b^* = 1 - s^* = \frac{\sqrt{2}}{2}.$$

Comparing this result with the competitive situation examined in question 1 shows that the gains from trade are not completely exploited by the intermediary. This is not surprising, given the monopolistic situation. But this has an interesting consequence: consider a buyer whose valuation b lies just below the competitive price $p^* = \frac{1}{2}$. In a competitive situation he obtains a zero surplus since he does not buy in the marketplace and since all the sellers with whom he could have traded (i.e., with a cost $s \leq b$) have gone to the marketplace. This is not true anymore with a monopolistic intermediary, who has set a bid price $\hat{s} = \frac{1}{2\sqrt{2}} < \frac{1}{2}$. Therefore if $b > \hat{s}$, the buyer obtains a positive expected surplus by searching for a seller with a cost parameter s between $\hat{s}$ and b.

Notes

1. This is not true if the bank can *securitize* its loans. However, asymmetric information limits the possibilities of securitization, as will be discussed later in this chapter. Without securitization bankruptcy issues become important. If the grocery store around the corner fails and is immediately replaced by another store, its customers essentially lose nothing. This is not the case if a deposit bank fails. This issue will be discussed in Chapter 9.

2. For instance in the case of N individuals confronted with simple independent risks, a single mutual insurance company offering N insurance contracts (one per individual) generates the same diversification that 2^N contingent markets would. Indeed, in the Arrow-Debreu framework of state contingent securities, complete markets are obtained when there is a contingent security for each state of the world. A state of the world is a complete description of the economy (i.e., which individuals have an accident, and which have no accident): there are 2^N of them, and therefore 2^N securities are needed. When N is large, this number becomes astronomical.

3. A more recent article by Holmström and Tirole (1995) gives a new justification of the liquidity provision activity by banks, related to moral hazard.

4. This is similar to Bester's (1985) solution to the credit rationing problem of Stiglitz and Weiss (1981), in which firms have to provide collateral to signal the quality of their project (see Chapter 5).

5. Notice, however, that *reputation* is another mechanism for solving the reliability problem. It applies in particular to rating agencies or security analysts, which are not included in this book's definition of FIs.

6. Gehrig (1993) studies an interesting model of trade with search costs, in which the introduction of a monopolistic intermediary surprisingly improves the situation of some traders (see problem 2.6.3).

7. This issue is still debated, in particular in connection with the Glass-Steagall Act in the United States. See, for instance, Mester (1992) and Kroszer and Rajan (1994).

8. This idea has been modeled for instance by Vale (1993).

9. In this simple version of the model, C_2^1 and C_1^2 are always optimally set to zero (since each type of consumer values consumption only at a particular date), so that the notations can be simplified: $C_1^1 = C_1, C_2^2 = C_2$.

10. This is equivalent to the condition $\frac{-Cu''(C)}{u'(C)} > 1$, which Diamond and Dybvig interpret as saying that the relative index of risk aversion is larger than one. The idea is that, starting from the market allocation ($C_1 = 1, C_2 = R$), depositors are willing to buy insurance against the risk of being of type 1. But risk aversion alone is not enough to imply this, because this liquidity insurance is costly: increasing expected consumption at $t = 1$ by ϵ (i.e., $\pi_1 C_1 = \pi_1 + \epsilon$) is obtained by decreasing long-term investment of the same amount, and therefore decreasing expected consumption at $t = 2$ by $R\epsilon$ (i.e., $\pi_2 C_2 = R(\pi_2 - \epsilon)$). Therefore, a stronger condition than just risk aversion is necessary: it is the condition that $C \to Cu'(C)$ is decreasing. Since there is no

aggregate uncertainty, a more natural interpretation of this condition is that the intertemporal elasticity of substitution is larger than 1.

11. For any integrable random variable $\tilde{x}$, the notation $E(\tilde{x})$ represents its expectation.

12. In this case, self-finance would be useless and costly: it would entail incomplete insurance for entrepreneurs.

13. This model uses the well-known fact that if $\tilde{x}$ is a normal random variable, then

$$E[-e^{-\rho\tilde{x}}] = -\exp[-\rho(E\tilde{x} - \frac{1}{2}\rho var\ (\tilde{x}))].$$

14. Leland and Pyle (1977) consider the case in which θ has a continuous distribution on some interval $[\underline{\theta}, \bar{\theta}]$, which implies the use of more sophisticated techniques.

15. To obtain a complete characterization of equilibria, the reader can check that two inefficient equilibria can arise:

- A pure strategy equilibrium in which only bad projects issue equity, and therefore $P = \theta_1$.
- A mixed strategy equilibrium in which $P = \theta_2 - \frac{1}{2}\rho\sigma^2$, and some good-quality projects (but not all of them) issue equity.

16. Haubrich (1989) considers an alternative way of preventing moral hazard, by assuming that the lender and the borrower are in a long-term relationship, in which truthful reporting is induced through punishment schemes that depend on the whole sequence of past messages. Systematic understatements of cash flows can thus be identified and punished. However, a crucial assumption made by Haubrich is the absence of discounting for the future.

17. A complete explanation of the concept of incentive compatibility and several examples are provided in Section 4.2. At this stage we only need this notion to express the fact that the bank cannot obtain higher profit by manipulating the value of the realized cash flow $\tilde{z}$.

18. This nonpecuniary penalty is designed in such a way that the total return to the bank is

$$\min(\sum_{i=1}^{n} \tilde{y}_i - nK, nR_D^n) + \max(nR_D^n + nK - \sum_{i=1}^{n} \tilde{y}_i, 0) = nR_D^n,$$

which is independent of the reported total cash flow $\sum_{i=1}^{n} \tilde{y}_i$. Therefore, the bank has no incentive to misreport its earnings.

19. This is true if stochastic auditing is ruled out. See problem 4.8.3 for a study of what happens if stochastic auding is possible.

20. Gorton (1996) has applied this idea to the banks themselves and tested it on a sample of U.S. banks that issued bank notes during the free banking era (1836–60). His results confirm the existence of a reputation effect.

21. This specification of moral hazard is probably more satisfactory than the one used in 2.5.1 and 2.5.2. Indeed, this previous specification relied on the awkward assumption that the success of an investment was verifiable, but not its return.

22. Von Thadden (1996) identifies an error in Sharpe's game theoretical analysis. Contrary to what Sharpe asserts, no pure strategy equilibria exist in the competition game between banks. The reason is a "winner's curse" problem similar to what happens in auction games. Von Thadden shows that instead mixed-strategy equilibria exist, implying a limited informational capture of borrowers in bank–firm relationships, interest rates above the market rate, and occasional switching of borrowers in equilibrium. Von Thadden argues that these predictions correspond more closely to observed behavior than those that would be generated by pure-strategy equilibria.

References

Akerlof, G. A. 1970. The market for lemons: Qualitative uncertainty and the market mechanism. *Quarterly Journal of Economics* 84:488–500.

Allen, F. 1990. The market for information and the origin of financial intermediation. *Journal of Financial Intermediation* 1:3–30.

Benston, G., and C. W. Smith. 1976. A transaction cost approach to the theory of financial intermediation. *Journal of Finance* 31:215–31.

Besanko, D., and G. Kanatas. 1993. Credit market equilibrium with bank monitoring and moral hazard. *Review of Financial Studies* 6:213–32.

Bester, H. 1985. Screening vs rationing in credit markets with imperfect information. *American Economic Review* 75:850–55.

Bhattacharya, S., and G. Chiesa. 1995. Proprietary information, financial intermediation and research incentives. *Journal of Financial Intermediation* 4:328–57.

Bhattacharya, S., and A. Thakor. 1993. Contemporary banking theory. *Journal of Financial Intermediation* 3:2–50.

Boot, A., and A. Thakor. 1995. Financial system architecture. Discussion paper no. 1197, Centre for Economic Policy Research, London.

Boyd, J., and E. Prescott. 1986. Financial intermediary-coalitions. *Journal of Economic Theory* 38:211–32.

Broecker, T. 1990. Credit worthiness tests and interbank competition. *Econometrica* 58:429–52.

Bryant, J. 1980. A model of reserves, bank runs and deposit insurance. *Journal of Banking and Finance* 43:749–61.

Calomiris, C. W., and C. M. Kahn. 1991. The role of demandable debt in structuring optimal banking arrangements. *American Economic Review* 81(3):497–513.

Campbell, T. S., and W. A. Kracaw. 1980. Information production, market signalling, and the theory of financial intermediation. *Journal of Finance* 35:863–82.

Cerasi, V., and S. Daltung. 1994. The optimal size of a bank: Costs and benefits of diversification. FMG discussion paper, London School of Economics, London.

Diamond, D. 1984. Financial intermediation and delegated monitoring. *Review of Economic Studies* 51:393–414.

———. 1991. Monitoring and reputation: The choice between bank loans and directly placed debt. *Journal of Political Economy* 99:689–721.

———. 1997. Liquidity, banks, and markets. University of Chicago. Mimeograph.

Diamond, D., and P. Dybvig. 1983. Bank runs, deposit insurance and liquidity. *Journal of Political Economy* 91:401–19.

Fama, E. 1980. Banking in the theory of finance. *Journal of Monetary Economics* 6(1):39–57.

Gale, D., and M. Hellwig. 1985. Incentive-compatible debt contracts: The one-period problem. *Review of Economic Studies* 52:647–63.

Gehrig, T. 1993. Intermediation in search markets. *Journal of Economics and Management Strategy* 2:97–120.

Gorton, G. 1996. Reputation formation in early bank note markets. *Journal of Political Economy* 104(2):346–97.

Gorton, G., and G. Pennacchi. 1990. Financial intermediaries and liquidity creation. *Journal of Finance* 45:49–71.

Greenbaum, S., G. Kanatas, and I. Venezia. 1989. Equilibrium loan pricing under the bank-client relationship. *Journal of Banking and Finance* 13:221–35.

Greenbaum, S. I., and A. V. Thakor. 1987. Bank funding modes: Securitization vs deposits. *Journal of Banking and Finance* 11:379–401.

Grossman, S. J., and J. Stiglitz. 1980. On the impossibility of informationally efficient markets. *American Economic Review* 70:393–408.

Gurley, J., and E. Shaw. 1960. *Money in the theory of finance.* Washington: Brookings Institution.

Haubrich, J. 1989. Financial intermediations, delegated monitoring and long-term relationships. *Journal of Banking and Finance* 13(1):9–20.

Hellwig, M. 1991. Banking, financial intermediation and corporate finance. In *European Financial Integration,* edited by A. Giovannini and C. Mayer. Cambridge: Cambridge University Press.

Holmström, B., and J. Tirole. 1993. Financial intermediation, loanable funds, and the real sector. IDEI, Toulouse University. Mimeograph.

————. 1995. Private and public supply of liquidity. Working paper, IDEI, Toulouse University.

James, C. 1987. Some evidence on the uniqueness of bank loans. *Journal of Financial Economics* 19(2):217–35.

Krasa, C. M., and A. P. Villamil. 1992. Monitoring the monitor: An incentive structure for a financial intermediary. *Journal of Economic Theory* 57:197–221.

Kroszner, R. S., and R. G. Rajan. 1994. Is the Glass-Steagall Act justified? A Study of the U.S. experience with universal banking before 1933. *American Economic Review* 84(4):810–32.

Leland, H. E., and D. H. Pyle. 1977. Informational asymmetries, financial structure and financial intermediation. *The Journal of Finance* 32:371–87.

Malinvaud, E. 1972. The allocation of individual risks in large economies. *Journal of Economic Theory* 5:312–28.

————. 1973. Markets for an exchange economy with individual risks. *Econometrica* 41:393–410.

Mester, L. J. 1992. Traditional and nontraditional banking: An information-theoretic approach. *Journal of Banking and Finance* 16(3):545–66.

Millon, M. H., and A. Thakor. 1985. Moral hazard and information sharing: A model of financial information gathering agencies. *Journal of Finance* 40(5):1403–22.

Padilla, J. A., and M. Pagano. 1993. Sharing default information as a borrower discipline device. CEMFI, Madrid. Mimeograph.

Pagano, M., and T. Jappelli. 1993. Information sharing in credit markets. *Journal of Finance* 48(5):1693–1718.

Pyle, D. 1971. On the theory of financial intermediation. *Journal of Finance* 26(3):737–47.

Rajan, R. G. 1992. Insiders and outsiders: The choice between informed and arm's-length debt. *Journal of Finance* 47(4):1367–1400.

Ramakrishnan, R. T. S., and A. V. Thakor. 1984. Information reliability and a theory of financial intermediation. *Review of Economic Studies* 51:415–32.

Repullo, R., and J. Suarez. 1995. Credit markets and real economic activity: A model of financial intermediation. CEMFI, Madrid. Mimeograph.

Rothschild, M., and J. Stiglitz. 1976. Equilibrium in competitive insurance markets. *Quarterly Journal of Economics* 11:629–49.

Sharpe, S. 1990. Asymmetric information, bank lending and implicit contracts: A stylized model of customer relationships. *Journal of Finance* 45(4):1069–87.

Spence, M. A. 1973. Job market signaling. *Quarterly Journal of Economics* 87(3):355–74.

Stiglitz, J., and A. Weiss. 1981. Credit rationing with imperfect information. *American Economic Review* 71:393–410.

Townsend, R. 1979. Optimal contracts and competitive markets with costly state verification. *Journal of Economic Theory* 21:417–25.

Vale, B. 1993. The dual role of demand deposits under asymmetric information. *Scandinavian Journal of Economics* 95(1):77–95.

Von Thadden, E. L. 1994. Optimal liquidity provision and dynamic incentive compatibility. Working paper no. 52, Centre for Economic Policy Research, London.

————. 1996. Asymmetric information, bank lending and implicit contracts: The winner's curse. Discussion paper, Basle University, Switzerland.

————. 1997. The term structure of investment and the banks' insurance function. *European Economic Review.*

Yafeh, Y., and Yosha, O. 1995. Large share holders and banks: Who monitors and how. Working paper, Brown University Department of Economics, Providence.

Yosha, O. 1995a. Information disclosure costs and the choice of financing source. *Journal of Financial Intermediation* 4:3–20.

————. 1995b. Arm's length financing and competition in product markets: A welfare analysis. Discussion paper, Tel Aviv University.

The previous chapter presented the asymmetric information justifications of financial intermediation; this chapter will focus on the second pillar of the microeconomic theory of banking, namely the Industrial Organization approach. For simplicity, some important specificities of banking activities will temporarily be ignored (essentially the risk and informational aspects of these activities, which are developed in the rest of the book). Although simplistic, this approach will provide a rich set of models for tackling different issues: monetary policy, market failures (network externalities, switching costs), and some aspects of banking regulation. This chapter will focus on the implications of modeling commercial banks as independent entities that optimally react to their environment, instead of simply considering the banking sector as a passive aggregate, as in the standard approach to monetary policy often found in macro textbooks.

As in the previous chapter, banks will be defined as financial intermediaries that *buy* securities of a certain type *(loans)* and *sell* securities of another type *(deposits)*.[1] This discussion will take as given the banking technology (i.e., the cost of managing these loans and deposits) and will look at the equilibrium of the banking sector under alternative specifications for the type of competition that prevails in this sector. The chapter will start with the polar cases of *perfect competition* (Section 3.1) and *monopoly* (Section 3.2) and show how they can be applied to study the impact of deposit rate regulations (Section 3.3). Then the discussion will move to alternative (and possibly more realistic) paradigms: *double Bertrand competition* (Section 3.4) and *monopolistic competition* (Section 3.5). Section 3.6 will be dedicated to the regulation of branch banking. The chapter will conclude with two appendices on empirical literature: Section 3.7 on the measurement of the market power of California banks and Section 3.8 on the measurement of banks' efficiency.

3.1 A Model of Perfect Competition in the Banking Sector

3.1.1 The Model

This chapter will model banking activity as the "production" of deposit and loan services, and banking technology will be represented by a cost function $C(D, L)$, interpreted as the cost of managing a volume D of deposits and a volume L of loans.[2] There are N different banks (indexed by $n = 1, \ldots, N$), and bank n has a cost function $C_n(D, L)$ that satisfies the usual assumptions of convexity (which implies, in particular, decreasing returns to scale) and regularity (C_n is twice differentiable).

To simplify notations, this discussion will often assume that the same technology is available to all banks ($C_n(D, L) = C(D, L)$ for all n), but this is not crucial. The typical balance sheet of a bank is therefore as follows:

Assets	Liabilities
R_n (reserves)	D_n (deposits)
L_n (loans)	

More precisely, the difference R_n between the volume of deposits D_n that bank n has collected and the volume of loans L_n that the bank has granted will be divided into two terms: cash reserves C_n (transferred by bank n on its account at the Central Bank) and the bank's (net) position M_n (positive or negative) on the interbank market. The difference between these two terms is that C_n typically bears no interest and is therefore optimally chosen at its minimum level defined by the regulator. C_n equals a proportion α of deposits. Thus for all n,

$$C_n = \alpha D_n. \tag{3.1}$$

The coefficient α of compulsory reserves may be used as a policy instrument through which the Central Bank will try to influence the quantity of money in circulation in the economy. To complete the picture, a description of the real sector is needed, which consists of three types of agents: the government (which includes the Central Bank), the firms, and the households. The role of commercial banks is to collect the savings S of households so as to finance the investment needs I of firms. Finally, the government finances its deficit G by issuing securities ΔB (Treasury bills)[3] and high-powered money ΔM_0 (the monetary base)[4] used by commercial banks to finance their compulsory reserves at the Central Bank. Since this model ignores currency (the cash holdings of households and the relations with foreign countries), money consists only of the sum of deposits collected by commercial banks ($D = \sum_{n=1}^{N} D_n$). Similarly, the monetary base M_0 equals the sum of the reserves of commercial banks on their accounts at the Central Bank (this is the equilibrium condition on the interbank market):

$$M_0 = \sum_{n=1}^{N} C_n = \alpha D. \tag{3.2}$$

In this simplistic framework, the increments in the aggregated balances of each category of agents are represented as follows:

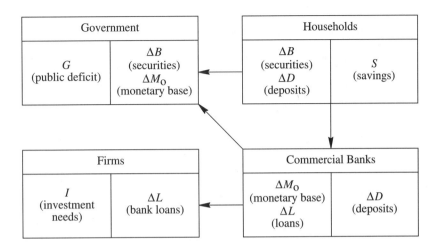

3.1.2   The Standard Approach: The Credit Multiplier

The usual description of monetary policy that can be found in elementary macroeconomics textbooks relies on this aggregate description. In this view, a change of the monetary base M_0 or an open market operation (i.e., a change in B) has a direct impact on money and credit, since this yields the following:

$$\Delta D = \frac{\Delta M_0}{\alpha} = \frac{G - \Delta B}{\alpha};$$

$$\Delta L = \Delta M_0 \left(\frac{1}{\alpha} - 1\right) = (G - \Delta B) \left(\frac{1}{\alpha} - 1\right). \tag{3.3}$$

The money multiplier is defined by the impact of a marginal change in the monetary base (or an open market operation)[5] on the quantity of money in circulation:

$$\frac{\partial D}{\partial M_0} = -\frac{\partial D}{\partial B} = \frac{1}{\alpha} > 0.$$

Similarly, the credit multiplier is defined as the impact on credit of such marginal changes:

$$\frac{\partial L}{\partial M_0} = -\frac{\partial L}{\partial B} = \frac{1}{\alpha} - 1 > 0.$$

The trouble with this simplistic description is that banks are taken as passive entities. Also, modern monetary policy is more accurately described as interventions on the rate r at which the Central Bank refinances commercial banks (which, for simplicity, will be assumed to equal the interbank rate). These interventions affect the behavior of commercial banks and therefore the equilibrium interest rates on deposits (r_D) and loans (r_L). To analyze these impacts we need to model the individual behavior of commercial banks.

3.1.3   The Behavior of Individual Banks in a Competitive Banking Sector

In a competitive model, banks are supposed to be price takers: they take as given the rate r_L of loans, the rate r_D of deposits, and the rate r on the interbank market. Taking into account the management costs, the profit of a bank will be given by

$$\pi = r_L L + r M - r_D D - C(D, L),$$

where M, the net position of the bank on the interbank market, is given by

$$M = (1 - \alpha)D - L. \tag{3.4}$$

Therefore, π can be rewritten as

$$\pi(D, L) = (r_L - r)L + (r(1 - \alpha) - r_D)D - C(D, L). \tag{3.5}$$

Thus the bank's profit is the sum of the intermediation margins on loans and deposits, net of management costs. Because of the assumptions on the cost function C, profit maximizing behavior is characterized by the first order conditions:

$$\begin{cases} \frac{\partial \pi}{\partial L} = (r_L - r) - \frac{\partial C}{\partial L}(D, L) = 0 \\ \frac{\partial \pi}{\partial D} = (r(1 - \alpha) - r_D) - \frac{\partial C}{\partial D}(D, L) = 0. \end{cases} \tag{3.6}$$

Result 3.1

1. A competitive bank will adjust its volume of loans and deposits in such a way that the corresponding intermediation margins, $r_L - r$ and $r(1 - \alpha) - r_D$, equal its marginal management costs.

2. As a consequence, an increase in r_D will entail a decrease in the bank's demand for deposits D. Similarly, an increase in r_L will entail an increase in the bank's supply of loans L. The cross-effects depend on the sign of $\frac{\partial^2 C}{\partial D \partial L}$: when $\frac{\partial^2 C}{\partial D \partial L} > 0$ (resp. < 0), an increase in r_L entails a decrease (resp. an increase) in D, and an increase in r_D entails a decrease (resp. an increase) in L. When costs are separable ($\frac{\partial^2 C}{\partial D \partial L} = 0$), cross-effects are nil.

The economic interpretation of the conditions on $\frac{\partial^2 C}{\partial L \partial D}$ is related to the notion of *economies of scope*. When $\frac{\partial^2 C}{\partial L \partial D} < 0$, an increase in L has the consequence of decreasing the marginal cost of deposits. This is a particular form of economies of scope, since it implies that a "universal" bank that jointly offers loans and deposits is more efficient than two separate entities, specialized respectively on loans and deposits. On the contrary, when $\frac{\partial^2 C}{\partial L \partial D} > 0$, there are *diseconomies of scope*.

Proof   Part 1 follows directly from 3.6. Part 2 is obtained by totally differentiating the same system of equations (that is, applying the implicit function theorem to 3.6). For instance, differentiating 3.6 with respect to r_L yields the following result:

$$\begin{cases} 1 & = & \frac{\partial^2 C}{\partial L \partial D} \frac{dD}{dr_L} + \frac{\partial^2 C}{\partial L^2} \frac{dL}{dr_L} \\ 0 & = & \frac{\partial^2 C}{\partial D^2} \frac{dD}{dr_L} + \frac{\partial^2 C}{\partial L \partial D} \frac{dL}{dr_L}. \end{cases}$$

The Cramer determinant of this system $(\Delta = (\frac{\partial^2 C}{\partial L \partial D})^2 - \frac{\partial^2 C}{\partial L^2} \cdot \frac{\partial^2 C}{\partial D^2})$ is negative, since C is convex. Solving this system by Cramer's formulas gives $\frac{dL}{dr_L} = -\frac{1}{\Delta} \frac{\partial^2 C}{\partial D^2}$ and $\frac{dD}{dr_L} = \frac{1}{\Delta} \frac{\partial^2 C}{\partial D \partial L}$. Therefore $\frac{dL}{dr_L}$ has the same sign as $\frac{\partial^2 C}{\partial D^2}$ (which is positive), and $\frac{dD}{dr_L}$ has the same sign as $-\frac{\partial^2 C}{\partial D \partial L}$. The consequences of a change in r_D are analyzed in exactly the same terms.   ∎

3.1.4   The Competitive Equilibrium of the Banking Sector

When there are N different banks (indexed by $n = 1, \ldots, N$), each of them will be characterized by a loan supply function $L^n(r_L, r_D, r)$ and a deposit demand function $D^n(r_L, r_D, r)$ defined as previously. Let $I(r_L)$ be the investment demand by firms (which, in this simple framework, is equal to their demand for loans, since they do not issue securities), and $S(r_D)$ the savings function of households. (Assume for simplicity that banking deposits and Treasury bills B are perfect substitutes for households: at equilibrium their interest rate is therefore the same.) The competitive equilibrium will be characterized by three equations:

$$I(r_L) = \sum_{n=1}^{N} L^n(r_L, r_D, r) \qquad \text{(loans market)} \qquad (3.7)$$

$$S(r_D) = B + \sum_{n=1}^{N} D^n(r_L, r_D, r) \qquad \text{(savings market)} \qquad (3.8)$$

$$\sum_{n=1}^{N} L^n(r_L, r_D, r) = (1 - \alpha) \sum_{n=1}^{N} D^n(r_L, r_D, r) \qquad \text{(interbank market)} \qquad (3.9)$$

where the third equation comes from the fact that the aggregate position of all banks on the interbank market is zero. More generally, a term corresponding to the injection (or drain) of cash by the Central Bank can be added to (or subtracted from) this equation, in which case r becomes a policy variable chosen by the Central Bank. Alternatively, r could be determined in the international capital markets. In both cases, equation 3.9 disappears.

In the case of constant marginal costs of intermediation ($C'_L \equiv \gamma_L, C'_D \equiv \gamma_D$), a simpler characterization of equilibrium is obtained, since the first two equations are replaced by a direct determination of r_L and r_D,[6] deduced from 3.6:

$$r_L = r + \gamma_L, \tag{3.10}$$

$$r_D = r(1 - \alpha) - \gamma_D. \tag{3.11}$$

Then the interest rate r on the interbank market is determined by the third equation:

$$S(r(1 - \alpha) - \gamma_D) - \frac{I(r + \gamma_L)}{1 - \alpha} = B. \tag{3.12}$$

The impact may now be determined of a marginal shift in the reserve coefficient α, or of an open market operation (change in the level of B) on the equilibrium level of interest rates r_L and r_D.

Result 3.2

1. An issue of Treasury bills by the government (an increase in B) entails a decrease in loans and deposits.[7] However, the absolute values are smaller than in the standard model of Section 3.1:

$$\left| \frac{\partial D}{\partial B} \right| < 1, \left| \frac{\partial L}{\partial B} \right| < 1 - \alpha.$$

2. If the reserve coefficient α increases, the volume of loans decreases, but the impact on deposits is ambiguous.[8]

Proof

1. Differentiating 3.12 with respect to B yields the following result:

$$\left\{ (1 - \alpha)S'(r_D) - \frac{I'(r_L)}{(1 - \alpha)} \right\} \frac{dr}{dB} = 1.$$

The impact on D of a change in B is now easily obtained, since

$$D(r_D) = S(r_D) - B.$$

Thus

$$\frac{\partial D}{\partial B} = S'(r_D)(1 - \alpha) \frac{dr}{dB} - 1 = \frac{1}{\frac{(1-\alpha)^2 S'(r_D)}{I'(r_L)} - 1}.$$

Since $S'(r_D) > 0$ and $I'(r_L) < 0$, then $\frac{\partial D}{\partial B} < 0$ and $\left| \frac{\partial D}{\partial B} \right| < 1$. As for the impact on L (which equals I), $L = (1 - \alpha)D$; therefore

$$\frac{\partial L}{\partial B} = (1 - \alpha)\frac{\partial D}{\partial B}.$$

Thus $\frac{\partial L}{\partial B} < 0$ and $\left|\frac{\partial L}{\partial B}\right| < 1 - \alpha$.

2. Differentiating 3.12 with respect to α,

$$\left\{(1 - \alpha)S'(r_D) - \frac{I'(r_L)}{1 - \alpha}\right\}\frac{dr}{d\alpha} = rS'(r_D) + \frac{I(r_L)}{(1 - \alpha)^2} > 0.$$

Since $S'(r_D) > 0$ and $I'(r_L) < 0$, $\frac{dr}{d\alpha} > 0$. Now, $r_L = r + \gamma_L$ and $r_D = r(1 - \alpha) - \gamma_D$. Therefore, if α increases, r_L also increases, and thus the volume of loans decreases. However, the impact on r_D (and deposits) is ambiguous:

$$\frac{dr_D}{d\alpha} = -r + (1 - \alpha)\frac{dr}{d\alpha}. \qquad\qquad \blacksquare$$

The second part of result 3.2 may be somewhat surprising given that the first order conditions state that the deposit rate is a decreasing function of the reserve coefficient α. But the interbank market rate here is endogenous, and equation 3.12 yields the result. If the extreme opposite assumption were made of an exogenous interbank market rate r (either controlled by the Central Bank through open market operations, or determined by the interest rate on international capital markets under a regime of fixed exchange rates), then the rate on loans would be unaffected by reserve requirements, and only the deposit rate would adjust, as easily seen from 3.10 and 3.11.

3.2   The Monti-Klein Model of a Monopolistic Bank

The assumption of perfect competition may not seem really appropriate for the banking sector, where there are important barriers to entry. An imperfect competition model (oligopoly) is probably more appropriate. For expository reasons, this discussion will first study the Monti-Klein model which, in its simplest version, is poles apart from the purely competitive model, since it considers a monopolistic bank.

3.2.1   The Original Model

The Monti-Klein model considers a monopolistic bank confronted with a downward sloping demand for loans $L(r_L)$ and an upward sloping supply of deposits $D(r_D)$. In fact, it will be more convenient to work with their inverse functions, $r_L(L)$ and $r_D(D)$. The bank's decision variables are L (the amount of loans) and D (the amount of deposits), since its level of equity is assumed to be given. Using the same assumptions and notations as before, the profit of the bank is easily adapted from 3.5, the only difference being that the bank now takes into account the influence of L on r_L (and of D on r_D). Assume that the bank still takes r as given, either because it is fixed by the Central Bank or because it is determined by the equilibrium rate on international capital markets:

$$\pi = \pi(L, D) = (r_L(L) - r)L + (r(1 - \alpha) - r_D(D))D - C(D, L). \quad (3.13)$$

The bank's profit is, as before, the sum of the intermediation margins on loans and on deposits minus management costs. In order for the maximum of π to be characterized by the first order conditions, assume that π is concave. The first order conditions are

$$\frac{\partial \pi}{\partial L} = r'_L(L)L + r_L - r - C'_L(D, L) = 0 \quad (3.14)$$

$$\frac{\partial \pi}{\partial D} = -r'_D(D)D + r(1 - \alpha) - r_D - C'_D(D, L) = 0 \quad (3.15)$$

Now the elasticities of the demand for loans and the supply of deposits are introduced:[9]

$$\varepsilon_L = -\frac{r_L L'(r_L)}{L(r_L)} > 0 \quad \text{and} \quad \varepsilon_D = \frac{r_D D'(r_D)}{D(r_D)} > 0.$$

The solution (r_L^*, r_D^*) of 3.14 and 3.15 can then be characterized by[10]

$$\frac{r_L^* - (r + C'_L)}{r_L^*} = \frac{1}{\varepsilon_L(r_L^*)}, \quad (3.16)$$

$$\frac{r(1 - \alpha) - C'_D - r_D^*}{r_D^*} = \frac{1}{\varepsilon_D(r_D^*)}. \quad (3.17)$$

These equations are simply the adaptation to the banking sector of the familiar equalities between Lerner indices (price minus cost divided by price) and inverse elasticities. The greater the market power of the bank on deposits (resp. loans), the smaller the elasticity and the higher the Lerner index. The competitive model corresponds to the limit case of infinite elasticities, which goes back to equation 3.6. Therefore the intuitive result is that intermediation margins are higher when banks have a higher market power.

Result 3.3 A monopolistic bank will set its volume of loans and deposits in such a way that the Lerner indices equal inverse elasticities.

An immediate consequence of this result is that intermediation margins will be adversely affected if substitutes to banking products appear on financial markets (for instance, when households have access to money market funds as substitutes for banking deposits, and when firms issue securities on financial markets as a substitute for bank loans).

Two other interesting consequences are the following

Result 3.4

1. If management costs are additive, the bank's decision problem is separable: the optimal deposit rate is independent of the characteristics of the loan market, and the optimal loan rate is independent of the characteristics of the deposit market.

2. Under the same assumption, if the interest rate r on the money market increases, both r_L^* and r_D^* increase.

Proof   Part 1 is obvious from 3.16 and 3.17. As far as 2 is concerned, consider equations 3.14 and 3.15, which implicitly define L^* and D^* as functions of r:

$$\frac{\partial \pi}{\partial L}(L^*(r), r) = \frac{\partial \pi}{\partial D}(D^*(r), r) = 0.$$

By differentiating these equations (again applying the implicit function theorem), the following result is obtained:

$$\frac{\partial^2 \pi}{\partial L^2}\frac{dL}{dr} + \frac{\partial^2 \pi}{\partial L \partial r} = 0$$

$$\frac{\partial^2 \pi}{\partial D^2}\frac{dD}{dr} + \frac{\partial^2 \pi}{\partial D \partial r} = 0.$$

Since π is concave, both $\frac{\partial^2 \pi}{\partial L^2}(r_L^*, r)$ and $\frac{\partial^2 \pi}{\partial D^2}(r_D^*, r)$ are negative. Therefore $\frac{dL}{dr}$ (resp. $\frac{dD}{dr}$) has the same sign as $\frac{\partial^2 \pi}{\partial L \partial r}$ (resp. $\frac{\partial^2 \pi}{\partial D \partial r}$). But now 3.14 and 3.15 yield the following:

$$\frac{\partial^2 \pi}{\partial L \partial r} = -1 < 0; \quad \frac{\partial^2 \pi}{\partial D \partial r} = 1 - \alpha > 0.$$

Consequently $\frac{dL^*(r)}{dr} < 0$ (resp. $\frac{dD^*(r)}{dr} > 0$). Since $L(r_L)$ (resp. $D(r_D)$) is a decreasing (resp. increasing) function, this yields $\frac{dr_L^*}{dr} > 0$ (resp. $\frac{dr_D^*}{dr} > 0$).   ∎

3.2.2   The Oligopolistic Version

Of course, one may question the practical relevance of these results, since the banking industry is clearly not controlled by a unique firm. In fact, the main interest of the Monti-Klein model is that it can easily be reinterpreted as a model of imperfect (Cournot) competition between a finite number N of banks, which is a more accurate description of reality.[11] Indeed, consider the case of N banks (indexed by $n = 1, \ldots, N$) supposed for simplicity to have the same cost function, taken to be linear:

$$C_n(D, L) = \gamma_D D + \gamma_L L, \qquad n = 1, \ldots, N.$$

A Cournot equilibrium of the banking industry is an N-tuple of vectors $(D_n^*, L_n^*)_{n=1,\dots,N}$ such that for every n, (D_n^*, L_n^*) maximizes the profit of bank n (taking the volume of deposits and loans of other banks as given). In other words, for every n, (D_n^*, L_n^*) solves

$$\max_{(D_n, L_n)} \left\{ (r_L(L_n + \sum_{m \neq n} L_m^*) - r)L_n + (r(1 - \alpha) - r_D(D_n + \sum_{m \neq n} D_m^*))D_n \right.$$

$$\left. - C(D_n, L_n) \right\}.$$

It is easy to see that there is a unique equilibrium, in which each bank sets $D_n^* = \frac{D^*}{N}$ and $L_n^* = \frac{L^*}{N}$. The first order conditions give

$$\begin{cases} \frac{\partial \pi_n}{\partial L_n} &= r_L'(L^*)\frac{L^*}{N} + r_L(L^*) - r - \gamma_L = 0 \\ \frac{\partial \pi_n}{\partial D_n} &= -r_D'(D^*)\frac{D^*}{N} + r(1 - \alpha) - r_D(D^*) - \gamma_D = 0. \end{cases}$$

These first order conditions can also be rewritten as

$$\frac{r_L^* - (r + \gamma_L)}{r_L^*} = \frac{1}{N\varepsilon_L(r_L^*)} \tag{3.18}$$

$$\frac{r(1 - \alpha) - \gamma_D - r_D^*}{r_D^*} = \frac{1}{N\varepsilon_D(r_D^*)}. \tag{3.19}$$

Comparing these with 3.16 and 3.17, one can see that the only difference between the monopoly case and the Cournot equilibrium is that the elasticities are multiplied by N. With this simple adaptation, the Monti-Klein model can thus be reinterpreted as a model of imperfect competition with two limiting cases: $N = 1$ (monopoly) and $N = +\infty$ (perfect competition). This will be done in the next section, which will apply this model to an analysis of deposit rate regulations.

Notice that equations 3.18 and 3.19 provide a possible test of imperfect competition on the banking sector. Indeed, from these equations, the sensitivity of r_L^* and r_D^* to changes in the money market rate r depends on N, which is a proxy for the intensity of competition ($N = 1$ may be interpreted as pure cartellization, whereas $N = +\infty$ corresponds to perfect competition). Assuming for simplicity that elasticities are constant,

$$\frac{\partial r_L^*}{\partial r} = \frac{1}{1 - \frac{1}{N\varepsilon_L}}, \text{ and } \frac{\partial r_D^*}{\partial r} = \frac{1 - \alpha}{1 + \frac{1}{N\varepsilon_D}}.$$

Therefore as the intensity of competition increases (N grows), r_L^* (resp. r_D^*) becomes less (resp. more) sensitive to changes in r.

Worthy of mention as a conclusion to this section is the contribution of De Palma and Gary-Bobo (1996), who introduce liquidation (or rather securitization) costs in a Cournot model of the loan market, in which banks may have different levels of capital. They show that these costs can generate non-concavities in the banks' objective functions, which in turn may provoke discontinuities of the aggregate credit supply function with respect to banks' capital.

3.2.3   Empirical Evidence

Although the Monti-Klein model presents a very simplified approach to the banking activity, it is clear that the model provides a series of conclusions that seem particularly natural and appealing, and that can be confronted with empirical evidence. Of course, there are also features of deposit contracts that the model cannot explain, but it seems reasonable too that market power will lead the banks to quote lower deposit rates and higher rates on loans. Indeed, the empirical findings (since Edwards's [1964] early contribution) show that the different interest rates charged on loans can be viewed as reflecting different elasticities of demand.

More recently, Neuberger and Zimmerman (1990) have also tested the validity of the model in their search for an explanation of the persistently lower rates on deposits in the state of California (what they call the "California rate mystery") using a sample of 430 banks over the period 1984 to 1987. The Monti-Klein model suggests an explanation in terms of market structure, since banking is more concentrated in California than in the rest of the United States. Still, an appropriate test of the model has to include some measure of the non-pecuniary part of the returns obtained by depositors, which the authors take to be the number of bank branches, complemented by, on the one hand, a measure of overhead expenses and, on the other hand, a measure of average salaries of bank employees, which may in part reflect the services to depositors. (See Appendix 3.7 for details.)

3.3   Analyzing the Impact of Deposit Rate Regulations

As an application of the Monti-Klein model, this section will study what happens when the regulator imposes a ceiling on deposit rates: $r_D \leq \bar{r}_D$. Such a restriction is not uncommon; known as "regulation Q" in the United States, it was imposed until April 1986. It still exists in several European countries (including Germany and France) and has been lifted only recently in others.[12]

One of the justifications for imposing regulation of deposit rates is the presumption that decreasing the cost of resources for banks will entail a decrease in the rates they charge to borrowers. This is based on the idea of markup pricing on behalf of the banks. In a more elaborate setup, as in the Monti-Klein model, this idea is incorrect, as will be shown.

As the last section showed, the discussion can be restricted, without loss of generality, to the monopoly case, the (symmetric) Cournot oligopoly being obtained by correcting elasticities by a multiplicative parameter. A second simplification is obtained, in the present context, by using interest rates as the strategic variables (instead of quantities). This is perfectly legitimate, since the profit function of the monopolistic bank can be written equivalently as

$$\pi(D, L) = (r_L(L) - r)L + (r - r_D(D))D - C(D, L),$$

or

$$\Pi(r_D, r_L) \stackrel{\text{def}}{=} (r_L - r)L(r_L) + (r - r_D)D(r_D) - C(D(r_D), L(r_L)),$$

where it is assumed for simplicity that $\alpha = 0$ (no compulsory reserves). Computing the first order condition for the unconstrained maximization of Π with respect to r_D and r_L yields, of course, the same equations as before:

$$\begin{cases} \dfrac{r_L^* - r - C_L'}{r_L^*} = \dfrac{1}{\varepsilon_L(r_L^*)} \\ \dfrac{r - C_D' - r_D^*}{r_D^*} = \dfrac{1}{\varepsilon_D(r_D^*)}. \end{cases}$$

When a ceiling $\bar{r}_D$ is imposed on deposit rates, the maximization program of the bank becomes

$$\begin{cases} \max \Pi(r_D, r_L) \\ r_D \leq \bar{r}_D. \end{cases}$$

Suppose that Π is concave, and denote by $(\hat{r}_D(\bar{r}_D), \hat{r}_L(\bar{r}_D))$ the solution of the previous program. Two cases have to be considered:

1. $r_D^* \leq \bar{r}_D$. The regulation is ineffective:

$$\hat{r}_D(\bar{r}_D) = r_D^*, \quad \hat{r}_L(\bar{r}_D) = r_L^*.$$

2. $r_D^* > \bar{r}_D$. This is of course the most interesting case, since (r_D^*, r_L^*) is no longer feasible. The new solution $(\bar{r}_D, \hat{r}_L)$ will satisfy the first order condition:

$$\frac{\partial \Pi}{\partial r_L}(\bar{r}_D, \hat{r}_L) = 0.$$

Because Π is concave, there is a unique such $\hat{r}_L$, and this equation defines $\hat{r}_L$ as an implicit function of the ceiling $\bar{r}_D$. Under the implicit function theorem,

$$\frac{\partial^2 \Pi}{\partial r_L^2} \frac{d\hat{r}_L}{d\bar{r}_D} + \frac{\partial^2 \Pi}{\partial r_L \partial r_D} = 0.$$

Since $\frac{\partial^2 \Pi}{\partial r_L^2}$ is negative, the sign of $\frac{d\hat{r}_L}{d\bar{r}_D}$ is equal to the sign of $\frac{\partial^2 \Pi}{\partial r_L \partial r_D}$.

Thus, the following has been proved:

LEMMA 3.1   A ceiling on deposit rates will induce a decrease in lending rates if and only if $\frac{\partial^2 \Pi}{\partial r_L \partial r_D} > 0$.

From the bank's viewpoint, the condition $\frac{\partial^2 \Pi}{\partial r_L \partial r_D} > 0$ (resp. < 0) corresponds to the case in which loans and deposits are substitutes (resp. complements) in the sense that when the volume of loans increases (i.e., when r_L decreases) the marginal profitability of collecting deposits decreases (resp. increases).

Under what assumptions is this condition satisfied? The following result provides the answer when the demand function for loans and the supply function of deposits are independent (i.e., L depends only on r_L, and D depends only on r_D):

Result 3.5   When the demand for loans and the supply of deposits are independent, and when banks have access to an infinitely elastic source of funds, a ceiling on deposit rates implies a decrease of lending rates if $\frac{\partial^2 C}{\partial D \partial L} > 0$. When the management cost function is separable $\left(\frac{\partial^2 C}{\partial D \partial L} = 0 \right)$, a ceiling on deposit rates has no effect on lending rates.

Proof   This is a direct consequence of lemma 3.1, once it is remarked that

$$\frac{\partial^2 \Pi}{\partial r_D \partial r_L} = -\frac{\partial^2 C}{\partial D \partial L} L'(r_L) D'(r_D), \text{ with } L' < 0 \text{ and } D' > 0. \qquad \blacksquare$$

This result means that the regulation of deposit rates may miss its objective, since in the simplest case (separable costs) a ceiling on deposit rates has no effect on lending rates. Moreover, the assumption that is needed for the informal justification of ceilings given to be correct (i.e., $\frac{\partial^2 C}{\partial D \partial L} > 0$) is precisely the opposite of the condition (cost complementarity, $\frac{\partial^2 C}{\partial D \partial L} < 0$) that is needed to explain the existence of universal banks. If $\frac{\partial^2 C}{\partial D \partial L}$ was positive, narrow banking would be more efficient.

Still, this disappointing result has been seen as a criticism of the Monti-Klein model, rather than a proof of the inappropriateness of deposit regulations as an indirect instrument for controlling loans. What happens if the assumptions of this model that were used in result 3.5 are changed?

First of all, if interdependence between loans and deposits is introduced, substitutability may appear in the profit function $\left(\frac{\partial^2 \Pi}{\partial r_L \partial r_D} > 0 \right)$. Consider for instance the case of constant marginal costs ($C'_L = \gamma_L$ and $C'_D = \gamma_D$). The new expression of the profit function is

$$\Pi(r_L, r_D) = (r_L - r - \gamma_L)L(r_L, r_D) + (r - r_D - \gamma_D)D(r_L, r_D).$$

By differentiating this expression with respect to r_L and r_D, the following condition for substitutability is obtained:

$$\frac{\partial L}{\partial r_D} - \frac{\partial D}{\partial r_L} + (r_L - r - \gamma_L)\frac{\partial^2 L}{\partial r_L \partial r_D} + (r - r_D - \gamma_D)\frac{\partial^2 D}{\partial r_L \partial r_D} > 0.$$

In particular, if the cross-derivatives of L and D are positive and large enough, substitutability may appear. However, there is no intuitive justification of this condition.[13]

Substitutability between loans and deposits may also appear if the money market rate varies when the (aggregate) reserves R of the banks (i.e., their net position on the money market) change. In that case the new expression of the profit of the (representative) bank is

$$\Pi(r_D, r_L) = r_L L(r_L) - r_D D(r_D) - \mathcal{C}(D(r_D), L(r_L)),$$

where $\mathcal{C}(D, L)$ represents the total cost of intermediation:

$$\mathcal{C}(D, L) \stackrel{\text{def}}{=} C(D, L) + (D - L)[r(D - L)].$$

The last term, which has the same sign as R (which equals $D - L$) represents the net income from money market operations. Substitutability of deposits and loans occurs when $\frac{\partial^2 \mathcal{C}}{\partial D \partial L} > 0$, which is equivalent to

$$\frac{\partial^2 C}{\partial D \partial L} > \{Rr''(R) + 2r'(R)\}. \tag{3.20}$$

This condition is satisfied, for instance, when management costs are separable $\left(\frac{\partial^2 C}{\partial D \partial L} = 0\right)$ and when the money market rate is decreasing ($r'(R) < 0$) and concave ($r''(R) \leq 0$) with respect to R.

Notice that this discussion has assumed that banks were risk neutral. This seems a reasonable assumption, since the bank portfolio is expected to be diversified. Nevertheless, it may be a good idea to take into account the fact that the bank itself may go bankrupt, and that its limited liability clause will then affect its supply of deposits. This point is developed by Dermine (1986). He shows that the separability of the bank's decision problem (result 3.4) may be lost when the bank has a nonzero probability of default. Problem 3.9.1 examines the core of Dermine's argument: separability is lost because depositors do not correctly price the bank's risk of default. As a consequence, the higher the bank's probability of default, the lower the cost of lending one additional unit. Since the probability of default is jointly determined by deposits and loans, the separability property is lost.

3.4 Double Bertrand Competition

The (generalized) Monti-Klein model, presented in Section 3.3 as a convenient description of imperfect competition in the banking industry, suffers from the same criticisms as the Cournot model from which it is adapted. In particular, as emphasized originally by Bertrand, prices (here rates) may be more appropriate strategic variables for describing firms' (here banks') behavior. As is well known, however, price competition à la Bertrand may go too far, since (1) existence of an equilibrium is not guaranteed, and (2) as soon as two firms are present, perfect competition is obtained. A classical compromise is to take into account capacity constraints à la Edgeworth.

As far as banks are concerned, these capacity constraints are not very natural to introduce. Therefore the Bertrand-Edgeworth paradigm does not seem very natural in the banking context. Moreover, considering the simplest case of constant marginal costs for managing loans and deposits, one may think that Bertrand competition will lead to the Walrasian equilibrium studied in Section 3.2. However, in the case of banks (or more generally intermediaries of any kind), things are more complex since we have *double competition,* i.e., simultaneous competition on outputs (loans) and inputs (deposits).

Stahl (1988) and Yanelle (1988, 1989) have studied this double Bertrand competition and shown that it may surprisingly give rise to outcomes that are different from the Walrasian equilibrium. This discussion will present their arguments in a simple framework and show that the timing of offers (the "rules" of the competition game) can be crucial.

This example will focus on the case of constant marginal costs, which can be normalized to zero without loss of generality. Denote by $L(r_L)$ the demand for loans and by $D(r_D)$ the supply of deposits. Since financial markets and reserve requirements are ignored, and constant (zero) marginal costs are assumed, the Walrasian equilibrium is simply characterized by

$$r_L = r_D = \hat{r},$$

where $\hat{r}$ is the unique solution of

$$L(r) = D(r).$$

In that case, financial intermediation is *neutral,* since the equilibrium is identical to a situation in which demands and supplies of funds would be confronted directly on a centralized market (without intermediaries). How could double Bertrand competition display nonneutrality? The answer comes from the absence (by assumption) of an infinitely elastic source of funds (money market). If there is no such source of funds, a bank can simply "corner" the loan market if it is able to attract the entirety of available deposits. (The word "corner" is used to highlight the analogy with the so-called corner strategies on futures markets.) A sequential timing is adopted in which competition takes place first on the deposit market and then on the loan market. Therefore *competition on the deposit market may boil down to auctioning the right of being a monopolist on the loan market.* Thus the Walrasian equilibrium ($r_L = r_D = \hat{r}$) may not be sustainable as a Bertrand equilibrium, since by offering a slightly higher rate on deposits ($r_D = \hat{r} + \varepsilon$) a single bank could deprive its competitors from their only source of funds, and subsequently behave as a monopolist on the loans market.

More specifically, Stahl (1988) is able to show that, when the elasticity of the demand for loans is high enough, the outcome of double Bertrand competition (in which competition takes place first in the deposit market) is not neutral. The equilibrium has the following features:

• Only one intermediary is active.

• The intermediation margin is positive ($r_L^* > r_D^*$), but all intermediaries (including the active one) make zero profit.

• The loan rate r_L^* is the one that maximizes the revenue from loans $(1 + r_L)L(r_L)$.

• r_D^* is defined implicitly by $(1 + r_D^*)D(r_D^*) = (1 + r_L^*)L(r_L^*)$.

• There is excess supply of deposits: $L(r_L^*) < D(r_D^*)$.

A few additional comments are in order. Notice first that zero profit and positive margins are consistent with each other, since the only active bank has idle reserves. Therefore there is a clear inefficiency in the allocation of funds. Note also that the equilibrium is similar to what would occur if depositors could collude: they would also charge the monopoly price r_L^* to borrowers, and the volume of credit would equal $L(r_L^*)$. The only difference is that depositors would not have to provide deposits in excess of the volume $L(r_L^*)$ needed for credit.

One could expect to find another equilibrium, symmetric to this one, in which borrowers extract all the revenue from depositors. But the symmetry breaks down, since it would imply negative (excess) reserves. In fact, to obtain such an equilibrium, borrowers would have to agree to be rationed in exchange for a lower rate on their loans, and then the game would be far more complex.

When rationing is introduced (that is, when each bank announces the maximum amount of deposits it is prepared to accept and of loans it is willing to grant), the equilibrium cannot be sustained any longer. Indeed, since the active bank has idle reserves (equal to $D(r_D^*) - L(r_L^*)$), by limiting deposits to $L(r_L^*)$ it will save on the cost of deposits and make a profit equal to $r_D^*(D(r_D^*) - L(r_L^*))$. Yanelle (1988) shows that in this case no pure strategy equilibrium exists.

By changing the rules of the competition game somewhat, a second type of nonneutral equilibrium can be obtained, *even in the absence of a limited supply of funds (deposits).* Assume that banks can borrow any amount from the money market at a given rate r, but that there is a fixed cost F of intermediation.

Firms can also borrow directly on financial markets, but at a higher rate $r + \alpha$. Therefore banks are potentially more efficient, provided their size is higher than a minimum level L_m defined by $\alpha L_m = F$. The size of individual loans is normalized to one, and the number of firms is assumed to be two. The interesting case occurs when $1 < L_m < 2$, so that a bank is viable only if it finances both firms. The timing of the game is as follows:

• At date 1, banks simultaneously announce lending rates $r_L^n (n = 1, \ldots, N)$.

• At date 2, firms simultaneously choose to apply for credit at a given bank or to borrow from the financial markets.

• At date 3, banks accept or reject credit applications.

Assume that firms' reservation rate is higher than $r + \alpha$, and that a firm that is rejected at date 3 cannot go to another bank or to the market. Therefore when a firm applies for credit from a bank at date 2, it has to be sure that this bank will not reject its application at date 3, in which case it would lose a valuable opportunity. This decision is based here only on efficiency considerations: a bank will operate if and only if it has enough loan applications. It is clear that no bank will ever announce a lending rate higher than $r + \alpha$ or smaller than $\underline{r} = r + \frac{F}{2}$, which is the minimal rate allowing a bank that finances both firms to cover its fixed cost. Then, independently of the lending rate the bank announces in this interval $[\underline{r}, r + \alpha]$, it will be viable if and only if it finances both firms. Therefore the stage 2 game is a pure coordination game between the firms, whose equilibria are easily characterized: both firms apply for credit at the same bank, or they both simultaneously tap the financial market. We thus have a multiplicity of subgame perfect equilibria for the whole game, in which banks set arbitrary lending rates between $\underline{r}$ and $r + \alpha$ and firms coordinate and apply for credit at the same bank. Notice, however, that if F was smaller, so that a bank of size 1 would be viable ($L_m < 1$), the coordination problem would disappear, and we would be back to classic Bertrand competition.

3.5   Monopolistic Competition

The concept of monopolistic competition, first introduced by Chamberlin (1933), has been extensively used in the theory of Industrial Organization. It can be summarized as follows: as soon as there is some degree of differentiation between the products sold by competing firms, price competition will lead to less extreme outcomes than in pure Bertrand models. One of the most popular models of monopolistic competition is the location model of Salop (1979), in which product differentiation is generated by transportation costs. This section will present successively three applications of the Salop model to the banking sector (in increasing order of complexity), designed to address three different questions: (1) Does free competition lead to an optimal number of banks (subsection 3.5.1)? (2) What is the impact of deposit rate regulation on credit rates (subsection 3.5.2)? (3) Does free competition lead to an appropriate level of interbank cooperation in automated teller machine (ATM) networks (subsection 3.5.3)?

3.5.1   Does Free Competition Lead to the Optimal Number of Banks?

The simplest formulation of the banking version of the Salop model considers a continuum of depositors, each endowed with one unit of cash, and uniformly distributed along a circle. There are n banks (indexed by $i = 1, \ldots, n$), located on the same circle, that collect the deposits from the public and invest them into a riskless technology (or security) with a constant rate of return r. Depositors do not have access to this technology; they can only deposit their money in a bank. Moreover, when each depositor does so, he or she incurs a transportation cost αx, proportional[14] to the distance x between the depositor's location and that of the bank.[15] The total length of the circle is normalized to one, and the total mass of depositors is denoted D.

Depositors being uniformly distributed, the optimal organization of the banking industry corresponds to a symmetric location of the n banks. The maximal distance traveled by a consumer is $\frac{1}{2n}$, and the sum of all depositors' transportation costs is

$$2n \int_0^{\frac{1}{2n}} \alpha x \, D \, dx = \frac{\alpha D}{4n}. \tag{3.21}$$

The unit cost of setting up a bank is denoted by F. The optimal number of banks is obtained by minimizing the sum of setup costs and transportation costs: $nF + \frac{\alpha D}{4n}$. Disregarding indivisibilities (i.e., the fact that n is an integer), the minimum of this expression is obtained when its derivative with respect to n vanishes:

$$F - \frac{\alpha D}{4n^2} = 0,$$

which gives:

$$n^* = \frac{1}{2} \sqrt{\frac{\alpha D}{F}}. \tag{3.22}$$

How many banks will appear if banking competition is completely free (no entry restrictions, no rate regulations)? To answer this question, consider that n banks enter simultaneously,[16] locate uniformly on the circle, and set deposit rates $r_D^1, \ldots, r_D^n$. To determine the volume D_i of deposits attracted by bank $i (i = 1, \ldots, n)$ in this situation, it is necessary to compute the location of the

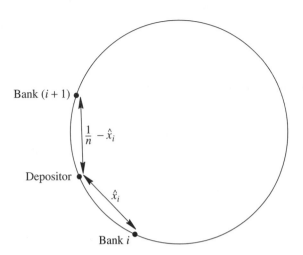

Figure 3.1
Location on the Salop Circle

"marginal depositor" who is indifferent about going to bank i or bank $i + 1$, as represented in Figure 3.1.

The distance $\hat{x}_i$ between this marginal depositor and bank i is defined by

$$r_D^i - \alpha \hat{x}_i = r_D^{i+1} - \alpha \left(\frac{1}{n} - \hat{x}_i \right). \tag{3.23}$$

Therefore,

$$\hat{x}_i = \frac{1}{2n} + \frac{r_D^i - r_D^{i+1}}{2\alpha},$$

and the total volume of deposits attracted by bank i is

$$D_i = D \left[\frac{1}{n} + \frac{2r_D^i - r_D^{i+1} - r_D^{i-1}}{2\alpha} \right].$$

(Since this example uses a circle, the following conventions are adopted: $r_D^{n+1} = r_D^1$ and $r_D^0 = r_D^n$.)

The profit of bank i is thus

$$\pi_i = D(r - r_D^i) \left(\frac{1}{n} + \frac{2r_D^i - r_D^{i+1} - r_D^{i-1}}{2\alpha} \right).$$

The equilibrium is obtained when for all i, r_D^i maximizes π_i (while other rates are kept constant). This is equivalent to

$$r - r_D^i = \frac{\alpha}{n} + \frac{2r_D^i - r_D^{i+1} - r_D^{i-1}}{2}, \qquad i = 1, \ldots, n. \tag{3.24}$$

It is easily seen that this linear system has a unique solution,

$$r_D^i = \ldots = r_D^n = r - \frac{\alpha}{n},$$

which gives the same profit to all the banks:

$$\pi_1 = \ldots = \pi_n = \frac{\alpha D}{n^2}.$$

Since there are no entry restrictions, the equilibrium number of banks (denoted n_e) will be obtained when this profit is equal to the setup cost F, which gives

$$n_e = \sqrt{\frac{\alpha D}{F}}. \tag{3.25}$$

A comparison with 3.22 shows immediately that free competition leads to too many banks. Consequently, there is scope for public intervention. The question is now to determine which type of regulation is appropriate. For instance, it is easy to see that, in such a context, imposing a reserve requirement on deposits is equivalent to decreasing the return rate r on the banks' assets. Formula 3.25 shows that this has no impact on the number of active banks at equilibrium. On the contrary, any measure leading directly (entry or branching restrictions) or indirectly (taxation, chartering fees, or capital requirements) to restricting the number of active banks will be welfare improving. This can be seen in particular as a justification of branching restrictions, which exist or have existed in many countries.[17] However, the robustness of this result[18] is questionable: other models of industries with differentiated products actually lead to too *few* products at equilibrium (see Chapter 7 in Tirole 1988 for a discussion of this issue).

3.5.2   The Impact of Deposit Rate Regulation on Credit Rates

Section 3.3, using the Monti-Klein model, concluded that, if the markets for deposits and loans are independent, the impact on loan rates of imposing a maximum deposit rate is determined by the properties of the cost function of the bank. In particular, if this cost function is separable between deposits and loans, the pricing of loans is independent of the deposit rates. Chiappori, Perez-Castrillo, and Verdier (1995) have studied the same question in a different context, in which the demands for loan and deposit services originate from the same consumers. They use an extension of the model of subsection 3.5.1, in which the credit activity is introduced. Depositors are also borrowers,[19] with an inelastic credit demand L (at the individual level). Assume $L < 1$. The total (net) utility of a typical consumer (that is, depositor-borrower) is therefore

$$U = (1 + r_D) - \alpha x_D - (1 + r_L)L - \beta x_L, \tag{3.26}$$

where x_D (resp. x_L) is the distance from the bank where the consumer's cash has been deposited (resp. where the consumer's loan has been granted), r_L is the loan rate, and β is the transportation cost parameter for loans.

Notice that transportation costs for loans and deposits may be different (for instance, because the frequencies of these transactions are different) and that, of course, the consumer may use different banks for deposits and loans (this issue will be discussed later).

A straightforward adaptation of the results of subsection 3.5.1 shows that if n banks enter, locate symmetrically on the circle, and compete in deposit rates and loan rates, the equilibrium is symmetric. All banks offer the same rates:

$$r_D^e = r - \frac{\alpha}{n}, \quad r_L^e = r + \frac{\beta}{nL}. \tag{3.27}$$

They share the market equally, and obtain a profit

$$\pi^e = \frac{D(\alpha + \beta)}{n^2}. \tag{3.28}$$

The number of active banks in a free entry equilibrium is determined by the equality between π and the entry cost F, which gives

$$n^e = \sqrt{\frac{D(\alpha + \beta)}{F}}. \tag{3.29}$$

It is also easy to see that loans and deposits are independently priced: if deposit rates are regulated (for instance, if r_D is fixed at zero), this has no impact on r_L. The only thing that changes is that banks make more profit on deposits, so that more banks enter, which is welfare decreasing.

However, another pattern appears if banks are allowed to offer "tied-up" contracts. Such contracts are defined by the fact that consumers can obtain credit from a bank only if they deposit their cash in the same bank (another possibility is that they get a lower credit rate if they do so). Chiappori, Perez-Castrillo, and Verdier (1995) show that such contracts would never emerge at equilibrium if banks were unregulated. However, if the remuneration of deposits is forbidden, attracting depositors is highly profitable to the banks. Therefore, they are ready to subsidize credit in order to do so.

Result 3.6   Under deposit rate regulation, banks will offer tied-up contracts with lower credit rates than in the unregulated case. Therefore the regulation is effective: it leads to decreasing credit rates.

If deposit rate regulation is maintained, a prohibition of tied-up contracts is welfare decreasing.[20]

Proof   Recall the expressions of the utility of a typical consumer:

$$U = 1 + r_D - \alpha x_D - (1 + r_L)L - \beta x_L,$$

and the profit of a typical bank:

$$\pi = 2D[\hat{x}_D(r - r_D) + L\hat{x}_L(r_L - r)],$$

where $\hat{x}_D$ (resp. $\hat{x}_L$) represents the distance between the bank and its marginal depositor (resp. borrower). For symmetry, this distance is assumed to be the same on both sides of the bank.

If deposit rates are regulated, $r_D = 0$. Moreover, if tied-up contracts are forbidden, depositors simply go to the closest bank, so that $\hat{x}_D = \frac{1}{2n}$. The equilibrium loan rates and profits are

$$r_L^0 = r + \frac{\beta}{nL}, \quad \pi^0 = \frac{D}{n}\left[r + \frac{\beta}{n}\right]. \tag{3.30}$$

Notice that $r_L^0 = r^L$, but $\pi^0 > \pi^e$ (compare with 3.28 and 3.29).

Suppose now that deposit rates are still regulated but that tied-up contracts are allowed. The previous situation ($r_L = r + \frac{\beta}{nL}$) is no longer an equilibrium. By offering a tied-up contact (deposit plus loan) at a slightly lower loan rate, a bank simultaneously gains more customers and a higher profit margin (since each deposit brings a rent r). Therefore all banks use such contracts so that all consumers choose the same bank for deposits and loans: $x_D = x_L$. The distance $\hat{x}$ between a bank and the marginal consumer is determined by

$$1 - (\alpha + \beta)\hat{x} - (1 + r_L)L = 1 - (\alpha + \beta)\left(\frac{1}{n} - \hat{x}\right) - (1 + r_L')L,$$

where r_L (resp. r_L') denotes the loan rate offered by the bank (resp. its neighbors). The following result is obtained:

$$\hat{x} = \frac{1}{2n} + \frac{L(r_L' - r_L)}{2(\alpha + \beta)}.$$

The expression of the bank's profit is

$$\pi = 2D\hat{x}(r + L(r_L - r)). \tag{3.31}$$

The maximization of π with respect to r_L (r_L' being fixed) is characterized by

$$\frac{1}{\pi}\frac{\partial \pi}{\partial r_L} = -\frac{L}{2\hat{x}(\alpha + \beta)} + \frac{L}{r + L(r_L - r)} = 0,$$

or

$$r_L = r - \frac{r - 2\hat{x}(\alpha + \beta)}{L}.$$

By symmetry, at equilibrium $\hat{x} = \frac{1}{2n}$, so that the new equilibrium loan rate is

$$r_L^1 = r - \frac{1}{L}\left(r - \frac{\alpha + \beta}{n}\right),$$

which can also be written

$$r_L^1 = \left(r + \frac{\beta}{Ln} \right) - \frac{1}{L} \left(r - \frac{\alpha}{n} \right), \tag{3.32}$$

$$= r_L^e - \frac{r_D^e}{L} < r_L^e. \tag{3.33}$$

This establishes the first part of result 3.6.

The proof of the second part simply results from the remark that 3.31 and 3.32 imply that the equilibrium profit with regulation and tied-up contracts equals π^e, the equilibrium profit in the absence of regulation.[21] As already remarked, if deposit rate regulation is maintained, while tied-up contracts are prohibited, the equilibrium profit is $\pi^1 > \pi^e$: therefore the equilibrium number of banks is higher and welfare is decreased.   ∎

3.5.3   Bank Network Compatibility

An interesting application of Salop's model is the contribution of Matutes and Padilla (1994).[22] Their model considers a two-stage game in which in the first period the banks choose whether they want to belong to some network (say, of ATMs), and in the second period they compete in prices (that is, deposit rates).

Compatibility has no physical cost and yields benefits to the depositors, so full compatibility is welfare maximizing. Still, full compatibility will never emerge as an equilibrium of the two-stage game. Indeed, the banks know that if they become fully compatible, stronger competition during the second stage will lower their profit, so there is an opportunity cost of compatibility.

For the case of three banks, it is possible to show (see problem 3.9.2) that if the equilibrium exists it can be either with three incompatible networks or with two banks sharing their network and leaving the third bank outside (which implies that an ex-ante symmetric situation will yield an asymmetric equilibrium outcome), so the equilibrium is not efficient.

In addition, the authors show that the existence of switching costs tends to reduce the incentives of banks to become compatible. Notice that this result may apply as well to other networks (for instance, in the emergence of clearing houses). The nonefficiency of equilibrium may justify public intervention.

3.6   Branch versus Unitary Banking

Another important debate in the history of banking regulation (particularly in the United States) has been whether banks should be allowed to possess large networks of branches (which some economists have considered to constitute a form of cartellization) or should be restricted to what has been called "unitary banking." In studying this question, this discussion will take into account the switching costs that consumers face when they change from one bank branch to another.

The existence of switching costs changes the time profile of competition. The main concept can be grasped through a simple, two-period model: if switching costs are high enough, customers are "locked in" during the second period and firms can charge them monopolistic prices. This has an influence on competition at period one. Ex ante (before customers choose the bank where they will be locked in during period two), banks will accept temporary losses during period one in order to attract customers that they will exploit during period two. At the competitive equilibrium, the second period rents will be exactly dissipated by the first period losses. This clearly differs from the standard marginal cost pricing behavior, and it gives a foretaste of the complexity of noncompetitive equilibria with switching costs.

To illustrate the importance of switching costs in modeling the banking sector, this discussion will summarize the arguments of Gale (1993) in his comparison of branch banking versus unitary banking. This summary will show that some generally held views on competition in the banking industry may be built on fragile ground. When switching costs and the nonobservable quality of banking services are taken into account, it is no longer clear that competition in its most desirable form can be identified with a large number of small banks.

Following Gale, consider the model of a city in which banks are infinitely lived, but depositors remain for only two periods. Suppose for simplicity that deposit rates are regulated, so that the only variable in which banks may differ is the quality of banking services. These banking services have the characteristics of an experience good, which means that depositors learn the quality of the service only of their own bank branch (after one period). Moreover, they will incur a switching cost if they change branches.

If the quality of banking services was observable ex ante, competition would lead banks to offer the efficient quality level q_C, which maximizes the difference between the utility of the depositors and the cost of the bank. However, this example assumes that this quality is observable only ex post. Then if switching costs are large enough, banks will behave as monopolists and offer the lowest quality level q_m that depositors will accept. This is indeed an equilibrium, since a deviating bank could attract the depositors of its competitors only by offering very high quality (needed to compensate depositors for the switching cost), which would be too costly.

Suppose now that the economy is composed of several cities, identical to the one just described. At each period, some fraction of the depositors is obliged to migrate from one city to another for exogenous reasons (such as labor mobility). In a unitary banking regime, these migrations do not alter the characteristics of the equilibrium just studied. When switching costs are high, banks offer services of a low quality level q_m. However, in a branch banking regime, the quality of banking services will be higher. Suppose that a bank has branches in several cities. Then the previous equilibrium will be destabilized if this bank increases slightly the quality of its services in all of its branches, therefore attracting the deposits of all migrant depositors.

The recent contribution of Cerasi (1995) uses a different framework from that of Gale. Cerasi's model is based on a specification of depositors' behavior inspired by Shaked and Sutton's (1982) model of market structure with multiproduct firms. This model is more general than Salop's because it captures the notion that the market size may increase with the total number of branches, whereas in Salop's model, an increase in the number of products (here, bank branches) only crowds the market further (at least when banks are not local monopolies). The idea is that, by increasing the number of branches, banks can enhance the demand of the public for deposit services. Cerasi shows that two types of symmetric equilibria may obtain: unit banking equilibria and branch banking equilibria. She shows that, regardless of the existence of scale economies in branching, unit banking equilibria obtain when the size of the market is small. Cerasi also studies the impact of deregulation (such as lifting branching restrictions or relaxing entry barriers). Interestingly, she shows that the impact of deregulation is not necessarily what is expected: by enhancing competition in the short run, deregulation may lead to the exit of unprofitable banks, which in the long run tends to increase concentration in the industry.

3.7   Appendix 1: Empirical Evidence

This appendix is based on Neuberger and Zimmerman (1990) (see subsection 3.2.3). Recall that Neuberger and Zimmerman estimate the impact of the elasticity of the deposit supply on the interest rates offered by banks for several categories of deposits. Using dummy variables, the authors correct for possible differences in regulation (limited branching or unit banking) that create an institutional barrier to entry.

Neuberger and Zimmerman analyze the following types of deposit contracts: Negotiable Order of Withdrawal (NOW), Money Market Deposit Account (MMDA), and Certificate of Deposit (CD) with either a short maturity (between 3 and 6 months) or a long maturity (2.5 years). Clearly, there is a higher rate of competition on the (national) market for long-maturity CDs than for the short-maturity ones, and these two products suffer from a more severe competition than MMDAs, which in turn will have a higher elasticity than NOW accounts.

As Table 3.1 shows, the results obtained support the main features of the Monti-Klein model. Indeed, as predicted by this model,

Table 3.1
Deposit Rate Regressions, 1984 to 1987

Independent Variable	Dependent Variable (rate in basis points)			
	(1) NOW (1986–87)	(2) MMDA	(3) 3–6-mo. CD	(4) 2.5-yr. CD
Constant	390.97**	101.06**	70.45**	169.75**
	(44.82)	(16.73)	(10.08)	(17.42)
3-Firm Concentration Ratio	−17.20**	−13.26**	−8.93*	−11.55
	(−4.54)	(−3.45)	(−2.00)	(−1.90)
Market Deposit Growth Rate	12.48**	16.97**	17.93**	35.61**
	(4.48)	(3.37)	(3.14)	(4.55)
Per Capita Bank Offices in State	0.60	8.27**	2.18	−0.33
	(0.49)	(6.48)	(1.47)	(−0.16)
Bank Assets	0.81**	0.74**	1.06**	0.66**
	(5.28)	(4.67)	(5.70)	(2.48)
Number of Branches	−0.10**	−0.06**	−0.09**	−0.01
	(−8.23)	(−4.92)	(−6.34)	(−0.57)
Retail Time as % of Total Deposits	−0.07	−0.46**	−0.18**	−0.05
	(−1.49)	(−9.68)	(−3.37)	(−0.71)
Overhead Expenses per $ Assets	−0.77	−1.25	−3.37**	−3.42**
	(−1.22)	(−1.87)	(−4.29)	(−3.05)
Average Salary	−0.84**	−1.79**	−1.39**	−1.15**
	(−7.78)	(−15.35)	(−10.28)	(−5.90)
Limited Branching Dummy	−6.62**	−3.73*	−7.00**	−5.18*
	(−4.50)	(−2.46)	(−3.97)	(−2.14)
Unit Banking Dummy	5.33*	19.88**	0.93	−3.02
	(2.28)	(8.62)	(0.35)	(−0.81)
Money Market Mutual Fund Rate	0.26**	0.83**	1.00**	1.00**
	(22.82)	(196.10)	(202.77)	(146.50)
California Dummy	−25.67**	−19.39**	−7.73*	−1.72
	(−8.20)	(−5.05)	(−2.11)	(−0.33)
R-Bar Squared	0.243	0.866	0.869	0.780
No. of Observations	3415	6573	6637	6475

Note: The symbol * (**) indicates a coefficient significantly different from 0 at the 5 (1)% level; t-statistics are in parentheses.
Source : Neuberger and Zimmerman (1990).

• the concentration ratio has a higher impact on the deposits that have a low elasticity.

• the number of branches is a relevant variable except for the 2.5-year CDs, and so is the average salary, but overhead expenses are not.

• the coefficient of the interbank market rate is higher when the elasticity of the deposit is higher.

Unfortunately, this model does not provide a complete explanation of the California rate mystery, since the California dummy still differs significantly from zero. However, it shows that intermediation margins are indeed related to the concentration of the banking sector, since the model explains roughly 10 basis points of the uncorrected statistical difference between California and the rest of the United States for NOW accounts, MMDAs, and 3-to-6-month CDs, and all of the difference for 2.5-year CDs.

3.8   Appendix 2 : Measuring the Activity of Banks

This book is primarily focused on theory, but this small appendix is dedicated to the empirical measurement of banks' activities. Obviously, it will be able to discuss only briefly the main directions of research that have been explored in the enormous literature on the estimation of banks' cost and production functions.[23] This discussion will distinguish three branches in this literature: the "production approach," the "intermediation approach," and the "modern approach." The first two approaches apply the classical microeconomic theory of the firm to the banking sector; they differ only in the specification of banks' activities. The third approach goes further and modifies the classical theory of the firm by incorporating some specificities of banks' activities, namely risk management and information processing, as well as some form of agency problems, which are crucial for explaining the role of financial intermediaries.

3.8.1   The Production Approach

The production approach, initiated by the contributions of Benston (1965a, b) and Bell and Murphy (1968),[24] describes banking activities as the production of services to depositors and borrowers. It suits well the case of a local branch that is "financially transparent" in the sense that the money collected from depositors is fully transferred to some main branch; similarly, all the money lent to borrowers is made available by the same main branch. The only outputs of the local branch are its services to depositors and borrowers, and its only inputs are labor and physical capital. Even though this approach already recognizes the multiproduct nature of banking activities, most authors have ignored the multiplicity of banking products because the techniques for measuring scale and scope economies were not well developed until Baumol, Panzar, and Willig (1982). The existence of the Functional Cost Analysis (FCA) program, conducted by the Federal Reserve system, allowed separate cost functions to be estimated for all product lines. This program provides disaggregated cost data for five categories of banking activities: demand deposits, term and savings deposits, real estate loans, consumer loans, and business loans.[25] Using these data, Benston and Bell and Murphy were able to estimate five different cost functions of the Cobb-Douglas type (one per activity):

$$\log C_i = \epsilon_i \log Q_i + a_i \log w_i + (1 - a_i) \log r_i + \text{constant}, \quad i = 1, \ldots 5,$$

where the variables C_i (total cost), Q_i (volume of output), w_i (wage rate, i.e., price of the first input, labor), and r_i (interest rate, i.e., price of the second input, physical capital) are given by the FCA data basis. The elasticities ϵ_i and a_i are estimated by least squares method.

Apart from the obvious criticism that the disaggregation of costs prevents the study of scope economies (as explained later), production approach suffers from a basic problem: what is the relevant measure of output volumes? Is it the number of accounts, the number of operations on these accounts, or the dollar amounts? The usual approach is to use the dollar amounts, which are more readily available, and to correct possible biases by introducing heterogeneity factors for homogenizing the data (size, activity, and composition of accounts).

Another difficulty is related to the Cobb-Douglas specification, for which average cost is monotonic (increasing if $\epsilon_i > 1$, decreasing if $\epsilon_i < 1$, constant if $\epsilon_i = 1$), which prevents the existence of an efficient size. A more convenient specification is the translog cost function, in which the logarithm of the cost is quadratic with respect to the logarithms of output and input prices.[26] This is the specification used by Benston, Hanweck, and Humphrey (1982), who find a U-shaped average cost function with an efficient size between 10 and 25 million dollars of deposits, which is surprisingly small. However, they use an aggregate measure of output, which may introduce an estimation bias (see M. Kim 1986).[27]

A natural extension is therefore to use a multiproduct cost function, which also allows the discussion of scope economies and cost complementarities. This approach has been followed, for instance, by Gilligan and Smirlock (1984); Gilligan, Smirlock, and Marshall (1984); Berger, Hanweck, and Humphrey (1987); and Kolari and Zardhooki (1987). The results are not very conclusive: there is no consistent evidence of either global economies of scope[28] or significant economies of scale above 100 million dollars of deposits (see Summary Table 1 in Clark 1988). However, there is some evidence of cost complementarities between loans and deposits or investments and loans (see Clark, Table 2).

3.8.2 The Intermediation Approach

The second strand of the literature differs from the previous one only by the specification of banking activities. It is in fact complementary to the production approach and is more appropriate to the case of a main branch, which is not directly in contact with customers and is in charge of "transforming" the money borrowed from depositors into the money lent to borrowers. This transformation activity, already discussed in Chapter 1, comes from the fact that deposits and loans have different characteristics: deposits are typically divisible, liquid, short-term and riskless; on the contrary, loans are typically indivisible, illiquid, long-term and risky. Also, the total volume of loans granted by the local branches is in general different from the total volume of deposits collected. Therefore, the main branch may have to borrow (or invest) on financial markets. In this approach, the inputs of the main branch are essentially financial capital (i.e., the deposits collected by local branches and the funds borrowed from financial markets), and the outputs are measured by the volume of loans and investments outstanding.[29]

This intermediation approach, already sketched by Benston, Hanweck, and Humphrey (1982), was explored on several data sets, notably Murray and White (1983) and H. Y. Kim (1986) for Canadian credit unions, Mester (1987) for California savings and loans, and M. Kim (1986) for Israeli banks. Surprisingly enough, the results obtained do not differ substantially from those of the production approach. This leaves open the question of which is the correct formulation of banking activities. An interesting answer is explored by Hancock (1991), who adopts the "user cost methodology." The core of this methodology is a linear regression of banks' profits on the real balances of the different items present in the banks' balance sheet, without presuming a priori which of these items correspond to outputs of the banks and which correspond to inputs.[30] In fact, it is the sign of the coefficients of the regression of the profit on the different balance sheet items that determines the separation: when these coefficients are positive they correspond to outputs (intuitively, the bank's profit increases when they increase), and when they are negative they correspond to inputs. On her data set, Hancock obtains the intuitively satisfactory result that loans and demand deposits are outputs,[31] whereas inputs are labor, physical capital, materials, and "cash" (which represents an aggregate comprising time deposits and borrowed money).

Finally, several contributions have tried to correct for the problematic behavior of the multiproduct translog cost function when some of the outputs tend toward zero (the logarithms become infinite). For instance, Hunter, Timme, and Yang (1990) use another specification (Minflex-Laurent) of the cost function, whereas McAllister and McManus (1992) adopt a nonparametric approach.

3.8.3   The Modern Approach

The novelty of the modern approach to the measurement of banks' activities consists in incorporating the specificities of these activities, namely risk management and information processing, into the classical theory of the firm, as well as taking into account some form of agency problems. This idea was already implicit in Mester (1991), who found evidence of X-inefficiency in California mutual savings and loans in 1982 (that is, prior to interest rate deregulation).[32] The idea is that the separation between owners and managers is larger in mutual than in stock companies, whereas regulation Q prevented additional profit from being passed on to depositors. Using post-deregulation data, Mester (1993) studies the impact of the Financial Institutions and Regulatory Reform Enforcement Act (FIRREA, 1989), which encouraged the conversion of many savings and loans from mutual (supposedly owned by depositors) to stock companies. Using an econometric technique called the "stochastic cost frontier model," she tries to evaluate the consequences of this change on X-inefficiency. Surprisingly, she finds that, on average, stock savings and loans are less efficient than mutuals, contrarily to what she found previously using the 1982 data. She also obtains other more easily interpretable results that are in line with modern theories of corporate structure: greater efficiency is positively correlated with higher capital-to-asset ratios (for stock savings and loans) and smaller reliance on uninsured deposits (for both stock and mutual savings and loans).

Another interesting article by the same author (Mester 1992) casts some doubt on the existence of economies of scope between what she calls "traditional" banking activities (such as granting credit to borrowers) and non-traditional activities that have emerged more recently (loans sales and securitization). In order to distinguish between the two, she separates the banks' portfolios into four categories of loans:

1. Loans originated or purchased before the current date, denoted t.
2. Loans originated at t and held.
3. Loans bought at t.
4. Loans originated at t and sold.

Surprisingly enough, she finds diseconomies of scope between the first two groups (which correspond to what could be called commercial banking) and the rest (which correspond more to investment banking). This suggests that arguments against the Glass-Steagall Act based on the existence of economies of scope are unfounded.[33]

The most innovative part of this new approach to the measure of bank activities is probably the series of papers by Hughes and Mester (1993a, b, 1994) that introduce the quality of banks' assets and the probability of banks' failure in the estimation of costs. Also, they introduce a possible discrepancy between the preferences of banks' managers and those of stockholders (i.e., profit maximization). If banks' managers are not risk neutral, they will typically choose a level of financial capital that is different from the cost minimizing one. This is indeed what Hughes and Mester (1994) find using data from 1989 and 1990 for United States banks with assets of more than $1 billion. As a consequence, there may be a systematic bias in previous measures of scope and scale economies in banking, which did not take into account the risk attitude of banks' managers. In Hughes and Mester (1993b), the authors correct for this bias and find constant returns to scale for mean-sized banks and diseconomies of scope for large banks. In their companion paper (Hughes and Mester 1993a) they explicitly incorporate the price of uninsured funds into the cost function. They find that for the largest banks, an increase in size (holding default risk and asset quality constant) significantly lowers the price of uninsured funds. They interpret this as empirical evidence for the "Too Big to Fail" doctrine.[34]

Finally, Berger and DeYoung (1997) examine the causality among loan quality, cost efficiency, and bank capital. Their results provide support for the "bad luck hypothesis," according to which high levels "of problem loans cause banks to increase spending on monitoring." They also find that "decreases in bank capital ratios generally precede increases in nonperforming loans . . . evidence that thinly capitalized banks may respond to moral hazard incentives by taking increased portfolio risks."

3.9   Problems

3.9.1   Extension of the Monti-Klein Model to the Case of Risky Loans (Adapted from Dermine 1986)

Modify the model of Section 3.2 by allowing borrowers to default. More specifically, suppose that the bank has lent L to one (representative) firm that has invested the amount in a risky technology of net (unit) return $\tilde{y}$. In the absence of collateral, the net (unit) return to the bank will be $\min(r_L, \tilde{y})$: when $\tilde{y} < r_L$, the firm defaults and the bank seizes the firm's assets, which are worth $(1 + \tilde{y})L$.

1. Assuming that the bank has no equity (in conformity with the model of Section 3.2), show that the bank itself will default if $\tilde{y}$ is below some threshold y^*. Compute y^*.

2. Assume risk neutrality and limited liability of the bank. Therefore the bank chooses the levels L^* of loans and D^* of deposits, which maximize the expectation of the positive part of its profit. (If this profit is negative, the bank defaults.) Write the first order conditions that characterize L^* and D^*.

3. Show that D^* is characterized by the same condition as in the Monti-Klein model.

4. On the contrary, show that L^* depends in general on what happens on the deposit side, so that the separability property is lost.

3.9.2   Compatibility between Banking Networks (Adapted from Matutes and Padilla 1994)

Consider a circular economy as described in subsection 3.5.1 with three symmetrically located banks, A, B, and C, each having an ATM. Competition is modeled by a two-stage game in which banks first decide whether their ATMs will be compatible and then compete in deposit rates. There are no costs of compatibility, and fixed costs and management costs are ignored. Let C_A denote the set of banks such that their ATMs are compatible with that of A (by convention $A \in C_A$).

For a depositor located at a distance x_j from bank j, the utility obtained by depositing its unit of cash in bank A is

$$r_A + k|C_A| - t x_A - T \min_{j \in C_A} x_j,$$

where r_A is A's offered deposit rate, $|C_A|$ is the number of elements of C_A, T is the transportation cost parameter for withdrawing cash, t is the transportation cost parameter for account management (which is necessarily to be done at bank A), and kn represents the benefits derived from the use of a network of n ATMs.

1. Consider first the two symmetric cases in which the ATMs are incompatible (resp. fully compatible) and confirm that each bank's profit will equal at equilibrium

$$\Pi = \frac{D}{3^2}(t + T) \quad (\text{resp. } \Pi = \frac{D}{3^2}t)$$

so that compatibility will always be dominated (for banks) by incompatibility if $T > 0$. Explain this result.

2. Assume now that A and B have compatible ATMs, whereas C's remains incompatible. Show that the profits of A and C are respectively

$$\Pi_A = D(r - r_A) \left[\frac{r_A - r_B}{2t} + \frac{r_A - r_C + k}{2(t + T)} + \frac{1}{3} \right]$$

$$\Pi_C = D(r - r_C) \left[\frac{2r_C - (r_A - r_B) - 2k}{2(t + T)} + \frac{1}{3} \right]$$

and that at the Nash equilibrium (which is symmetric for A and B), margins are given by

$$r - r_A = r - r_B = \frac{[3k + 5(t + T)]t}{3(5t + 2T)}$$

$$r - r_C = \frac{-3k(2t + T) + (t + T)(5t + T)}{3(5t + 2T)}.$$

Confirm that the value of A's profit in equilibrium equals

$$\Pi_A = \frac{D}{2 \cdot 3^2} t \frac{(2t + T)}{t + T} \left[\frac{3k + 5(t + T)}{5t + 2T} \right]^2.$$

3. Show that for some values of t, T and k, partial compatiblity will be preferred to incompatibility (hint: set $\frac{3k+5(t+T)}{5t+2T} = \frac{3}{2}$).

3.10   Solutions

3.10.1   Extension of the Monti-Klein Model to the Case of Risky Loans

1. The profit of the bank becomes

$$\tilde{\pi}(L, D, \tilde{y}) = [\min(r_L(L), \tilde{y}) - r]L + [r - r_D(D)]D.$$

The threshold y^* corresponds to the value of $\tilde{y}$ such that $\tilde{\pi}$ vanishes (L and
D being given):

$$y^* = r - [r - r_D(D)]\frac{D}{L}.$$

2. The objective function of the bank is

$$\pi(L, D) = E[\max(0, \tilde{\pi}(L, D, \tilde{y}))].$$

The first order conditions are

$$\frac{\partial \pi}{\partial D} = E\left[\frac{\partial \tilde{\pi}}{\partial D}(L, D, \tilde{y})\, \mathbb{1}_{\tilde{y}>y^*}\right] = 0,$$

$$\frac{\partial \pi}{\partial L} = E\left[\frac{\partial \tilde{\pi}}{\partial L}(L, D, \tilde{y})\, \mathbb{1}_{\tilde{y}>y^*}\right] = 0,$$

where $\mathbb{1}_A$ denotes the characteristic function of the set A, with

$$\frac{\partial \tilde{\pi}}{\partial D}(L, D, \tilde{y}) = r - r_D - Dr_D'$$

and

$$\frac{\partial \tilde{\pi}}{\partial L} = \begin{cases} r_L - r + Lr_L' & \text{if } \tilde{y} > r_L \\ \tilde{y} - r & \text{if } \tilde{y} < r_L. \end{cases}$$

3. The expression of $\frac{\partial \tilde{\pi}}{\partial D}$ is independent of $\tilde{y}$. Therefore D^* is characterized as
before by the condition

$$r - r_D(D^*) = D^* r_D'(D^*),$$

which does not depend on what happens on the loan side.

4. The determination of L^* is more complex:

$$0 = \frac{\partial \pi}{\partial L} = (r_L - r + Lr_L')\, \text{Proba}\, (\tilde{y} > r_L) + E\left[(\tilde{y} - r)\, \mathbb{1}_{y^* < \tilde{y} < r_L}\right].$$

The second term, if it does not vanish, introduces a relation between deposits and loans, since y^* depends on D.

3.10.2   Compatibility between Banking Networks

1. The problem is exactly the one studied in subsection 3.5.1, with $n = 3$, $\alpha = t + T$ for the incompatibility case and $\alpha = t$ for the case of full compatibility.

2. On the B side of A, the marginal depositor for A will be indifferent between depositing in A or in B if he is at a distance x of A (and $\frac{1}{3} - x$ of B) such that

$$r_A + 2k - tx - T \min(x, \frac{1}{3} - x) = r_B + 2k - t(\frac{1}{3} - x) - T \min(x, \frac{1}{3} - x).$$

This condition simplifies into

$$x = \frac{r_A - r_B + t/3}{2t}.$$

On the C side of A, the marginal depositor will be defined similarly by a distance y such that

$$r_A + 2k - (t + T)y = r_C + k - (t + T)\left(\frac{1}{3} - y\right),$$

yielding

$$y = \frac{r_A - r_C + k + \frac{1}{3}(t + T)}{2(t + T)}.$$

Therefore A's supply of deposits equals $D(x + y)$, and its profit is $D(r - r_A)(x + y)$.

The marginal depositor for bank C will be obtained similarly as

$$x' = \left[(r_C - r_A - k + \frac{1}{3}(t + T)\right] / 2(t + T)$$

$$y' = \left[r_C - r_B - k + \frac{1}{3}(t + T)\right] / 2(t + T)$$

and its profit equals $\Pi_C = D(r - r_C)(x' + y')$.

First order conditions for A and C yield respectively

$$-\left[\frac{r_A - r_B}{2t} + \frac{r_A - r_C + k}{2(t + T)} + \frac{1}{3}\right] + (r - r_A)\frac{1}{2}\left[\frac{1}{t} + \frac{1}{t + T}\right] = 0$$

and

$$-\left[\frac{2r_C - (r_A + r_B) - 2k}{2(t + T)} + \frac{1}{3}\right] + (r - r_C)\left[\frac{1}{t + T}\right] = 0.$$

By symmetry, $r_A = r_B$. Moreover, changing variables by setting $r - r_A = u$ and $r - r_C = v$ yields the following system of equations:

$$u\left[3 + \frac{T}{t}\right] - v = k + 2(t + T)/3$$

$$-u + 2v = -k + (t + T)/3$$

Its solution gives the result indicated.

3. It suffices to show that the profits under partial compatibility are higher than the ones obtained under incompatibility for the two banks, say A and B, that decide to share their networks:

$$\frac{1}{2.3^2}t\frac{(2t + T)}{t + T}\left[\frac{3k + 5(t + T)}{5t + 2T}\right]^2 > \frac{1}{3^2}(t + T).$$

Setting $\frac{3k + 5(t+T)}{5t + 2T} = \frac{3}{2}$ implies that $3k = 5t/2 - 2T$, which is consistent with the condition $r - r_C > 0$.

Taking $T = \alpha t$, it must be shown that the equality

$$\frac{1}{2}\frac{t^2(2 + \alpha)}{t(1 + \alpha)}\left(\frac{3}{2}\right)^2 > t(1 + \alpha)$$

holds for some values of α. But this is equivalent to

$$(2 + \alpha)3^2 > 2^3(1 + \alpha)^2,$$

which is true for a value of α that is sufficiently small.

Notes

1. Indeed, granting a loan is like buying a security issued by the borrower. Similarly, collecting deposits is like issuing securities. However, this discussion will conform with the more traditional view of a bank "buying" funds from depositors and "selling" them to borrowers. It will therefore speak of a *demand* for loans by borrowers and a *supply* of deposits by households.

2. Sealey and Lindley (1977) were among the first to use the microeconomic theory of the firm to build a rigorous model of banks' production functions. In their approach, banks can be described as multi-unit firms that use labor and physical capital as inputs for producing different financial services for depositors and borrowers. The main specificity of banks (or more generally depository financial institutions) with respect to industrial firms is that their outputs (namely these financial services) can be measured only indirectly, through the volumes of deposits D and loans L they generate. The "apparent" cost function $C(D, L)$ of the bank is obtained by finding the efficient combination of inputs that generate a given vector (D, L) (see also Section 3.8).

3. As usual, the symbol Δ refers to increments in stock variables.

4. The monetary base is the sum of currency in circulation plus reserves held by the banks at the Central Bank.

5. In this simple model, an issue of Treasury bills is equivalent to a decrease in the monetary base.

6. As usual with constant returns to scale, equilibrium is possible only when profit margins are zero.

7. The comparison with the standard approach of the credit multiplier is complicated by the fact that the monetary base M_O is no longer considered as a policy instrument. The focus is now on open market operations (i.e., changes in B) that were equivalent to changes in M_O of the same amount and opposite sign in the simple model put forth in subsection 3.1.2.

8. As simple as it is, this result regarding the endogeneity of interbank interest rates has empirical implications in terms of making cross-country comparisons of the cost of financial services. If this cost is measured by the difference $r_L - r$, as is done for instance in Price Waterhouse (1988) a bias will be introduced as soon as there are differences in the reserve requirement coefficients in the different countries. Indeed, the cost of financial services in countries with high reserve requirements will be overestimated.

9. The minus sign is only there to ensure that the elasticity ε_L is positive, which is the more usual and more convenient convention.

10. As usual, we assume that ε_L is greater than 1, otherwise the bank's problem may not have a solution.

11. The alternative model of price competition à la Bertrand is examined in Section 3.4.

12. Notice, though, that imposing a restriction on the rates does not mean that the restriction will be respected for the real return for depositors. Assume indeed that banks can modulate the quality of nonpecuniary services provided to depositors. Then, *the first effect of a ceiling on deposit rates is that banks will increase the quality of these services.*

13. Notice, though, that $\frac{\partial L}{\partial r_D} > 0$ and $\frac{\partial D}{\partial r_L} < 0$ are satisfied, at the *level of an individual bank,* in some models (such as the monopolistic competition model of Chiappori, Perez-Castrillo, and Verdier 1995, studied in subsection 3.5.2.)

14. This assumption is not important; any increasing convex cost function would lead to the same results.

15. This location model can also be interpreted in a more abstract fashion: suppose depositors have different preferences about the mix of services to be provided by their bank. Each depositor prefers a specific combination of banking services. Transportation costs then correspond to the utility loss associated with consuming the mix of services offered by a bank, instead of one's preferred combination.

16. The assumption of sequential entry, although more natural, would enormously complicate the analysis, since banks would not always locate uniformly.

17. In this simplistic model, each bank has one branch. However, the example can be easily extended to a case in which banks have several branches. If these branches are not adjacent, the equilibrium deposit rates are unchanged, and the results still hold.

18. It is nothing but the adaptation to the banking context of the "proliferation" result of Salop (1979), who had in mind a different context: industries with differentiated products such as breakfast cereal brands.

19. It may seem strange that a consumer simultaneously borrows (at a high rate) and lends (at a low rate), instead of netting out the position. However, this is very common in practice. The reader is invited to determine why this is the case.

20. Chiappori, Perez-Castrillo, and Verdier (1995) also study the impact of tied-up contracts on the efficiency of monetary policy.

21. In fact tied-up contracts allow banks to "bypass" the regulation: the total subsidy to each borrower-depositor equals the forgone interest on this deposit.

22. More recently, Bouckaert and Degryse (1995) have also used the Salop model for modeling "phonebanking" (i.e., the option that some banks offer some of their customers to deal with them by phone, which obviously reduces transaction costs). Similarly, Degryse (1996) studies the impact on banking competition of the possibility of offering remote access to banking services.

23. This literature is surveyed for instance in Benston (1965b); Benston, Hanweck, and Humphrey (1982); and Clark (1988). See also Hancock (1991) and Kolari and Zardhooki (1987).

24. Strictly speaking, the first contribution was apparently Alhadeff (1954), who studied in particular scale economies in the California banking industry.

25. Several problems arise with the FCA data. First, all cost disaggregation methods contain some elements of arbitrariness. Second, a selection bias exists, since the FCA program is voluntary: large

banks are dramatically under-represented (see Clark 1988). Finally, cost complementarities among outputs are ignored.

26. This is a natural generalization of the Cobb-Douglas specification, in which the logarithm of the cost is a linear function of the logarithms of output and input prices.

27. There are criticisms of the translog cost function as well (see, e.g., McAllister and McManus 1993).

28. Formally, economies of scope arise when it is less costly to produce a vector of outputs together rather than separately. A particular example is the case of cost complementarities between two outputs i and j, meaning that the marginal cost $\frac{\partial C}{\partial q_i}$ of output i decreases with the volume of output q_j: mathematically, $\frac{\partial^2 C}{\partial q_i \partial q_j} < 0$. For further elaboration, see Sharkey (1982).

29. Notice that contrary to the case of industrial firms, whose input and output data are obtained from their income statements, the input and output volumes of banks are obtained from their balance sheets.

30. This question arises in the banking sector, because of the debate on deposits: are they inputs or outputs of banks? Most studies consider them as *inputs,* but it would be more natural to model banks as *producers* of deposit services. Sealey and Lindley (1977) consider deposits as an intermediate input, "produced" by the bank by offering means of payment services to depositors, and later used by the bank for producing loans.

31. However, Hughes and Mester (1993a,b) developed another test to determine whether deposits are outputs or inputs. They estimate a variable cost function with fixed levels of deposits, and the derivative of this function with respect to these levels. They find that these derivatives are negative, which they interpret to mean that deposits are inputs. This is because an increase in the level of one input, holding outputs constant, should reduce the amount spent on other inputs.

32. "X-inefficiency" is defined as the peculiar form of inefficiency that arises, not for techno-logical reasons but for organizational reasons, when the interests of managers and workers are not perfectly in line with those of owners. Berger and Mester (forthcoming) examine the possible sources of such inefficiencies for a sample of U.S. banks from 1990 to 1995.

33. The Glass-Steagall Act is discussed in Chapter 9, Section 3.

34. The Too Big to Fail doctrine asserts that the government cannot accept the failure of large banks. This is justified either by political reasons or by the fear of "systemic risk" (i.e., the risk of spread of the failure to other banks). This doctrine obviously generates moral hazard (the managers of large banks can take more risks, on the presumption that their banks will be rescued in case of problems), so regulatory authorities officially refuse the doctrine and adopt a position of "constructive ambiguity." For a formal discussion of these issues, see Rochet and Tirole (1996).

References

Baumol, W. J., J. C. Panzar, and R. P. Willig. 1982. *Contestable markets and the theory of industrial structure.* San Diego: Harcourt Brace Jovanovich.

Bell, F. W., and N. B. Murphy. 1968. Economies of scale and division of labor in commercial banking. *National Banking Review* 5:131–39.

Benston, G. J. 1965a. Branch banking and economies of scale. *Journal of Finance* 20:312–31.

———. 1965b. Economies of scale and marginal costs in banking operations. *National Banking Review* 2:507–49.

Benston, G. J., G. A. Hanweck, and D. Humphrey. 1982. Scale economies in banking. *Journal of Money, Credit, and Banking* 14(1):435–546.

Berger, A. N., and R. DeYoung. Forthcoming. Problem loans and cost efficiency in commercial banks. *Journal of Banking and Finance.*

Berger, A. N., G. A. Hanweck, and D. B. Humphrey. 1987. Competitive viability in banking: Scale, scope, and product mix economies. *Journal of Monetary Economics* 20(3):501–20.

Berger, A. N., and L. Mester. Forthcoming. Inside the black box: What explains differences in the efficiency of financial institutions. *Journal of Banking and Finance.*

Bouckaert, J., and H. Degryse. 1995. Phonebanking. *European Economic Review* 39(2):229–44.

Cerasi, V. 1995. A model of retail banking competition. London School of Economics. Duplicated.

Chamberlin, E. 1933. *Theory of monopolistic competition.* Cambridge: Harvard University Printing Office.

Chiappori, P. A., D. Perez-Castrillo, and F. Verdier. 1995. Spatial competition in the banking system, localization, cross-subsidies and the regulation of interest rates. *European Economic Review* 39(5):889–919.

Clark, J. A. 1988. Economies of scale and scope at depository financial institutions: A review of the literature. *Economic Review* (Federal Reserve Bank of Kansas City), September (73):16–33.

Degryse, H. Forthcoming. On the interaction between vertical and horizontal product differentiation: An application to banking. *Journal of Industrial Economics.*

De Palma, A., and R. Gary-Bobo. 1996. Coordination failures in the Cournot approach to deregulated bank competition. University of Paris, Cergy-Pontoise. Mimeograph.

Dermine, J. 1986. Deposit rates, credit rates and bank capital: The Monti-Klein model revisited. *Journal of Banking and Finance* 10:99–114.

Edwards, F. 1964. *Review of Economics and Statistics,* August, 294–300.

Gale, D. 1993. Branch banking, unitary banking and competition. Department of Economics, Boston University. Mimeograph.

Gilligan, T. W., and M. L. Smirlock. 1984. An empirical study of joint production and scale economies in commercial banking. *Journal of Banking and Finance* 8(1):67–77.

Gilligan, T., M. L. Smirlock, and W. Marshall. 1984. Scale and scope economies in the multiproduct banking firm. *Journal of Monetary Economics* 13(3):393–405.

Hancock, D. 1991. *A theory of production for the financial firm.* Norwell, Mass: Kluwer Academic Publishers.

Hughes, J. P., and L. J. Mester. 1993a. A quality and risk-adjusted cost function for banks: Evidence on the Too-Big-to-Fail doctrine. *Journal of Productivity Analysis* 4(3):293–315.

———. 1993b. Accounting for the demand for financial capital and risk-taking in bank cost functions. Working paper no. 93-17, Federal Reserve Bank of Philadelphia, Economic Research Division.

———. 1994. Bank managers' objectives. Working paper no. 94-8, Federal Reserve Bank of Philadelphia, Economic Research Division.

Hunter, W. C., S. G. Timme, and Won Keun Yang. 1990. An examination of cost subadditivity and multiproduct production in large US banks. *Journal of Money, Credit, and Banking* 22:504–25.

Kim, H. Y. 1986. Economies of scale and economies of scope in multiproduct financial institutions: Further evidence from credit unions. A note. *Journal of Money, Credit, and Banking* 18(2):220–26.

Kim, M. 1986. Banking technology and the existence of a consistent output aggregate. *Journal of Monetary Economics* 18(2):181–95.

Klein, M. 1971. A theory of the banking firm. *Journal of Money, Credit, and Banking* 3:205–18.

Kolari, J., and A. Zardhooki. 1987. *Bank costs, structure and performance.* Lexington, Mass.: D. C. Heath.

Matutes, C., and J. Padilla. 1994. Shared ATM networks and banking competition. *European Economic Review* 38(5):1113–38.

McAllister, P. H., and D. A. McManus. 1992. Diversification and risk in banking: Evidence from ex post returns. Board of Governors of the Federal Reserve System Finance and Economics Discussion Series no. 201, Federal Reserve Board, Washington, D.C.

Mester, L. 1987. A multiproduct cost study of savings and loans. *Journal of Finance* 42(2):423–45.

———. 1991. Agency costs among savings and loans. *Journal of Financial Intermediation* 1(3):257–78.

———. 1992. Traditional and nontraditional banking: An information-theoretic approach. *Journal of Banking and Finance* 16(3):545–66.

————. 1993. Efficiency in the savings and loans industry. *Journal of Banking and Finance* 17(2–3):267–86.

Monti, M. 1972. Deposit, credit, and interest rate determination under alternative bank objectives. In *Mathematical methods in investment and finance,* edited by G. P. Szego and K. Shell. Amsterdam: North-Holland.

Murray, J. D., and R. W. White. 1983. Economies of scale and economies of scope in multi-product financial institutions: A study of British Columbia credit unions. *Journal of Finance* 38(3):887–902.

Neuberger, J., and G. Zimmerman. 1990. Bank pricing of retail deposit accounts and "the California rate mystery." *Economic Review (Federal Reserve Bank of San Francisco).* 0(2):3–16.

Price Waterhouse. 1988. The cost of non-Europe in financial markets. London: Price-Waterhouse.

Rochet, J. C., and J. Tirole. 1996. Interbank lending and systemic risk. *Journal of Money, Credit, and Banking* 28(4):733–62.

Salop, S. 1979. Monopolistic competition with outside goods. *Bell Journal of Economics* 10(1):141–56.

Sealey, C. W., and J. T. Lindley. 1977. Inputs, outputs, and a theory of production and cost at depository financial institutions. *Journal of Finance* 32:1251–66.

Shaked, A., and J. Sutton. 1982. Relaxing price competition through product differentiation. *Review of Economic Studies* 49:3–13.

Sharkey, W. 1982. *The theory of natural monopoly.* Cambridge: Cambridge University Press.

Stahl, D. O. 1988. Bertrand competition for inputs and Walrasian outcomes. *American Economic Review* 78(1):189–201.

Tirole, J. 1988. *The theory of industrial organization.* Cambridge: MIT Press.

Yanelle, M. O. 1988. The strategic analysis of intermediation. PhD. diss., University of Bonn.

————. 1989. The strategic analysis of intermediation. *European Economic Review* 33(2/3):294–301.

When a bank grants a loan to a borrower, both parties typically sign a contract. Ideally, it would be useful to specify in this contract all the obligations of the two parties in every possible future contingency. Even in the case of a one-period contract, this would mean writing down a complete list of these contingencies (states of nature) at the end of the period and specifying, for each of these contingencies, the amount of the repayment to the lender. In a dynamic (multi-period) setting, things are even more complicated. A complete contingent contract would have to specify as well, in every state of nature and at every interim date,

1. the amount of repayment or (possibly) the amount of additional loan,

2. the interest rate on the remaining debt,

3. a possible adjustment in the collateral required by the lender, and

4. the actions (in particular investment decisions) to be undertaken by the borrower.

In practice, debt contracts are much less complex. In general, repayment obligations (points 1 and 2) and collateral (point 3) are specified for the whole duration of the contract, whereas actions to be taken (point 4) are left to the borrower. Sometimes, however, some covenants are stipulated, and sometimes default is declared, in which case creditors take over. Therefore, loan contracts are much less flexible than one could expect, in particular because writing a complete contingent contract would be prohibitively costly.

These issues are crucial in corporate finance, because they explain the use of second best financial contracts. Harris and Raviv (1991, 1992) provide interesting surveys of these questions, with particular attention to the famous results of Myers and Majluf (1984) and Jensen and Meckling (1976). The objective here is more limited; this chapter will discuss only the aspects of the lender–borrower relationship that concern banking, thus leaving aside the issues related to the financial structure of firms.

Section 4.1 will present the benchmark case of symmetric information, in which the characteristics of the loan contract are determined only by risk-sharing considerations. The discussion will show that this is not enough to explain all the features of bank loans. Then Section 4.2 will study one of the most popular paradigms for explaining the lack of flexibility of loan contracts, namely the costly state verification model of Townsend (1979), further developed by Gale and Hellwig (1985). In this model it is assumed that the lender cannot observe the result y of the investment made by the borrower, unless a costly audit is performed. In that case, incentive compatibility conditions imply that, absent auditing, the repayment cannot depend on y. Typically, the optimal contract is such that an audit takes place only when the cash flows are so low that the (fixed) agreed repayment is not feasible. This is interpreted as failure, in which case the lender seizes all the cash flows.

Another interesting issue involves the incentives to repay in a dynamic context (Section 4.3). The discussion of this question will start with the case of corporate debt, as studied by Bolton and Scharfstein (1990) (subsection 4.3.1). It will then proceed to the study of strategic debt service, first for a sovereign debtor (subsection 4.3.2) and then for a private debtor with inalienable human capital (subsection 4.3.3).

Section 4.4 will be specifically dedicated to the subject of moral hazard, and Section 4.5 will present two examples of the incomplete contract approach. As a complement, Section 4.6 will study the possible use of collateral and loan size as devices for screening heterogenous borrowers.

4.1   Why Risk Sharing Does Not Explain All the Features of Bank Loans

This section will present the simple model of the lender–borrower relationship that will be used throughout this chapter and will study the benchmark case of symmetric information. In this case, the analysis focuses on optimal risk sharing between the two parties, the lender (or investor) and the borrower (or entrepreneur). Assume only one good and two dates.

At date 0 the borrower has the possibility to invest some quantity L (assumed to be fixed) of the good, which will produce in return a random quantity $\tilde{y}$ of the same good at date 1. For simplicity, assume that the borrower has no private resources at date 0 and borrows L from the lender. Therefore L designates the amount of the loan. For simplicity again, assume that both agents consume only at date 1, and that their preferences are characterized by Von Neumann–Morgenstern (VNM) utility functions u_L (for the lender) and u_B (for the borrower), assumed to be twice continuously differentiable, concave, and strictly increasing.

4.1.1   Optimal Contracts When Cash Flows Are Observable

If the result $\tilde{y}$ of the investment is observable by both agents (a situation of symmetric information), these agents can sign a contract specifying in advance how they will share $\tilde{y}$ at date 1. This sharing rule is completely determined once the repayment $R(y)$ to the lender is specified as a function of the realization y of $\tilde{y}$. The borrower then gets $y - R(y)$. In most cases it is reasonable to require positive consumption for both agents (which may be interpreted as introducing limited liability constraints):

$$0 \leq R(y) \leq y$$

for all y in the support of $\tilde{y}$. The family of optimal debt contracts (under symmetric information) can be obtained parametrically as the solution of the following program $\mathcal{P}_0$:

$$\max_{R(\cdot)} E u_B(\tilde{y} - R(\tilde{y}))$$

$$s.t. E u_L(R(\tilde{y})) \geq U_L^0 \tag{4.1}$$

$$0 \leq R(y) \leq y, \tag{4.2}$$

where the parameter U_L^0 denotes the expected utility demanded by the lender (individual rationality level). Since u_B and u_L are monotonic, it is easy to see that 4.1 will always be binding. Notice that optimal contracts could be obtained as well by maximizing the expected utility of the lender under an individual rationality constraint for the borrower (plus limited liability constraints). Therefore the lender and the borrower play completely symmetric roles, and the features of optimal contracts will be determined purely by risk-sharing considerations and limited liability constraints. When the latter constraints are not binding, it is easy to see that the solution of $\mathcal{P}_0$ is characterized by the equality of marginal rates of substitution across states for the two agents. For all y_1 and y_2 in the support of $\tilde{y}$, one must have

$$\frac{u_L'[R(y_1)]}{u_L'[R(y_2)]} = \frac{u_B'[y_1 - R(y_1)]}{u_B'[y_2 - R(y_2)]}, \tag{4.3}$$

or, put in another way, the ratio of the marginal utilities of the two agents is a constant μ in the support of $\tilde{y}$. For all y in this support,

$$\frac{u_B'(y - R(y))}{u_L'(R(y))} = \mu. \tag{4.4}$$

Of course, μ depends on the individual rationality level U_L^0 demanded by the lender. If the logarithm of equation 4.4 is differentiated with respect to y, the following result is obtained for all y in the support of $\tilde{y}$:

$$\frac{u_B''}{u_B'}(y - R(y))(1 - R'(y)) - \frac{u_L''}{u_L'}(R(y))R'(y) = 0.$$

This gives a relation between $R'(y)$ and the absolute indexes of risk aversion of the two agents, defined by

$$I_B(x) = -\frac{u_B''(x)}{u_B'(x)} \quad \text{and} \quad I_L(x) = -\frac{u_L''(x)}{u_L'(x)}.$$

A classical result is obtained that can be traced back to Wilson (1968):

Result 4.1   When limited liability constraints are not binding, optimal debt contracts under symmetric information are characterized by the condition

$$R'(y) = \frac{I_B(y - R(y))}{I_B(y - R(y)) + I_L(R(y))}.$$

This result can be easily interpreted:[1] the sensitivity of the repayment $R(y)$ to the result y is high when the borrower is more risk averse than the lender ($\frac{I_B}{I_L}$ large) and low in the reverse case. This finding is not very satisfactory in the banking context. Indeed, banks typically have large, diversified portfolios, which means that in general they are approximatively neutral vis-à-vis the small risks of individual loans. But then, result 4.1 suggests that $R'(y)$ should be close to one, whereas the typical bank loan involves instead a constant repayment ($R(y) \equiv R$). In fact, when limited liability is introduced, the repayment function of a typical bank loan becomes $R(y) = \min(y, R)$. This is what is usually called the standard debt contract, in which the borrower promises a fixed repayment R, and the bank seizes the entire cash flow y when the borrower cannot repay R.

As has just been shown, risk sharing alone cannot explain the widespread use of such contracts. This leads to abandonment of the symmetrical treatment of the lender and the borrower. Later sections will introduce a fundamental asymmetry between them, by considering that the observation of $\tilde{y}$ by the lender is costly (Section 4.2) or even impossible (Section 4.3). Before that, the following discussion will examine some possible extensions and applications of the above result.

4.1.2 Extensions and Applications of the Risk-Sharing Paradigm

The previous result characterized the optimal risk-sharing contracts when the cash flow y was observable. The analysis can be extended to any source of risk, provided it is observable. Such an extension will not provide a deeper insight into risk sharing, since the model is formally the same. Still, it has practical implications for the design of loan contracts that are worth mentioning:

• When inflation is taken into account, the borrower's and the lender's utilities are functions of real (as opposed to nominal) cash flows. Then it is easy to show that the optimal repayment (in real terms) is independent of the price level, i.e., that there is a full price indexation of the repayment.

• When the cost of funds for the lender is stochastic (and thus there is interest rate risk), the optimal contract is such that the repayments are contingent on the interest rate.[2] Here the utilities of the two agents would be $u_B(y - R(y, r))$ and $u_L(R(y, r) - L(1 + r))$. The equivalent of result 4.1 would be

$$\frac{\partial R}{\partial r} = \frac{I_L}{I_B + I_L} L,$$

which means that interest rate risk is shared in inverse proportion to the agents' absolute risk aversion index.

• If the borrower's income is not directly observable, the lender will try to collect indirect information about this income. In fact, the optimal contract will make the repayments contingent on the observable variables that are the most informative on the borrower's income.

The recent innovations in the U.S. mortgage market can be better understood in the light of these risk-sharing considerations. When inflation was moderate, the standard fixed payment mortgage implied real repayment flows decreasing over time, but when the rate of inflation became high, indexation was to be brought in. This may explain why *graduated payment mortgages* (with mortgage payments rising at some specified rate), and *price level adjusted mortgages* (with full price indexation of mortgage payments) were introduced.[3] *Shared-appreciation mortgages* (in which the lender assumes some fraction of the risk on the value of the house) can also be analyzed along the same lines (see Alm and Follain 1982, Statman 1982, and Artus and Freixas 1990).

4.2   Costly State Verification

Following the articles of Townsend (1979) and Gale and Hellwig (1985), this section will modify the model of Section 4.1 by assuming that the realization y of $\tilde{y}$ is not observable by the lender unless the lender undertakes an audit, which costs γ. The rules of the contract to be signed between the lender and the borrower are now more complex: in particular, the contract has to specify when an audit will be undertaken and how its result will affect the payment to the lender. Using the *revelation principle* (see for instance Fudenberg and Tirole 1991 or Mas Colell, Whinston, and Green 1995), the contract may be described (without loss of generality) by a revelation mechanism in which the borrower is asked to report y, and in which the rules of the mechanism are designed in such a way that it is always in the interest of the borrower to report truthfully. Therefore the contract can be described as

• *a repayment function* $\hat{y} \rightarrow R(\hat{y})$ (transfer promised by the borrower to the lender, as a function of the report $\hat{y}$ sent by the borrower),

• *an auditing rule,* identified as a set S of reports of the borrower for which the lender undertakes an audit,

• a *penalty (or reward) function* $P(y, \hat{y})$ specifying a possible additional transfer between the borrower and the lender after the audit, and depending on the result y of the audit and on the report $\hat{y}$ previously sent by the borrower.

This array $(R(\cdot), S, P(\cdot, \cdot))$ specifies a *direct revelation mechanism* in the language of contract theory. This mechanism has to fulfil the incentive compatibility (IC) constraints, ensuring that truthful reporting $(\hat{y} = y)$ is a dominant strategy. The next subsection first will characterize the set of incentive compatible mechanisms. It then will show that the efficient incentive compatible contracts are simply standard debt contracts. It will also study what happens when borrowers can falsify their reports. Finally, it will present a two-period extension of the costly state verification model put forth by Chang (1990).

4.2.1 Incentive Compatible Contracts

In a first step it is easy to see that $P(y, \hat{y})$ can be taken as arbitrarily large for $\hat{y} \neq y$ and normalized to zero for $\hat{y} = y$. In other words, it is easy to prevent untruthful reporting in the auditing region, and therefore (this is in fact a convention) truthful reporting need not be rewarded.

A second remark is that the repayment function is necessarily constant on the complement of S, since otherwise the borrower could cheat by announcing the message that corresponds to the minimum repayment on the no-audit zone. Denote by R the (constant) value of this repayment function on the complement of S.

A third remark is that R cannot be smaller than the maximum repayment possible on S. Otherwise, the borrower would have an interest, for some realizations of y in S, in reporting a message in the no-audit region, and paying R; therefore, the mechanism would not be incentive compatible. To summarize:

Result 4.2a   A debt contract is incentive compatible if and only if there exists a constant R such that

$$\begin{cases} \forall y \notin S & R(y) \equiv R \\ \forall y \in S & R(y) \leq R. \end{cases}$$

4.2.2 Efficient Incentive Compatible Contracts

The next task is to select, among these incentive compatible debt contracts, those that are efficient. Assume that both agents are risk neutral, so that risk-sharing considerations are irrelevant. Efficient incentive compatible debt contracts are then obtained by minimizing the probability of an audit for a fixed expected repayment, or equivalently by maximizing the expected repayment for a fixed probability of an audit. In view of result 4.2a, for a given expected repayment $E[R(y)]$, an incentive compatible debt contract will be efficient only if $R(y)$ is maximum in the audit region. The efficient incentive compatible debt contracts will be such that

• $\forall y \in S$ $R(y) = \min(y, R)$ (maximum repayment in the audit zone, taking into account limited liability and incentive compatibility constraints), and

• $S' = \{y, y < R\}$, which means that an audit will take place only when reimbursement is less than R (bankruptcy).

This can be interpreted as a standard debt contract

Result 4.2b   If both agents are risk neutral, any efficient incentive compatible debt contract is a standard debt contract.

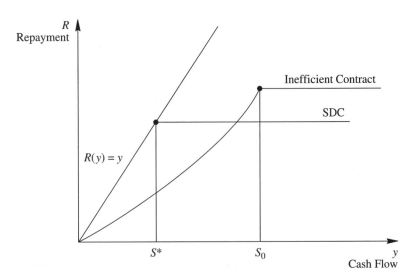

Figure 4.1
Optimality of the Standard Debt Contract under Costly State Verification

Figure 4.1 illustrates the result by comparing incentive compatible contracts giving the same expected repayment for the borrower.

If risk aversion is introduced, optimal contracts are more complex and do not always correspond to standard debt contracts. Moreover, even if agents are risk neutral, standard debt contracts can be dominated if the situation allows for stochastic auditing procedures (see problem 4.7.4). Also, it may not be easy for the lender to commit to an audit when the borrower defaults.[4]

A related result establishing the optimality of standard debt contracts was previously obtained by Diamond (1984) within a similar context of risk neutrality. The objective is also to obtain truthful revelation of the borrower's cash flows y. The difference is that in Diamond's model cash flows are not observable (or equivalently, auditing costs are infinite), so that mechanisms have to be defined only for $y \notin S$. But result 4.2a shows that this implies a constant repayment R, which has to be smaller than the smallest possible value of y. To go beyond this uninteresting case, Diamond assumes that the contract may also include a nonpecuniary cost $\varphi(y)$ that the lender can inflict on the borrower (for instance, a loss of reputation). This modifies the incentive compatibility condition, which now becomes

$$R(y) + \varphi(y) = R,$$

and is interpreted as the indifference of the borrower to announce any cash flow level, since the total (pecuniary plus nonpecuniary) cost is constant.

Efficient contracts, then, are those that minimize the expected nonpecuniary cost. This leads to minimizing the set S on which $\varphi(y) > 0$ and to take the

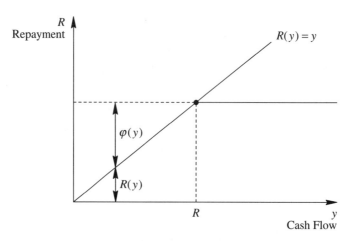

Figure 4.2
Optimality of the Standard Debt Contract under Nonpecuniary Costs of Bankruptcy

minimum possible value $\varphi(y)$; that is, $\varphi(y) = R - y$. A standard debt contract is thus obtained, as shown in Figure 4.2. Notice, though, that to some extent the introduction of a nonpecuniary cost means a violation of the limited liability constraint as it is usually understood.

4.2.3 Efficient Falsification-Proof Contracts

This subsection will briefly address the issue of falsification, which arises when the borrower can manipulate the reported cash flow at a certain cost. This model will keep exactly the same framework and the notations that have already been introduced, but assume that there is a cost $c(y, \hat{y})$ incurred by the borrower for reporting $\hat{y}$ when y has occurred (with $c(y, y) = 0$, which means that truthful reporting is costless). Lacker and Weinberg (1989) address this problem in a general setting. The aim here is simply to illustrate how falsification may alter the characteristics of the optimal repayment function $R(\hat{y})$.

Assume[5] that the cost of falsification is $c(y, \hat{y}) = \gamma|y - \hat{y}|$, where γ is positive but smaller than 1. A borrower who reports $\hat{y}$ after obtaining y obtains the following profit:

$$\pi_B = y - R(\hat{y}) - \gamma|y - \hat{y}|.$$

The mechanism will be falsification proof if for all y, this expression has a maximum for $\hat{y} = y$ (no falsification). Since π_B has a kink for $\hat{y} = y$, this is equivalent to requiring that for all y,

$$-\gamma \leq R'(y) \leq \gamma. \tag{4.5}$$

Because of limited liability constraints, $R(0)$ necessarily equals 0, which, together with 4.5, implies that for all y,

$$R(y) \leq \gamma y.$$

The maximum expected repayment for the lender is therefore $\gamma E(y)$. The possibility of falsification thus imposes a severe constraint on the projects that can be funded. If L represents the size of the loan and r the interest rate demanded by the bank, a necessary condition for funding is

$$\gamma E(y) \geq (1+r)L. \tag{4.6}$$

If this condition is satisfied, funding is possible, and the characteristics of the optimal repayment function can be investigated. The most realistic case is when the borrower is risk averse, whereas the lender is risk neutral. Risk-sharing considerations alone would lead to a repayment function such that $R'(y)$ equals 1 (see result 4.1); this violates the no-falsification constraint (4.5). In fact, the optimal falsification proof contract is such that $R'(y)$ is as close as possible to 1.[6] The following result is obtained:

$$R(y) = \max(0, \gamma y - \alpha),$$

where α is a positive number.

4.2.4 Dynamic Debt Contracts with Costly State Verification

This subsection will present the results obtained by Chang (1990), who studies a two-period extension of the model of Townsend and of Gale and Hellwig. Consider an entrepreneur who has to invest 1 at date $t = 0$, this investment producing random independent cash flows $\tilde{y}_1$ at date $t = 1$ and $\tilde{y}_2$ at date $t = 2$. These cash flows are not observable by the lender without incurring an auditing cost $\gamma_t(x_t)$ $t = 1, 2$, where $\gamma_t(\cdot)$ is a nondecreasing function and x_t represents the total value of the firm's assets at date t. Since it is assumed that the entrepreneur has no other source of funds (both at $t = 0$ and at $t = 1$), x_1 equals y_1 and x_2 equals y_2 plus (possibly) the earnings retained at date $t = 1$. Other simplifying assumptions are the absence of discounting (the risk-free rate equals zero) and the impossibility of paying dividends at $t = 1$ or perquisites to the firm's managers (another interpretation is that there are no outside stockholders). This setup allows us to determine the optimal debt contracts under risk neutrality, that is, contracts that minimize the expected costs of an audit for a given expected repayment to the lender. Use of the revelation principle will again allow the definition of a contract that directly depends on the values the agents announce for y_1 and y_2. That is, a general contract will specify $(R_1(y_1), D_1(y_1), R_2(y_1, y_2), D_2(y_1, y_2))$, where R_t represents period t

payments to the lender and D_t the dichotomic variable for auditing: $D_t = 1$ if an audit occurs at date t, and $D_t = 0$ otherwise.

Since nothing happens after date 2, and using the standard backward induction argument, the results of the static model may be applied to this date: the second stage of an optimal contract is necessarily a standard debt contract, i.e., it specifies a contractual repayment $R_2(y_1, y_2) = R_2(y_1)$ that is independent of y_2. An audit takes place at date 2 if and only if the total assets of the firm $y_1 - R_1(y_1) + y_2$ are less than R_2, in which case the lender seizes these assets. That is, an audit takes place at date 2 if and only if $R_1(y_1) + R_2(y_1) > y_1 + y_2$, i.e., if total liability exceeds the sum of cash flows. The only characteristics of the contract that remain to be derived concern date 1, namely the auditing rule $D_1(y_1)$ and required repayment $R_1(y_1)$, subject to the incentive compatibility constraints:

- $R_1(y_1) + R_2(y_1)$ equals a constant M on the no-audit set.
- $R_1(y_1) + R_2(y_1)$ is less than M on the audit set.

If verification costs were constant, it would never pay to audit the firm during the first period, since the firm's cash flows cannot be diverted away. The problem becomes interesting only when it is assumed that the verification cost y_2 is strictly increasing with the size of the firm's assets. It is easy to see then that it is never optimal to let the firm retain some of its earnings at date 1, because this would increase period 2 auditing costs. Since limited liability is required, optimality implies that the lender seizes the whole first period cash flow in the audit region. Therefore, there exists a threshold M such that:

$$\forall y_1 \leq M : \; R_1(y_1) = y_1.$$

Under the additional assumption that the distribution of $\tilde{y}$ exhibits a decreasing hazard rate, Chang (1990) is able to show that the optimal contract can be described as follows:

- When $y_1 \leq m$, an audit takes place, $R_1(y_1) = y_1$, and the borrower is required to repay his remaining liability $M - y_1$ at date 2 (if he can).
- When $m < y_1 < M$, there is no audit, but the borrower repays as much as he can at $t = 1$:

$$R_1(y_1) = y_1; \quad R_2(y_1) = M - y_1.$$

- When $y_1 \geq M$, all debt is repaid at $t = 1$.

The optimal dynamic contract can therefore be interpreted as a two-period standard debt contract with an early repayment option at date 1.

4.3   Incentives to Repay

This section will consider a more extreme framework than the costly state verification paradigm. Assume here that an audit is simply impossible, and the borrower will repay only when incentives are present to do so. Subsection 4.3.1 will start with the general model of Bolton and Scharfstein (1990), who assume that the returns of the borrower's investment are not verifiable by a third party (and thus are noncontractible). Then subsection 4.3.2 will examine the specific case of a sovereign debtor, considering the contributions of Allen (1983) and Eaton and Gersovitz (1981). Finally, subsection 4.3.3 will study the case in which the borrower is an entrepreneur who cannot alienate his or her human capital (Hart and Moore 1994), so that the use of collateral is justified.

4.3.1   Threat of Termination

Bolton and Scharfstein (1990) study a repeated borrower–lender relationship in which the threat of termination by the lender provides incentives for the borrower to repay the loan.[7] In its simplest formulation, their model considers an entrepreneur who owns a technology that transforms a fixed amount L into a random cash flow $\tilde{y}$. This technology can be used repeatedly, at discrete dates $t = 0, 1 \ldots$, and cash flows are independently identically distributed (i.i.d.) across dates. The entrepreneur has no resources of his own and can invest at a given date only if a bank grants him a loan. For simplicity, assume risk neutrality and no discounting, and assume that $E(\tilde{y}) > L$. Therefore, in a world of symmetric information, the investment would be undertaken. However, the realized cash flows are not observable by the bank (or verifiable by a court of justice). This may lead the bank to refuse to grant the loan. For example, Bolton and Scharfstein examine a case in which the cash flows $\tilde{y}_t$ can take only two values, high ($\bar{y}$) or low ($\underline{y}$), and they assume that $L > \underline{y}$. Then, the borrower can always pretend that $\tilde{y} = \underline{y}$, which is therefore the maximum repayment that the bank can enforce. In a one-shot relationship, there would be no lending, since it would lead to a deficit of (at least) $L - \underline{y}$ for the bank.

However, in a two-period relationship, the bank can commit to renew (at $t = 2$) the initial loan if the firm repays $R > \underline{y}$ at the end of period 1 (which can occur only if $\tilde{y}_1 = \bar{y}$). Of course, at the end of period 2 the firm will be in the same situation as in a one-shot relationship, and will always repay the minimum possible amount. Therefore, the bank knows that it will lose money at $t = 2$ (if the second loan is granted), but the first repayment R can be sufficiently high to compensate for this loss. More specifically, the expected present value of the bank profit is

$$\pi = -L + P(\tilde{y}_1 = \underline{y})\underline{y} + P(\tilde{y}_1 = \bar{y})(R - L + \underline{y}),$$

which can also be written

$$\pi = \underline{y} - L + P(\tilde{y}_1 = \bar{y})(R - L).$$

The bank will sign the two-period contract if π is nonnegative, or if

$$R \geq L + \frac{L - \underline{y}}{P(\tilde{y}_1 = \bar{y})}. \tag{4.7}$$

It must be confirmed that the borrower has incentives to repay when $\tilde{y}_1 = \bar{y}$:

$$-R + P(\tilde{y}_2 = \bar{y})(\bar{y} - \underline{y}) \geq -\underline{y},$$

which is equivalent to

$$R \leq E(\tilde{y}). \tag{4.8}$$

Therefore, any repayment R that satisfies both conditions 4.7 and 4.8 will be acceptable to the lender. Such a repayment exists if and only if

$$L - \underline{y} \leq P(\tilde{y}_1 = \bar{y})(E(\tilde{y}) - L). \tag{4.9}$$

If this condition is satisfied, the threat of termination provides the incentives to repay in a two-period model. Gromb (1994) provides a detailed analysis of an extension of this model to several periods. (See also Dewatripont and Maskin 1995.)

It is interesting to remark that this model and Diamond's (1984) share the assumption that lenders cannot observe cash flows. Diamond's solution is based on the existence of a nonpecuniary cost. In Bolton and Scharfstein, the incentives are brought in through the threat not to lend in the future. Haubrich (1989) combines the two types of mechanisms in an infinite horizon model with no discounting. When the dynamic contract is used, this means that the lender devises a test that catches an agent who systematically cheats (in an infinite horizon model with no discounting, cheating a finite number of times is irrelevant). Unlucky people will almost never be punished. Also, punishment need not entail a cessation of credit but may take the form of higher interest rates.

4.3.2   Strategic Debt Repayment: The Case of a Sovereign Debtor

Consider a very simple stationary model inspired by Allen (1983), in which a sovereign country makes an investment funded by a foreign bank loan L. This allows the country to produce output $f(L)$, assumed to be sufficient to repay $(1 + r)L$. The static profit of the country is

$$\pi = f(L) - (1 + r)L \geq 0,$$

where r is the (exogenous) riskless interest rate. The country's demand for capital L_D (obtained by maximizing π) is given by the usual condition on marginal productivity:

$$f'(L_D) = 1 + r.$$

Assume that the country is able to repudiate its debt at any moment,[8] in which case it cannot obtain a new loan anymore: no renegotiation is possible.[9] Of course, the country could default only once, and live in autarky ever after, by simply reinvesting some fraction of its production. Assume that this is not possible, and take this as the reduced form of a more complex model in which a lag occurs between the moment at which investment is made and the moment at which the nonstorable output is obtained.[10]

The opportunity cost of default equals the present value of forgone profits (for simplicity, consider an infinite time horizon):

$$V(L) = \sum_{t=1}^{\infty} \beta^t (f(L) - (1+r)L) = \frac{\beta}{1-\beta}(f(L) - (1+r)L),$$

with $0 < \beta < 1$.

For the country to repay, it must have incentives to do so. That is, the cost of repayment has to be inferior to the opportunity cost of default:

$$(1+r)L \leq V(L).$$

This is equivalent to

$$(1+r)L \leq \beta f(L).$$

Assuming (as in Figure 4.3) that there are decreasing returns to scale, this inequality holds for $L \leq \hat{L}$, where $\hat{L}$ is the maximum loan size that satisfies this inequality. When β is large enough, the optimal loan L_D will be feasible, as in Figure 4.3. However, when β is small, $\hat{L}$ may be smaller than L_D and the firm will be rationed.

Following Eaton and Gersovitz (1981), this discussion now will elaborate on the previous model by studying a more complete infinite horizon stationary model in which the borrowing country is characterized by an exogenous (stochastic) output process $\tilde{y}_t$ (assumed to be independently and identically distributed on a bounded interval) and by an objective function

$$U = E(\sum_{t=0}^{+\infty} \beta^t u(C_t)),$$

where C_t represents absorption ("consumption") at date t and u is a VNM utility function with the usual properties ($u' > 0$, $u'' < 0$, and u bounded

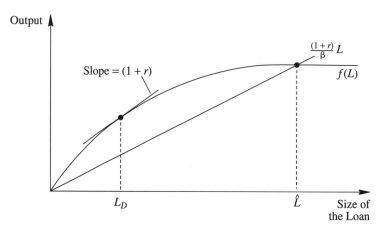

Figure 4.3
Underinvestment in the Case of a Strategic Debtor (Allen 1983)

above). For simplicity, assume that borrowing occurs only on *even* dates, and repayment is always due at the next period (short-term borrowing). The lender may set a limit on the borrowing capacity, or more generally restrict the amount b that is borrowed, which is captured by the condition $b \in B$ where the set B is chosen by the lender. Another assumption is that default is followed by definitive exclusion from future borrowing (no forgiveness).[11] In that case, the continuation payoff for the borrower corresponds to autarky:

$$U_d = E(\sum_{t=0}^{+\infty} \beta^t u(\tilde{y}_t)) = \frac{Eu(\tilde{y})}{1 - \beta},$$

where U_d stands for the utility of defaulting. Assuming that repayment is always feasible, strategic default will occur if and only if

$$u(y) + \beta U_d > u(y - R) + \beta V_r,$$

where V_r represents the continuation payoff associated with repaying the loan during the current period (and defaulting later if it is optimal to do so). V_r will be computed later. For the moment, notice that the condition for strategic default can also be written

$$\psi(y, R) = u(y) - u(y - R) > \beta(V_r - U_d).$$

Since u is concave, this condition is satisfied if and only if y is less than some cutoff point denoted as $\varphi(R)$. Indeed, u' is decreasing, and therefore $\frac{\partial \psi}{\partial y}$ is negative. Since $\psi(\varphi(R), R) = \beta(V_r - U_d)$, φ' will have the same sign as $-\frac{\partial \psi}{\partial y} / \frac{\partial \psi}{\partial R}$. It is already known that $\frac{\partial \psi}{\partial y} < 0$. Moreover, the fact that u is increasing implies $\frac{\partial \psi}{\partial R} > 0$. Therefore, φ has to be increasing. In other words, strategic default will occur (as expected) when output is low (bad times) and will be more likely when debt is high. Under the dynamic programming principle (provided default has not occurred previously), for any given level y of current output, the country will choose to borrow the amount $b(y)$ that solves

$$\max_{b \in B} \{u(y+b) + \beta E_{y'}[\max(u(y') + \beta U_d, u(y' - R(b))$$

$$+ \beta V_r]\} = V(y), \tag{4.10}$$

where $V(y)$ represents the (optimal) value function for the borrower, $R(\cdot)$ is the repayment function, and y' is the unknown future output. The expression inside the expectation symbol represents the continuation payoff, after strategic debt servicing at the next period.

Assume that the lenders are risk neutral and have a competitive behavior. An equilibrium in the credit market will then be characterized by a value function $V(y)$, a borrowing decision $b(y)$, a cutoff point $\varphi(R)$ (these three functions together characterize the borrower's behavior), and a repayment function $R(b)$ such that

- condition 4.10 is satisfied, where the maximum is attained for $b = b(y)$ and V_r equals $E[V(\tilde{y})]$ (optimal borrowing decision).

- $y < \varphi(R) \Leftrightarrow u(y) + \beta U_d > u(y - R) + \beta V_r$ and repudiation occurs exactly in that case (optimal repudiation decision).

- for all b in B, $R(b) = \frac{(1+r)b}{P\{\tilde{y} > \varphi(R(b))\}}$ where r represents the risk-free rate at which risk neutral lenders can refinance their loans (zero profit condition for lenders).

Depending on the parameters, the set B may be bounded or not. Indeed, there is no reason why the function $E(R) = RP\{\tilde{y} > \varphi(R)\}$ should increase up to infinity. If $E(R)$ reaches a maximum, then there will be a maximum amount that the country can borrow.

Result 4.3   At a competitive equilibrium of the credit market, the following propositions hold true:

- Strategic default occurs when current output is low relative to outstanding debt ($y < \varphi(R)$).

- The probability of strategic default increases with the volume of outstanding debt (φ is increasing).

- The nominal interest rate $\frac{R(b)}{b}$ increases with b.

Proof   The only thing not already proven in the text is the last property. Recall that $R(b)$ is defined implicitly by

$$R(b) = \frac{(1+r)b}{P\{\tilde{y} > \varphi(R(b))\}}.$$

Therefore,

$$\frac{R(b)}{b} = \frac{1+r}{P\{\tilde{y} > \varphi(R(b))\}}.$$

φ and R are increasing. Therefore, this is also the case for $\frac{R(b)}{b}$.   ∎

Another noteworthy property of this equilibrium is that it typically exhibits "credit rationing," at least in the following sense: if borrowers were confronted with a linear repayment schedule (i.e., in which the interest rate is independent of the size of the loan), they would sometimes want to borrow more than what they get at the equilibrium discussed earlier.[12] This comes from the nonconvexity of preferences due to the repudiation option (for more details, see Eaton and Gersovitz 1981).

It is worth noticing that although this model is not based on any idea of reputation building, it can be subject to a criticism of Bulow and Rogoff (1989) for reputation models. Indeed, Bulow and Rogoff use a simple arbitrage argument in order to show that reputation alone is not enough to ensure debt repayment. This argument can be perfectly adapted to the setting used by Eaton and Gersovitz.

The argument of Bulow and Rogoff can be summarized as follows. Two types of contracts are available to the country for smoothing its consumption. A "reputation contract" is one in which the country receives a loan in exchange for a state contingent repayment. On the other hand, a "cash-in-advance contract" is one in which the country makes an initial payment in exchange for a series of state contingent payments. Since in a cash-in-advance contract the country bears the credit risk, a foreign "investor" will always accept it, and thus will act as an insurance company vis-à-vis the country's macroeconomic risk. Bulow and Rogoff show that if the country's future repayments have a positive expected present discounted value, the country will be better off by ceasing payment on its reputation contract and starting a series of cash-in-advance contracts that will replicate the initial contract at a lower cost.

As a consequence, the threat faced by the defaulting country (of being excluded from the credit market) loses its strength. The borrower's choice then is not to repay or to face income fluctuations without any possibility of borrowing, but rather to repay or to pay cash for an insurance mechanism. Bulow and Rogoff show that default dominates repayment. Consequently, absent penalties to the defaulting countries that will exclude them from access to the insurance mechanism, the credit market will be nonexistent.

4.3.3 Private Debtors and the Inalienability of Human Capital

Turn now to the case of a nonsovereign debtor. In contrast with the previous case, if a nonsovereign borrower defaults, the creditor is able to liquidate the project. As such, this is merely an extension of the previous models that would simply modify the conditions previously obtained but not their economic interpretation. Instead, this discussion will stress the limitations that strategic debt service imposes on the time structure of repayments. In order to do so, consider the repayment of an initial loan over a finite horizon T rather than the problem of renewed lending examined before.

Hart and Moore (1994) stress as the main characteristic of a debt contract the fact that it cannot impose on the entrepreneur any restriction on the freedom to walk away. This noncommitment for the entrepreneur not to withdraw human capital from the investment project will imply that (1) some profitable projects will not be funded and (2) the time profile of repayments will be affected by the liquidation value of the project.

To see this, consider a risk neutral entrepreneur who wants to invest an amount I in a project that yields a certain stream of (discounted) cash flows $y_t, t = 1, \ldots, T$. If the entrepreneur is not cash constrained, she will invest if and only if

$$I \leq \sum y_t,$$

where $\sum y_t$ is the present value of the project (the riskless rate of interest is normalized to zero). The case that will be focused on is, of course, the one in which there is a cash constraint and the project has to be funded by a debt contract. If additional subsequent loans are ruled out, the time profile for the repayment $R_t(t = 1, \ldots, T)$ is constrained by the limited liability clause:

$$0 \leq R_t \leq y_t \qquad t = 1, \ldots, T.$$

Since the entrepreneur cannot commit not to walk away from the project, she will use this possibility in a strategical way. Therefore, the situation must be modeled as a game. At any time the debtor can threaten to end the contract, possibly incurring an opportunity cost, since future cash flows will be lost or reduced. If this threat is credible, then the creditor and the debtor will enter into a bargaining game in which the creditor will obtain at least the liquidation value of the investment project, but may obtain more if the project is not liquidated.

A crucial element is how the bargaining game is solved, i.e., how the bargaining power is allocated between the two parties (players). This discussion will examine in turn the two extreme cases in which all the bargaining power belongs to either the creditor or the debtor. Denote by V_t the value of the project to the creditor if the entrepreneur quits. V_t may represent collateral, the liquidation value of the assets, or the net present value of the project if a new manager has to implement it.

• Consider first the case in which the bank has all the bargaining power.[13] This implies that it obtains $\sum_{\tau=t}^{T} y_\tau$ if debt is repudiated at time t. Now any project satisfying the limited liability constraint will be repudiation-proof. The maximum amount of debt that a project can raise will be $\sum_{\tau=1}^{T} y_\tau$, and therefore a project will be funded if and only if its net present value is nonnegative.

• Next, assume that the entrepreneur has all the bargaining power. Then, a debt repayment scheme will be repudiation-proof if

$$\sum_{\tau=t}^{T} R_\tau \leq V_t, \qquad t = 1, \dots, T.$$

Indeed, in this case repudiation cannot improve the debtor's position, since she will never gain from entering the bargaining process. The project will be undertaken only if there is a loan contract such that the present value of repayments exceeds the volume L of the loan, and if the entrepreneur has enough wealth to finance the investment:

$$L \leq \sum_{t=1}^{T} R_t \quad \text{and} \quad W + L \geq I,$$

where R_t is the repudiation-proof repayment scheme, and W the wealth of the entrepreneur. Clearly, some profitable investment projects will be overlooked because the nonappropriability of human capital reduces the amount of *credible* repayment flows.

As intuition suggests, between these two extreme assumptions on the allocation of bargaining power, repudiation-proof repayment schemes will be obtained that will imply some inefficiency for the credit allocation. More generally,

Result 4.4   The noncommitment of human capital to a project puts an upper bound on the total future indebtness of an entrepreneur.

This inefficiency result appears only in a dynamic setting. It shows why banks may be concerned not only with the net present value of cash flows but also with the projects' collateral. In addition, as mentioned by Hart and Moore (1994, p.842), it corresponds to the advice practitioners often give to "lend long if the loan is supported by durable collateral," and to "match assets with liabilities."

4.4   Moral Hazard

It is characteristic of the banking industry for banks to behave as a sleeping partner in their usual relationship with borrowers.[14] For this reason, it seems natural to assume that banks ignore the actions the borrowers are taking in order to obtain the highest return. This is typically a moral hazard setup: the borrower has to take an action that will affect the return to the borrower, yet the borrower has no control over this action that is not observable.

Chapter 2 presented a simple model of the credit market with moral hazard. This discussion will involve a more complex model with continuous returns, as inspired by Innes (1987), who uses it to determine the shape of the optimal repayment function. A crucial assumption will be the limited liability of the borrower.[15]

Following Innes, consider a static borrower–lender relationship in which the borrower's return $\tilde{y}$ is continuous (instead of binomial as in the simple example of Chapter 2) and its distribution is influenced by an action e ("effort") undertaken by the borrower and nonobservable by the lender. Assume that both agents are risk neutral. Given a contract $R(\cdot)$, the borrower will choose the effort level e^* that maximizes net expected utility:

$$V(R, e) = \int (y - R(y)) f(y, e) dy - \psi(e),$$

where $f(y, e)$ is the density function of y for a given e, and ψ is a convex increasing function, representing the pecuniary equivalent of the cost of effort for the borrower. By definition of e^*,

$$\forall e \quad V(R, e) \leq V(R, e^*).$$

Given an individual rationality level U_L^0 demanded by the lender, the optimal contract will be such that it maximizes the utility of the borrower, under the effort constraint and the usual limited liability and individual rationality constraints.

Therefore the program to be solved is

$$(\mathscr{P}) \begin{cases} \max V(R, e^*) \\ 0 \leq R(y) \leq y & \forall y \\ V(R, e) \leq V(R, e^*) & \forall e \\ E[R(y)|e^*] \geq U_L^0. \end{cases}$$

Result 4.5   If for all $e_1 > e_2$, the likelihood ratio $\frac{f(y,e_1)}{f(y,e_2)}$ is an increasing function of y (monotone likelihood ratio (MLR)),[16] the optimal repayment function is always of the following type

$$\begin{cases} R(y) = 0 & \text{for } y \geq y^* \\ R(y) = y & \text{for } y < y^*. \end{cases}$$

Figure 4.4 shows the shape of the optimal repayment function.

The MLR property (see Holmström 1979) means that the result y of the investment is a good signal for the effort level: the higher y is, the higher

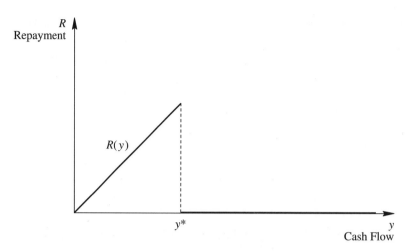

Figure 4.4
Optimal Contract in the Innes (1987) Moral Hazard Model

the relative likelihood will be that the effort has been high rather than low. Therefore, the intuition behind result 4.5 is that the best way to provide correct incentives for effort is to give to the agent maximal reward ($R(y) = 0$) when the result is good ($y \geq y^*$) and maximal penalty ($R(y) = y$) when the result is bad ($y < y^*$) (for a formal proof, see problem 4.7.3). Unfortunately, this type of contract is not frequently seen in practice. Innes (1987) has studied what happens if one restricts the problem further by requiring that the repayment function is nondecreasing in y.[17] In that case, Innes shows that the optimal contract is a standard debt contract.

Dionne and Viala (1992, 1994) have studied the lender–borrower relationship in which there is simultaneously moral hazard and costly state verification. Their model is a synthesis of those of Innes and Townsend, Gale, and Hellwig. They look for Pareto optimal contracts among the contracts that satisfy incentive compatibility (see subsection 4.2.1) and induce the borrower to the optimal level of effort. Under the MLR property, they show that any optimal contract is a combination of a debt contract and a "bonus contract" like those obtained in result 4.5. Thus, any optimal repayment function is characterized by two thresholds R and y^*, with $R(y^*)$ such that

$$\begin{cases} R(y) = \min(y, R) & \text{for } y < y^* \\ R(y) = 0 & \text{for } y \geq y^*. \end{cases}$$

Several articles have studied moral hazard in a dynamical context, such as Diamond (1991) (see Chapter 2). In such a context banks can offer multiperiod contracts, possibly involving cross-subsidies across periods. This implies that the bank commitment is crucial here, since banks would be better off by simply reneging on their promise to renew the loans of successful borrowers.

This important issue has to be addressed in a general setting. Indeed, as emphasized by Boot, Thakor, and Udell (1991), if a firm has to make a nonobservable investment before obtaining the funds to finance a project, lack of commitment on behalf of the bank to grant a loan with prespecified terms will reduce the level of nonobservable investment below the efficient one.

Why would a financial intermediary commit? There are two main reasons why the bank may prefer honoring the contract to the "take the money and run" alternative: either (1) the probability of successful legal recourse by the borrower may be sufficiently high (Boot, Thakor, and Udell 1991) or (2) the bank may have built a reputation for honoring its contracts. In this last case it is interesting to notice that the bank may still choose to "liquefy reputational capital" rather than to face an important (capital) loss in financially impaired states, a point emphasized by Boot, Greenbaum, and Thakor (1993).

Another important aspect of the relationship between banks and corporate borrowers is that the firms with close ties to banks seem to be less liquidity constrained in their investment behavior than independent firms. Hoshi, Kashyap, and Scharfstein (1993) provide empirical evidence for this phenomenon when they study the Japanese "Keiretsu," which are conglomerates that closely associate banks and industrial firms. Similar results are obtained on German data (for the period 1973 through 1984) by Elston (1995).

4.5   The Incomplete Contract Approach

Economic theory establishes that writing complete contracts (i.e., contracts that are potentially contingent on all future states of nature) can only improve efficiency, because it allows for complete risk sharing across these future states of nature. Still, complete contracts are not seen in practice and, even more at odds with this theory, renegotiations often occur after a contract has been signed. A typical example is when a firm goes bankrupt, which triggers a bargaining process involving all the claim holders. Such a situation seems to indicate that it was ex ante too difficult to describe all the events that would lead to bankruptcy and all the actions that the firm should take in each of them.

Incomplete contracts theory recognizes this fact and allows modeling of this type of situation. An important case is when the states of nature are observable by the two parties to the contract but are not *verifiable*, which means that a third party would not be able to observe the state of nature that has occurred, as happens in the models of Bolton and Scharfstein (1990) and Hart and Moore (1996) (sections 4.31 and 4.3.3). Consequently, a contingent contract, if written, would not have any legal value, since no court would be able to determine the (contingent) obligations of either party.

An incomplete contract will typically involve some delegation and allocation to one of the parties of the power to choose among a predetermined set of actions (investment choice, renewal of a loan, issuing new shares) and will make this power contingent on the realization of a verifiable signal. Thus, for instance, a contract may specify that, in case of default, creditors will take over the firm.

However, in general these verifiable signals are not perfectly correlated with the nonverifiable states of nature. Typically, the agent in charge will act according to its own objective function and may not choose the most efficient course of action. In such a case, there is scope for renegotiation. Of course, agents will rationally anticipate this from the start.

The objective of this section is not to study all the incomplete contract models[18] that have dealt with the borrower–lender relationship, but briefly to present some recent contributions so as to give a flavor of how incomplete contracts might improve the understanding of the lender–borrower relationship.

A general conclusion of these models is that the design of contracts should be such that it limits the tendency of agents to behave inefficiently. This implies, for instance, a different interpretation of bankruptcy, which plays a role because it allocates control to a different party, or because it is a credible threat that gives an incentive to the agent in charge to choose the efficient action.[19] As a simple example in the spirit of Hart and Moore (1995), imagine that a firm's managers are "empire builders" who have a preference for investing independently of the investment's net present value when this net present value is observable but not verifiable. If the firm has available cash flows it will always invest; if instead it has to make a debt repayment, it will be cash constrained and banks will finance only the profitable investment projects. The debt structure will be useful because it restricts the freedom of the managers to choose investments (for details, see problem 4.7.4).

This section will study two examples: the first, inspired by Bolton and Freixas (1994), builds on the idea that depositors delegate to the bank the right to renegotiate the loans granted to borrowers. The second, inspired by Gorton and Kahn (1993), will shed some light on why bank loans frequently include covenants that may give the right to the bank to call the loan back, sometimes triggering liquidation.

4.5.1 Delegated Renegotiation

A crucial difference between financial markets and financial intermediaries (FIs) comes from their different powers of renegotiation. Indeed, if an FI is viewed as a coalition of depositors, the interest of such a coalition is that the power to renegotiate is not dispersed among multiple individual lenders but centralized in the financial institution. Depositors can be seen as delegating their renegotiation power to the intermediary. This idea is backed by the stylized fact that it is much more costly for a firm to renegotiate the terms of a bond it has placed in the public than it is for a bank to renegotiate a loan.

Bolton and Freixas (1994) build on this idea to develop a model of financial intermediation that is consistent with the changes observed in the firms' debt composition through the business cycle. This discussion will take a simplified approach, abstracting from the main purpose of their paper, in order to illustrate the pros and cons of renegotiation in a very simple framework. A similar idea is used by Chemmanur and Fulghieri (1994). This discussion will simply show how renegotiation may be attractive or not, depending on the firms' characteristics. In that way the difference between publicly issued debt and bank loans will be illustrated. Namely it will be shown that even if the bank lending contract is efficient it may fail to be feasible, whereas the public debt contract will work out.

Consider a three-period investment model in which at time 0 a risk neutral firm issues debt and invests one unit of money in a project. As a result, at times 1 and 2 it will obtain cash flows y_1 and y_2, which can be high (y_H) or low (y_L). Their realization is summarized by a variable, called the state of nature, that can take four possible values: (H, H), (H, L), (L, H), and (L, L).

Assume that the state of nature is completely revealed at time $t = 1$ (so that time 2 cash flow is perfectly known one period ahead). Assume also that the state of nature is not verifiable even if both parties (the borrower and the lender) observe it. Nevertheless, since cash flows are at least equal to y_L, this part of the cash flow is verifiable. Take time 1 and time 2 cash flows to be independently identically distributed, with a probability p of obtaining y_H. In addition, assume a zero interest rate (equivalently, all cash flows are already discounted).

In this context the contract between borrowers and lenders cannot be made contingent on the nonverifiable cash flow. Therefore it is equivalent to a standard debt contract, in which the power to liquidate the firm is given to the lender in case the promised repayment is not made. In this case the lender obtains a first-period liquidation value A.

When the project is terminated, its liquidation value is zero. Under these assumptions, the second-period repayment can be set equal to the verifiable amount y_L.[20]

If $y_L > A$, then the bank's threat to liquidate in case of default is not credible. Therefore the firm will always pretend to be unsuccessful and the total repayment to the bank will equal only $2y_L$. If $y_L < \frac{1}{2}$, the market for loans breaks down.

On the other hand, assume that bond holders are unable to renegotiate so that they always liquidate the firm when it reports y_L. This occurs when the firm is indeed unsuccessful at $t = 1$ (i.e., in states of nature $[L, H]$ and $[L, L]$, but also in state $[H, L]$ [strategic default]). However, when the state is (H, H), the firm prefers to repay R (provided, of course, $R < y_H$), since it obtains $(y_H - R) + (y_H - y_L)$ instead of $y_H - y_L$.

Hence the commitment to liquidate, even if it is inefficient, allows the financial markets to work provided that

$$p^2(R + y_L) + (1 - p^2)(A + y_L) > 1.$$

Therefore, the ex-post benefits of renegotiation are here the reason for the (ex-ante) breakdown of the market for loans.

4.5.2 The Efficiency of Bank Loan Covenants

As has been mentioned, renegotiation between the parties plays a key role when contracts are incomplete. Indeed, the two parties know the contract is not efficient ex post. Therefore, since they are better off renegotiating the terms of the contract (such as the share of cash flows accruing to each party and repayments), they cannot credibly commit not to renegotiate. In a debt contract, the debtor may (credibly) take an inefficient or risky action that will decrease the net present value of the project undertaken while increasing the debtors' profit at the expense of the creditor. Clearly, in such a situation, renegotiation may improve efficiency.

This idea is explored by Gorton and Kahn (1993) (GK) so as to justify the difference between a bank loan and the issue of public debt. (Another interesting contribution is Bester 1994 which uses the incomplete-contract approach to justify the role of collateral in debt contracts.) Indeed, private placements and bank loans usually include more detailed and more restrictive covenants than publicly placed bonds. According to GK, the difference between bank loans and publicly issued debt is that bank loans contain embedded options that allow the bank to call back the loan. Since this will trigger renegotiation, it might be Pareto-improving in an incomplete contract environment.

The role of covenants is emphasized because they allow the bank to renegotiate the loan efficiently. The role of the collateral's liquidation value is also important because, as seen in subsection 4.4.2, the liquidation threat is credible only if it allows the bank to obtain a higher return.

This presentation will drastically simplify GK with the consequence that some of their results will be omitted.

Assume that both the bank and the firm are risk neutral, and that the sequence of events is the following:

Date 0: The firm borrows one unit of money to finance a project, agreeing to repay R at date $t = 2$.

Date 1: A nonverifiable signal z is observed by the firm and the bank. The bank and the firm can renegotiate the loan terms. This happens in particular if the bank threatens to liquidate the project and if this threat is credible.

Date 2: The firm chooses a new investment project (either G or B). A verifiable return from this project is obtained and shared between the bank and the firm.

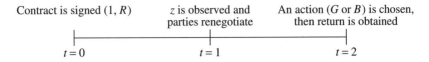

Figure 4.5
The Time Line of Events in the Model of Gorton and Kahn (1993)

Figure 4.5 represents the time line of events.

The following nonobservable investment technology choice will illustrate the period 2 moral hazard problem. For a given value of the parameter z ($z \geq 0$), the firm has a choice between investment projects G and B, whose returns are given by

$$\begin{cases} zy_i + A_2 \text{ with probability } p_i \\ A_2 \text{ with probability } 1 - p_i \end{cases} \qquad i = G, B$$

where A_2 is the period 2 liquidation value of the project. The standard assumptions, $p_G y_G > p_B y_B$, $y_G < y_B$, generate moral hazard.

For a given repayment $R_0 (R_0 > A_2)$, the firm's optimal project choice i^* will be to choose project G if and only if $p_G(zy_G + A_2 - R_0) \geq p_B(zy_B + A_2 - R_0)$, which is equivalent to[21]

$$\frac{R_0 - A_2}{z} \leq \hat{R}, \tag{4.11}$$

where $\hat{R} = \frac{p_G y_G - p_B y_B}{p_G - p_B}$.

By setting $r = (R_0 - A_2)/z$, equation 4.11 can be rewritten as $r \leq \hat{R}$.

As a consequence, in the absence of renegotiation, there exists a critical level z^* defined by $R_0 - A_2 \equiv \hat{R} z^*$ such that if $z < z^*$ (that is, if the project is to perform poorly in period 2), then project B will be chosen, which is inefficient.

Let A_1 be the early liquidation value of the project, which is assumed to be superior to A_2. Clearly, for low values of z it is efficient to liquidate the project at time $t = 1$. As a consequence, in the absence of renegotiation, the expected gross return on the loan will be

$$1 + \rho(R) = \text{Prob } [z > z^*](p_G R_0 + (1 - p_G)A_2)$$
$$+ \text{ prob } [z < z^*][p_B R_0 + (1 - p_B)A_2].$$

Setting $\rho(R)$ equal to the riskless rate of return, the value of the initial repayment R_0 at equilibrium can be determined.

Such a contract will bring in *two sources of inefficiency: the use of the inefficient technology B and the absence of efficient early liquidation for low values of z.*

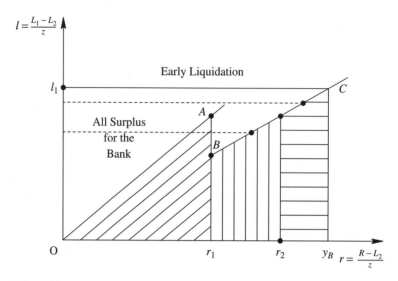

Figure 4.6
Different Types of Equilibria in the Gorton-Kahn (1993) Model (with Dashed Areas Corresponding to Debt Forgiveness, or Pareto-Improving Renegotiation)

Now this discussion will consider the case in which the bank is able to call the loan at date $t = 1$, and solve for the perfect Nash equilibria of the game. The solution to this problem will proceed by backward induction.

The bank may renegotiate the terms of the loan either by decreasing the amount R (debt forgiveness) or by increasing it. But in this case it can do so only if the threat to liquidate is credible, that is, if the original contract repayment R_0 is such that

$$A_1 > p_{i*}R_0 + (1 - p_{i*})A_2, \tag{4.12}$$

where $i^* \in \{G, B\}$ represents the project that the firm would choose (which depends on z).

Introducing the new notation $\ell = (A_1 - A_2)/z$, this condition can be written as

$$\ell > p_{i*}r. \tag{4.13}$$

If 4.13 is not satisfied, the liquidation threat is not credible.

Now all the different types of solutions will be analyzed by locating them in the (ℓ, r) space. To begin with, 4.13 is not satisfied in the vertical dashed area of Figure 4.6 that is below the truncated line OABC.

To simplify the renegotiation game, assume that the bank has all the bargaining power. Consequently, if 4.13 holds, the bank will impose the repayment $\tilde{R}$ for which it obtains the maximum expected return. This could be either $\tilde{R} = z\hat{R}$

or $\tilde{R} = zy_B$. The case examined here will be $p_G\hat{R} < p_By_B$ so that the bank will prefer to set $\tilde{R} = zy_B$.[22]

To study the solutions of the game when liquidation is a credible threat, define ℓ_1 as the threshold $\ell_1 = p_By_B$. Depending on the level of ℓ, two different cases may occur:

1. If $\ell > \ell_1$, early liquidation is the bank's best strategy, since $\ell > \ell_1$ is equivalent to $A_1 > p_Bzy_B + A_2$. Notice that this is only second best efficient, since the choice of the efficient project G would have been preferred.

2. If $\ell \leq \ell_1$, and r is such that early liquidation is credible, the bank will set $\tilde{R} = zy_b + A_2$.

Finally, if liquidation is not credible, there is still room for a Pareto-improving renegotiation: the bank may still be willing to negotiate a reduction in debt if this increases its expected return. This will happen for r in the interval (r_1, r_2) and l below BC (horizontally and vertically dashed areas) where the bank will choose $r = r_1$, that is $\tilde{R} = z\hat{R} + A_2$.

Thus, there are three possible outcomes of the renegotiation process:

1. For low z the bank loan covenants allow for early liquidation, which improves efficiency.

2. For intermediate z the bank loan allows for renegotiation with an increase in repayment, which (if all the bargaining power is given to the bank) may leave the firm with a zero profit.

3. For a higher z the bank loan may lead to debt forgiveness.

The possibility of renegotiation improves efficiency: indeed, the project is liquidated only when its net present value is inferior to its liquidation value,[23] and debt forgiveness allows a switch from the inefficient to the efficient project. In all the other cases the project choice is not affected by renegotiation; only the distribution of the cash flows between the agents is.

To summarize, GK offers a justification of bank loans (as opposed to public debt), based on the existence of covenants that may trigger renegotiation. As the authors argue, this is a new justification for the existence of banks.[24] Ex-ante screening of borrowers or ex-post monitoring of projects, which are alternative justifications, would not be satisfactory in explaining why banks are typically not junior claimants or even equity holders. They would also be unsatisfactory in explaining why bank loans contain multiple embedded options (covenants).

Berlin and Mester (1992) address a similar issue within a more abstract model. According to their model, the bank loans introduce covenants not because covenants allow the bank to call back the loan as GK argues, but because the bank wants to restrict the set of actions the firm can take. Namely, the bank does not want the firm to "gamble for resurrection." But of course, such a restriction aimed at a firm in distress may decrease the firm's growth opportunities if it is successful. Accordingly, Berlin and Mester define an incomplete contract model in which the bank might observe a noisy signal indicating whether the firm has been successful or not, and if the signal is received by the borrower the contract will be renegotiated if it has been successful. The result they obtained seems intuitive: when renegotiation is possible, covenants should be more stringent. Since renegotiation of a public bond issue is extremely costly, this would explain why bank loan covenants are more restrictive than bond covenants.

4.6   Collateral and Loan Size as Devices for Screening Heterogenous Borrowers

This section will assume the existence of different categories of borrowers, represented by a "risk parameter" θ. If this parameter θ was common knowledge, the optimal contract (corresponding to a given individual rationality level U_L^0 for the lender) would be obtained as in Section 4.1 by solving program $\mathcal{P}_0$ for each value of θ. In the particular case of exponential utilities (see note 1), the optimal equity participation coefficient α would be constant, but the repayment R would be higher for higher risks.

In fact, it is often more realistic to assume that θ is observed only by the borrower, in which case the previous contract (with the interest rate conditional on θ) cannot be implemented: unless other considerations are introduced, all borrowers would claim to be in the lowest risk category, in order to pay the minimum interest rate. As a consequence, the lender would be bound to disregard the declaration of the borrower and to charge a uniform interest rate.

This section will examine how some flexibility can be reintroduced by offering to the population of borrowers a whole menu of contracts with different provisions.[25] For example, the lender can offer different loan contracts with variable collateral requirements (as in Bester 1985), the interest rate being a decreasing function of the collateral. Another possibility is to offer different loans of variable sizes (as in Freixas and Laffont 1990), the interest rate being now an increasing function of the size of the loan. More complex menus can also be offered (as in Besanko and Thakor 1987) and the menus may specify how the terms of the contract depend upon observed variables (Webb 1991), but this discussion will concentrate for simplicity on these two examples, since they clearly illustrate ways in which the lender can obtain a self-selection of heterogenous borrowers. Notice, however, that the precise characteristics of the contracts that will be obtained are sensitive to the specification of risks distribution. (Chapter 5 will come back to this point.)

This discussion will first consider the case of binomial risks, where an investment (of a given size) can either fail ($\tilde{y} = 0$) or succeed ($\tilde{y} = y$). The risk parameter θ represents the probability of failure. Therefore a higher θ means an increasing risk in the sense of first order stochastic dominance. For simplicity, the example will assume that there are only two categories of borrowers: "low risks," θ^L, and "high risks," θ^H (with $\theta^L < \theta^H$). The proportions v^k ($k = L, H$) of borrowers of each type are common knowledge. All agents are risk neutral.

4.6.1   The Role of Collateral

Assume that borrowers can initially put down some collateral C. The lender can thus offer a menu of loan contracts $\{(C^k, R^k)\ k = L, H\}$, where the repayment R^k in case of success depends on the collateral C^k put down by the borrower. If the project fails ($\tilde{y} = 0$) the lender can liquidate this collateral: the borrower loses C^k, whereas the lender gets only δC^k (with $\delta < 1$). Thus there is a cost of liquidation,[26] $(1 - \delta)C^k$, which is assumed to be proportional to the size of the collateral. If, on the other hand, the project succeeds ($\tilde{y} = y$), there is no liquidation: the lender obtains R^k and the borrower gets $(y - R^k)$.

The menu of contracts offered by the lender will depend on the outside opportunities of borrowers (represented by their reservation utilities U^k, $k = L, H$) and on the relative bargaining powers of the two parties. This example assumes that all bargaining power is concentrated in the hands of the lender. For example, in the benchmark case of symmetric information (i.e., when the lender is able to observe θ), the lender will offer contracts such that the individual rationality constraints of each type of borrowers are binding:

$$(1 - \theta^k)(y - R^k) - \theta^k C^k = U^k \quad (k = L, H).$$

The corresponding indifference curves in the (C, R) plane, denoted $\Delta^k (k = L, H)$, are represented in Figure 4.7.

The inequality $\theta^H > \theta^L$ implies that Δ^H is steeper than Δ^L (assuming that the intersection of the two indifference curves P lies in the positive quadrant, which means that $\frac{U^L}{1 - \theta^L} \geq \frac{U^H}{1 - \theta^H}$).[27] Since liquidation is costly, the contracts preferred by the lender on each of these lines are (respectively) M and N, which both correspond to the absence of collateral ($C = 0$).

Of course, if θ is not observable by the lender, and if contracts do not differ in their collateral ($C = 0$), both types of borrowers will claim to be low risks and choose contract N. The average expected return to the lender will be $(1 - \bar{\theta})R^L$, where R^L is the maximum repayment that is acceptable to type L borrowers:[28]

$$R^L = y - \frac{U^L}{1 - \theta^L},$$

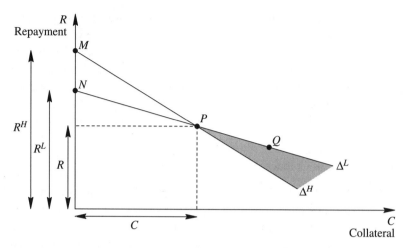

Figure 4.7
The Borrowers' Indifference Curves: Δ^L for Low Risks, Δ^H for High Risks

and $\bar{\theta}$ denotes the average probability of failure in the population of borrowers:

$$\bar{\theta} \stackrel{\text{def}}{=} v^L \theta^L + v^H \theta^H.$$

In this situation, high risks obtain an "informational rent," since their expected utility is higher than what they would get if low risks were absent, in which case they would have to repay the higher amount:

$$R^H = y - \frac{U^H}{1 - \theta^H}.$$

A lender who wants high risks to repay R^H must offer simultaneously another contract, designed specifically for low risks and requiring a collateral C and a repayment R such that

$$(1 - \theta^H)(y - R^H) \geq (1 - \theta^H)(y - R) - \theta^H C$$

(i.e., high risks prefer contract M to the new contract $P = (C, R)$) and

$$(1 - \theta^L)(y - R) - \theta^L C \geq U^L$$

(i.e., low risks accept this new contract).[29] The set of contracts satisfying these two conditions is represented by the shaded area in Figure 4.7. Obviously (since collateral is costly), it would be inefficient to design a contract in which both types are required to pledge some collateral. Indeed, the only role of collateral is to allow for self-selection between the two types of risks. Intuitively, the choice between the two types of contracts depends on what the agent would answer to the question, Do you want to bet a collateral C that you will not fail,

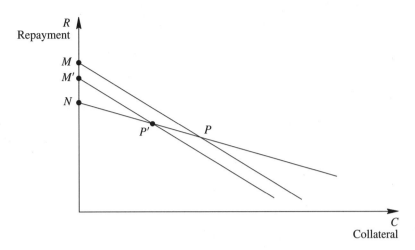

Figure 4.8
The Optimal Menu of Loan Contracts

against a reduction in interest rates? Only low-risk borrowers will take that bet. Figure 4.7 uses indifference curves to examine the borrowers' choice between the two contracts (that is, if they would take the bet) for any two points. A menu of (two) contracts will allow discrimination between the two types of borrowers if each of them chooses the contract that he prefers (that is closer to the origin). Thus, for instance, the menu (M, Q) is a discriminating one. Clearly it is not efficient, since low-risk borrowers are offering too much (costly) collateral. Starting from this point, the lender's profit may be increased under these constraints by offering (M, P) where P is the intersection of Δ^L and Δ^H in Figure 4.7. To improve on the menu of contracts (M, P), consider the point (M', P') in Figure 4.8.

By accepting that high-risk borrowers receive an informational rent (they repay M' instead of M), which implies a loss for the lender, the amount of collateral decreases, and this implies a gain for the lender. The optimal set of contracts will thus be obtained at a pair such as pair (M', P') in Figure 4.8, where P' lies between N and P. The exact location of P' will be determined by the proportions v^H and v^L. In particular, when v^L tends toward 1, (N, N) of Figure 4.1 will be the optimal set of contracts, (i.e., a single contract will be offered to both types of borrowers) and when v^L tends toward 0, it will be (M, P).

Result 4.6   The optimal menu of loan contracts combining repayment and collateral is such that

• high risks pay a high interest rate but are not required to put down any collateral (no distortion at the top).

• low risks have to put down some collateral but pay a lower interest rate.

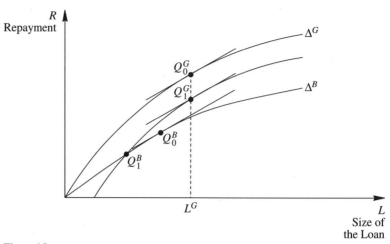

Figure 4.9
Optimal Pairs of Loan Contracts in the (Size, Repayment) Plane (with Lines Representing Isoprofit Curves of the Lender)

4.6.2   Loans with Variable Size

A second illustration is obtained when the size L of the loan is allowed to vary. The return of a loan L to a borrower of type $k(k = B, G)$ is now equal to $\tilde{\theta}^k f(L)$, where $\tilde{\theta}^k$ is a random variable (where by definition $E(\tilde{\theta}^k) \overset{\text{def}}{=} \theta^k$), and $f(\cdot)$ is a production function with decreasing returns to scale ($f' > 0$, $f'' < 0$). Investments now differ by their average returns, higher for "good" projects G than for "bad" projects $B(\theta^G \geq \theta^B)$. No collateral is required anymore, but repayments depend on the size of the loan. In the benchmark case of symmetric information, the optimal menu of contracts $\{(L^k, R^k), k = B, G\}$ is obtained by maximizing the expected profit of the lender under the individual rationality constraint of the borrower. Denoting by r the opportunity cost of funds (the interest rate paid by the lender when refinancing the loan), the following result is obtained:

$$\begin{cases} \max R^k - (1 + r)L^k \\ \text{under } \theta^k f(L^k) - R^k \geq U^k. \end{cases}$$

For simplicity, the probability of default is assumed to be zero ($\forall t \in \text{Supp } \tilde{\theta}^k$, $tf(L^k) \geq R^k$). The optimal pair of contracts under symmetric information is represented in Figure 4.9 by Q_0^G and Q_0^B (assuming $U^B = U^G = 0$).

Of course if θ is not observable by the lender, all borrowers will choose Q_0^B, and good risks will obtain a higher utility than if bad risks were absent. In order to obtain a better allocation and to extract some surplus from these good risks, the lender will offer two choices: a bigger loan with a higher repayment (Q_1^G) and a smaller loan with a lower repayment (Q_1^B). If the proportion of good risks v^G is high enough, this is the optimal solution for the lender. As before, if v^G tends toward 1, the optimal menu will be $(0, Q_0^G)$, and if it tends toward 0, the optimal menu will be (Q_0^B, Q_2^G), with (Q_2^G) on the same isoprofit curve as Q_0^B.

Result 4.7   If the proportion of good risks is high enough, the optimal menu of loan contracts combining repayment and loan size is such that

• good risks obtain a larger loan and pay a higher repayment. They benefit from an informational rent.

• bad risks pay a lower repayment but obtain a smaller loan. There is no distortion at the top: the size of the loan obtained by good risks is efficient.

The design of self-selection mechanisms to improve credit allocation in an asymmetric information setting has been widely studied. For instance, Webb (1992) considers an environment in which the lenders sequentially invest in two projects, so that truthful reporting of cash flows and costly auditing (depending on the reported cash flows) is necessary at every period. Then, it is possible to make the terms of borrowing during the second period depend on the reported first-period cash flows. By so doing, auditing can be reduced, and this implies that long-term lending may dominate short-term lending because the expected cost of auditing is lower.

Another interesting application of self-selection mechanisms is the study of securitization. One of the main characteristics of securitization is that it is associated with credit enhancement (see problem 4.7.6). In this way it is possible to save on screening costs: the deposit funding mode implies higher screening costs and a lower level of risk, since in case of failure the investors will share the full amount of the bank's capital. Consequently the choice between the deposit funding mode and securitization will depend on screening costs on the one hand and the investors' risk aversion on the other hand.

4.7   Problems

4.7.1   Optimal Risk Sharing with Symmetric Information

Using the notations of Section 4.1 and neglecting limited liability constraints, optimal debt contracts can be obtained by solving the following problem:

$$\begin{cases} \max_{R(\cdot)} Eu_B(\tilde{y} - R(\tilde{y})) \\ \text{under } Eu_L(R(\tilde{y})) \geq U_L^0. \end{cases}$$

1. If μ denotes the Lagrange multiplier associated with the individual rationality constraint, show that for all y in the support of $\tilde{y}$, $R(y)$ can be obtained by maximizing $u_B(y - R) + \mu u_L(R)$ with respect to R.

2. Prove condition 4.4: $\forall \mu \in \text{Supp } \tilde{y}$: $\dfrac{u_B'(y - R(y))}{u_L'(R(y))} = \mu$.

3. Prove condition 4.3: $\forall y_1, y_2 \in \text{Supp } \tilde{y}$: $\dfrac{u_L'[R(y_1)]}{u_L'[R(y_2)]} = \dfrac{u_B'[y_1 - R(y_1)]}{u_B'[y_2 - R(y_2)]}$.

4. When limited liability constraints are introduced ($0 \leq R(y) \leq y$), show that the characterization becomes

$$R(y) = 0 \quad \text{if} \quad u'_B(y) \geq \mu u'_L(0),$$
$$R(y) = y \quad \text{if} \quad u'_B(0) \leq \mu u'_L(y),$$

and $\frac{u'_B(y-R(y))}{u'_L(R(y))} = \mu$ in the other cases.

4.7.2 Optimal Debt Contracts with Moral Hazard (Adapted from Innes 1987)

Recall the notations of Section 4.4:

- $f(y, e)$ denotes the density of $\tilde{y}$ when the effort level is e.
- $\psi(e)$ represents (the pecuniary equivalent of) the cost of effort for the borrower.
- $V(R, e)$ is the expected utility of the (risk neutral) borrower, as a function of the repayment schedule $R(\cdot)$ and the effort level e:

$$V(R, e) = \int (y - R(y)) f(y, e) dy - \psi(e).$$

Given U_L^0, the individual rationality level of the lender, the (second best) optimal contract $R(\cdot)$ and effort level e will be obtained as the solution of

$$(\mathscr{P}) \begin{cases} \max_{(R,e)} V(R, e) \\ 0 \leq R(y) \leq y & \forall y \\ V(R, e') \leq V(R, e) & \forall e' \\ \int R(y) f(y, e) dy \geq U_L^0. \end{cases}$$

A simpler program is obtained by replacing the incentive compatibility constraint with the first order condition of the borrower's problem which determines the borrower's effort choice:

$$V_e(R, e) = \int (y - R(y)) f_e(y, e) dy - \psi'(e) = 0.$$

When V is concave in e, it is legitimate to use this first order approach (as proved in Rogerson 1985). The simpler program is equivalent to $\mathscr{P}$, and the optimal contract $R(\cdot)$ can be obtained by maximizing the Lagrangian for each y:

$$\begin{aligned} \max_{0 \leq R(y) \leq y} \mathcal{L}(R(y), y) \quad &= \quad [y - R(y)][f(y, e) + \mu f_e(y, e)] \\ &+ \quad \lambda R(y) f(y, e), \end{aligned}$$

where μ and λ denote respectively the Lagrange multipliers associated with the first order condition of the borrower's problem and with the individual rationality constraint of the lender.

1. Show that the optimal contract is such that

$$\begin{cases} R(y) = y & \text{if} \quad (\lambda - 1)f(y, e) > \mu f_e(y, e) \\ R(y) = 0 & \text{if} \quad (\lambda - 1)f(y, e) < \mu f_e(y, e). \end{cases}$$

2. Show that the monotone likelihood property ($\forall e_1 > e_2 \ y \to \frac{f(y,e_1)}{f(y,e_2)}$ is increasing) implies that $y \to \frac{f_e(y,e)}{f(y,e)}$ is also increasing.

3. Assuming that $\mu > 0$, show that the optimal contract involves a cutoff level y^*, with a maximum penalty ($R(y) = y$) when y is less than y^* and a maximum reward ($R(y) = 0$) when y is greater than y^*.

4.7.3   The Optimality of Stochastic Auditing Schemes

Consider a simple version of the Townsend model (lender–borrower relationship with costly state verification) in which the cash flow $\tilde{y}$ obtained by the borrower at the second period can take only two values: a high value y_H (with probability p_H) and a low value y_L (with probability $p_L = 1 - p_H$). The lender is risk neutral, but the borrower is risk averse: she has a concave VNM utility function u. The optimal contract is found by maximizing the expected repayment to the lender (net of auditing costs) under incentive compatibility and individual rationality constraints for the borrower. The status quo utility level of the borrower is denoted $u(C_0)$ (with $C_0 > 0$), and the audit cost γ. Finally, the borrower has limited liability: the maximum penalty that can be inflicted on her if she lies (i.e., reports y_L when y_H has occurred) is confiscation of y_H.

1. Compute the optimal contract when the borrower is always audited. Show that it is useless to audit if state y_H is useless.

2. Suppose for the moment that the borrower is always audited when she reports y_L. Show that the optimal contract gives a constant consumption level to the borrower: $C_H = C_L = C_0$.

3. Suppose now that the lender can credibly commit to a stochastic auditing policy: audit with probability $q \in [0, 1]$ when the borrower reports y_L. Show that the incentive compatibility constraint is equivalent to

$$q \geq q^* = \frac{u(C_L + y_H - y_L) - u(C_H)}{u(C_L + y_H - y_L) - u(0)}.$$

4. Show that the optimal q is never equal to 1 (write the first order condition).

4.7.4   The Role of Hard Claims in Constraining Management (Adapted from Hart and Moore 1995)

Consider a firm whose managers are empire builders in the sense that they always choose to implement investment projects provided they are not cash constrained. The objective is to show that the firm's indebtedness will help discipline their behavior.

Assume that all agents are risk neutral, and normalize the interest rate to zero. Consider a firm, characterized by current cash flow y and a debt R, that has at time $t = 1$ an investment opportunity of cost I and return y_I to be obtained with certainty at time $t = 2$. Managers will invest in the project regardless of its Net Present Value (NPV) if $y > R + I$; if this is not the case, they will turn to a bank for a loan that will be obtained only if the future cash flows (derived from the project or obtained independently) are superior to the investment.

If the firm defaults $(R > y)$, then there is a bankruptcy cost c and the firm is liquidated (no renegotiation).

1. Show that if the NPV of the investment is always positive, then setting $R = 0$ (all equity firm) will maximize the value of the firm.

2. Show that if y equals some constant $\bar{y}$ with probability 1, then $R = \bar{y}$ is optimal.

3. Assume the firm obtains deterministic cash flows $\bar{y}_1, \bar{y}_2$ during periods 1 and 2 respectively, independently of its investment choice. Show that using short-term debt with repayment $R_1 = \bar{y}_1$ and long-term debt with repayment $R_2 = \bar{y}_2$ will lead to the best investment policy.

4.7.5 Collateral and Rationing (Adapted from Besanko and Thakor 1987)

With the notations used in Section 4.5, assume $U^L = U^H$ and show that if collateral is costly, a monopoly that is funding its loans at the interbank rate r will offer a contract characterized by $C^H = C^L$ and $R^H = R^L = R$.

1. Compute the two values R can take depending on whether both types of agents borrow or not. (Hint: The intersection point p is not in the positive quadrant.) Show that for a low proportion of high-risk borrowers, v^H, the contract will be designed in order to attract only low risks.

2. Consider now a competitive setting in which low-risk borrowers have only a wealth level W to be posted as collateral, and the contracts $(R^H, 0)$ and (R^L, W), which yield a zero profit for the bank, are such that both borrowers prefer (R^L, W) (i.e., the collateral is too low to allow for self-selection). Introduce the probabilities π^K for a type k borrower to be rationed, so that the new mechanisms become (π^K, R^K, C^K) for $K = L, H$. Show that the condition $\pi^L > 0$ is necessary to obtain an incentive compatible mechanism.

4.7.6 Securitization (Adapted from Greenbaum and Thakor 1987)

One of the main characteristics of securitization is that the investor usually obtains the return from a loan and credit enhancement to limit the credit risk. This exercise will show how credit enhancement can be used to allow for truthful revelation of credit risk, with better risks buying more credit enhancement, as is usual in loan securitization.

Consider an economy in which risk neutral firms have an investment project with a return X in case of success, which occurs with probability p, and a zero return in case of failure (probability $1 - p$). The probability p is known to the firms but not to the investors.

Banks offer credit contracts characterized by different levels of credit enhancement θ, where θ is the fraction of the initially promised repayment $R(\theta)$ that the investor will receive if the firm project fails. A credit contract will specify the fee paid by the firm $Q(\theta)$ corresponding to the level of θ and the repayment $R(\theta) - Q(\theta)$ to the investor through the bank. Consequently, a contract will define a mechanism $(R(\theta(\hat{p})), Q(\theta(\hat{p})))$ associating with the announced probability of success $\hat{p}$ a level of credit enhancement and the corresponding insurance fee and repayment to final investors.

1. Write the first and second order conditions for the contract to be incentive compatible.

2. Write the individual rationality (IR) constraint for the bank-insurer.

3. Assume the IR constraint holds with equality. By differentiating it, show that the mechanism is such that

   - better risks tend to buy more credit enhancement.
   - interest repayments R decrease with the guarantee θ.

4.8 Solutions

4.8.1 Optimal Risk Sharing with Symmetric Information

1. The Lagrangian of the problem is simply

$$\mathcal{L} = Eu_B(\tilde{y} - R(\tilde{y})) + \mu(Eu_L(R(\tilde{y})) - U_L^0).$$

The maximization with respect to $R(\cdot)$ can be performed separately for each value of y, leading to maximizing $u_B(y - R) + \mu u_L(R)$ with respect to R.

2. $R(y)$ is therefore defined implicitly by the first order condition:

$$-u'_B(y - R(y)) + \mu u'_L(R(y)) = 0,$$

which gives condition 4.4.

3. 4.3 is immediately deduced by applying 4.4 to y, and y_2.

4. When the constraint $0 \le R(y) \le y$ is added, the first order condition changes only when $R(y) = 0$ or y, in which case it becomes

$$\begin{cases} -u'_B(y) + \mu u'_L(0) \leq 0 & \text{if} \quad R(y) = 0 \\ -u'_B(0) + \mu u'_L(y) \geq 0 & \text{if} \quad R(y) = y. \end{cases}$$

4.8.2 Optimal Debt Contracts with Moral Hazard

1. To obtain the optimal contract, it is necessary only to maximize the Lagrangian $\mathcal{L}$ with respect to $R(y)$ for a given y. But $\mathcal{L}$ is linear with respect to $R(y)$. Therefore, if the coefficient affecting $R(y)$ is positive, that is, if

$$(\lambda - 1)f(y, e) - \mu f_e(y, e) > 0,$$

then $\mathcal{L}$ is increasing and the maximum is obtained for $R(y) = y$. Conversely, if the coefficient is negative, $R(y) = 0$ is obtained.

2. Since $\frac{f(y,e_1)}{f(y,e_2)}$ is increasing in y, so is the function $\frac{1}{e_1 - e_2}(\frac{f(y,e_1)}{f(y,e_2)} - 1)$. When e_1 tends toward e_2, the limit of this function will also be increasing in y. But this limit is $\frac{f_e(y,e_2)}{f(y,e_2)}$.

3. The result obtained in problem 1 shows that the optimal function $R(y)$ is characterized by

$$R(y) = y \text{ for } \frac{f_e(y, e)}{f(y, e)} < \frac{\lambda - 1}{\mu}$$

$$R(y) = 0 \text{ for } \frac{f_e(y, e)}{f(y, e)} > \frac{\lambda - 1}{\mu}.$$

Since f_e/f is continuous and increasing in y, there is a unique y^* such that $\frac{f_e(y^*, e)}{f(y^*, e)} \equiv \frac{\lambda - 1}{\mu}$, and therefore the solution will be given by

$$R(y) = \begin{cases} y & y < y^*, \\ 0 & y > y^*. \end{cases}$$

4.8.3 The Optimality of Stochastic Auditing Schemes

1, 2. If the borrower is always audited, the asymmetric information problem disappears and the optimal contract gives a constant consumption level to the borrower (because of risk aversion): $C_H = C_L = C_0$. This implies that the repayment to the lender is higher when $\tilde{y} = y_H$. Therefore the borrower has no interest in reporting y_H when $\tilde{y} = y_L$, and it is useless to audit when the borrower reports y_H.

3. When the borrower is caught cheating, it is optimal for the lender to use the maximal penalty (i.e., to confiscate all her cash flow). Therefore, the incentive compatibility (IC) constraint is equivalent to

$$u(C_H) \geq qu(0) + (1 - q)u(C_L + y_H - y_L), \text{ or}$$
$$q \geq q^* = \frac{u(C_L + y_H - y_L) - u(C_H)}{u(C_L + y_H - y_L) - u(0)}.$$

4. If the optimal q was equal to one, question 2 would imply that $C_L = C_H = C_0 > 0$. Therefore the critical level q^* would be strictly smaller than $q(= 1)$ and the IC constraint would not be binding, which is inefficient. Thus the optimal probability of auditing is strictly less than 1. By writing the first order conditions of the corresponding optimization program, it is easily shown that $C_H > C_L$. The reason is that q^* is a decreasing function of C_H: by increasing C_H, the lender can audit less often.

4.8.4   The Role of Hard Claims in Constraining Management

The firm's value V is the (present) expected value of its cash flows. This has to be computed in three different cases:

$$
\begin{aligned}
y < R \qquad\qquad & V = y - c \\
R \le y < R + I \qquad\qquad & V = y + Max(y_I - I, 0) \\
R + I \le y \qquad\qquad & V = y + y_I - I,
\end{aligned}
$$

so that

$$
V = E(y) - cF(R) + \int_{R \le y < R+I} Max(y_I - I, 0) f(y, y_I, I) dy\, dy_I\, dI
$$

$$
+ \int_{y \ge R+I} (y_I - I) f(y, y_I, I) dy\, dy_I\, dI,
$$

where $f(y, y_I, I)$ is the joint density function of (y, y_I, I), and $F(t)$ is the cumulative marginal distribution of y.

1. If $y_I - I < 0$ occurs with probability zero,

$$
V = E(y) - cF(R) + \int_R^\infty \left(\int (y_I - I) f(y, y_I, I) dy_I\, dI \right) dy
$$

and $\frac{\partial V}{\partial R} = -cf(R) - \int (y_I - I) f(R, y_I, I) dy_I\, dI < 0$, so that $R = 0$ maximizes V.

2. The efficient investment policy is to invest if and only if $E(y_I) \ge I$. Setting $R = \bar{y}$, then $F(R) = 0$ and the event $\{y \ge R + I\}$ occurs with probability zero (assuming $I > 0$). Thus the efficient investment policy is followed, because of the availability of bank funding.

3. Again setting $R_1 = \bar{y}_1$ and $R_2 = \bar{y}_2$, the banks will fund the project if and only if $y_I > I$. Notice that $R_2 < \bar{y}_2$ would lead to an inferior investment policy.

4.8.5   Collateral and Rationing

1. First compute the full-information solution. If each borrower is at its reservation level, then

$$(1 - \theta^L)(y - R^L) - \theta^L C^L = U$$

$$(1 - \theta^H)(y - R^H) - \theta^H C^H = U.$$

Using $\theta^L < \theta^H$, the two indifference curves may be drawn:

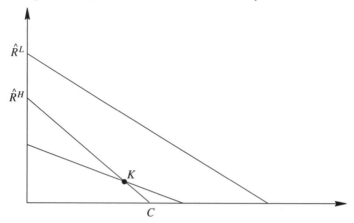

The optimal contract would be $(\hat{R}_L, 0)$ and $(\hat{R}_H, 0)$. With imperfect informa-tion there is no way to discriminate between the two types of borrowers using the level of collateral, because starting from $(\hat{R}^H, 0)$ for the two types, any con-tract with a higher collateral (as K) would be separating but would yield the monopoly a lower return.

Consequently, if there is adverse selection, the monopoly will prefer a con-tract $(\hat{R}_H, 0)$ designed to attract both types of borrowers over a contract $\hat{R}^L$ to attract only the low-risk ones, if

$$(1 - \bar{\theta})\hat{R}^H - r > v^L[(1 - \theta^L)\hat{R}^L - r_g],$$

where $\bar{\theta} = v^L \theta^L + v^H \theta^H$.

This is equivalent to

$$v^H(1 - \theta^H)(\hat{R}^H - r) - v^L(1 - \theta^L)(\hat{R}^L - \hat{R}^H) > 0;$$

that is, the gain obtained on the H type borrowers has to be superior to the opportunity cost of quoting a lower rate of interest $\hat{R}_H$. For a low v^H this expression will be negative, and the monopoly will lend only to the low-risk borrowers at the high interest rate.

2. The IC constraint for the high-risk borrowers is

$$(1 - \pi^H)(1 - \theta^H)(y - R^H) \geq (1 - \pi^L)\{(1 - \theta^H)(y - R^L) - \theta^H W\},$$

but W is too low to allow for separation, that is,

$$(1 - \theta^H)(y - R^H) < (1 - \theta^H)(y - R^L) - \theta^H W.$$

The first inequality can be obtained only if $1 - \pi^L < 1 - \pi^H$, that is, $\pi^L > \pi^H$. Thus, $\pi^L > 0$.

4.8.6 Securitization

1. The firm objective function is

$$p[X - R(\theta(\hat{p}))] - Q(\theta(\hat{p})).$$

Consequently, maximization with respect to $\hat{p}$ yields at point $p = \hat{p}$ the following first order condition:

$$(-pR'(\theta(p)) - Q'(\theta(\hat{p})))\frac{d\theta}{dp} = 0. \tag{IC}$$

Since the first order condition holds for every p, it may be differentiated and replaced in the second order condition, which yields

$$-R'(\theta(p))\frac{d\theta}{dp} > 0.$$

2. The fee has to equal the expected value of the repayments made to the investor in case of failure, so that

$$Q(\theta(p)) = (1 - p)\theta(p)R(\theta(p)). \tag{IR}$$

3. Differentiation of IR implies

$$[Q'(\theta(p)) - (1 - p)(R(\theta(p)) + \theta(p)R'(\theta(p)))]\frac{d\theta}{dp} = -\theta(p)R(\theta(p)).$$

Replacing the first order conditions (IC),

$$(1 - p)R(\theta(p))\frac{d\theta}{dp} = \theta(p)R(\theta(p)) - [pR'(\theta(p)) + (1 - p)R'(\theta(p))\theta(p)]\frac{d\theta}{dp}.$$

Due to the second order conditions, the right side of this equality is positive, implying $\frac{d\theta}{dp} > 0$, so that better risks tend to buy more credit enhancement. Using this in the second order condition yields the result $R'(\theta) < 0$, that is, interest repayments decrease with the guarantee θ.

Notes

1. When utilities are exponential ($u_i(x) = -e^{-\rho_i x}$, $i = B, L$), the absolute indexes of risk aversion are constant ($I_i \equiv \rho_i$). In this case the optimal repayment function has the simple form $R(y) = \alpha y + \beta$ (with $\alpha = \frac{\rho_B}{\rho_B + \rho_L}$), which can be obtained as a combination of a standard debt contract (with nominal debt R) and an equity participation (i.e., the bank gets a fraction α of the shares). The total repayment is then

$$R(y) = R + \alpha(y - R).$$

However, this interpretation neglects the control rights associated with an equity participation.

2. We do not consider contracts stipulating that the borrowers could be rationed. (See Fried and Howitt 1980 on that issue.)

3. Another, complementary, explanation may be the existence of regulations on the ratio of mortgage payments to income.

4. Khalil and Parigi (forthcoming) argue that the size of a loan is an important determinant of the incentive to audit in a costly state verification framework. When banks cannot credibly commit to auditing a defaulting loan, it can be useful for them to increase that loan's size and use this as a commitment device.

5. Lacker and Weinberg (1989) take an asymmetric cost function which they justify by arguing that only understating the true value of cash flows can be of interest. The slightly more general formulation discussed here allows proof that this is indeed a property of the solution.

6. This is the case at least when the limited liability constraint of the lender is not binding.

7. Another interesting article that addresses the issue of termination is Stiglitz and Weiss (1983), in which the possibility of renegotiation is introduced.

8. Of course, lenders can retaliate to some extent when they are backed by their home country. Thus they may be able to impose commercial sanctions on the defaulting country.

9. See Gale and Hellwig (1989) for a game theoretic approach to this issue. See Eaton, Gersovitz, and Stiglitz (1986) for a general overview of this topic.

10. Nevertheless, this implies that if the country receives no loan, production is impossible, an assumption that is not needed in the model of Eaton and Gersovitz (1981) that will be examined hereafter.

11. Innocuous as it may seem, this is a restriction on the equilibrium concept used for solving the game.

12. In fact, the next chapter will argue that this should not be called credit rationing, which explains the use of quotation marks for the term.

13. The effect of the negotiation that follows default on debt structure is emphasized by Bolton and Scharfstein 1996, among others.

14. Regulation may even give incentives so that banks do not interfere with the choice of investment projects by the firms.

15. As is well known, in a principal–agent relationship in which the agent is risk neutral and has unlimited liability, moral hazard problems become trivial and are solved by making the agent (borrower) pay a fixed amount to the principal (lender) and become a residual claimant in the project.

16. To understand the MLR property, consider the case of two effort levels e_1 and e_2, with $e_1 > e_2$. Under Bayes' formula the (posterior) probability of a high effort level (e_1) conditional on y is

$$P[e_1|y] = \frac{P(e_1)f(y|e_1)}{P(e_1)f(y|e_1) + P(e_2)f(y|e_2)},$$

or

$$P[e_1|y] = \frac{1}{1 + \frac{P(e_2)}{P(e_1)} \cdot \frac{f(y|e_2)}{f(y|e_1)}}.$$

Under the MLR property, this function increases with y: a higher return indicates a greater likelihood of high effort.

17. This is justified if the entrepreneur has access to an alternative source of (short-term) borrowing. Indeed, if $R(y)$ is not increasing (as in result 4.5), the entrepreneur with a return y below the threshold y^* could borrow ($y^* - y$) and declare a result y^*. Thus the borrower would have nothing to repay except the short-term loan $y^* - y$.

18. An interesting survey of this area is provided in Tirole (1994).

19. A seminal article on this question is Aghion and Bolton (1992).

20. In view of the models of Stiglitz and Weiss (1983) and Bolton and Scharfstein (1990) this is not at all obvious: there could be an incentive for the firm to repay during period 1 if period 2 profits are sufficiently large. The reader can easily prove that this is not so in the present context.

21. By convention, assume that in case of equality G is chosen.

22. The case $p_G \hat{R} \geq p_B y_B$ is left to the reader. It will lead to more frequent debt forgiveness.

23. This is not always so in Gorton and Kahn (1993). They show, indeed, that inefficient liquidation may occur in a more general model.

24. See Chapter 2.

25. See Myerson (1979) for the general analysis of this class of problem.

26. Liquidation costs are important in explaining why loans are not always 100 percent collateralized.

27. The alternative case is studied in Besanko and Thakor (1987) and in problem 4.7.5.

28. It is assumed that lenders will be satisfied with this return. If they are not and increase the lending rate they could obtain $(1 - \theta^H) R^H$, but this can be still worse and could result in no lending at all. This is related to the lemon problem of Akerlof (1970), and in the banking literature to the credit rationing paper of Stiglitz and Weiss (1981) (see Chapter 5).

29. The other self-selection constraint,

$$(1 - \theta^L)(y - R) - \theta^L C \geq (1 - \theta^L)(y - R^H),$$

is trivially satisfied, since low risks obtain utility U^L with the contract $(R^L, 0)$. Therefore $(R^H, 0)$ is not individually rational.

References

Aghion, P., and P. Bolton. 1992. An incomplete contract approach to financial contracting. *Review of Economic Studies* 59:473–94.

Akerlof, G. A. 1970. The market for "lemons": Quality uncertainty and the market mechanism. *Quarterly Journal of Economics* 84(3): 488–500.

Allen, F. 1983. Credit rationing and payment incentives. *Review of Economic Studies* 50(4):639–46.

Alm, J., and Follain, J. R., Jr. 1982. Alternative mortgage instruments, the tilt problem and consumer welfare. *Journal of Financial and Quantitative Analysis* 19(March):113–26.

Artus, P., and X. Freixas. 1990. Le partage de risque prêteur-emprunteur: Une approche en termes de contrats contingents. *Finance* 11:7–28.

Berlin, M., and L. Mester. 1992. Debt covenants and renegotiation. *Journal of Financial Intermediation* 2:95–133.

Besanko, D., and A. V. Thakor. 1987. Collateral and rationing: Sorting equilibria in monopolistic and competitive credit markets. *International Economic Review* 28:671–90.

Bester, H. 1985. Screening vs rationing in credit markets with imperfect information. *American Economic Review* 57:850–55.

———. 1994. The role of collateral in a model of debt renegotiation. *Journal of Money, Credit, and Banking* 26(1):72–86.

Bolton, P., and X. Freixas. 1994. Direct bond financing, financial intermediation, and investment. Universitat Pompeu Fabra, Barcelona. Mimeograph.

Bolton, P., and D. Scharfstein. 1990. A theory of predation based on agency problems in financial contracting. *American Economic Review* 80(1):93–106.

———. 1996. Optimal debt structure and the number of creditors. *Journal of Political Economy* 104(1):1–25.

Boot, A., S. Greenbaum, and A. Thakor. 1993. Reputation and discretion in financial contracting. *The American Economic Review* 83(5):1165–83.

Boot, A., A. Thakor, and G. Udell. 1991. Credible commitments, contract enforcement problems and banks: Intermediation as credible insurance. *Journal of Banking and Finance* 15:605–32.

Bulow, J., and Rogoff, K. 1989. Sovereign debt: Is to forgive to forget? *American Economic Review* 79(1):43–50.

Chang, C. 1990. The dynamic structure of optimal debt contracts. *Journal of Economic Theory* 52:68–86.

Chemmanur, T. J., and P. Fulghieri. 1994. Reputation, renegotiation, and the choice between bank loans and publicly traded debt. *Review of Financial Studies* 7(3):475–506.

Dewatripont, M., and E. Maskin. 1995. Credit and efficiency in centralized and decentralized economies. *Review of Economic Studies* 62(4):541–56.

Diamond, D. 1984. Financial intermediation and delegated monitoring. *Review of Economic Studies* 51:393–414.

———. 1991. Monitoring and reputation: The choice between bank loans and directly placed debt. *Journal of Political Economy* 99:689–721.

———. 1992. Seniority and maturity structure of debt contracts. *Journal of Financial Economics* 33:341–68.

Dionne, G., and P. Viala. 1992. Optimal design of financial contracts and moral hazard. Université de Montréal. Mimeograph.

———. 1994. Moral hazard, renegotiation and debt. *Economics Letters* 46:113–19.

Eaton J., and M. Gersovitz. 1981. Debt with potential repudiation: Theoretical and empirical analysis. *Review of Economic Studies* 48:289–309.

Eaton, J., M. Gersovitz, and J. Stiglitz. 1986. On the pure theory of country risk. *European Economic Review* June:481–513.

Elston, J. A. 1995. Banks, finance, and investment in Germany: A review article. *Small Business Economics* 7(6):475–79.

Freixas, X., and J. J. Laffont. 1990. Optimal banking contracts. In *Essays in honor of Edmond Malinvaud*, Vol. 2, *Macroeconomics*, edited by P. Champsaur et al. Cambridge: MIT Press.

Fried, J., and P. Howitt. 1980. Credit rationing and implicit contract theory. *Journal of Money, Credit, and Banking* 12:471–87.

Fudenberg, D., and J. Tirole. 1991. *Game theory.* Cambridge: MIT Press.

Gale, D., and M. Hellwig. 1985. Incentive compatible debt contracts: The one-period problem. *Review of Economic Studies* L11:647–63.

———. 1989. Repudiation and renegotiation: The case of sovereign debt. *International Economic Review* 30(1):3–31.

Gorton, G., and J. Kahn. 1993. The design of bank loan contracts, collateral, and renegotiation. Working paper no. 4273, National Bureau of Economic Research, Cambridge, Mass.

Greenbaum, S., and A. Thakor. 1987. Bank funding modes: Securitization versus deposits. *Journal of Banking and Finance* 11:379–401.

Gromb, D. 1994. Contributions à l'economie financiere et industrielle. PhD. diss. Laboratoire d'Econométrie de l'Ecole Polytechnique, Paris.

Harris, M., and A. Raviv. 1991a. The theory of capital structure. *Journal of Finance* 46(1):297–355.

———. 1992. Financial contracting theory. In *Advances in economic theory: Sixth World Congress*, Vol. 2, edited by J. J. Laffont. Econometric Society Monographs no. 21. Cambridge: Cambridge University Press, 64–150.

Hart, O. 1995. Firms, contracts and financial structure. Paper presented at Clarendon Lectures. Oxford: Oxford University Press.

Hart, O., and J. Moore. 1989. Default and renegotiation: A dynamic model of debt. MIT Discussion paper no. 520, Cambridge.

———. 1994. A theory of debt based on the inalienability of human capital. *Quarterly Journal of Economics* 109:841–79.

———. 1995. Debt and seniority: An analysis of the role of hard claims in constraining management. *American Economics Review* 85:567–85.

Haubrich, J. 1989. Financial intermediation: Delegated monitoring and long term relationships. *Journal of Banking and Finance* 13(1):9–20.

Holmström, B. 1979. Moral hazard and observability. *Bell Journal of Economics* 10:74–91.

Hoshi, T., D. Scharfstein, and A. K. Kashyap. 1993. The choice between public and private debt: An analysis of post-deregulation corporate financing in Japan. Working paper no. 4421, National Bureau of Economic Research, Cambridge, Mass.

Innes, R. D. 1990. Limited liability and incentive contracting with ex-ante action choices. *Journal of Economic Theory* 52(1):45–67.

Jensen, M., and N. Meckling. 1976. Theory of the firm: Managerial behavior, agency costs and ownership structure. *Journal of Financial Economics* 3(4):305–60.

Kahlil, F., and B. Parigi. Forthcoming. The loan size as a commitment device. *International Economic Review.*

Lacker, J., and J. Weinberg. 1989. Optimal contracts under costly state falsification. *Journal of Political Economy* 97(6):1345–63.

Mas Colell, A., M. D. Whinston, and J. Green. 1995. *Microeconomic theory.* Oxford: Oxford University Press.

Myers, S. C., and N. Majluf. 1984. Corporate financing and investment decisions when firms have information that investors do not have. *Journal of Financial Economics* 13:187–221.

Myerson, R. 1979. Incentive compatibility and the bargaining problem. *Econometrica* 47(1):61–73.

Rogerson, W. 1985. The first-order approach to principal-agent problems. *Econometrica* 53(6):1357–67.

Statman, M. 1982. Fixed rate or index-linked mortgages from the borrower's point of view: A note. *Journal of Finance and Quantitative Analysis* XVII:(3)451–57.

Stiglitz, J. E., and A. Weiss. 1981. Credit rationing in markets with imperfect information. *American Economic Review* 71(3):393–410.

———. 1983. Incentive effects of terminations: Applications to the credit and labor markets. *American Economic Review* 73(5):912–27.

Tirole, J. Forthcoming. Incomplete contracts: Where do we stand? *Econometrica.*

Townsend, R. 1979. Optimal contracts and competitive markets with costly state verification. *Journal of Economic Theory* 21:265–93.

Webb, D. C. 1991. Long term financial contracts can mitigate the adverse selection problem in project financing. *International Economic Review* 32(2):305–20.

———. 1992. Two-period financial contracts with private information and costly state verification. *Quarterly Journal of Economics* 107(3):1113–23.

Wilson R. 1968. On the theory of syndicates. *Econometrica* 36:119–32.

The preceding chapter extensively analyzed the characteristics of a loan contract as a complex relationship between a borrower and a lender. This chapter turns to the credit market to examine the formation of equilibrium interest rates when multiple borrowers and lenders compete.

It is important to notice that, even if a partial equilibrium framework is adopted, the usual graphical analysis of supply and demand does not work in the context of the credit market. The reason is that the credit supply function may well be backward bending for high levels of the interest rate. As a consequence, demand and supply curves may not intersect, which means that a new equilibrium concept (less demanding than the usual market clearing condition) has to be designed to describe the outcome of a competitive credit market. Typically it involves a situation of *credit rationing* (i.e., the demand for credit exceeds supply at the prevailing interest rate).

Credit rationing has been the subject of a vast amount of literature: for instance, it has been taken as a postulate in the *availability doctrine* developed in the early 1950s.[1] However, before the clarifying contributions of Baltensperger (1978), Keeton (1979), and more recently De Meza and Webb (1992), there was no clear-cut definition of equilibrium credit rationing. This situation resulted in some confusion. Therefore, Section 5.1 will define credit rationing and explain the exact circumstances in which it occurs. Section 5.2 will then pinpoint the reason behind this phenomenon, namely the backward bending credit supply curve. Section 5.3 will show that this backward bending supply curve can be explained by adverse selection (Stiglitz and Weiss 1981). However, Section 5.4 will show that if collateral can be used as a screening device, credit rationing disappears (Bester 1985). Finally, moral hazard can also lead to credit rationing, as will be discussed in Section 5.5.

5.1   Definition of Equilibrium Credit Rationing

Following Baltensperger (1978), this discussion will speak of *equilibrium credit rationing* as occurring whenever *some borrower's demand for credit is turned down, even if this borrower is willing to pay all the price and nonprice elements of the loan contract.*[2]

The phrase "price elements of the loan contract" obviously means the interest rate charged by the bank, which is assumed to be unconstrained by the government. Of course, if there is a ceiling on credit rates, rationing can occur, but this is hardly surprising and not specific to the credit market. This discussion will explain situations in which the demand for credit exceeds supply even though the banks could increase interest rates.

However, loan contracts are not only characterized by their interest rate, but also, as emphasized by Baltensperger (1976), by "nonprice elements" such as collateral requirements. If a borrower is turned down because he does not have enough collateral, this cannot be denominated as credit rationing. Similarly, it is important to understand that credit is not a perfectly divisible good. Consequently, the fact that a borrower would be ready to borrow more at a given interest rate does not necessarily mean that he is rationed. Lending more to an individual borrower may increase the risk for the bank, and therefore the equilibrium interest rate may be a nonlinear function of the loan size. As a consequence, if the price of loans did not depend on the amount lent, the firms would not take into account the marginal cost of their loans, and this would result in inefficiency. (This point is developed in problem 5.6.2, following De Meza and Webb 1992).

The difference between the rejection of borrowers who do not meet these nonprice elements and credit rationing may appear more clearly in the context of complete contingent markets. In such a context, credit rationing is impossible, since any borrower (say, a firm) can borrow up to the net present value of all the future cash flows he can generate in the future. For instance, Freimer and Gordon (1965) study a situation in which these future cash flows depend on the size of the investment. When returns to scale are decreasing, there is a maximum amount that the bank is ready to lend at a given interest rate; yet, this should not be called credit rationing.

Another common use of the term "credit rationing" is when some categories of borrowers are totally excluded from the credit market. This phenomenon, known as "redlining," occurs because these borrowers do not have enough future cash flows or collateral to match their demand for credit. Again, this is not equilibrium credit rationing.

Finally, any institutional restrictions that can prevent lenders from offering differentiated conditions to heterogenous borrowers, such as ceilings on interest rates or "discriminatory" pricing, may lead to "disequilibrium" credit rationing. For instance, Smith (1972) shows that rationing may be Pareto-improving when firms have different equity-to-assets ratios and banks have to demand the same interest rate from all of them. Similarly, Jaffee and Modigliani (1969) show that a monopolistic bank that cannot use price discrimination (because of regulation) will typically ration those borrowers for which it would set higher rates in the absence of regulation. Using a related model, Blackwell and Santomero (1982) emphasize the fact that rationing concerns essentially the firms with a higher demand elasticity. Therefore the model predicts that larger firms (which have access to alternative sources of financing) will more likely be rationed, which seems contradicted by casual empiricism. Finally, Cukierman (1978) uses a similar model to examine the macroeconomic implications of credit rationing (see Devinney 1986 and Jaffee and Stiglitz 1990 for an overview).

5.2   The Backward Bending Supply of Credit

This section will show how equilibrium credit rationing can appear as soon as the expected return on a bank loan (for a given category of borrowers) is not a monotonic function of the nominal rate of this loan, as represented in Figure 5.1 below.

For the moment, this discussion will take this property as given (it will be explained in the next section) and explore its consequences on banks' behavior. First of all, consider the credit market for a completely specified category of loans (including all the observable characteristics of borrowers). The next thing to specify is the type of competition that prevails.

For example, a monopolistic bank facing the return schedule of Figure 5.1 will never offer an interest rate above R^*. This explains why a monopolistic bank may prefer to ration credit applicants. To understand why a competitive equilibrium of the banking sector may also lead to credit rationing, the aggregate demand and supply of loans must be examined. The aggregate demand analysis is straightforward. The aggregate supply is more involved because it depends on the behavior of depositors. Assuming that the depositors know the relationship between the quoted interest rate R and the banks' rate of return ρ, a supply of deposits increasing in the rate of return will determine a supply of loans on behalf of the banks that is backward bending (see Hodgman 1960).

Figure 5.2 shows how credit rationing may occur. If the demand schedule is L_1^D, a competitive equilibrium exists, characterized by the equality of supply and demand, so that the nominal rate R_1 clears the market. On the other hand, if

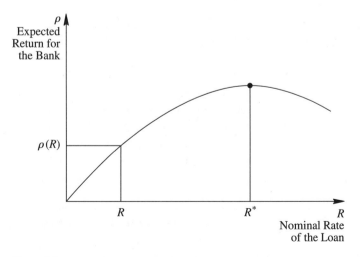

Figure 5.1
Expected Return for the Bank as a Function of the Nominal Rate of the Loan

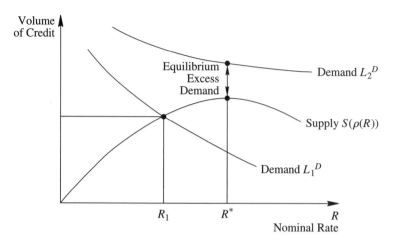

Figure 5.2
Equilibrium Credit Rationing

the demand schedule is L_2^D, the supply and demand curves do not intersect. An equilibrium with credit rationing will then occur, characterized by the interest rate R^* and zero profit for the banks.

Although competition between banks is not explicitly modeled by Stiglitz and Weiss (1981) in game theory terms, the implicit rules of the game are that banks are price setters on the credit market and quantity setters on the deposit market. In other words, they simultaneously choose a capacity (demand for deposits) and a nominal loan rate in such a way that their profit is maximized, taking as given the return demanded by depositors and the loan rates set by other banks.

The equilibrium that prevails in this case is characterized by type II credit rationing (see note 2); that is, only some randomly selected applicants will obtain the loan they demand. This is of course due to the assumption of indivisibility of the investment projects. If instead the projects were divisible, the type of credit rationing that would prevail would depend on the technology of borrowers: under decreasing returns to scale it would be of type I, and under increasing returns to scale rationing would be of type II. Notice that supply and demand could intersect at an interest rate $\hat{R}$ superior to R^*. In that case, any bank could benefit from decreasing its interest rates if it was not bound to serve all credit applicants and the market clearing level $\hat{R}$ would not be sustainable.

5.3   How Adverse Selection Can Lead to a Backward Bending Supply of Credit

So far, this discussion has taken as a postulate that the credit supply function could be backward bending for high levels of interest rates. More precisely, it has been assumed that the expected return ρ on a loan was not always a monotonic function of the nominal rate R of this loan. This section will show how this result can be explained by asymmetric information (following Stiglitz and Weiss 1981), who attribute it to adverse selection). Section 5.5 will show that moral hazard can lead to the same kind of result.

5.3.1   The Model of Stiglitz and Weiss (1981)

The basic assumption of Stiglitz and Weiss (1981) is that borrowers differ by a risk parameter θ, which is privately observed. The bank knows only the statistical distribution of θ among the population of potential borrowers. The crucial ingredient is that the characteristics of the loan offered by the bank will affect the composition of the population of firms that actually apply for the loan. In the model of Stiglitz and Weiss, all firms are assumed to bring the same amount of collateral C, which can therefore not be used as a screening device. Being unable to observe θ, the banks cannot discriminate among firms. They offer the same standard debt contract, in which all firms have to repay a fixed amount R (if they can) or their cash flow will be seized by the bank. Concerning unsecured loans, each firm will obtain a profit π that is related to its cash flow y by the familiar expression

$$\pi(y) = \max(0, y - R).$$

More generally, if a collateral C is introduced, the profit function becomes

$$\pi(y) = \max(-C, y - R).$$

A crucial property needed by Stiglitz and Weiss is that $E[\pi(y) \mid \theta]$ be an increasing function of θ. Since the profit function is convex (as shown by Figure 5.3), this property is satisfied if higher θs indicate riskier distributions of cash flows (in the sense of Rothschild and Stiglitz 1970). Notice that the convexity of the profit function comes from the rules of the standard debt contract, which are here exogenously given.[3]

5.3.2   Risk Characteristics of Loan Applicants

Assume that firms have a reservation level $\bar{\pi}$ for their expected profits, so that below that level they will not be interested in developing the project financed by the bank loan. For instance, $\bar{\pi}$ could be the level of profits the firm can obtain with another source of funds or another project. Since projects are indivisible, the total demand for loans is given by the number of firms with expected profits higher than $\bar{\pi}$. Since $E(\pi(y) \mid \theta)$ is increasing in θ, there is at most one value θ^* that satisfies

$$E(\pi(y) \mid \theta^*) = \bar{\pi}.$$

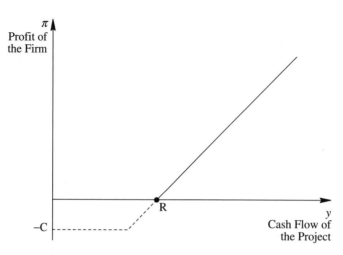

Figure 5.3
The Profit of the Firm as a Function of the Cash Flow of the Project

Focus on the case where this value exists (disregarding both cases where either all firms demand credit or none of them does), so that the demand for loans is determined by the population of firms with values of θ in the interval $[\theta^*, \bar{\theta}]$.

Consider now the banks' expected profits. They depend on the amount of the repayment R and the distribution of the cash flows of the firms applying for a loan. The effect of an increase in interest rates on the banks' expected profit is therefore twofold. On the one hand, it increases the profit the bank makes on any individual loan granted to a given firm θ. On the other hand, since it decreases $E(\pi(y) \mid \theta)$ for every θ, it has to increase θ^*, so the population of firms that demand a loan becomes more risky. Thus, as usual an increase in the interest rate decreases the demand for loans, but this happens because the less risky firms drop out of the market. As a consequence, an increase in the interest rate *need not* necessarily increase the banks' expected profits. This will depend on which of the two effects dominates: the direct effect of the interest rate increase for a given population of borrowing firms, or the indirect effect of changing the risk of this population. The distribution of θ, consequently, will play an important role on that account. For some of these distributions the banks' expected return on loans will be single peaked, with a maximum for a repayment R^*, and this results in the nonmonotonic profile shown in Figure 5.1.

Coming back to the previous assumptions, recall that banks cannot a priori distinguish between firms. Yet, in general, the banks will try to find devices in order to sort out firms. If banks find a way to distinguish between different classes of risk, the peaks of the expected return functions will occur at different levels in each of these classes, and therefore credit rationing will occur only in (at most) one of them. This has led Riley (1987) to think that rationing as explained by the Stiglitz-Weiss model would not be observed frequently. Still, Stiglitz and Weiss never claimed that the type of credit rationing their model described was frequent, nor that it was likely, but only that it *could* occur in a *competitive* framework.

A second assumption that is crucial in order to obtain the result is that the parameter θ ranks firms by increasing risk.[4] If, for instance, the probability distribution for the firms' cash flows is instead ranked according to first order stochastic dominance, an increase in interest rates would *decrease* the average risk of the population of borrowers, and consequently credit rationing would never occur at the equilibrium interest rate (see, for instance, De Meza and Webb 1987).

Finally, it has been assumed that the function relating the banks' expected return to the quoted interest rate was single peaked. This is not a consequence of previous assumptions, but only a possibility. If this function is increasing, the equilibrium will be without credit rationing.

Still, perhaps the main criticism that could be addressed to the Stiglitz-Weiss model is the fact that the debt contracts that are used are exogenously given and do not allow for any sorting mechanism. The subsequent contributions presented in Section 5.4 will explore this direction.

Another interesting contribution is that of Williamson (1987), who offers an alternative theoretical explanation of credit rationing that is based on the costly state verification paradigm of Townsend (1979) and Gale and Hellwig (1985) (studied in Chapter 4). This theoretical explanation has two merits: it justifies the use of the standard debt contract (which is optimal in this context, as shown in Chapter 4), and it does not require additional assumptions on the distribution of returns. Indeed, let $\tilde{x}$ denote the random return of the borrower's project, assumed to be unobservable by the lender, except when the lender performs an audit that costs γ. If R denotes the nominal unit repayment (one plus the nominal interest rate) of the debt contract, and if $\tilde{x}$ has a density $f(x)$, continuous and positive on its support $[\underline{x}, \bar{x}]$, then the return to the lender (as a function of R) has the following expression:

$$\rho(R) = \int_{\underline{x}}^{R} (x - \gamma) f(x) dx + \int_{R}^{\bar{x}} R f(x) dx.$$

Since f is continuous, ρ is (continuously) differentiable, and

$$\rho'(R) = (R - \gamma) f(R) - R f(R) + \int_{R}^{\bar{x}} f(x) dx$$

$$= -\gamma f(R) + \int_{R}^{\bar{x}} f(x) dx.$$

For R close enough to $\bar{x}$, this is negative (since $f(\bar{x}) > 0$). Therefore ρ has an interior maximum, and equilibrium credit rationing may arise. To summarize Williamson's simple argument, when failure is costly to the lender, an increase in the nominal rate of a loan may decrease the net return to the bank, since it increases the probability of failure of the borrower.

5.4   Collateral as a Sorting Device

A banker facing a heterogenous distribution of potential borrowers may benefit from discriminating among them. The fact that the banker is unable to identify the borrowers will lead the banker to consider sorting devices constructed in such a way that each type of borrower will choose a specific type of contract. Self-selection of clients will result from product differentiation. This idea has been explored, for instance, by Mussa and Rosen (1978) in the case of a monopoly for a durable good and by Rothschild and Stiglitz (1976) in the case of a competitive insurance market.

A natural way to model this strategy of the bank in the credit market is to consider a menu of contracts[5] $\gamma_i = (R_i, C_i)_{i \in I}$ specifying, together with an interest rate R_i, a collateral requirement C_i. This idea has been explored by Wette (1983), Bester (1985, 1987), Chan and Kanatas (1985), and Deshons and Freixas (1987). We follow Bester (1985), which uses a model with only two values for θ ($\theta \in \{\theta_a, \theta_b\}$), where θ_b is a higher risk than θ_a, in the sense of Rothschild and Stiglitz.[6]

In Bester's model, the wealth constraint is not binding and collateral has a cost, so the perfectly secured loan solution is inefficient. The strategy of each bank is to offer (equal or) different contracts γ_a, γ_b. Competition on each of these contracts implies that expected profit is zero for each of them, so that

$$\rho_a(\gamma_a) = \rho_b(\gamma_b) = r_0,$$

where ρ_a is the expected return computed with a's cash flow distribution (and similarly for ρ_b) and r_0 is the banks' cost of funds.

A priori, two types of Nash equilibria can obtain: separating equilibria, where different borrowers choose different contracts, and pooling equilibria.

A *separating equilibrium* is defined as a pair of (distinct) contracts (γ_a^*, γ_b^*) such that

1. γ_a^* is preferred by low-risk firms and γ_b^* is preferred by high-risk firms (self-selection constraints).

2. no bank is able to offer another contract on which it obtains an expected rate of return higher than r_0.

3. $\rho_a(\gamma_a^*) = \rho_b(\gamma_b^*) = r_0$.

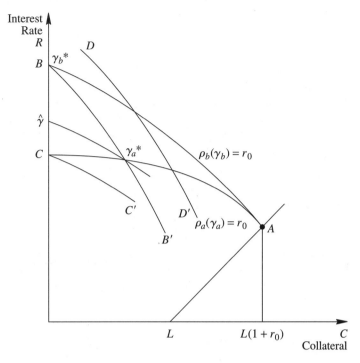

Figure 5.4
Separating Equilibrium in the Bester Model 1: The Only Candidate Is (γ_a^*, γ_b^*)

A *pooling equilibrium* would be defined in the same way when $\gamma^* = \gamma_a^* = \gamma_b^*$ (both types of firms choose the same contract), so that the expected return of the contract γ^*, denoted $\rho_{a+b}(\gamma^*)$, is estimated with the whole population of firms. The analogue to condition 3 will be written as $\rho_{a+b}(\gamma^*) = r_0$.

Bester establishes that if an equilibrium exists it entails no credit rationing. This point can be proved by using a figure in the (C, R) plane.

Banks will prefer contracts with higher collateral C and interest rates R, whereas firms will prefer contracts with lower collateral and interest rates. Notice that the isoprofit of the bank and the borrower curves are different, since the existence of a cost for pledging (or monitoring) the collateral implies that this is not a zero sum game.

In Figure 5.4 the AB curve (resp. AC) represents the locus of all contracts that would entail zero expected profit for the bank if they were chosen only by the type b (resp. type a) borrowers. The curves BB' and DD' are type b isoprofit curves. Notice that an additional unit of collateral costs more to the firm than what the bank will obtain from it. Therefore, the decrease in interest rate that compensates for a unit increase in collateral will be greater for the firm than for the bank. This explains why the BB' curve is steeper than the AB curve. (Notice that if there was no such pledging cost the AB and BB' curves would merge.)

Isoprofit curves corresponding to type b firms are above and on the right of those for the type a firms, since the former are riskier and the firms' profits are a convex function of the cash flow they obtain, as in the Stiglitz-Weiss model.

To establish that the contracts γ_a^* and γ_b^* define a separating equilibrium requires confirming that γ_a^* is preferred by type a firms and γ_b^* by type b firms. This is clearly the case, since the two contracts are indifferent from b's point of view, and type a firms strictly prefer γ_a^* given their lower risk. On the other hand, condition 3 is satisfied, since each contract is on the bank's zero profit curve.

Finally, it is necessary to confirm that condition 2 of the definition is satisfied, both for separating and for pooling contracts:

• First, no separating pair of contracts dominates (γ_a^*, γ_b^*). Indeed, γ_b^* is the contract preferred by b types on the zero profit curve; no other contract γ_b can attract them and make a positive profit. On the other hand, for a contract γ_a to be preferred by a and make zero profit, it should be on the left of γ_a^* and on the AC locus. Therefore it would also attract all type b borrowers and the bank would suffer a loss.

• Second, the zero profit condition for a pooling contract $(\rho_{a+b}(\gamma) = r_0)$ defines a curve $A\tilde{\gamma}$ (see Figure 5.5). On this curve both a and b prefer $\tilde{\gamma}$, so that

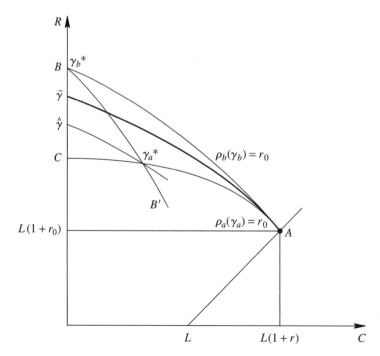

Figure 5.5
Separating Equilibrium in the Bester Model 2: The Case of Existence

$\tilde{\gamma}$ is the only candidate as a pooling contract. If the indifference curve for type a borrowers that goes through γ_a^* intersects the vertical axis at a point $\hat{\gamma}$ below $\tilde{\gamma}$ (as represented in Figure 5.5), then a will stick to γ_a^* and the contract (γ_a^*, γ_b^*) is the only separating equilibrium. If, on the contrary, $\hat{\gamma}$ is above $\tilde{\gamma}$, then the equilibrium does not exist, because it is possible to design contracts γ_a that will attract only type a borrowers and make a profit. The reasons why the equilibrium fails to exist are exactly the same as in Rothschild and Stiglitz (1976): $\tilde{\gamma}$ is not an equilibrium because it can be destabilized by a separating contract, yet the separating equilibrium is itself dominated by the pooling contract $\tilde{\gamma}$.

To summarize, Bester's model shows that if the equilibrium exists, no credit rationing will occur, because collateral is used in order to sort out the different (nonobservable) types of borrowers. Thus, again, going from an equilibrium with only a price characteristic to another in which contracts contain nonprice components (namely collateral) may prevent credit rationing from occurring.

In some cases, the amount of collateral needed for the equilibrium to be separating may be superior to the agent's wealth. This does not imply a return to the Stiglitz-Weiss case, as has been pointed out by Besanko and Thakor (1987). Besanko and Thakor use a slightly different framework, in which agent a's cash flow distribution is "less risky" in the sense of first order stochastic dominance. Figure 5.5 shows that a contract (R^a, W) to the left of γ^* on the AC curve will also be preferred by agent b. Still, the class of mechanisms (i.e., contracts) may be enriched by introducing the possibility of a stochastic rationing. If the agents demanding contract (R^a, W) are rationed, this might have a stronger effect on type b borrowers (who may stick to contract γ_b^*) than on the type a ones, to which contract b is of little interest. In that way separation is restored (provided W is not too low), and a competitive equilibrium is obtained in which the less risky agents are rationed, which is surprising.

However, the game theory formulation of competition in contracts is not completely satisfactory, in particular because equilibrium may fail to exist (at least in pure strategies). This has led Hellwig (1987) to examine more complex games in which the banks can reject some applicants, after having observed all the contracts offered and the choices of borrowers. Hellwig shows that an equilibrium always exists, and more importantly it may be a pooling equilibrium, which reintroduces the possibility of credit rationing.[7]

A related contribution is that of Pagano and Japelli (1993), who provide a theoretical analysis of the functioning of "credit bureaus," which are cooperative organizations among lenders designed for exchanging information about the credit history of borrowers. Membership in a credit bureau gives access to more information about potential borrowers, in exchange for the lender's own private information about its former customers. Their model predicts that the incentive to share information is greater when the underlying credit market is deep, the mobility of borrowers is high, and competition among banks is limited by entry cost or regulatory factors (such as entry restrictions or limits to branching).

5.5   Credit Rationing Due to Moral Hazard

In general, lenders will not participate in the management of the projects they finance. This may come from a self-imposed policy decision of financial institutions, aimed at preserving their reputation, or because the law may penalize such a behavior by lowering the rank of the bank in the creditors line in case of bankruptcy, if it is proved to have been involved in the management of the bankrupt firm.

Consequently, it is not always easy for the lender to enforce a particular use for the credit granted to the firm.[8] Nor is it easy to ascertain whether the firm has the capacity to repay. This is the main source of moral hazard problems in credit activities.

These moral hazard problems may lead to credit rationing exactly in the same way as adverse selection does. Moral hazard may generate a nonmonotonic relationship between quoted interest rates and expected rates of return, as in the Stiglitz-Weiss model, and therefore lead to equilibrium credit rationing.

This section will model two different types of moral hazard. The first is based on a model by Bester and Hellwig (1987) in which the firm is free to choose its technology (and therefore the cash flow distribution), and the second is based on the Jaffee and Russell (1976) contribution, in which the firm's capacity to repay the loan can be manipulated.

5.5.1   Nonobservable Technology Choice

Consider, as in subsection 2.5.1, a firm that has a choice between a "good" technology, which produces G (for a unit investment) with probability π_G (and zero otherwise), and a "bad" technology, which produces B with probability π_B.

Assume that the good technology has a higher expected return,

$$\pi_G G > \pi_B B,$$

but the cash flow in case of success is higher for the bad technology:

$$B > G,$$

which implies that $\pi_B < \pi_G$. Therefore the bad technology is riskier than the good one.

The loan contract specifies the amount R to be repaid by the firm in case of success. Since the size of the loan is normalized to one, R can be interpreted as (one plus) the interest rate of the loan.

The technology choice by the firm is then straightforward. The good technology will be chosen if and only if

$$\pi_G(G - R) \geq \pi_B(B - R).$$

Defining $\hat{R} = (\pi_G G - \pi_B B)/(\pi_G - \pi_B)$, this is equivalent to say

$$R \leq \hat{R}.$$

It is therefore easy to determine the expected return on the loan for the bank as a function of the repayment required; it is represented in Figure 5.6. For values of R lower than $\hat{R}$, expected repayment is $\pi_G R$, and for values of R higher than $\hat{R}$, it is equal to $\pi_B R$. The region $R > B$ is not interesting, since the repayment cannot exceed B and therefore expected repayment is constant in this region and equal to $\pi_B B$.

In order to close the model, the supply of credit must be introduced, as a function of expected repayment ρ. The simplest specification corresponds to an infinitely elastic supply of funds (that is, when ρ is equal to some constant ρ^*). In that case there may be two equilibria (when $\pi_B \hat{R} < \rho^* < \pi_B X_B$) as shown in Figures 5.6 and 5.7. Both R_1 and R_2 are interest rates at which the credit market clears. This is crucially related to the assumption of price-taking behavior by banks, because if lenders were price setters, R_2 would not be an

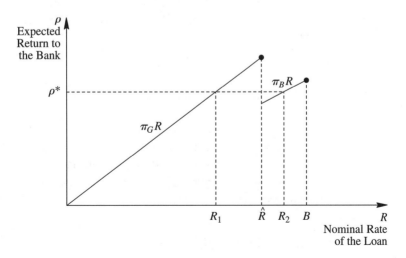

Figure 5.6
Expected Return to the Bank as a Function of R in the Bester-Hellwig Model Case I

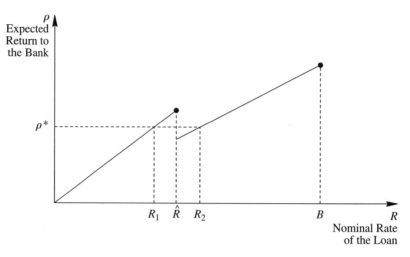

Figure 5.7
Expected Return to the Bank as a Function of R in the Bester-Hellwig Model Case II

equilibrium interest rate. By offering a loan rate $R_1 + \varepsilon$ just above R_1 (ε is positive and small), a bank could attract all borrowers and make a positive profit. In any case, equilibrium credit rationing cannot occur when the supply of funds is infinitely elastic, since markets will clear.

Assuming, as usual, that the deposit supply function $S(\rho)$ is not infinitely elastic, the function $S(\rho(R))$ is not increasing but reaches a global maximum at point $\hat{R}$ for the Bester-Hellwig model case I (Figure 5.6) and a local maximum at point $\hat{R}$ for case II (Figure 5.7). The credit market may then clear or not exactly as it happens in the Stiglitz-Weiss model (see Figure 5.2).

Rationing will occur for a supply function that is strictly increasing in the expected return ρ if

$$D > S(\rho(\hat{R})),$$

where D is the (inelastic) demand for credit on the project for a quoted interest rate equal to $\hat{R}$.

This simple model gives the main intuition on how moral hazard may lead to credit rationing. It may be extended to include collateral in the specification of the loan contract. This results in a modification of the incentives for choosing between the two investment projects. It is easily shown that the previous result holds true provided that $\hat{R}$ is replaced by $\hat{R} + C$, where C is the value of the collateral.

5.5.2 Nonobservable Capacity to Repay

Jaffee and Russell (1976) model a simple situation in which the borrower has a choice whether to repay or to default: it is assumed that repayment of the loan is not enforceable. The problem of borrower j consists in choosing between a repayment R_j or paying some exogenous nonpecuniary cost of default D_j. Therefore, depending on the value of the borrower's cash flows y_j, the following are possibilities:

1. $R_j > y_j$, and the firm is forced to default.

2. $y_j > R_j$ and $D_j > R_j$, and the firm chooses to repay.

3. $y_j > R_j > D_j$, and the firm chooses to default (strategic default).

If the value of D_j is observable by the bank, the bank may limit its loan so that the incentive to repay is preserved, $R_j \leq D_j$. Therefore, a threshold for the value of the repayment is obtained beyond which the expected return of the bank decreases. As in the previous models, this leads to credit rationing. If D_j does not depend on the amount of the loan, rationing is of type I.

It is straightforward to extend the model to the case in which the values of D_j are not observable by the bank. In this case the bank faces the same problem as in the Stiglitz-Weiss model, although the reason is now moral hazard. Indeed, an increase in the nominal interest rate would increase the bank's expected return provided it did not affect the incentives to repay. Since it does in fact affect the incentives to repay for a fraction of the borrowers' population, the question is which of the two effects dominates. If the bank's expected return is not a monotonic function of the nominal rate of the loan, credit rationing may occur.

5.6   Problems

5.6.1   The Model of Mankiw (1986)

Consider an economy à la Stiglitz and Weiss in which each firm θ has an investment technology in which one unit investment returns X_θ with probability $(1 - \theta)$ and zero with probability θ. Firms invest only if they have a strictly positive expected profit. The parameter θ follows a uniform distribution on $[0, 1]$.

Assume $(1 - \theta)X_\theta = \bar{X}$ so that all the projects have the same expected return, and higher θs indicate riskier projects as in Stiglitz and Weiss.

1. Compute the expected return for each repayment level R fixed in the loan contract, assuming that there is no collateral.

2. Assume that investors are able to obtain an exogenous riskless return r. Characterize the different types of equilibria that can be obtained, depending on the level of r.

5.6.2   Efficient Credit Rationing (Adapted from De Meza and Webb 1992)

Consider an economy with risk neutral agents in which firms (assumed to have no internal source of funds) develop projects that succeed in the state of nature

S_G (good) and fail in the state of nature S_B (bad), in which case the investment returns less than its cost. Let p_j, $j = G, B$, denote the probability of these two events. The expected return on the project when a loan of size k is obtained is

$$p_G f(k, S_G) + p_B f(k, S_B),$$

where f is the production function, conditional on the state of nature.

Competitive risk neutral banks fund the project provided they obtain at least the exogenous rate of return r.

Let r_L denote the interest rate due on the loans when the firm is successful. In the bad state of nature, the bank seizes all the output.

1. Show that if firms act as price takers in the credit market and if $f(k, S_B)$ is not linear in k, the allocation will not be efficient.

2. Show that if the banks competed in nonlinear prices (interest rates) on loans the efficiency would be restored.

3. If the equilibrium described in problem 2 prevails, when is there "apparent" credit rationing?

5.6.3   Too Much Investment (Adapted from De Meza and Webb 1987)

Consider an economy in which a continuum of risk neutral agents endowed with the same wealth W have access to an investment project that yields y with probability p and 0 with probability $1 - p$. The agents differ in their probability of success p, which ranges in the interval $[0, 1]$ and has a distribution with density $f(p)$. The investment requires a capital I superior to W so that agents will have to obtain a loan $L = I - W$. The supply of loanable funds (deposits) is an increasing function $S(r)$ of the money market interest rate r, which is assumed to be equal to the riskless rate.

Assume first that funding is done through a standard debt contract. In the perfect information case:

1. Write the agent's individual rationality constraint given that the agent has the choice between investing I or depositing W.

2. Write the equations determining the equilibrium money market rate r, the marginal investor, and the zero (marginal) profit for the bank.

3. Confirm that only projects with positive net present value will be implemented.

Assume now that p is not observable, so that R cannot depend on p.

4. Compute the equilibrium interest rate $\hat{r}$ and the probability of success $\hat{p}$ of the marginal investor. Show that there is overinvestment.

5.7   Solutions

5.7.1   The Model of Mankiw (1986)

1. Firm θ will demand a loan if $X_\theta - R > 0$ (that is, if $\theta > 1 - \bar{X}/R$). Only the risky firms in $[1 - \bar{X}/R, 1]$ ask for a loan, and the total amount lent equals $\bar{X}/R$. When $\bar{X} > R$, all the firms obtain a loan.

The expected return for the bank is thus

$$\rho = \frac{R}{\bar{X}} \{ \int_{1-\frac{\bar{X}}{R}}^{1} (1 - \theta) R d\theta \} = \frac{\bar{X}}{2},$$

if $\bar{X} \le R$, and

$$\rho = \frac{R}{2} \quad \text{if} \quad \bar{X} > R.$$

2. If $r \le \frac{\bar{X}}{2}$, the equilibrium (nominal) rate is $R = 2r$. However, if $r > \bar{X}/2$, the market for credit collapses: the unique equilibrium involves no trade.

5.7.2   Efficient Credit Rationing

1. The banks' zero profit condition can be written as

$$p_G(1 + r_L)k + p_B f(k, S_B) = (1 + r)k. \tag{5.1}$$

The firm maximizes its expected profit, given that it will not get anything in state S_B and taking r_L as exogenously given:

$$\max_{k} p_G[f(k, S_G) - (1 + r_L)k],$$

which leads to the first order condition

$$\frac{\partial f}{\partial k}(k, S_G) = 1 + r_L. \tag{5.2}$$

However, the efficient amount of capital is the one for which the following equality is obtained:

$$p_G \frac{\partial f}{\partial k}(k, S_G) + p_B \frac{\partial f}{\partial k}(k, S_B) = 1 + r. \tag{5.3}$$

Now, replacing r_L given by 5.2 in 5.1, and dividing by k,

$$p_G \frac{\partial f}{\partial k}(k, S_G) + \frac{p_B}{k} f(k, S_B) = 1 + r,$$

so that 5.3 does not hold except when $f(k, S_B)$ is linear in k.

2. Assume that banks can compete in nonlinear prices. Bertrand competition implies that $r_L(k)$ will be set in such a way that the bank's zero profit condition (5.1) is satisfied for all k. Then the firm's profit is just equal to the total surplus:

$$p_G f(k, S_G) + p_B f(k, S_B) - (1 + r)k,$$

and efficiency of equilibrium is warranted.

3. "Apparent" rationing means that, at the equilibrium loan rate $r_L(k^*)$, firms would like to borrow more. Given 5.2, this is satisfied if and only if

$$\frac{\partial f}{\partial k}(k^*, S_G) > 1 + r_L(k^*).$$

Using the equations that define k^* and $r_L(k^*)$,

$$\begin{cases} p_G \frac{\partial f}{\partial k}(k^*, S_G) + p_B \frac{\partial f}{\partial k}(k^*, S_B) = 1 + r \\ p_G(1 + r_L(k^*)) + p_B \frac{f(k^*, S_B)}{k^*} = 1 + r. \end{cases}$$

Therefore, apparent rationing occurs exactly when

$$\frac{\partial f}{\partial k}(k^*, S_B) < \frac{f(k^*, S_B)}{k^*}.$$

However, as proved in problem 2, this credit rationing is efficient.

5.7.3   Too Much Investment

1. The individual rationality constraint is

$$p(y - R(p)) \geq (1 + r)W. \tag{5.4}$$

2. For the marginal investor 5.4 holds with equality, and in addition the bank's zero profit condition (for each p) implies

$$pR(p) = (1 + r)L. \tag{5.5}$$

Therefore 5.4 is satisfied when

$$p \geq \bar{p}(r) \stackrel{\text{def}}{=} \frac{(1 + r)}{p}(W + L),$$

and the demand for credit is

$$D(r) = \int_{\bar{p}(r)}^{1} f(p)dp.$$

The market clearing condition is

$$\int_{\bar{p}(r)}^{1} f(p)dp = S(r). \tag{5.6}$$

3. Notice that adding 5.4 and 5.5 yields

$$py \geq (1+r)I,$$

so that only profitable projects are funded.

4. $\hat{p}$ and $\hat{r}$ are jointly defined by

$$\hat{p}(y - \hat{r}) = (1+r)W,$$

and $\quad \hat{r}\dfrac{\int_{\hat{p}}^{1} pf(p)dp}{1 - F(\hat{p})} = (1+r)L.$

Adding these two equalities yields

$$\hat{p}y + \hat{r}\frac{\int_{\hat{p}}^{1}(p - \hat{p})f(p)dp}{1 - F(\hat{p})} = (1+r)I.$$

The integral is clearly positive. Therefore $\hat{p}y < (1+r)I$, which means that there is overinvestment.

Notes

1. According to this doctrine, banks are limited by the availability of the funds they can attract. Therefore credit is always rationed: the credit market equilibrium is purely determined by the supply conditions. In such a context, monetary policy would be very effective; changes in the money supply would have direct effects on credit, instead of indirect effects channeled via changes in interest rates. However, this theory suffers from a major drawback: it does not explain why banks cannot increase their interest rates to equate demand with supply and make more profit. For a discussion of the availability doctrine, see Baltensperger and Devinney (1985) or the introduction of Clemenz (1986).

2. Following Keeton (1979), one can distinguish two types of rationing :

   a. *Type I rationing* occurs when there is a partial or complete rationing of all the borrowers within a given group.

   b. *Type II rationing* occurs within a group that is homogenous from the lender's standpoint, so that ex post some borrowers of this group obtain the loan they demand while others are rationed.

   To see the difference between type I and type II rationing, assume that $2N$ borrowers with demand equal to 1 face a supply of N. Type I rationing would imply that each borrower obtains $\frac{1}{2}$ unit. Type II would imply that N borrowers randomly selected out of the $2N$ potential ones obtain 1 unit.

3. Different justifications have been presented in Chapter 4.

4. Recall that Rothschild and Stiglitz (1970) have defined this notion as follows: Let $\tilde{y}_1$ and $\tilde{y}_2$ be two random variables; $\tilde{y}_1$ is more risky than $\tilde{y}_2$ if and only if for all concave functions $u(\cdot)$, $Eu(\tilde{y}_1) \leq Eu(\tilde{y}_2)$. In economic terms, it means that any risk averse investor would prefer the random return $\tilde{y}_2$ to $\tilde{y}_1$.

5. This was shown in Chapter 4. As Chapter 4 also showed, there are other possible menus of contracts, in particular those linking repayments to the loan size. These types of contracts, which lead to similar results, have been explored by Milde and Riley (1988).

6. The extension to n types of risk is modeled in Bester (1987). The problems in modeling loans that are backed by collateral are that

- collateral may be limited by the entrepreneur's wealth and

- if there is no such limit, the optimal contracts may involve a 100 percent collateral, so that imperfect information becomes irrelevant. The solution is to introduce a cost of collateral, as in Bester (1985, 1987).

7. Since Hellwig's game is a sequential game under asymmetric information, he must use the concept of Perfect Bayesian Equilibrium and some sophisticated refinement criteria. For a clear presentation of these concepts, see for instance, Fudenberg and Tirole (1991). Interesting discussions of game theory modelings of the credit market may be found in Clemenz (1986) and Clemenz and Ritthaler (1992).

8. Notorious exceptions are mortgage loans and project financing. But even inventory financing that theoretically could be easily observed by banks has, in practice, an important record of fraud on the part of the borrowing firms.

References

Baltensperger, E. 1976. The borrower-lender relationship, competitive equilibrium and the theory of hedonic prices. *American Economic Review* 66(3):401–5.

———. 1978. Credit rationing: Issues and questions. *Journal of Money, Credit, and Banking* 10(2):170–83.

Baltensperger, E., and T. Devinney. 1985. Credit rationing theory: A survey and synthesis. *Zeitschrift für die gesamte Staatswissenschaft* 141(4):475–502.

Besanko, D., and A. Thakor. 1987. Collateral and rationing: Sorting equilibria in monopolistic and competitive credit markets. *International Economic Review* 28(3):671–89.

Bester, H. 1985. Screening vs rationing in credit markets with imperfect information. *American Economic Review* 75(4):850–55.

———. 1987. The role of collateral in credit markets with imperfect information. *European Economic Review* 31(4):887–99.

Bester, H., and M. Hellwig. 1987. Moral hazard and equilibrium credit rationing. In *Agency theory, information and incentives,* edited by Bamberg, G., and K. Spremann. Heidelberg: Springer Verlag.

Blackwell, N., and A. Santomero. 1982. Bank credit rationing and the customer relation. *Journal of Monetary Economics* 9(1):121–29.

Chan, Y., and G. Kanatas. 1985. Asymmetric valuations and the role of collateral in loan agreements. *Journal of Money, Credit, and Banking* 17(1):84–95.

Clemenz, G. 1986. *Credit markets with asymmetric information.* Lecture Notes in Economics and Mathematical Systems. Berlin: Springer Verlag.

Clemenz, G., and M. Ritthaler. 1992. Credit markets with asymmetric information: A survey. *Finnish Economic Papers* 5(1):12–26.

Cukierman, A. 1978. The horizontal integration of the banking firm, credit rationing and monetary policy. *Review of Economic Studies* 45(1):165–78.

De Meza, D., and D. Webb. 1987. Too much investment: A problem of asymmetric information. *Quarterly Journal of Economics* 102(2):281–92.

———. 1992. Efficient credit rationing. *European Economic Review* 36(6):1277–90.

Deshons, M., and X. Freixas. 1987. Le role de la garantie dans les contrats de prêt bancaire. *Finance* 8(1):7–32.

Devinney, T. 1986. *Rationing in a theory of the banking firm.* Studies in Contemporary Economics Series. Berlin: Springer Verlag.

Freimer, M., and M. Gordon. 1965. Why bankers ration credit. *Quarterly Journal of Economics* 79:397–410.

Fudenberg, D., and J. Tirole. 1991. Game theory. Boston: MIT Press.

Gale, D., and M. Hellwig. 1985. Incentive compatible debt contracts: The one-period problem. *Review of Economic Studies* L11:647–63.

Hellwig, M. 1987. Some recent developments in the theory of competition in markets with adverse selection. *European Economic Review* 31(1/2):319–25.

Hodgman, D. 1960. Credit risk and credit rationing. *Quarterly Journal of Economics* 74:258–78.

Jaffee, D., and F. Modigliani. 1969. A theory and test of credit rationing. *American Economic Review* 59:850–72.

Jaffee, D., and T. Russell. 1976. Imperfect information, uncertainty and credit rationing. *Quarterly Journal of Economics* 90:651–66.

Jaffee, D., and J. Stiglitz. 1990. Credit rationing. Chap. 16 in *Handbook of monetary economics,* Vol. II, edited by B. M. Friedman and F. H. Hahn. Amsterdam: Elsevier Science Publication.

Keeton, W. 1979. *Equilibrium credit rationing.* New York: Garland Press.

Mankiw, G. 1986. The allocation of credit and financial collapse. *Quarterly Journal of Economics* 101(3):455–70.

Milde, H., and J. Riley. 1988. Signaling in credit markets. *Quarterly Journal of Economics* 103(1):101–130.

Mussa, M., and S. Rosen. 1978. Monopoly and product quality. *Journal of Economic Theory* 18(2):301–17.

Pagano, M., and T. Japelli. 1993. Information sharing in the consumer credit market. *Journal of Finance* 48(5):1693–1718.

Riley, J. 1987. Credit rationing: A further remark. *American Economic Review* 77(1):224–27.

Rothschild, M., and J. Stiglitz. 1970. Increasing risk: A definition. *Journal of Economic Theory* 2(3):225–43.

———. 1976. Equilibrium in competitive insurance markets: An essay on the economics of imperfect informations. *Quarterly Journal of Economics* 90(4):630–49.

Smith, V. L. 1972. A theory and test of credit rationing: Some generalizations. *American Economic Review* 62:66–76.

Stiglitz, J., and A. Weiss. 1981. Credit rationing in markets with imperfect information. *American Economic Review* 71(3):393–410.

———. 1983. Incentive effects of terminations: Applications to the credit and labor markets. *American Economic Review* 73(5):912–27.

Townsend, R. 1979. Optimal contracts and competitive markets with costly state verification. *Journal of Economic Theory* 21:265–93.

Wette H. 1983. Collateral in credit rationing in markets with imperfect information: A note. *American Economic Review* 73(3):442–45.

Williamson, S. 1987. Costly monitoring, loan contracts, and equilibrium credit rationing. *Quarterly Journal of Economics* 102(1):135–45.

It may seem strange to devote a chapter of this book to *macroeconomic* issues, since the discussion so far has focused explicitly on the microeconomic approach to banking and has essentially ignored the traditional textbook material on money and banking in macroeconomic equilibrium. Nevertheless, the last ten years or so have witnessed a partial rejection of this traditional material. This trend is the result of the promising development of theoretical literature on the macroeconomic implications of the *same financial imperfections* that are studied in detail in this book and that have been used to explain the role of banks and financial intermediaries (see Gertler 1988 for a first overview). Although this theoretical literature has not really stabilized yet, in particular because it has not been convincingly supported by empirical evidence, it is important to be aware of some of its results.

After a short historical perspective on the macroeconomic consequences of financial markets' imperfections (Section 6.1), this chapter will study five issues:

1. The transmission channels of monetary policy (Section 6.2)

2. The fragility of the financial system (Section 6.3)

3. The existence of financial cycles (Section 6.4)

4. The real effects of financial intermediation (Section 6.5)

5. The impact of financial intermediation on growth (Section 6.6).

6.1 A Short Historical Perspective

In the first issue of *Econometrica,* Irving Fisher (1933) argued that the severity of the economic downturn during the Great Depression resulted from the poor performance of financial markets. He defined the concept of *debt deflation:* when borrowers (firms) are highly leveraged, a small shock that affects their productivity or their net wealth can trigger a series of bankruptcies, which generate a decrease in investment, in demand, and as a consequence, in prices. This aggravates the real indebtedness of the productive sector, which may provoke a further series of failures, with a cumulative effect.

This viewpoint was later reinforced by the Gurley-Shaw (1955) theory according to which *financial intermediaries* play a critical role in facilitating the circulation of loanable funds between savers and borrowers. Also in line with this view is the finding by Goldsmith (1969) that a positive correlation exists between economic growth and the degree of sophistication and development of the financial sector.

Following the publication by Friedman and Schwartz (1963) of their monetary history of the United States, the idea that *money supply* was the key financial aggregate gained wide support. Friedman and Schwartz found a high positive correlation between money supply and output, especially during the Great Depression. They argued therefore that banks did matter insofar as they create money. This is in line with the conclusions of simple IS/LM macro models, in which the money supply is assumed to be controlled by the Central Bank—a crucial simplifying assumption. In fact (as Section 6.2 will discuss), even if the Central Bank can control the money base, the other components of the money supply adjust to changes in interest rates. As a consequence, the stock of money is in fact less important for macroeconomic performance than the *financial capacity* of the economy, defined as the aggregate volume of credit that lenders are ready to grant to borrowers. Therefore, in response to Friedman and Schwartz's "money view," the alternative position was to emphasize the "credit view."

After the 1960s, and following Modigliani and Miller's (1958) contribution, the view that "finance is a veil" became widely accepted. If the financial structure of firms is irrelevant, and if financial intermediaries are redundant, then monetary policy can have only a transitory impact on real variables, through unanticipated changes in the money supply. In all the *real business cycle models* that were developed subsequently, finance does not play any role.

The comeback of financial aspects in macro models started in the early 1980s. Following an earlier study by Mishkin (1978), Bernanke (1983) analyzed the relative importance of monetary versus financial factors in the Great Depression. His central conclusion was that monetary forces alone were "quantitatively insufficient" to explain the Depression's depth and persistence, and that the collapse of the financial system (half of the U.S. banks failed between 1930 and 1933, and the financial markets crashed worldwide) was an important factor. Therefore, the decline in the money stock seems in fact to have been less important than argued by Friedman and Schwartz. Bernanke tested the two explanations (the breakdown in banking having affected borrowers who did not have access to security markets versus the decline in money supply) and concluded in favor of the first. Thus, this piece of empirical evidence gave support to the credit view, which argued that financial markets appeared to be imperfect, so the Modigliani-Miller assumptions did not hold and finance did matter.

The following sections will study the different theoretical arguments that support this view, starting with those that aim to explain the transmission channels of the monetary policy.

6.2   The Transmission Channels of Monetary Policy

It is important to recognize that the precise mechanisms through which the monetary policy of Central Banks affects real activity are not completely understood.[1] Before discussing these mechanisms, and without going into institutional descriptions that are outside the scope of the book,[2] recall the main methods used by Central Banks to supply liquidity to the banking system. Although the detailed procedures differ, most Central Banks of developed countries primarily use the same instrument, namely an "auction of reserves on a repurchase basis against collateral of securities" (Schnadt 1993, 123). In addition to these operations, banks are permitted, on their own initiative, to obtain short-term advances from the Central Bank. Of course, the cost of these advances typically exceeds the interest rate on the regular open-market auctions of reserves. This facility may be systematically offered, as in France and Germany, or frequently rationed as in the United States. Bank reserves are also traded on a secondary market (the interbank market or the federal funds market in the United States). Finally, a wider set of markets for liquidity (the so-called money market) exists in which other financial institutions and large nonfinancial firms intervene.

Roughly speaking, two different views on the mechanisms of monetary policy still coexist among economists. The *money view* (presented in subsection 6.2.1) essentially asserts that only banks' liabilities (money) matter. The *credit view* (presented in subsection 6.2.2) insists on the importance of bank loans, as opposed to other sources of funds for borrowers. Subsection 6.2.3 will compare the two views by judging the pertinence of the assumptions they require and by examining some empirical evidence. Finally, subsection 6.2.4 will depart from the standard money-multiplier model and will introduce the topic of endogenous money.

6.2.1   The Money Channel

In its simplest formulation, the money channel can be described in the standard IS/LM model; that is, in a world with one good, two assets (money D and bonds B) and four types of agents: households, firms, banks, and the government.[3] The real income of households (y) and the interest rate on bonds (r_B) determine (real) savings $S(y, r_B)$, which are allocated between the two assets:

$$S(y, r_B) = D^h(y, r_B) + B^h(y, r_B), \tag{6.1}$$
$$\underset{+\ \ +}{} \quad \underset{+\ \ -}{} \quad \underset{+\ \ +}{}$$

where superscript h refers to households, and $+$ or $-$ indicates the postulated signs of partial derivatives. Similarly, the investment demand of firms $I(r_B)$[4] is financed through bonds:

$$I(r_B) = B^f(r_B), \tag{6.2}$$

where superscript f refers to firms. The modeling of banks is simplistic: they issue deposits D^b, purchase bonds B^b, and hold reserves R, with the following balance constraint:

$$R + B^b = D^b. \tag{6.3}$$

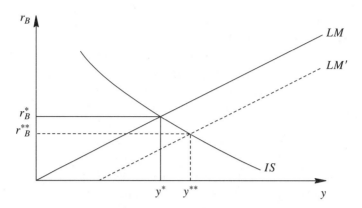

Figure 6.1
The Consequences of Increasing Reserves in the IS/LM Model

In the simpler story, banks are completely passive. B^b and D^b are determined by the reserve rate α required by the Central Bank ($R = \alpha D^b$), implying

$$D^b = \frac{R}{\alpha}, \text{ and } B^b = \frac{R(1-\alpha)}{\alpha}. \tag{6.4}$$

Finally, the last agent is the governement, which finances real expenditures G by the reserves R borrowed from banks and by issuing bonds B^g:

$$G = R + B^g. \tag{6.5}$$

Using Walras's law, two equations are enough to characterize the equilibrium levels of the endogenous variables y and r_B:

$$R = \alpha D^h(y, r_B) \tag{6.6}$$

(equilibrium on the money market) and

$$I(r_B) + G = S(y, r_B) \tag{6.7}$$

(equilibrium on the goods market).

Under the assumptions regarding the signs of partial derivatives, the traditional textbook analysis of the Keynesian model is obtained, in which 6.6 and 6.7 correspond respectively to the LM and IS curves.

The effect of monetary policy is then clear-cut: if the Central Bank increases R or decreases B^g (liquidity injection),[5] the LM curve moves downward (see Figure 6.1), but the IS curve is unaffected. Therefore, activity is enhanced (y increases) and the interest rate decreases.

The implicit assumptions that are needed for this analysis to hold are as follows:

- A1: Prices do not adjust instantaneously to offset changes in the (nominal) quantity of money.

- A2: The Central Bank can directly influence the nominal quantity of *money* by adjusting reserves.

- A3: Loans and bonds are *perfect* substitutes for the borrowers (therefore, explicitly introducing banks is unnecessary).

The following discussion will explore what happens if assumptions A2 and A3 are modified.

6.2.2   Credit View

Following Bernanke and Blinder (1988) (see also Bernanke and Blinder 1987), the previous model will be modified by introducing bank loans as an imperfect substitute for bonds.[6] The interest rate on bank loans is denoted r_L. The behavior of households (equation 6.1) is not modified, but that of firms and banks is now more complex. Firms have now two possibilities for financing their investments, so that 6.2 is replaced by

$$I(r_B, r_L) = B^f(r_B, r_L) + L^f(r_B, r_L). \tag{6.8}$$
$$\underset{-\quad -}{} \quad \underset{-\quad +}{} \quad \underset{+\quad -}{}$$

Similarly, banks now have three assets (reserves, loans, and bonds), so 6.3 is replaced by

$$R + L^b + B^b = D^b. \tag{6.9}$$

As before, the quantity of money is exogenously determined by the multiplier mechanism: $D^b = \frac{R}{\alpha}$. The allocation of loanable funds $D^b - R(= R(\frac{1-\alpha}{\alpha}))$ by banks results from their portfolio optimization (which is not explicitly modeled by Bernanke and Blinder):

$$\begin{cases} L^b &= \mu(r_B, r_L)R \\ & \underset{-\ +}{} \\ B^b &= \nu(r_B, r_L)R, \\ & \underset{+\ -}{} \end{cases} \tag{6.10}$$

with $\mu(r_B, r_L) + \nu(r_B, r_L) = \frac{1-\alpha}{\alpha}$. The money market equilibrium (equation 6.6, LM curve) is the same as before, but equation 6.7 (IS curve) has to be replaced by a system of two equations:

$$I(r_B, r_L) + G = S(y, r_B) \tag{6.11}$$
$$\underset{-\quad -}{} \qquad \underset{+\quad +}{}$$

(equilibrium on the goods market) and

$$L^f(r_B, r_L) = \mu(r_B, r_L)R \tag{6.12}$$
$$\underset{+\quad -}{} \quad \underset{-\quad +}{}$$

(equilibrium on the credit market).

Using the assumptions regarding the signs of partial derivatives, equation 6.12 can be solved for r_L:

$$r_L = \phi(r_B, R). \tag{6.13}$$
$$\underset{+\ \ -}{}$$

Injecting equation 6.13 in 6.11 yields what Bernanke and Blinder call the commodities and credit (CC) curve:

$$I(r_B, \phi(r_B, R)) + G = S(y, r_B). \tag{6.14}$$
$$\underset{-\ \ -\ +\ -}{} \qquad \underset{+\ +}{}$$

The main difference between the current and the previous case is that R appears in the CC curve but was absent from the IS curve. The following result is obtained:

Result 6.1   An increase in bank reserves has two effects in the Bernanke-Blinder model:

1. As in the previous case, the quantity of money increases (the LM curve shifts downward).

2. In addition, the volume of credit increases, which enhances the demand for investment by firms (the CC curve shifts upward).

As a result, activity is enhanced (y increases) but the effect on r_B is ambiguous.[7]

Proof   The proof is obvious from Figure 6.2.   ■

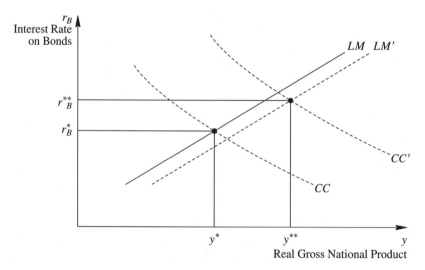

Figure 6.2
The Credit Channel of Monetary Policy

A first important consequence of this result is that monetary policy can have important real effects without substantially affecting the interest rate r_B. If banks have more access to reserves, they can increase their credit supply to firms, which can in turn invest more without significantly changing their demand for bonds.

A second important consequence concerns the relevance of monetary policy indicators. If the Central Bank cannot directly and instantaneously observe the impact of its policy on real activity but has to rely on financial indicators (money, interest rates, and credit) the question is, which of these financial variables gives the best forecast of real activity and should therefore be used as a target? In the money view, all three variables are perfectly correlated. In the credit view, credit should be the target. The following discussion will focus on the relevance of the assumptions that are implicit in the credit view and the empirical work on the question, closely following Kashyap and Stein (1993).

6.2.3   Credit View versus Money View: Relevance of the Assumptions and Empirical Evidence

The implicit assumptions behind the credit view are as follows:[8]

• A1: Prices do not adjust instantaneously to offset changes in the (nominal) quantity of money.

• A'2: The Central Bank can directly influence the volume of *credit* by adjusting bank reserves.

• A'3: Loans and securities are *imperfect* sustitutes both for borrowers and for banks.

Assumption A1 is common to both views of monetary policy. The early explanations of A'2 (the so-called availability doctrine of Roosa 1951) relied on credit rationing. Modern arguments (related to imperfect information and the monitoring role of banks) explain the assumption without credit rationing: as Chapter 2 showed, firms having insufficient capital or reputation cannot issue direct debt and therefore rely on credit from financial intermediaries. This is confirmed by empirical evidence: James (1987) shows that bank credit is more expensive than direct debt, which indicates that there is "something special" in bank services to borrowers. Similarly, Hoshi, Kashyap, and Scharfstein (1991) show that Japanese firms with close banking ties are less likely to be liquidity constrained. However, as pointed out by Kashyap and Stein (1993), financial intermediaries other than banks (such as finance companies, which do not hold Central Bank reserves) could in principle provide the same services. Even if these nonbank intermediaries do not appear to have a large share of the credit market, they could effectively be the "marginal" lenders in the economy, which would supply credit to the economy when the Central Bank restricts liquidity, thus undermining assumption A'2. This does not seems to be the case, probably because of the "lock-in" effect (Sharpe 1990, Rajan 1992, and Slovin, Sushka, and Polonchek 1993): because of informational asymmetries, borrowers cannot switch from one lender to another without cost.

However, one may wonder whether in the future, nonbanks could drive depository institutions out of the credit market, implementing effectively a narrow banking solution. As Gorton and Penacchi (1990) argue, this is conceivable, since "the sum of outstanding Treasury bills and non-financial commercial paper is now (in the US) roughly twice as large as the level of checkable bank deposits" (quoted by Kashyap and Stein 1993, 18).

Finally, even if one accepts the view that loans and securities are not perfect substitutes for borrowers, they could be viewed as such by banks. For instance, Romer and Romer (1990) argue that the supply of large-denomination Certificates of Deposits (CDs) (which are not subject to reserves) addressed to any given bank is perfectly elastic at the current market rate. However, this is not confirmed by casual empiricism: a nonnegligible interest spread exists between CDs and Treasury bills (T-bills) of the same characteristics. Moreover, these spreads appear to be strongly dependent on the banks' ratings given by the rating agencies. Cook and Rowe (1986) (quoted by Kashyap and Stein 1993) give the example of Continental Illinois, which experienced a large increase in its CD rates before going bankrupt.

Another explanation for the imperfect substitutability between loans and securities (here essentially T-bills), documented by Bernanke and Gertler (1987), is that banks use T-bills as a buffer against liquidity shocks. This is confirmed by the fact that large banks hold significantly fewer T-bills than the average (Kashyap and Stein 1993, 20).

This discussion will conclude with a look at some empirical work on the subject of the credit view versus the money view. Strong evidence seems to exist in favor of a high correlation between credit supply and economic activity. As already mentioned, Bernanke's influential study of the Great Depression in the United States (1983) attributes its depth and persistence to the crisis experienced by the U.S. banking sector at that time. Similar conclusions are obtained for other periods and other countries (Bernanke and James 1991, Schreft 1990, Bernanke 1986).

Another important empirical issue is whether monetary policy really influences credit supply (assumption A'2) more than money supply (assumption A2). Several studies (King 1986, Romer and Romer 1990, Ramey 1992) have found that loans adjust gradually to changes in monetary policy but that money changes more rapidly and is correlatively a better predictor of output. Kashyap, Stein, and Wilcox (1993) go further and examine the impact of monetary policy on the composition of firms' borrowing (i.e., its repartition between bank loans and commercial paper). They find that an episode of restrictive monetary policy is typically followed by a raise in commercial paper issuance and a decline in bank loans. Using cross-sectional data, Gertler and Gilchrist (1992) show that in such a case external financing of large firms actually *increases* (both commercial paper and bank loans) and that it is the small firms that pay the burden, since they experience a large decrease in bank loans, which are essentially their only source of external finance.

6.2.4   Endogenous Money

The discussion thus far has worked with a standard, but caricatural, description of monetary policy: the money multiplier mechanism, which assumes that the compulsory reserves coefficient α is fixed, and the quantity of money in the economy is completely determined by the money base (i.e., compulsory reserves R). As Chapter 3 showed, this is not satisfactory, for at least two reasons:

1. Because banks' deposits are now remunerated in most countries, their supply is not independent of interest rates; money is endogenous.

2. The modern instruments of monetary policy are interest rates and not the monetary base.

These two aspects will now be introduced in a simple extension of the Bernanke-Blinder model based on Grimaud (1994). The main differences are that banking deposits are now remunerated (at an interest rate r_D) and that banks are explicitly modeled as profit maximizers. For convenience, this discussion uses the competitive model of the banking sector described in Chapter 3 (Section 3.2) and will assume constant marginal costs γ_D and γ_L of managing deposits and loans. The equilibrium equations on the credit and deposit market are then simply

$$r_L = r + \gamma_L \tag{6.15}$$

and

$$r_D = r(1 - \alpha) - \gamma_D, \tag{6.16}$$

where r denotes the interest rate on the interbank market.[9] Moreover, banks have access simultaneously to the bond market and to the interbank market and behave competitively. Thus, assuming that all banks are solvent, the interest rates on these two markets must be equal:

$$r_B = r.$$

The following new expressions for the LM curve show how the Bernanke-Blinder results are modified by introducing endogenous money:

$$R = \alpha D^h(y, r_B, r_D). \tag{6.17}$$
$$+ \;\; - \;\; +$$

The only difference between the new expression and 6.6 is that the quantity of money now depends on r_D, which is itself determined by the deposit market equilibrium condition 6.16. The new expression for the LM curve is therefore

$$R = \alpha D^h(y, r_B, (1 - \alpha)r_B - \gamma_D). \tag{6.18}$$

Note that this modified LM curve is not necessarily increasing in the (r_B, y) plane. Indeed, differentiating 6.18 yields the slope of this curve:

$$\left(\frac{dy}{dr_B}\right)_{LM} = -\frac{1}{\underset{+}{\frac{\partial D^h}{\partial y}}} \left\{ \underset{-}{\frac{\partial D^h}{\partial r_B}} + (1 - \alpha)\underset{+}{\frac{\partial D^h}{\partial r_D}} \right\}.$$

If the demand for money is very sensitive to the deposit rate r_D, this expression can be negative, which means that the LM curve can very well be decreasing.

Recall the second constitutive element of the Bernanke-Blinder model, namely the CC curve. This curve is obtained from the IS equation,

$$I(r_B, r_L) + G = S(y, r_B, r_D), \tag{6.19}$$

by incorporating the equilibrium values of r_L and r_D as a function of r_B. Notice that savings now depend on r_D. The following result is obtained:

$$I(r_B, r_B + \gamma_L) + G = S(y, r_B, r_B(1 - \alpha) - \gamma_D). \tag{6.20}$$

Under the given assumptions, this curve is decreasing in the (y, r_B) plane. An important difference between this curve and the CC curve of Bernanke and Blinder (equation 6.14) is that this curve is independent of R. This modifies the consequences of an increase in bank reserves.

Result 6.2   If the modified LM curve is increasing, then an increase in bank reserves (liquidity injection) has the following consequences:

• Activity is enhanced (y increases), and the interest rate on bonds r_B decreases.

• As a consequence, interest rates on both credit r_L and deposits r_D decrease, and the quantity of money increases.

This result also holds true as soon as the slope of the LM curve, $(\frac{dy}{dr_B})_{LM}$, is not "too negative." When it becomes smaller (higher in absolute value) than $(\frac{dy}{dr_B})_{CC}$ (this can occur if the demand for money is very elastic to r_D), the consequences of a liquidity injection are completely reversed: output y decreases, and money and interest rates r_B, r_L, and r_D increase. The reason is that, in this case, the demand for money is so sensitive to the variations of r_D that an increase in the stock of money means that all interest rates increase.

Suppose now that the Central Bank determines the interbank rate r and that banks choose their own reserves (according to equation 6.18). This is more in line with the actual conduct of monetary policy in most countries. In the competitive model of the banking sector (with constant marginal costs of intermediation), the movements of all interest rates are exactly proportional to those of the interbank market:

$$r_B = r, \ r_L = r + \gamma_L, \ r_D = (1 - \alpha)r - \gamma_D.$$

The impact of r on y is directly obtained from 6.20:

$$I(r, r + \gamma_L) + G = S(y, r, r(1 - \alpha) - \gamma_D).$$

In particular, a decrease in r is always followed by an increase in output y. However, the impact on money is ambiguous; it depends on the sign of the slope of $(\frac{dy}{dr_B})_{LM}$.

6.3   The Fragility of the Financial System

The two articles that will be presented in this section examine the conditions under which an economy may experience a brutal contraction of credit and, as a consequence, of activity. In each case, this phenomenon is related to asymmetric information. Subsection 6.3.1 will discuss the simpler model of Mankiw (1986), in which, because of adverse selection, the credit market may collapse after a small increase in the money market rate (which is the cost of banks' refinancing). Subsection 6.3.2 will then study the contribution of Bernanke and Gertler (1990), who show that, because of moral hazard, the general financial conditions (credit worthiness of borrowers, or banks' solvency) can affect macroeconomic performance.

6.3.1   Financial Collapse Due to Adverse Selection

Mankiw (1986) considers a credit market with adverse selection, in the spirit of Stiglitz and Weiss (1981). There is a continuum population of risk neutral borrowers, parameterized by the characteristics (X, p) of their investment project. Each project costs one unit of money; its return is $\frac{X}{p}$ with probability p (success) and zero with probability $(1 - p)$ (failure). X is thus the expected return on the project. Risk neutral banks offer standard debt contracts (with limited liability); repayment is thus R in case of success and zero in case of failure. Since (X, p) is private information of the borrower, R cannot be conditioned on it. As a consequence, bankers are confronted with adverse

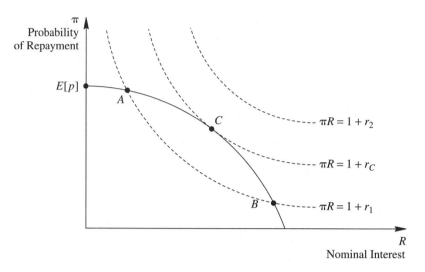

Figure 6.3
Equilibria of the Credit Market. The dashed lines correspond to the bank's isoprofit curves for different values of the money market rate r. The solid line represents the probability of repayment as a function of the nominal interest factor R.

selection: the firms that apply for credit are the more risky ones. Indeed, a firm of characteristics (X, p) will apply for credit if and only if its expected gain $X - pR$ exceeds its reservation utility U_0, which can be interpreted as what it can gain on other activities (to simplify notations, assume $U_0 = 0$). The average probability of repayment $\pi(R)$ in the population of borrowers is a decreasing function of R:

$$\pi(R) = E\left[p|p < \frac{X}{R}\right].$$ (6.21)

Notice in particular that $\pi(0) = E[p]$ and that $\lim_{R \to +\infty} \pi(R) = 0$. If r denotes the money market or interbank rate (assumed to be exogenous), the equilibrium condition on the credit market is

$$\pi(R)R = 1 + r.$$ (6.22)

As Figure 6.3 shows, there is a possibility of 0, 1, or 2 equilibria (or even more if the function $R \to \pi(R)$ is badly behaved).

For $r = r_1$, there are two equilibria: A is stable, and B is unstable.[10] For $r = r_2$, there is no equilibrium (in fact, a no-trade equilibrium). The equation $r = r_C$ corresponds to a critical situation: a unique equilibrium C, which vanishes as soon as there is a small increase in r. Mankiw interprets this as the possibility of a financial collapse (notice, though, that such a financial collapse may be second best efficient).

A concluding remark on this model may be of interest, even if unrelated to the macroeconomic perspective adopted here. Mankiw also shows that even when the credit market has a stable equilibrium (as in A), it does not correspond to a welfare maximum. Indeed, let $W(R)$ represent the social welfare as a function of the interest rate on credit. Since all agents are risk neutral, $W(R)$ is simply equal to the sum of excess expected returns $X - (1 + r)$ of the projects that are financed ($X \geq pR$):

$$W(R) = E\left[[(X - (1 + r)] \mathbb{1}_{\{X \geq pR\}}\right]. \tag{6.23}$$

Therefore, a small decrease in R enhances welfare if and only if, for the population of marginal borrowers (that is, the less risky, with $X = pR$), the average of excess returns $[X - (1 + r)]$ (which is also equal on that population to $pR - (1 + r)$) is positive. This is the case at the equilibrium rate R^*, since it is defined by the fact that the average of excess returns $pR - (1 + r)$ on *all* borrowers ($pR \leq X$) is zero. As a consequence, there is scope for public intervention, for example credit subsidies or loan guarantees provided by the government.

6.3.2   Financial Fragility and Economic Performance

The Model of Bernanke and Gertler (1990)

Elaborating on Boyd and Prescott (1986) (see chapter 2), Bernanke and Gertler (1990) study a two period ($t = 1, 2$) general equilibrium model, with an infinite number of agents, who can be entrepreneurs (in proportion μ) or households (in proportion $1 - \mu$). Bernanke and Gertler consider two versions of the model, one in which the type of agents is publicly observable and one in which it is not. The second version will be studied here. All agents are risk neutral and have access to a riskless (storage) technology: 1 unit of the (unique) good at $t = 1$ becomes $(1 + r)$ units at $t = 2$. The average initial endowment is normalized to 1, but that of entrepreneurs (ω_e) is less than one. Since investment requires 1 unit of the good, they will have to borrow from households.

Each entrepreneur owns a risky technology: 1 unit of the good at $t = 1$ becomes X units (at $t = 2$) with probability p, and 0 with probability $(1 - p)$. The initial wealth ω of each entrepreneur (with $E(\omega) = \omega_e$) is publicly observable, but p is unknown a priori: it is only privately observable by the entrepreneur after an "evaluation" (screening) that costs him an effort whose monetary equivalent is C. After the screening has been made, the entrepreneur decides to undertake the project (i.e., invest 1) if p is large enough.

The First Best Allocation

Obviously, the projects that are funded in the first best allocation do not depend on the distribution of initial endowments. Assume the following notations:

- $h(p)$ denotes the density function of p on $[0, 1]$ and $H(p)$ its cumulative distribution.

- $A(p_0) = E[p|p \geq p_0]$ (average success probability conditionally on $p \geq p_0$).

Among the projects that are screened, only those with a positive expected excess return will be undertaken ($pX > 1 + r$). This gives the cutoff probability p^* under which projects are not financed:

$$p^* = \frac{1+r}{X}. \tag{6.24}$$

Now screening a project (which costs the entrepreneur C) gives an option on future investment. To compute the value of this option requires determining the expected profit the firm obtains if it chooses not to screen. The value is $\max(E(p)X, 1 + r)$, but this discussion will assume that $E(p)X < 1 + r$, so that, absent screening, the firms would use the storage technology.

Now consider instead the case in which the firm screens. The firm's profit will be $E_p[\max pX, (1 + r)]$. Consequently, the value of screening is the increment of profit $V = E[\max(pX - 1, -r, 0)]$ that accrues to the firm choosing to screen. Therefore screening will take place (for all projects) if and only if

$$C < V \stackrel{\text{def}}{=} E_p[\max(0, pX - 1 - r)], \tag{6.25}$$

which will be assumed to hold true. As a consequence, all projects will be screened. Therefore the aggregate economic variables (per capita) are given by

$$I^* = \mu(1 - H(p^*)) \qquad \text{(investment)}$$
$$q^* = 1 + r + \mu(V - C) \quad \text{(output, net of screening costs)}.$$

The investment of firms is financed in part on their own wealth, $\mu\omega_e(1 - H(p^*))$, and in part by households' savings S^*, which equal the firms' demand for funds:

$$S^* = \mu(1 - \omega_e)(1 - H(p^*)).$$

The rest of initial endowments is stored: $\mu\omega_e H(p^*)$ by firms and $\{1 - \mu(1 - H(p^*))\}$ by households. This first best allocation will be implemented if all entrepreneurs have a sufficient endowment, $\omega \geq 1$.

Introducing Credit Constraints and Limited Liability

Now assume that (at least some fraction of) entrepreneurs cannot self-finance their projects ($\omega < 1$). They have to find a lender (a household) to fund the remaining part $(1 - \omega)$[11] and sign with the lender a contract specifying the repayment R in case of success. The lender knows that, because of limited liability, there will be no repayment in case of failure. It is assumed that

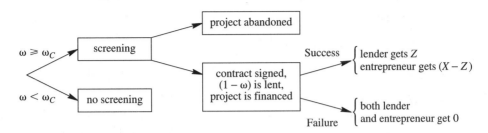

Figure 6.4
Timing in the Bernanke-Gertler (1990) Model

the contract is signed after screening takes place, that is, after the borrower observes p, but that borrowers cannot credibly communicate the value of p.

The timing is therefore as in Figure 6.4.

In this setup, a loan contract is completely described by the amount $(1 - \omega)$ to be lent and the amount R (which will depend on ω) to be repaid in case of success. The characteristics of the contract determine the minimum cutoff probability $\hat{p}(\omega)$ required by the entrepreneur to implement the project. It is given by

$$(X - R(\omega))\hat{p}(\omega) = (1 + r)\omega. \tag{6.26}$$

The equilibrium contract will be determined by 6.26 and the zero profit condition for lenders:[12]

$$A(\hat{p}(\omega))R(\omega) = (1 + r)(1 - \omega). \tag{6.27}$$

The option value of the screening technology becomes

$$V(\omega) = E_p[\max(0, p(X - R(\omega)) - (1 + r)\omega)] = \int_{\hat{p}(\omega)}^{1} (p(X - R(\omega))$$
$$- (1 + r)\omega)h(p)dp.$$

Using 6.27, $R(\omega)$ can be eliminated, and $V(\omega)$ appears to be equal to the expected surplus for p above the cutoff point $\hat{p}(\omega)$:

$$V(\omega) = E_p[(pX - (1 + r))\,\mathbb{1}_{\{p > \hat{p}(\omega)\}}] = \int_{\hat{p}(\omega)}^{1} (pX - (1 + r))h(p)dp. \tag{6.28}$$

Result 6.3   The consequences of moral hazard and limited liability are as follows:

1. There is overinvestment (among projects that have been screened):

$$\hat{p}(\omega) \leq p^* = \frac{1 + r}{X} \quad \text{(with equality when } \omega = 1).$$

2. There is a critical value ω_C of firms' wealth under which projects are not screened. ω_C is defined implicitly by $V(\omega_C) = C$.[13] Firms with $\omega < \omega_C$ will prefer to invest in the storage technology.

3. The nominal interest rate $r(\omega) \stackrel{\text{def}}{=} \frac{R(\omega)}{1-\omega}$ is a decreasing function of ω.

Proof   When $\omega = 1$, equation 6.27 implies $R(1) = 0$, and 6.26 immediately gives that $\hat{p}(1) = p^*$. All the properties stated in result 6.3 are easy consequences of the fact that $\hat{p}(\omega)$ is a nondecreasing function of ω, a property that will be proved hereafter. Indeed,

- Item 1 comes from the fact that $\hat{p}(\omega) \leq \hat{p}(1) = p^*$, or equivalently $\hat{p}(\omega)X - 1 - r < 0$.

- Item 2 comes from the fact that

$$\frac{dV}{d\omega} = -h(\hat{p}(\omega))(\hat{p}(\omega)X - 1 - r)\frac{d\hat{p}}{d\omega} > 0 \text{ (since } \hat{p}(\omega)X - r < 0),$$

and $V(1) = V > C$, by assumption.

Now for a firm with endowment ω such that $\omega < \omega_C$, the project will not be screened, and the expected return from implementing the project will be $E(p)X$, inferior to $1 + r$. Lending to the firm against a promised repayment $R(\omega)$ may be profitable only if $\frac{E(p)R(\omega)}{1-\omega} \geq 1 + r$. But in this case the firm will obtain a return from the project inferior to $1 + r$.

- Item 3 comes from equation 6.27, remembering that $p \to A(p)$ is increasing:

$$r(\omega) = \frac{1+r}{A(\hat{p}(\omega))}.$$

To establish that $\hat{p}(\omega)$ is indeed increasing, apply the implicit function theorem to the system 6.26 and 6.27:

$$\begin{cases} [X - R(\omega)]\frac{d\hat{p}}{d\omega} - \frac{dR}{d\omega}\hat{p} = 1 + r \\ A'(\hat{p})R\frac{d\hat{p}}{d\omega} + A(\hat{p})\frac{dR}{d\omega} = -1 + r. \end{cases}$$

Multiplying the first equation by $A(\hat{p})$ and the second by $\hat{p}$, and adding them, yields

$$\{A(\hat{p})\underbrace{[X - R(\omega)]}_{>0} + \underbrace{\hat{p}A'(\hat{p})R}_{>0}\}\frac{d\hat{p}}{d\omega} = 1 + r\underbrace{[A(\hat{p}) - \hat{p}]}_{>0}.$$

Therefore $\frac{d\hat{p}}{d\omega} > 0$ and the proof is complete.   ∎

To obtain a better understanding of what is underlying result 6.3, consider the benchmark case in which there is perfect information on p, so that the repayment, $R(\omega, p)$, is made contingent also on this variable. It is easy to show that, as expected, the cutoff probability is then p^*. Therefore, it is the adverse selection on p that is causing overinvestment and inefficiency. The reason this happens is that a higher p implies lower repayments, so that $R(\omega, 1) < R(\omega, p) < R(\omega, p^*)$ for $p > p^*$. If these different payments are replaced by their average $R(\omega)$, this results in taxing high probability firms and subsidizing low probability ones. As a consequence of this subsidy (due to adverse selection), low probability firms will be willing to implement the project even for low (inefficient) values of p, that is, in the range $(\hat{p}(\omega), p^*)$.

Macroeconomic Implications

This subsection will discuss the macroeconomic consequences of result 6.3 by computing the general equilibrium of this economy. Let $F(\omega)$ denote the distribution function of the firms' wealth, with associated density $f(\omega)$ and support $[\omega_0, \omega_1]$. The interesting case is when

$$\omega_0 < \omega_C < \omega_1,$$

that is, when the firms with ω between ω_0 and ω_C are actually credit constrained.

The expected output (net of screening costs) of a firm of wealth ω is

$$q(\omega) = r\omega \text{ if } \omega < \omega_C$$
$$= r\omega + V(\omega) - C \text{ if } \omega > \omega_C.$$

The aggregate economic variables (per capita) are

$$I = \mu \int_{\omega_C}^{\omega_1} (1 - H(\hat{p}(\omega))) dF(\omega) \quad \text{(investment)}$$

$$S = \mu \int_{\omega_C}^{\omega_1} (1 - \omega)(1 - H(\hat{p}(\omega))) dF(\omega) \quad \text{(households' savings)}$$

$$q = r + \mu \int_{\omega_C}^{\omega_1} (V(\omega) - C) dF(\omega) \quad \text{(output)}$$

(remember that μ denotes the proportion of entrepreneurs), to be compared with their first-best levels:

$$I^* = \mu(1 - H(p^*))$$

$$S^* = \mu(1 - \omega_e)(1 - H(p^*))$$

$$q^* = r + \mu(V - C).$$

Therefore, it appears that the global performance (output q and investment I) of this economy does not depend only on the "fundamentals" of investment (i.e., p^*, μ, V, and C) but also on the financial situation of firms (captured here by the distribution of their initial wealth ω). In particular, when many entrepreneurs have low wealth (i.e., when $F(\omega_C)$ is close to one, or ω_C close to ω_1) investment and output will be low even if the fundamentals are good. This situation is described by Bernanke and Gertler as "financial fragility." Moreover, if there is a shock on the distribution of ω such that ω_1 falls below ω_C, a *collapse* of investment will occur as a result of the poor financial condition of firms.

Bernanke and Gertler proceed to discuss the policy implications of their results. For instance, if the types of agents are not observable (the case discussed here), they show that a tax on successful investment projects (used to subsidize households) will be welfare improving. This is because entrepreneurs tend to invest in too many projects ($\hat{p}(\omega) < p^*$); therefore, by reducing the profitability of investments, a tax makes entrepreneurs more selective. However, this positive effect is counterbalanced by a reduction of the screening activity (because the value of the option is reduced by the tax). In the case in which types are observable, a more interesting welfare improving policy consists in subsidizing entrepreneurs by taxing households. This could be interpreted as bailing out debtors (as in the least developed countries [LDC] debt crisis) or as lending money to "illiquid" entrepreneurs. Bernanke and Gertler extend the interpretation of their results to justify the lender of last resort policy of the Central Bank, aimed at protecting financial institutions from liquidity shocks.

6.4   Financial Cycles and Fluctuations

This section will explore the possible explanation of business cycles and economic fluctuations that can be attributed to financial constraints or imperfections. Fluctuations of macroeconomic variables (output, investment, employment) are not surprising per se, as soon as the "fundamentals" of the economy (i.e., productivity and demand parameters) randomly fluctuate across time. However, traditional theories find it difficult to explain two qualitative properties of empirical data: macroeconomic variables seem to fluctuate much more than the fundamentals, and they typically exhibit autocorrelation and cyclical behavior, which seems to indicate that transitory shocks may have persistent effects. Understanding these phenomena is important not only as a theoretical question, but also in providing possible recommendations for economic policy. In particular these issues are crucial to explain if and how monetary and fiscal policies can have real effects both in the short run (stabilization) and in the long run (growth). Two possible explanations of financial cycles will be given in the present section: the first relies on bankruptcy constraints (Farmer 1984), and the second focuses on the role of real assets as collateral (Kiyotaki and Moore 1995).[14]

6.4.1   Bankruptcy Constraints

Farmer (1984) offers a new theory of the business cycle that combines two ingredients: imperfection of credit markets due to asymmetric information and nonexistence of a complete system of futures markets due to overlapping generations.

The Model

The model is an infinite horizon overlapping generations model, with an alternation of production periods $P_t (t = 1, 2, \ldots, \infty)$ and market periods $M_t (t = 1, 2, \ldots, \infty)$. Each agent lives for 2 production periods and 3 market periods: agents of generation t are born at M_{t-1} and die at M_{t+1}. There are two goods, labor and a consumption good that can also be used as capital and stored until the next period. Production takes place on distinct "islands" (with one worker per island and no mobility of labor but perfect mobility of capital) with a Leontief technology. If a worker on a given island receives capital k_t at period P_t, his or her net production is

$$y_t = (1 + s_t) \min(k_t, l_t) - \delta k_t l_t, \tag{6.29}$$

where $l_t \in \{0, 1\}$ denotes labor supply, $\delta > 0$ captures the depreciation of capital, and s_t (productivity shock known only by the worker) represents the realization of a random variable with density $h(s)$ on a support normalized to $[0, 1]$. These realizations are identically independently distributed across workers (islands).

At period M_{t-1}, the newly born agents (generation t) sign labor contracts with capitalists (generation $t - 1$), which specify labor supply for period P_t and the sharing of output at period M_t. Workers consume C_t^0 and invest their savings in capital (i.e., they sign labor contracts with generation $t + 1$) or in government bonds, with a guaranteed real return ρ_t. At period M_{t+1}, the generation t consume $\tilde{C}_{t+1}$, the real returns of their portfolios, and die. Preferences are represented by a utility function $u(C_t^0, E\tilde{C}_{t+1})$ where u is concave increasing.

Optimal Contracts

In a perfect world without asymmetric information, each production unit would receive one unit of capital, workers would be active exactly when $1 + s_t \geq \delta$, and they would be perfectly insured by capitalists. In other words, they would receive w when inactive and would repay $1 + s_t - w$ when active. In the imperfect world in which s_t is the private observation of the worker, the promised repayment can depend only on whether he is active or not (incentive compatibility constraint). Moreover, limited liability implies that no repayment is feasible when the worker is inactive (bankruptcy constraint). Therefore the optimal contract repayment can only take two values: the worker repays R

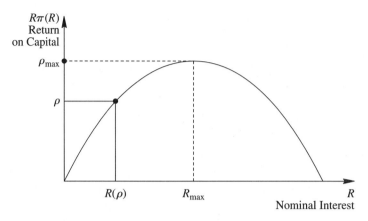

Figure 6.5
Return on Capital as a Function of the Nominal Interest Factor

(nominal interest factor) when he is active and nothing when he is not. As usual, the nominal interest rate influences the probability of repayment:

$$\pi(R) \overset{\text{def}}{=} \text{Proba}\,\{y_t \geq R\} = \text{Proba}\,\{s_t \geq \delta + R - 1\}.$$

To fix ideas, assume that workers have all the bargaining power, so that the nominal interest factor will be the minimum rate such that the lenders' expected return exceeds the gross return ρ on government bonds:

$$R(e) = \min\{x/x\pi(x) = \rho\}. \tag{6.30}$$

Thus, to some extent the situation is the same as in Mankiw (1986), in which the nominal interest rate $R(\rho)$ can be defined as above for $\rho \in [0, \rho_{\max}]$ (see Figure 6.5).

Macroeconomic Equilibrium

By the law of large numbers, the average productivity of labor over all islands is constant: it is equal to $(1 + \bar{s})$ where $\bar{s}$ is the mathematical expectation of $\tilde{s}_t$. First best optimality would require that all workers with productivities above $\delta - 1$ be active. Moreover, because of the Leontief technology and because capital has to be invested before s_t is known, there is no flexibility on capital allocation: each island should receive one unit of capital. The first best production level is therefore

$$Y^* = K \left[\int_{\delta}^{1} (1 + s - \delta)h(s)ds \right], \tag{6.31}$$

where K is the total stock of capital.

Without the bankruptcy constraint, this could be implemented by requiring workers to repay ρ regardless of whether they are active or not. Because of this bankruptcy constraint, the repayment R is exigible only if the worker is active, which distorts the participation decision. Indeed, the effective production level is a decreasing function of the nominal interest factor R:

$$Y(R) \stackrel{\text{def}}{=} K \left[\int_{\delta+R}^{1} (1 + s - \delta - R)h(s)ds \right], \tag{6.32}$$

where R is itself a function of ρ, defined by relation 6.30.

Finally, ρ is determined by the equilibrium on the asset market. At period M_t, the asset demand $a(W_t)$ of an individual member of generation t is determined by

$$\max_{a} u(\tilde{W}_t - a, \rho_{t+1}a), \tag{6.33}$$

where

$$\tilde{W}_t = \max(0, 1 + \tilde{s}_t - \delta - R(\rho_t)) \tag{6.34}$$

denotes the (random) wealth of this individual. To fix ideas, consider the following specification:

$$u(C_0, C_1) = \sqrt{C_0} + \sqrt{C_1},$$

for which the individual asset demand is easily found:

$$a \stackrel{\text{def}}{=} a(W_t) = \frac{W_t \rho_{t+1}}{1 + \rho_{t+1}}.$$

Then the aggregate asset demand at date t is

$$A(\rho_t, \rho_{t+1}) = \frac{\rho_{t+1}}{1 + \rho_{t+1}} Y(R(\rho_t)),$$

which is denoted by

$$A(\rho_t, \rho_{t+1}) = A_1(\rho_{t+1})A_2(\rho_t),$$

where A_1 is increasing and A_2 is decreasing (notice that R is increasing in ρ and Y is decreasing in R). The asset market equilibrium (which determines by Walras's law the equilibrium of the whole economy) will then be defined as a sequence $\{\rho_t^*\}_{t=0}^{\infty}$ of interest factors such that, for all t,

$$A_1(\rho_{t+1}^*)A_2(\rho_t^*) = K_t + B_t, \tag{6.35}$$

where K_t represents the stock of private capital and B_t is the stock of government debt. Because of the Leontief technology, the demand for capital is inelastic: $K_t \equiv K$. If the government adopts a stationary policy ($B_t \equiv B$), the dynamic path of equilibrium interest rates is given by

$$\rho_{t+1}^* = \psi(\rho_t^*) \stackrel{\text{def}}{=} A_1^{-1} \left[\frac{K+B}{A_2(\rho_t^*)} \right] = \frac{1}{\frac{A_2(\rho_t^*)}{K+B} - 1}. \tag{6.36}$$

Notice that, absent the bankruptcy constraint, the aggregate asset demand would be $A_1(\rho_{t+1})Y^*$ and the equilibrium interest rate would be constant:

$$A_1(\rho_{t+1})Y^* = K + B \Rightarrow \rho_{t+1} \equiv \rho \stackrel{\text{def}}{=} \frac{1}{\frac{Y^*}{K+B} - 1}.$$

Moreover, the borrowing policy of the government (which determines B_t) would affect only the (nominal) interest rate ρ_{t+1} and not the output Y^*. Because of the bankruptcy constraint, things are very different here. A positive shock on interest rates at date t can have a persistent effect, even though both the productivity of capital and the supply of financial assets ($K_t + B_t$) remain constant. This is easy to deduce from equation 6.35 (or 6.36): if ρ_t increases, the effective production level $Y[R(\rho_t)]$ decreases, which negatively affects the wealth of generation t. As a consequence, the rate of return demanded by this generation for buying the (constant) stock of assets increases. It is also interesting to notice that the borrowing policy of the government (represented here by B) has a long-term impact on the aggregate production level, since the latter depends on the steady state interest factor ρ^* determined by the equation

$$A_1(\rho^*)A_2(\rho^*) = K + B.$$

To summarize, the essence of Farmer's (1984) contribution is to point out the complex real effects of financial contracting. Once asymmetric information and limited liability are introduced, Farmer shows that today's productivity shocks will affect tomorrow's interest rates. As a consequence, real aggregate variables depend not only on current shocks but also on all the history of the past ones.

6.4.2 Credit Cycles

Kiyotaki and Moore (1995) consider an economy in which credit cycles appear because of two ingredients: some firms are credit constrained and they use their productive assets as collateral. The authors show how, borrowing possibilities being limited by collateral, small productivity shocks can trigger credit cycles. In a perfect capital market, a negative shock on the return of the productive asset would only make the value of this asset decrease until a new equilibrium is reached. But when loans are collateralized (and firms are credit constrained), the amount borrowed is determined by the value of collateral; therefore the decrease in the price of the productive asset will also have a negative impact on the firms' investment. This effect is cumulative: a decrease in the firms' investment decreases future revenues of firms, their net worth falls, and investment is decreased further until the price of the asset is so low that it starts being sold to firms that are not credit constrained, or used for other purposes.

This discussion will use a simplified version of the model of Kiyotaki and Moore, inspired by Tirole (1994). The economy is composed of (a large number of) risk neutral infinitely lived agents who seek to maximize the discounted sum of their expected consumptions (i.e., $E[\sum_{t=0}^{+\infty} \beta^t C_t]$). There are only two goods: a nonstorable physical good used for consumption and production, and a capital good (real estate) used as collateral by borrowers and also as a productive asset. There are two classes of agents: entrepreneurs who own the technology and the productive asset (say, the land), and lenders who receive endowments of the consumption good. Therefore entrepreneurs have to borrow all the consumption good they invest in their projects. The technology is of the Leontief type with constant returns to scale: with one unit of the consumption good and λ units of land invested at date t, each entrepreneur obtains X units of the consumption good at date $t + 1$.

The use of collateral can be justified in many ways. Still, the simplest one is to use Hart and Moore's (1994) idea of inalienability of human capital discussed in Chapter 4. In a one-period contract, even if the loan is riskless it must be fully collateralized to prevent renegotiation of the terms of the contract.

Assuming that the loan must be fully collateralized means in the present context that the amount of future debt cannot exceed the future value of land. If k_t is the amount of land the borrower owns during period t and q_{t+1} is the future price of land (which is perfectly forecasted by lenders), the amount of the loan b_t must be such that the borrower's total liability at date $t + 1$ ($b_t(1 + r)$, where $r = \frac{1}{\beta} - 1$ is the riskless rate) is less than the future value of collateral $k_t q_{t+1}$:

$$b_t \leq \frac{k_t q_{t+1}}{1 + r}. \tag{6.37}$$

Assume this constraint holds with equality, which corresponds to Fisher's idea of credit constrained investment.

Assume also that there is an alternative use for land; the land can be lent to another category of agents for other purposes such as residential real estate. The (inverse) demand for residential real estate determines the rental price h_t as a function of the total supply of residential real estate. Since the total stock of real estate is fixed, the rental rate h_t is an increasing function of the quantity A_t of real estate used for production. For simplicity, take a linear specification for this inverse demand function:

$$h_t = m(A_t + h_0). \tag{6.38}$$

It remains to determine A_t and the equilibrium price of the asset, q_t.

Let A denote the total stock of land available, which is assumed to be held by entrepreneurs. Since investment is credit constrained, the quantity A_t of land that is used for the productive activity is simply λ times the total amount that firms are able to borrow (i.e., $\frac{Aq_{t+1}}{1+r}$). Consequently,

$$A_t = \frac{\lambda A q_{t+1}}{1+r}.$$

Notice therefore that the aggregate borrowing capacity is determined by the future price of land q_{t+1}. The last ingredient to introduce before solving for the equilibrium dynamics is the no-arbitrage condition: the net return on land must equal the riskless rate r. This determines the relation between q_t and q_{t+1}. Indeed, by buying one unit of land at date t an entrepreneur is able to borrow a quantity $q_{t+1}/(1+r)$ of the consumption good. Investing this in the production process, she obtains a unit return of $X - (1+r)$, provided she dedicates a fraction λ of the land for production. The rest of the land $(1 - \frac{\lambda q_{t+1}}{1+r})$ is used for rental. Consequently the no-arbitrage condition yields

$$q_{t+1} + (X - (1+r))\frac{q_{t+1}}{1+r} + h_t\left(1 - \frac{\lambda q_{t+1}}{1+r}\right) = (1+r)q_t. \tag{6.39}$$

Replacing h_t by its value and rearranging terms yields

$$q_t = a q_{t+1}^2 + b q_{t+1} + c \stackrel{\text{def}}{=} \phi(q_{t+1}) \tag{6.40}$$

with

$$a = -\frac{\lambda^2}{(1+r)^3}mA; \quad b = \frac{X - \lambda_m[A - h_0]}{(1+r)^2}; \quad c = \frac{mh_0}{1+r}.$$

For a stable cycle of order 2 to obtain, two values $q_1^*, q_2^*(q_1^* \neq q_2^*)$ must be found such that

$$q_2^* = \phi(q_1^*) \quad \text{and} \quad q_1^* = \phi(q_2^*).$$

It is easy to see that the dynamical system defined by 6.40 has a stable cycle of order 2 under the following conditions (see Figure 6.6):

$$\begin{cases} 4ac + 4 < (b-1)^2 \\ c > -\frac{b+1}{a} > 0. \end{cases}$$

The economic mechanism that generates the cyclical behavior (and the stable cycle ABAB) in the neighborhood of the steady state E_1 corresponds to the debt deflation theory described by Fisher in his early contribution. Indeed, starting from E_1, assume there is a negative shock on the real estate equilibrium price that was initially q^* and becomes $q_0 < q^*$. A priori this has two impacts on the price $\phi(q)$ at which the asset will be resold during the next period (this price is given by the no-arbitrage condition): on the one hand, less profit will

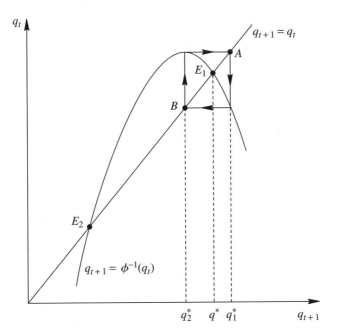

Figure 6.6
A Stable Credit Cycle. (A,B) is a stable cycle; E_1 and E_2 are steady states (E_2 is unstable).

be made on the productive activity (since the value of assets susceptible to be used as collateral decreases, the financial constraint becomes more stringent), but on the other hand, more profit will be made on the rental activity. It turns out that in a neighborhood of E_1, ϕ^{-1} is decreasing, so the first effect dominates. Moreover, on the left of q^*, $\phi^{-1}(q) > q$, so the negative shock on q^* will entail an increase in the real estate price at the next date: $q_1^* = \phi^{-1} > q^* > q_2^*$. The cyclical behavior comes from the fact that at the right of q^*, $\phi^{-1}(q) < q$, so

$$q_2^* = \phi^{-1}(q_1^*) < q^* < q_1^*.$$

In other words, once the real estate price has increased to q_1^* (that is, above the equilibrium price q^*), the second effect dominates, and q is again pulled down below q^*. The crucial element for this result is the fact that when firms are credit constrained, the demand for the productive asset is an *increasing* function of its price.

6.5   The Real Effects of Financial Intermediation

Briefly recall the features of the Holmström-Tirole (1994) model studied in Chapter 2. In the simplest version of this model, firms have to find external finance for their investment (of fixed size I), but there is a moral hazard problem:

firms' managers may choose a bad project (with a low probability of success p_L) instead of a good project (with a high probability of success p_H) because the bad project gives them a private benefit B. However, if the firm is monitored by a bank, and the monitoring costs C, this private benefit is decreased to b, with $b + C < B$. The moral hazard problem can be solved without monitoring if firms have enough cash assets A that they can invest in their projects. This happens when condition 2.33 of Chapter 2 (recalled for convenience) is satisfied:

$$A \geq \bar{A}(\rho) = I - \frac{p_H}{\rho}\left(R - \frac{B}{p_H - p_L}\right). \tag{6.41}$$

Here R denotes the repayment on the loan in case of success and ρ is the return (1+ interest rate) that investors can obtain on the financial markets. If the firm's assets are not worth enough, so that 6.41 is not satisfied, the moral hazard problem may be solved by bank lending: a bank lends I_m to the firm, which is financed partly by its own funds and partly by borrowing $I - I_m - A$ on the financial markets. This happens when

$$\underline{A}(\beta, \rho) \leq A < \bar{A}(\rho),$$

where β denotes the gross return (one plus net return) on bank loans, and recalling 2.36,

$$\underline{A}(\beta, \rho) = I - I_m(\beta) - \frac{p_H}{\rho}\left[R - \frac{b + C}{p_H - p_L}\right], \tag{6.42}$$

with

$$I_m(\beta) = \frac{p_H C}{\beta(p_H - p_L)}.$$

Finally, β is determined by the equilibrium equation of the market for banking capital:

$$K_m = [G(\bar{A}(\rho)) - G(\underline{A}(\beta, \rho))]I_m(\beta). \tag{6.43}$$

Here G is the distribution function of the firms' assets A, and $I_m(\beta)$ equals the portion of each loan that is financed by the bank's own wealth, while ρ is determined by the equilibrium condition on the financial market: the savings supply $S(\rho)$ equals the demand for funds $D(\beta, \rho, C)$, defined by

$$D(\beta, \rho, C) = \int_{\underline{A}(\beta, \rho)}^{\bar{A}(\rho)} (I - I_m - A)f(A)dA + \int_{\bar{A}(\rho)}^{\bar{A}} (I - A)f(A)dA. \tag{6.44}$$

Figure 6.7 represents the segmentation of firms into three categories: those that cannot find external finance, those that obtain bank loans, and those that are funded directly in the financial markets.

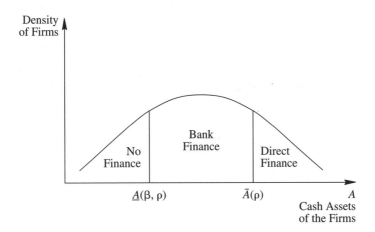

Figure 6.7
Repartition between the Two Types of Finance among Firms

Holmström and Tirole consider three types of financial shocks: a *credit crunch* (which corresponds to a decrease in K_m, the capital of the banking industry), a *collateral squeeze* (which corresponds to a negative shock on firms' assets), and a *savings squeeze* (which corresponds to a downward shift in the function S). They show in particular the following properties:

Result 6.4 Let ρ and β denote the equilibrium returns on financial markets and on bank loans, respectively. Then:

- A credit crunch decreases ρ and increases β.
- A collateral squeeze decreases ρ and β.
- A savings squeeze increases ρ and decreases β.

Proof The proof is easily deduced from 6.44 and is left to the reader. ∎

6.6 Financial Structure and Economic Development

The empirical relationship between financial structure and economic development has been studied by many authors, who have emphasized the strong positive correlation between the level of financial "superstructure" and the rate of growth of the economy. In fact, if it is argued that financial intermediation can be justified on efficiency grounds (as was done in Chapter 2), then economic development and the level of financial intermediation will reinforce one another. Understanding this is crucial to assess the different contributions in the recent theoretical literature on the macroeconomic effects of financial intermediation.

Of course, the general idea that growth is related to financial structure is not a new one, since it goes back at least to Schumpeter (1961) and Gerschenkron (1992). Nevertheless, the specific results that have been obtained more recently are based precisely on the asymmetric information hypothesis explored previously. Therefore, although this is not a topic that will be developed here, the reader may be interested in exploring the work of Greenwood and Jovanovic (1990) and Bencivenga and Smith (1991), which are classical references.

Both models show that financial intermediaries tend to stimulate growth. In Greenwood and Jovanovic intermediation arises endogenously, and as in Boyd and Prescott (1986), the role of intermediaries is to screen the projects. If the return is sufficiently high, the investment is realized; otherwise the intermediary invests only in safe assets. In this way, the existence of financial intermediaries results in a better screening of projects, which fosters a higher rate of growth. The model of Bencivenga and Smith is more in line with the liquidity insurance models of Diamond and Dybvig (1983). In these models, financial intermediation not only facilitates the allocation of savings to productive investments, but also leads to a lower rate of unnecessary project liquidation, which improves efficiency and promotes growth.

Sussman and Zeira (1995) extend the delegated monitoring model of Diamond (1984) by including an element of horizontal differentiation, namely transportation costs. They show that this can be the source of a feedback effect between real economic development and financial development. They test their model on U.S. cross-state aggregate banking data, and show that the cost of financial intermediation is indeed lower in states with higher output per capita. For an interesting survey of the relations between financial intermediation and economic development, see King and Levine (1993).

Notes

1. Chapter 3 showed that the industrial organization of the banking sector could have a strong influence on these mechanisms.

2. In addition to already-cited textbooks on money, an excellent recent reference is Schnadt (1993).

3. This model is the same as the one developed in Chapter 3, subsection 3.1.1.

4. Investment could also depend on y, without changing the reasoning.

5. If G is held constant, the budget constraint of the government (equation 6.5) implies that any increase in R is accompanied by an equal decrease in B^g.

6. This approach can be justified by the arguments developed in Chapters 2 and 4.

7. This complex effect of money on interest rates is also analyzed in a different setting by Fuerst (1992).

8. Compare these assumptions with A1 through A3 in subsection 6.2.1.

9. These equations were numbered 3.10 and 3.11 in Chapter 3.

10. Notice that there are two equilibria because of the assumption that banks are price takers. If the discussion assumed instead, as in the Stiglitz-Weiss model, that banks are price setters, then

only A would remain an equilibrium. By quoting a rate just smaller than the one corresponding to B, a bank could obtain a positive profit.

11. The cost of screening is assumed to be nonmonetary. That is, C is the monetary equivalent of the cost of effort needed for screening projects.

12. Notice that when $\omega < 1$, $\hat{p}(\omega)$ is different from the best cutoff $p^* = \frac{r}{X}$. Indeed, if $\hat{p}(\omega)$ was equal to p^*, 6.26 would imply $p^* R(\omega) = r(1 - \omega)$, which should be equal to $A(p^*)R(\omega)$ according to 6.27. Since $A(p^*) > p^*$, this is possible only when $R(\omega) = 1 - \omega = 0$, contradicting $\omega < 1$.

13. When $V(0) \geq C$, all projects are screened. This discussion focuses on the more interesting case in which $C > V(0)$.

14. Related alternative explanations are given by Scheinkman and Weiss (1986), Williamson (1987), and Bernanke and Gertler (1989).

References

Bencivenga, V. R., and B. D. Smith. 1991. Financial intermediation and endogenous growth. *Review of Economic Studies* 58(2):195–209.

Bernanke, B. 1983. Non monetary effects of the financial crisis in propagation of the great depression. *American Economic Review* 73(3):257–76.

———. 1986. Alternative explanations of the money-income correlation. *Carnegie Rochester Conference Series on Public Policy* 25(0):49–99.

Bernanke, B., and A. Blinder. 1987. Banking and macroeconomic equilibrium. In *New approaches to monetary economics,* edited by W. Barnett and K. Singleton. Cambridge: Cambridge University Press.

———. 1988. Credit, money and aggregate demand. *American Economic Review* 78(2):435–39.

Bernanke, B., and M. Gertler. 1987. Banking in general equilibrium. In *New approaches to monetary economics,* edited by W. Barnett and K. Singleton. Cambridge: Cambridge University Press.

———. 1989. Agency cost, net worth and business fluctuations. *American Economic Review* 79(1):14–31.

———. 1990. Financial fragility and economic performance. *Quarterly Journal of Economics* 105(1):87–114.

Bernanke, B., and H. James. 1991. The gold standard, deflation, and financial crisis in the great depression: An international comparison. In *Financial markets and financial crises: A National Bureau of Economic Research Project report,* edited by R. Hubbard. Chicago: University of Chicago Press.

Boyd, J., and E. Prescott. 1986. Financial intermediary coalitions. *Journal of Economic Theory* 38(2):211–32.

Cook, T., and T. Rowe. 1986. *Instruments of the money market,* 6th edition. Richmond, Va.: Federal Reserve Bank of Richmond.

Diamond, D. 1984. Financial intermediation and delegated monitoring. *Review of Economic Studies* 51(3):393–414.

Diamond, D., and P. Dybvig. 1983. Bank runs, deposit insurance, and liquidity. *Journal of Political Economy* 91(3):401–19.

Farmer, R. 1984. New theory of aggregate supply. *American Economic Review* 74(5):920–30.

Fisher, I. 1933. The debt-deflation theory of great depressions. *Econometrica,* no. 1 (October):337–57.

Friedman, M., and A. Schwartz. 1963. *A monetary history of the United States, 1867–1960.* Princeton, N.J.: Princeton University Press.

Fuerst, T. 1992. Liquidity, loanable funds, and real activity. *Journal of Monetary Economics* 29(1):3–24.

Gerschenkron, A. 1992. Economic backwardness in historical perspective. In *The sociology of economic life,* edited by M. Granovetter and R. Swedberg. Boulder, Colo.: Westview Press. Article first published in 1952.

Gertler, M. 1988. Financial structure and aggregate economic activity: An overview. *Journal of Money, Credit, and Banking* 20(3):559–88.

Gertler, M., and S. Gilchrist. 1992. Monetary policy, business cycles and the behavior of small manufacturing firms. New York University Economic Research Report, 92-108. New York: New York University.

Goldsmith, R. 1969. *Financial structure and development.* New Haven: Yale University Press.

Gorton, G., and G. Penacchi. 1990. Financial innovation and the provision of liquidity services. Wharton School, Pittsburgh, Pa. Mimeograph.

Greenwood, J., and B. Jovanovic. 1990. Financial development, growth and the distribution of income. *Journal of Political Economy* 98(5):1076–1107.

Grimaud, A. 1994. Intermédiation financière, politique de base, politique de taux et monnaie endogène: Un modèle synthétique. GREMAQ-IDEI, University of Toulouse. Mimeograph.

Gurley, J., and E. Shaw. 1955. Financial aspects of economic development. *American Economic Review* 65:515–38.

————. 1960. *Money in the theory of finance.* Washington, D.C.: Brookings Institution.

Hart, O., and J. Moore. 1994. A theory of debt based on the inalienability of human capital. *Quarterly Journal of Economics* 109(4):841–79.

Holmström, B., and J. Tirole. 1994. Financial intermediation, loanable funds and the real sector. Working paper, IDEI, University of Toulouse.

Hoshi, T., A. Kashyap, and D. Scharfstein. 1991. Corporate structure, liquidity, and investment: Evidence from Japanese industrial groups. *Quarterly Journal of Economics* 106(1):33–60.

James, C. 1987. Some evidence on the uniqueness of bank loans. *Journal of Financial Economics* 19(2):217–326.

Kashyap, A., and J. Stein. 1993. Monetary policy and bank lending. Working paper no. 4317, National Bureau of Economic Research, Cambridge.

Kashyap, A., J. C. Stein, and D. W. Wilcox. 1993. Monetary policy and credit conditions: Evidence from the composition of external finance. *American Economic Review* 83(1):79–98.

King, R. G., and R. Levine. 1993. Financial intermediation and economic development. In *Capital markets and financial intermediation,* edited by C. Mayer and X. Vives. Cambridge: Cambridge University Press.

King, S. 1986. Monetary transmission: Through bank loans or bank liabilities? *Journal of Money, Credit, and Banking* 18(3):290–303.

Kiyotaki, N., and J. Moore. 1995. Credit cycles. Discussion paper no. 205, Financial Market Group, London School of Economics.

Mankiw, G. 1986. The allocation of credit and financial collapse. *Quarterly Journal of Economics* 101(3):455–70.

Mishkin, F. 1978. The household balance sheet and the great depression. *Journal of Economic History* 38(4):918–37.

Modigliani, F., and M. Miller. 1958. The cost of capital, corporation finance and the theory of investment. *American Economic Review* 68(June):261–97.

Rajan, R. 1992. Insiders and outsiders: The choice between relationship and arm's length debt. *Journal of Finance* 47(1):1367–1400.

Ramey, V. 1992. How important is the credit channel of monetary transmission. University of California, San Diego. Mimeograph.

Romer, C. D., and D. H. Romer. 1990. New evidence on the monetary transmission mechanism. In *Brookings papers on economic activity,* Vol. 1, 149–98.

Roosa, R. V. 1951. Interest rates and the central bank. In *Money, trade and economic growth: Essays in honor of John H. Williams.* New York: MacMillan.

Scheinkman, J., and L. Weiss. 1986. Borrowing constraints and aggregate economic activity. *Econometrica* 54(1):23–45.

Schnadt, N. 1993. The domestic money markets of the UK, France, Germany and the US. FMG, London School of Economics. Duplicated.

Schreft, S. L. 1990. Credit controls: 1980. *Economic Review* (Federal Reserve Bank of Richmond) 76(6):25–55.

Schumpeter, J. 1961. The theory of economic development, translated by R. Opie. 1934. Reprint, New York: Oxford University Press.

Sharpe, S. 1990. Asymmetric information, bank lending and implicit contracts: A stylized model of customer relationships. *Journal of Finance* 45(4):1069–87.

Slovin, M., M. Sushka, and J. Polonchek. 1993. The value of bank durability: Borrowers as bank stakeholders. *Journal of Finance* 48(1):247–66.

Stiglitz, J., and L. Weiss. 1981. Credit rationing in markets with imperfect information. *American Economic Review* 71(June):393–410.

Sussman, O., and J. Zeira. 1995. Banking and development. Discussion paper no. 1127, Centre for Economic Policy Research, London.

Tirole, J. 1994. Lecture notes. IDEI, Toulouse.

Williamson, S. D. 1987. Financial intermediation, business failures, and real business cycles. *Journal of Political Economy* 95(6):1196–216.

Bank panics were a recurrent phenomenon in the United States until 1934. Indeed, because of its decentralized regulation, the U.S. market has quite a record of bank failures, individual bank runs, and generalized bank panics. According to Kemmerer (1910), the country experienced 21 bank panics between 1890 and 1908. Similarly, Friedman and Schwartz (1963) enumerate 5 bank panics between 1929 and 1933,[1] the most severe period in the financial history of the United States. Miron (1986) extensively documents this phenomenon, recalling its seasonal pattern prior to the founding of the Federal Reserve System (the Fed), and providing some impressive figures: during the period 1890 through 1908, he estimates the probability of a bank panic in a given year to be almost one in three. Morever, whereas the average yearly growth rate of real gross national product (GNP) was 3.75 during this period, Miron finds that if the years in which a bank panic occurred (or following a bank panic) are taken out of the sample,[2] the average growth rate becomes 6.82 percent.

Similar phenomena affected England before the establishment of a Central Bank, as well as other European countries (Bordo 1990, Eichengreen and Portes 1987). Therefore, it seems that without regulation, bank runs and bank panics are inherent to the nature of banking, and more specifically to the fractional reserve system. Indeed, bank deposit contracts usually allow depositors to dispose of a nominal amount on demand. As soon as a fraction of these deposits is used for financing illiquid and risky loans or investments, there is a possibility of a liquidity crisis. The natural questions this chapter will try to answer are whether such deposit contracts are efficient and whether the fractional reserve system is justified, *in spite of the possibility of bank runs*.

Most theoretical models have addressed this question in an aggregate framework, representing the whole banking industry by a unique entity. However, it is important to distinguish between *bank runs*, which affect an individual bank, and *bank panics*, which concern the whole banking industry, and as a consequence the payment system.[3]

The conventional explanation for a bank run is that when depositors observe large withdrawals from their bank, they fear bankruptcy and respond by withdrawing their own deposits. Withdrawals in excess of the current expected demand for liquidity generate a negative externality for the bank experiencing the liquidity shortage, since they imply an increase in the bank's probability of failure. But they can also generate an externality for the whole banking system if the agents view the failure as a symptom of difficulties occuring throughout the industry.

In such a case, a bank run may develop into a bank panic. Bagehot (1873) was one of the first to analyze how the Central Bank could prevent such contagion by playing the part of a Lender of Last Resort. The last section of this chapter is devoted to this question. The other sections are organized as follows: Section 7.1 will recall the model of liquidity insurance presented in

Section 2.2, and Section 7.2 will introduce a fractional reserve banking system. Section 7.3 will study the stability of this fractional reserve system and other institutional arrangements. Section 7.4 will study cases in which bank runs can be efficient. Section 7.5 will be dedicated to the management of idiosyncratic liquidity shocks, whereas Section 7.6 will examine that of nondiversifiable liquidity shocks.

7.1   Banking Deposits and Liquidity Insurance

This section will recall the simple model of liquidity insurance (inspired by Bryant 1980, 1981, and Diamond and Dybvig 1983) introduced in Chapter 2. It will then discuss different institutional arrangements that can provide this liquidity insurance to individual economic agents.

7.1.1   A Model of Liquidity Insurance

Consider a one-good, three-period economy in which a continuum of agents, each endowed with one unit of good at date $t = 0$, want to consume at dates $t = 1$ and $t = 2$. These agents are ex-ante identical, but they are subject to independently identically distributed liquidity shocks in the following sense: with some probability $\pi_i (i = 1, 2,$ with $\pi_1 + \pi_2 = 1)$, they need to consume at date $t = i$. The utility of agents of type $i = 1$ (impatient consumers) is $u(C_1)$, whereas that of agents type $i = 2$ (patient consumers) is $\rho u(C_2)$ where $\rho < 1$ is a discount factor. Ex ante all agents have the same utility:

$$U = \pi_1 u(C_1) + \rho \pi_2 u(C_2). \tag{7.1}$$

Assume that u is increasing and concave.

There is a storage technology that allows transfer of the good without cost from one date to another. More importantly, there is also a long-term illiquid technology (with constant returns to scale): one unit invested at $t = 0$ gives a return $R > 1$ at $t = 2$. The term "illiquid" reflects the fact that investments in this long-term technology give a low return $L < 1$ if they are liquidated prematurely at $t = 1$. This section will determine the characteristics of the optimal (symmetric) allocation. It will begin by studying two benchmarks: the autarkic situation and the allocation obtained when a financial market is opened.

7.1.2   Autarky

Autarky corresponds to the absence of trade between agents. Each of them independently chooses at $t = 0$ the level I of his investment in the long-term technology and stores the rest (i.e., $1 - I$). In the case of a liquidity shock at date $t = 1$, the investment is liquidated, yielding a consumption level

$$C_1 = LI + 1 - I. \tag{7.2}$$

In the case of a liquidity shock at date $t = 2$, the consumption level obtained is

$$C_2 = RI + 1 - I. \tag{7.3}$$

At date $t = 0$, consumers choose I so as to maximize U under constraints 7.2 and 7.3. Notice that, since $L < 1 < R$, then $C_1 \leq 1$ and $C_2 \leq R$, with at least one strict inequality. This comes from the fact that the investment decision is always ex-post inefficient with a positive probability: if $i = 1$ the efficient decision is $I = 0$, whereas it is $I = 1$ if $i = 2$. This inefficiency can be mitigated by opening a financial market.

7.1.3   The Allocation Obtained When a Financial Market Is Opened

Suppose that a bond market is opened at $t = 1$, whereby p units of good at $t = 1$ are exchanged against the promise to receive one unit of good at $t = 2$. The consumption levels obtained by each consumer at dates 1 and 2 become

$$C_1 = pRI + 1 - I \tag{7.4}$$

and

$$C_2 = RI + \frac{1-I}{p}. \tag{7.5}$$

In the first case, the impatient agent has sold RI bonds (instead of liquidating his long-term investment), whereas in the second case the patient agent has bought $\frac{1-I}{p}$ bonds at $t = 1$ (instead of storing the good for another period). Notice that $C_1 = pC_2$ and that the utility of the agent can have only a nontrivial maximum when $pR = 1$. Therefore the equilibrium price of bonds is $p = \frac{1}{R}$ and the allocation obtained is $C_1 = 1$, $C_2 = R$, which Pareto dominates the autarkic allocation. This is because the existence of a financial market ensures that the investment decisions are efficient. However, this market allocation is not Pareto optimal in general, because liquidity risk is not properly allocated.

7.1.4   The Optimal (Symmetric) Allocation

Agents being ex-ante identical, it is legitimate to focus on the (unique) symmetric optimal allocation obtained by

$$\mathcal{P}_1 \begin{cases} \max_{C_1,C_2,I} U = \pi_1 u(C_1) + \rho \pi_2 u(C_2) \\ \text{under the constraints} \\ \pi_1 C_1 = 1 - I & (7.6) \\ \pi_2 C_2 = RI. & (7.7) \end{cases}$$

Replacing C_1 and C_2 by their values given by 7.6 and 7.7, U becomes a function of the single variable I:

$$U(I) = \pi_1 u \left(\frac{1 - I}{\pi_1} \right) + \rho \pi_2 u \left(\frac{RI}{\pi_2} \right).$$

The solution (C_1^*, C_2^*, I^*) of $\mathcal{P}_1$ is thus determined by the constraints 7.6 and 7.7 and the first order condition:

$$-u'(C_1^*) + \rho R u'(C_2^*) = 0. \tag{7.8}$$

In general, the market allocation $(C_1 = 1,\ C_2 = R,\ I = \pi_2)$ does not satisfy 7.8 (except in the peculiar case in which $u'(1) = \rho R u'(R)$). An interesting situation arises when $u'(1) > \rho R u'(R)$.[4] In this case, impatient consumers get more in the optimal allocation than in the market equilibrium ($C_1^* > 1$): they need to be insured against a liquidity shock at $t = 1$. The next section will show how a fractional reserve banking system can provide this liquidity insurance.

7.2   A Fractional Reserve Banking System

This section will study how the optimal allocation characterized in the previous seciton can be implemented by a fractional reserve banking system in which banks collect the endowments of consumers (deposits) and invest a fraction of them in long-term investments while offering depositors the possibility of withdrawal on demand. A deposit contract (C_1, C_2) specifies the amounts C_1 and C_2 that can be withdrawn respectively at dates $t = 1, 2$ for a unit deposit at $t = 0$. Competition between banks leads them to offer the optimal feasible deposit contract (C_1^*, C_2^*) characterized earlier. A crucial question is whether this fractional reserve system is stable, that is, whether the banks will be able to fulfill their contractual obligations. This depends very much on the behavior of patient consumers, which in turn depends on their anticipations about the safety of their bank.

Consider first the case of a patient consumer who anticipates that the bank will be able to fulfill its obligations. The consumer has the choice between withdrawing C_2^* at date $t = 2$ or withdrawing C_1^* at date $t = 1$ and storing it until $t = 2$. Equation 7.8 shows that

$$C_2^* \geq C_1^* \Leftrightarrow \rho R \geq 1.$$

Therefore if $\rho R < 1$ there is no hope of implementing the optimal allocation through a deposit contract; such a contract will always be destabilized by the early withdrawal of patient consumers. This discussion will concentrate on the more interesting opposite case, $\rho R \geq 1$. If the patient consumer trusts her bank, she will always prefer to withdraw at $t = 2$. By the law of large numbers, the proportion of withdrawals at $t = 1$ will be exactly π_1. This determines the amount $\pi_1 C_1^*$ of liquid reserves that the bank has to make in order to avoid premature liquidation. With these reserves, the bank will be solvent with probability one and the consumers' expectations will be fulfilled. Thus there is an equilibrium of the banking economy that implements the optimal allocation. However, another equilibrium also exists, which leads to an inefficient allocation.

Suppose the patient consumer anticipates that all other patient consumers want to withdraw at $t = 1$. The bank will be forced to liquidate its long-term investments, yielding a total value of assets $\pi_1 C_1^* + (1 - \pi_1 C_1^*)L$, which is clearly less than the total value of its liabilities (i.e., C_1^*). In the absence of other institutional arrangements, the bank will fail and nothing will be left at $t = 2$. In this case the optimal strategy for a patient consumer is to withdraw at $t = 1$, which means that the initial expectations of the consumer are self-fulfilling. In other words, there is a second Nash equilibrium[5] of the withdrawal game in which all consumers withdraw at $t = 1$ and the bank is liquidated: this is what is called an inefficient bank run.

Result 7.1   In a fractional reserve banking system in which investment returns are high enough ($R > 1/\rho$), two possible situations may arise at equilibrium:

1. An efficient allocation, when patient depositors trust the bank and withdraw only at $t = 2$

2. An inefficient bank run, when all depositors withdraw at $t = 1$.

7.3   The Stability of the Fractional Reserve System and Alternative Institutional Arrangements

7.3.1   The Causes of Instability

As was just shown, the fractional reserve banking system leads to an optimal allocation only if patient consumers do not withdraw early. There are two reasons why they might want to withdraw:

1. If the relative return of date 2 deposits with respect to date 1 deposits (i.e., $C_2^*/C_1^* - 1$) is less than what they can obtain elsewhere, either by storage (as in the present model) or more generally by reinvesting in financial markets as in Von Thadden (1995), then patient depositors will prefer to withdraw early. If consumers' types were observable, this could be avoided by forbidding patient consumers to withdraw early. In practice, however, liquidity needs are not publicly observable, and incentive compatibility constraints must be

introduced. In a continuous time extension of the Bryant-Diamond-Dybvig model, Von Thadden (1995) shows that these incentive compatibility constraints are *always* binding somewhere, which severely limits the provision of liquidity insurance that can be obtained through a fractional reserve banking system.

2. The literature has paid more attention to a second cause of instability, arising from the fact that the game between depositors has two equilibria, one efficient and one inefficient. The inefficient equilibrium arises only when there is a coordination failure among depositors, coming from a lack of confidence in their bank. In any case, theoreticians dislike multiple equilibria, and they have tried to offer selection devices. For instance, Anderlini (1989) suggests a recourse to exogenous uncertainty ("sun-spots") to determine which equilibrium will prevail. This might explain sudden confidence crises in real-world banking systems. On the other hand, Postlewaite and Vives (1987) suggest that some agents may observe signals that give them some information about the likelihood of a bank run (see problem 7.8.2): these are "information-based" bank runs. The following subsections will discuss several institutional arrangements that have been proposed to solve the instability problem of the fractional reserve system.

7.3.2   A First Remedy to Instability: Narrow Banking

A natural way to prevent the instability of the banking system is to require that *under any possible circumstance* all banks can fulfill their contractual obligations. This is guaranteed, for instance, if the bank is required to have a reserve ratio of 100 percent, which means that its liquid reserves $(1 - I)$ are at least equal to C_1, the maximum possible amount of withdrawals at date 1.[6] This is in line with the narrow bank proposal (discussed in detail in Chapter 9), according to which the maturity structure of banks' assets should be perfectly matched with that of their liabilities. In the present context, this means that the deposit contract (C_1, C_2) offered by the bank must satisfy $C_1 \leq 1 - I$ and $C_2 \leq RI$. Eliminating I yields the "budget constraint" that a narrow bank must satisfy:

$$C_1 + \frac{C_2}{R} \leq 1.$$

This is clearly much more restrictive than the constraints on a bank allowed to perform the maturity transformation activity:

$$\pi_1 C_1 + \pi_2 \frac{C_2}{R} \leq 1.$$

It is even more restrictive than the budget constraint associated with autarky:

$$(R - 1)C_1 + (1 - L) \leq R - L.$$

The best deposit contract (C_1, C_2) that can offer such a narrow bank is defined by

$$\mathcal{P}_2 \begin{cases} \max_{I,C_1,C_2} U = \pi_1 u(C_1) + \rho \pi_2 u(C_2) \\ \text{under the constraints} \\ C_1 \leq 1 - I, C_2 \leq RI. \end{cases}$$

As remarked by Wallace (1988, 1996), the solution of $\mathcal{P}_2$ is obviously dominated by that of $\mathcal{P}_1$. In fact, it is even dominated by the autarkic situation, which will be obtained if a milder version of the narrow banking proposal is adopted, in which the banks are allowed to liquidate some of their assets in order to satisfy unexpected withdrawals. If the bank has offered the deposit contract (C_1, C_2), the amount I invested in the long-term technology now must be such that

$$C_1 \leq LI + (1 - I)$$

(i.e., the liquidation value of the bank's assets at $t = 1$ covers the maximum possible amount of withdrawals). Similarly, at $t = 2$,

$$C_2 \leq RI + 1 - I,$$

which means a return to the autarkic situation. Finally, the more modern (and weaker) version of narrow banking suggests replacing banks by money market funds that use the deposits they collect to buy (riskless) financial securities. It is easy to see that the best deposit contract that can be offered by such a money market fund is the market equilibrium that was characterized in subsection 7.1.2. Therefore, even with the milder version of money market funds (or "monetary service companies"), the narrow banking proposal is exactly antagonistic to the efficient provision of liquidity insurance. It remains to see whether this efficient provision can be obtained under institutional arrangements that would guarantee the stability of the banking system.

7.3.3   Regulatory Responses: Suspension of Convertibility or Deposit Insurance

If liquidity shocks are perfectly diversifiable and if the proportion[7] π_1 of impatient consumers is known, it is easy to get rid of the coordination problem that gives rise to inefficient bank runs. For instance, the bank could announce that it will not serve more than $\pi_1 C_1^*$ withdrawals at date $t = 1$. After this threshold, convertibility is suspended. Patient consumers therefore know that the bank will be able to satisfy its engagements at date 2 and thus they have no interest in withdrawing at date 1. The threat of a bank run disappears.[8]

An equivalent way to get rid of inefficient bank runs is to insure depositors. In this case, even if the bank is not able to fulfill its obligations depositors receive the full value of their deposits, the difference being paid by a new institution, the Deposit Insurance System, financed by insurance premiums paid ex ante by the bank (or by taxes, if the system is publicly run). In the present simple framework, the existence of deposit insurance is enough to get rid of bank failures, which means that the Deposit Insurance System never has to intervene and that the insurance premiums are actually nil. Still, it is worth noting that the effects of deposit insurance may be more difficult to analyze in a three-period model with moral hazard, such as Freeman's (1988).

The equivalence between these two systems breaks down as soon as one allows for a variability of the proportion π_i. In that case, the equilibrium without bank runs is characterized by a random amount of period 1 withdrawals. But since the level of investment has been already chosen, if the realized value of π_1 is too high, the investment in the long-run technology will have to be liquidated at a loss. Consequently the bank will not be able to meet its obligations during period 2. On the other hand, if π_1 is too low, the level of investment is also too low, and again period 2 depositors will not obtain the promised return. More generally, any type of regulation that is intended to cope with random withdrawals will have to take into account the fact that period 2 returns are contingent on period 1 withdrawals. In such a case it is inefficient to set a critical level of liquidity demand (i.e., type 1 deposits) that triggers the suspension of convertibility. If this level is $\hat{f}$, a realization of π_1 with $\pi_1 > \hat{f}$ implies that type 1 agents will be rationed. Conversely, a realization with $\pi_1 < \hat{f}$ implies that a bank run may still develop, since type 2 agents are actually too numerous in relation to the promised return, given the amount the bank has invested. Thus, even if it is true that the suspension of convertibility will eliminate bank runs, it will do so at a cost, since the deposit contracts will then be less efficient as a risk-sharing instrument.

Deposit insurance, on the contrary, will allow for a contingent allocation. For instance, if the Deposit Insurance System is publicly run and financed by taxes, the government can levy a tax based on the realization of π_1. If the analysis is restricted to the case in which no discrimination is allowed, so that the tax rate will be the same across agents (which will lead to an inferior allocation of risks), this tax can be interpreted as resulting from the adjustment of the period 1 price of the good (inflationary tax). Of course, as pointed out by Wallace (1988) this is only possible if the potential taxpayers have not already consumed the good.

7.3.4   Jacklin's Proposal: Equity versus Deposits

Since a demand deposit economy achieves better risk sharing than a market economy but is vulnerable to bank runs, it is interesting to investigate whether other contractual arrangements achieve the same allocations without being prone to bank runs. Jacklin (1987) has shown that sometimes equity can do as well as deposit contracts.

Instead of the mutual bank of the previous section, consider a banking firm distributing a dividend d during period 1. Its shares can be traded during period 1, once agents know their types. Each share gives a right to $R(1-d)$ consumption units at time 2. The price p of the ex-dividend share in terms of period 1 consumption good will be given by the market equilibrium, but this will depend on d. Therefore, changing the value of d affects the period 1 utilities of the agents, so that this mechanism will also allow for some improvement of the ex-ante expected utility with respect to the market economy.

In an equity economy with dividend d and a price p for the ex-dividend share, the behavior of each type of agent is easy to determine. Type 1 agents (impatient consumers) receive their dividend and sell their share,

$$C_1 = d + p, \tag{7.9}$$

whereas type 2 agents (patient consumers) use their dividend d to buy $\frac{d}{p}$ new shares, which gives them, at date $t = 2$,

$$C_2 = (1 + \frac{d}{p})R(1-d). \tag{7.10}$$

The price p is determined by equality of supply and demand of shares:

$$\pi_1 = \pi_2 \frac{d}{p}, \tag{7.11}$$

which gives $p = \frac{\pi_2 d}{\pi_1}$ and

$$C_1 = \frac{d}{\pi_1}, \quad C_2 = \frac{R(1-d)}{\pi_2}. \tag{7.12}$$

Finally, the level of d is determined ex ante (at $t = 0$) by stockholders, who unanimously choose it so as to maximize U under the constraints 7.12. Eliminating d between these constraints yields the same "budget constraint" as for deposit contracts:

$$\pi_1 C_1 + \pi_2 \frac{C_2}{R} = 1.$$

Therefore, in the particularly simple specification adopted here, the second best optimum (C_1^*, C_2^*) can also be obtained by "participation" contracts in which consumers are stockholders of the bank instead of depositors. The advantage of these participation contracts is that they are immune to bank runs. However, for more general specifications of agent utilities, Jacklin shows that equity contracts can be dominated by efficient deposit contracts, yielding a trade-off between stability and efficiency, since deposit contracts can be destabilized by bank runs. The reason for this domination is that equity contracts are necessarily *coalitionally incentive compatible* in the sense that they are immune to early withdrawals (deviations) of *coalitions* of patient consumers, whereas deposit contracts are only *individually incentive compatible*. If agents are allowed to trade their deposit contracts, these contracts become equivalent to equity contracts.

This discussion illustrates that the explicative power of the Bryant-Diamond-Dybvig theory of liquidity insurance depends heavily on the implicit assumption of a limited access of agents to financial markets. In a recent contribution, Holmström and Tirole (1996) offer a new theory of liquidity provision by banks that does not suffer from this drawback.

7.4   Efficient Bank Runs

In the models examined up to now, the investment returns are certain. This implies that bank runs have a purely speculative origin. Yet, not only is it reasonable to think that leakage of bad performance of bank loan portfolios should trigger bank runs, but also the empirical evidence on bank runs seems to point in that direction. Thus, bank runs could also have a fundamental origin, motivated by the expectation of poor performance of the banks.

To understand fundamental bank runs, there is no need to model explicitly the chain of events that trigger a fundamental bank run when agents uniformly perceive a "bad" signal on the bank return during period 1: type 2 agents will then choose between the two types of contracts that are offered, knowing that the period 2 withdrawal will be lower than what has been promised. They will all prefer the contract with the higher period 1 return. As Jacklin and Bhattacharya (1988) state, the information on future returns modifies the relevant incentive compatible constraint, and therefore agents of type 2 may prefer the type 1 deposit. As such, a bank run would not be very different from the bankruptcy of a firm, and would occur because the bank is worth more dead than alive. The interesting issue arises when both speculative and fundamental bank runs may occur, so that the majority of agents can identify only ex post what has been the bank's performance.

Gorton (1985) suggests a simple model in which all agents have identical preferences. During period 1, the agents obtain information on the expected return on deposits during period 2. If the expected return on deposits is lower than the expected return on the currency, there is a (fundamental) bank run. This simple structure enables Gorton to provide a rationale for the suspension of convertibility when there is asymmetric information on the period 2 return on deposits. To do so, it suffices to assume that the banks are able to pay a verification cost to transmit the true value of the expected return to the depositors. If there is a bank run on a solvent bank, the bank is able to suspend convertibility and pay the verification cost, which is Pareto superior (see problem 7.8.3

for a simplified version of Gorton's model). This explains "a curious aspect of suspension . . . that despite its explicit illegality, neither banks, depositors nor the courts opposed it at any time" (Gorton 1985, 177).

Chari and Jagannathan (1988) consider a model close to the one of Diamond and Dybvig, in which they introduce a random return on investment that may be observed by some of the type 2 agents. If the signal that the agents receive indicates a poor performance, this makes them prefer the type 1 deposit that is less sensitive to the variations in period 2 returns. The agents observe the total amount of withdrawals and use this information to decide their own action (withdraw or wait). Since the proportion of type 1 agents is not observable, it is impossible for an uninformed type 2 depositor to distinguish if the origin of the large withdrawal he observes comes from informed type 2 agents or simply from a large proportion of type 1 agents. The rational expectations equilibrium that is obtained therefore combines fundamental bank runs (the ones that are justified by the poor performance of the bank) and speculative bank runs that develop as in the Diamond-Dybvig model, but here they are triggered by the fear of poor performance, anticipated by informed traders.[9] Notice that this model assumes that the management keeps the bank open even if this implies a decrease in its net wealth. If managers have proper incentives and maximize the bank's value, then fundamental bank runs will never occur, and then speculative bank runs will not occur either. Under limited liability, the bank's manager may have an incentive to keep running the bank if the risk is sufficiently high, since the value of equity may be increased by so doing, even if the total value of the bank is decreased. As reported in Benston et al. (1986), this "gambling for resurrection" behavior is frequently observed when a bank faces a crisis. Therefore, although it is unattractive from a theoretical viewpoint, this assumption is consistent with casual empiricism.

Two other contributions extend the Diamond-Dybvig framework to deal with the effect of the banks' performance. Still, they do not focus directly on bank runs, but rather on the risk sharing provided by demand deposit contracts in this framework.

Jacklin and Bhattacharya (1988) address the question of the relative performance of equity versus demand deposit economies, given the existence of type 2 agents who are informed on the bank's future return, in a model in which liquidation of the long-run technology is impossible ($L = 0$). In an equity economy, this means that the equilibrium prices will be fully revealing; in a demand deposit equilibrium, with suspension of convertibility, this implies that there is rationing on type 1 deposits, so that these deposits are shared between type 1 and informed type 2 agents. Comparison for specific values of the model's parameters of the relative performance shows that for a lower dispersion of returns demand deposits would perform better, whereas for a large dispersion the equity economy allocation should be preferred. Still, the demand deposit contract can be improved if it is required to be incentive compatible after type 2 agents become informed (Alonso 1991).

Gorton and Pennacchi (1990)[10] also consider that some of the type 2 agents are informed, but the agents' behavior is not competitive, so the prices of an equity economy are not fully revealing. Informed traders benefit from trading in the equity market. Demand deposit contracts emerge then because they are riskless, so their value cannot be affected by informed trading. Gorton and Pennacchi establish that in equilibrium uninformed traders invest in deposits and informed traders invest in equity of the financial intermediary, so there is no other market for equity. In that way, the authors elaborate on Jacklin's (1987) contention that equity could perform as well as demand deposit contracts.

7.5   Interbank Markets and the Management of Idiosyncratic Liquidity Shocks

Until now the discussion has maintained the convenient fiction that there was only one collective mutual bank. This section will drop this assumption and focus on the problems that arise precisely because of the multiplicity of banks.[11] These problems are again based on the coexistence of demand deposits on the liability side with nonmarketable loans on the asset side.

7.5.1   The Model of Bhattacharya and Gale (1987)

The Bhattacharya-Gale model is a variant of that of Diamond and Dybvig in which, to keep things simple, it is assumed that $L = 0$ (liquidation is impossible) and that the consumption good cannot be stored, so there are no bank runs. The novelty is that there are now several banks that are confronted with i.i.d. liquidity shocks in the sense that their proportion of patient consumers (who withdraw at date 1) can be π_L or π_H (with $\pi_L < \pi_H$) with respective probabilities p_L and p_H. Again to keep things simple, assume that there is a large number of banks, so liquidity shocks are completely diversifiable; the proportion of banks with few (i.e., π_L) early withdrawals is exactly p_L.

In an autarkic situation (absence of trade between the banks), each bank is completely restricted by its ex-ante choice of investment I: the bank can offer only contingent deposit contracts $C_1(\pi) = \frac{1-I}{\pi}$, $C_2(\pi) = \frac{IR}{1-\pi}$, where π can be π_L or π_H. Therefore depositors bear the liquidity risk of their bank. This risk can be eliminated by opening an interbank market, which can decentralize the optimal allocation, obtained by solving

$$\begin{cases} \max_{I, C_1^k, C_2^k} \sum_{k=L,H} p_k[\pi_k u(C_1^k) + \rho(1-\pi_k)u(C_2^k)] \\ \sum_{k=L,H} p_k \pi_k C_1^k = 1 - I \\ \sum_{k=L,H} p_k(1-\pi_k)C_2^k = IR, \end{cases}$$

where (C_1^k, C_2^k) is the deposit contract offered by a bank of "type" k, $k = L, H$.

The solution to this problem satisfies

$$C_1^k \equiv C_1^* = \frac{1 - I^*}{\pi_a} \qquad C_2^k \equiv C_2^* = \frac{I^* R}{1 - \pi_a}, \qquad k = L, H, \qquad (7.13)$$

where $\pi_a = p_L \pi_L + p_H \pi_H$ is the average proportion of early withdrawals across all banks. Equations 7.13 show that consumers are now completely insured against the liquidity risk faced by their bank: C_1 and C_2 are independent of k.

7.5.2   The Role of the Interbank Market

The implementation of this allocation by the interbank market is realized as follows: banks of type $k = L$ face fewer early withdrawals than the average; therefore they have excess liquidity $M_L = 1 - I^* - \pi_L C_1^*$. On the contrary, banks of type $k = H$ have liquidity needs $M_H = \pi_H C_1^* - (1 - I^*)$. Conditions 7.13 imply that on aggregate, supply and demand of liquidity are perfectly matched:

$$p_L M_L = p_H M_H.$$

At date 2, banks of type $k = H$ will, on the contrary, have excess liquidities that they will use to repay the interbank loan they obtained at date 1. The interest rate r on the interbank market will thus be determined by equalling this repayment with $(1 + r)M_H$, where M_H is the amount of the loan obtained at date 1:

$$(1 + r)M_H = I^* R - (1 - \pi_H)C_2^*.$$

Easy computations yield the following:

$$1 + r = \left(\frac{\pi_a}{1 - \pi_a} \right) \left(\frac{I^*}{1 - I^*} \right) R. \qquad (7.14)$$

7.5.3   The Case of Unobservable Liquidity Shocks

Bhattacharya and Gale also study the more difficult case in which the liquidity shock (i.e., the type k of the bank) and the investment of the bank in the illiquid technology are not publicly observed. In that case, the first best allocation derived earlier will typically not be implementable. Suppose, for instance, that the equilibrium interest rate r on the interbank market (defined by 7.14) is smaller than $R - 1$. Then all banks will have an interest in declaring that they are of type H, since this will entitle them to an interbank loan that they will use for investing in the illiquid technology, obtaining a positive excess return $R - (1 + r)$. To prevent this, the second best solution will involve imperfect insurance of depositors (in the sense that $C_1^L < C_1^H$ and $C_2^L > C_2^H$) and overinvestment with respect to the first best solution I^*. This case occurs when liquidity shocks are small, which can be shown to imply that the interest rate r defined by 7.14 is smaller than $R - 1$.

Symmetrically, when liquidity shocks are large, then $1 + r > R$, and the second best solution involves, on the contrary, underinvestment and reverse ordering of the consumption profiles.[12]

7.6   Aggregate Liquidity Shocks

This section will discuss the more complex case of nondiversifiable liquidity shocks, following the contribution of Hellwig (1994),[13] who studies the allocation of interest rate risk in an extension of the Bryant-Diamond-Dybvig model.

7.6.1   The Model of Hellwig (1994)

The main difference between the Hellwig model and the model presented in Section 7.1 is that Hellwig introduces interest rate risk. More specifically, there are three possible technologies (all with constant returns to scale):

• A short-term investment at date 0 that yields a return $r_1 = 1$ at date 1 (storage technology).

• A long-term investment at date 0 that yields a return $R > 1$ as of date 2, but can also be liquidated at date 1, for a return $L < 1$.

• A short-term investment at date 1 that yields a random return $\tilde{r}_2 \geq 1$ at date 2. $\tilde{r}_2$ is observed only at date 1.

Therefore, the only additional element with respect to the Bryant-Diamond-Dybvig paradigm is the third technology, which dominates storage between $t = 1$ and $t = 2$ (since $\tilde{r}_2 \geq 1$), but which has an unknown return as of date 0. Therefore the allocation of resources is now more complex to characterize:

• It may be useful to liquidate some fraction ℓ of the long-term investment I when the reinvestment opportunities are good (i.e., when $\tilde{r}_2$ is larger than $\frac{R}{L}$).

• The consumption profile (C_1, C_2) may also depend on $\tilde{r}_2$ (i.e., depositors may bear some of the interest rate risk). For instance, when $\tilde{r}_2$ is large, some quantity $x(\tilde{r}_2)$ of the available consumption good can be invested in the short-term technology rather than used for immediate consumption by impatient consumers.

7.6.2   Efficient Risk Allocation

The optimal allocation[14] is obtained by solving

$$
\mathcal{P}_3 \begin{cases} \max\ E[\pi_1 u(C_1(\tilde{r}_2)) + \pi_2 u(C_2(\tilde{r}_2))] \\ \pi_1 C_1(\tilde{r}_2) + x(\tilde{r}_2) = 1 - I + L\ell(\tilde{r}_2) & (7.15) \\ \pi_2 C_2(\tilde{r}_2) = R(I - \ell(\tilde{r}_2)) + \tilde{r}_2 x(\tilde{r}_2) & (7.16) \\ 0 \le \ell(\tilde{r}_2) \le 1 - I & (7.17) \end{cases}
$$

Whereas in general the complete characterization of the solution of $\mathcal{P}_3$ is complex, a simplification occurs with the additional assumption that $L\tilde{r}_2 \le R$. In that case, it is never optimal (in the best allocation) to liquidate some of the long-term investment and to reinvest it in the short-term technology; it is thus natural to set $\ell(\tilde{r}_2) \equiv 0$. Then $x(\tilde{r}_2)$ can be eliminated between 7.15 and 7.16, yielding a unique budget constraint:

$$
\pi_1 C_1(\tilde{r}_2) + \frac{\pi_2}{\tilde{r}_2} C_2(\tilde{r}_2) = 1 + \left(\frac{R}{\tilde{r}_2} - 1\right) I. \tag{7.18}
$$

However, keep in mind the fact that $x(\tilde{r}_2)$ cannot be negative, which gives another constraint:

$$
\pi_1 C_1(\tilde{r}_2) \le 1 - I.
$$

At this stage, it is useful to introduce the following notation: let $(C_1^*(r_2, M), C_2^*(r_2, M))$ denote the solution of

$$
\begin{cases} \max\ \pi_1 u(C_1) + \pi_2 u(C_2) \\ \pi_1 C_1 + \frac{\pi_2 C_2}{r_2} = M. \end{cases}
$$

With this notation, the solution of $\mathcal{P}_3$ is easy to characterize:

1. When $\tilde{r}_2$ is large enough (greater than a threshold r_2^*), some investment takes places at $t = 1 (x(\tilde{r}_2) > 0)$:

$$
\begin{cases} C_1(\tilde{r}_2) & = & C_1^*(\tilde{r}_2, 1 + (\frac{R}{\tilde{r}_1} - 1)I), \\ C_2(\tilde{r}_2) & = & C_2^*(\tilde{r}_2, 1 + \left(\frac{R}{\tilde{r}_2} - 1\right) I). \end{cases} \tag{7.19}
$$

2. When $\tilde{r}_2 \le r_2^*$, no investment takes place at $t = 1$, and depositors bear no interest rate risk:

$$
\begin{cases} C_1(\tilde{r}_2) & = & \frac{1-I}{\pi_1} \\ C_2(\tilde{r}_2) & = & \frac{RI}{\pi_2} \end{cases} \tag{7.20}
$$

In other words, when the investment opportunities are good enough at $t = 1$ $(\tilde{r}_2 \ge r_2^*)$, it is optimal to let depositors bear some risk, even though a complete immunization would be possible, since the allocation defined by 7.20 is always feasible.

7.6.3 Second Best Allocations under Asymmetric Information

Now assume that liquidity needs are privately observed by depositors, so an incentive compatibility constraint must be added to $\mathcal{P}_3$:

$$C_2(\tilde{r}_2) \geq \tilde{r}_2 C_1(\tilde{r}_2). \tag{7.21}$$

Constraint 7.21 simply means that patient consumers (type 2) do not gain by withdrawing their deposits at date 1 and reinvesting them in the short-term technology. Hellwig obtains a complete characterization of the solution of the new program ($\mathcal{P}_3$ plus constraint 7.21) and shows in particular that for large enough L, it might be desirable to liquidate some of the long-term investment at $t = 1$ and reinvest it in the short-term technology (i.e., $\ell(\tilde{r}_2) > 0$), even though this is technologically inefficient (since $L\tilde{r}_2 \leq R$). This discussion will focus on the other case (when L is small). Assume also that $C \to Cu'(C)$ is decreasing. This assumption implies that $C_1^*(r_2, M)$ is always less than $r_2 C_1^*(r_2, M)$, which suggests that the incentive compatibility condition will play a key role in determining the solution. Indeed, Hellwig shows that the allocation of consumption is in this case independent of the utility function (except indirectly through the determination of I). More specifically, the solution is determined as follows:

1. When $\tilde{r}_2$ is large enough (greater than another threshold $\hat{r}_2$), the incentive compatibility constraints are binding. As a result, depositors bear some interest rate risk:

$$\begin{cases} C_1(\tilde{r}_2) &= 1 + \left(\frac{R}{\tilde{r}_2} - 1\right) I \\ C_2(\tilde{r}_2) &= \tilde{r}_2 C_1(\tilde{r}_2). \end{cases}$$

2. When $\tilde{r}_2 \leq \hat{r}_2$, there is no investment at $t = 1$, and the solution is again defined by 7.20.

Hellwig's results show in particular that, contrary to what is done most frequently in practice, depositors should bear some interest rate risk. There are two reasons for that:

1. As shown by optimal risk-sharing formulas,[15] nondiversifiable risks should be borne by all agents, including depositors, in proportion to their risk tolerance.

2. In a second best situation, incentive compatibility constraints may be binding: if banks want to prevent patient depositors from withdrawing early and reinvesting, banks have to provide their depositors with at least the rate of return they can obtain on financial markets.

7.7   Systemic Risk and the Lender of Last Resort: A Historical Perspective

Following the ideas of Bagehot (1873), the Central Banks of most countries have adopted a position of Lender of Last Resort (LLR), in the sense that, under certain conditions, commercial banks facing liquidity problems can turn to them for obtaining short-term loans. The justification given to this system is that the market mechanism is not sufficient to provide commercial banks with insurance against liquidity shocks. This section will start with a quick review of Bagehot's doctrine and of the criticisms that have addressed it. Then it will examine some historical evidence about the efficiency of the LLR system in preventing systemic risk.

7.7.1   Four Views on the LLR Role

The idea that market mechanisms cannot insure against liquidity shocks has to be based on arguments that sustain the existence of a market failure. The classical argument has been forcefully put forward by Bagehot, emphasizing the difficulty a bank will face if it must transmit credible information to the market during a crisis. In his own words, "Every banker knows that if he has to prove that he is worthy of credit, however good may be his argument, in fact his credit is gone" (p. 68). The classical "price" argument, which would imply that an increase in interest rates would compensate the lenders for the increased risk they take when lending to a bank facing a crisis, may in fact act as a signal of an unsound position and therefore discourage the potential lenders. Market failure can thus be traced to asymmetric information on the banks' solvency.

The idea of the role of the Central Bank as the LLR is associated with the work of Bagehot. But his argument is far from being unchallenged. Following are four views on the role of the LLR:

1. As the outstanding representative of the so-called classical school, Bagehot argues that

   a. The LLR has a role in lending to illiquid solvent financial institutions.

   b. these loans must be at a penalty rate, so that financial institutions cannot use the loans to fund their current lending operations.

   c. the lending must be open to solvent financial institutions provided they have good collateral (valued at prepanic prices).

   d. the LLR must make clear in advance its readiness to lend any amount to an institution that fulfills the conditions on solvency and collateral (credibility).

Three other views oppose the classical one, as suggested by Bordo (1990):

2. Goodhart (1987, 1995) asserts that the clear-cut distinction between illiquidity and insolvency is a myth, because the banks that require the assistance

of the LLR are already under suspicion of being insolvent. The existence of contagion is the additional argument that may induce the systematic rescue of *any* bank.

3. The view of Goodfriend and King (1988) is poles apart from the previous one. They argue that the LLR functions must be restricted to the use of open market operations. Humphrey (1986) even claims that this would have also been Bagehot's viewpoint had he known of open market operations.

4. Proponents of free banking do not challenge the existence of market failure but suggest that the market still would lead to a better allocation than a public LLR would.

A second issue that divides academics is the classical view that the rules governing LLR behavior should be clearly stated. Most of the time, this is opposed by Central Bankers. In the United States, for instance, the Fed has always stressed that discounting is a privilege and not a right. The supporters of this view base their argument on the fact that ambiguity in the policy will help to bring in some market discipline (in contradiction with the view also held by Central Bankers that disclosure could have a destabilizing effect on the payment system). In fact, the effect of ambiguity is a transfer of wealth from small to large banks, because there is no ambiguity regarding the fact that large institutions are "too big to fail." Thus, ambiguity is to some extent illusory and is equivalent to repaying all large banks' liabilities and rescuing only the solvent ones among the small (if they are able to prove that they are solvent).

It is clear that these positions should result from social welfare maximization, taking into account asymmetric (or costly) information and all the externalities that the behavior of the LLR may have: contagion, panics, and effects on securities markets, as well as the moral hazard problem. Therefore, at least theoretically, the differences among the views of the LLR's role and behavior could be traced to differences in the appreciation of, say, the social cost of individual bank failure, bank panics, and contagion effects.[16]

7.7.2 The Effect of LLR and Other Partial Arrangements

The evidence on the effect of the creation of an LLR mechanism points unambiguously to the conclusion that it has helped to avoid bank panics. Miron (1986), Bordo (1990), and Eichengreen and Portes (1987), among others, have obtained results that support this view.[17] These results have been reached through different types of analysis: either by examining the result of the creation of the LLR in a given country, thus assuming the ceteris paribus clause for changes in the banking system, or by comparing different countries and assuming that the ceteris paribus clause is satisfied for other factors affecting the frequency of financial panics. It is also true that by monitoring the banks' solvency and payment system, the LLR mitigates the risk of contagion, the importance of which has been emphasized by Aharony and Swary (1983), Humphrey (1986), Guttentag and Herring (1987), Herring and Vankudre (1987), and Saunders (1987).

The evidence obtained by Miron (1986) on the effect of the creation of the Federal Reserve Board in the United States shows the importance it has had on limiting bank runs. Prior to its founding, autumn and spring were the stringent money quarters, during which panics tended to occur. The founding of the Fed provided the U.S. economy with a lender of last resort, and the frequency of bank panics immediately decreased. The change in seasonality patterns for both the interest rates and the loan-reserve ratio[18] confirms the importance of the founding of the Fed as a way out of seasonal liquidity triggered bank panics. Between 1915 and 1928, the banking system experienced no financial panics, although several recessions occurred during the subperiods 1918–19, 1920–21, 1923–24 and 1926–27, of which the 1920–21 recession was quite severe. Miron makes a simple test using a Bernoulli distribution. He estimates that prior to the founding of the Fed the probability of having a panic during a given year was 0.316. This implies that the probability of having no bank panic during the fourteen years 1914–28 was only 0.005. Miron rejects the hypothesis of no change in the frequency of panics at the 99 percent level of confidence.

On the other hand, the panics observed during the 1929–33 period may be considered as providing an argument against the effectiveness of the LLR policy. Still, it is clear that during that period the Fed did not conduct the open market operations necessary to provide banks with adequate reserves. According to Friedman and Schwartz (1963), the series of bank failures that produced an unprecedented decline in the money stock could have been prevented. Meltzer (1986) makes the same point. According to him, "the worst cases of financial panics arose because the central bank did not follow Bagehotian principles" (p. 83).

Bordo (1990) examines the changes that occurred in the United States and in the United Kingdom before and after the creation of an LLR system. Before 1866, the Bank of England tended to react by protecting its own gold reserves, which could even worsen panics. After that date, the Bank of England adopted Bagehot's policy and thus "prevented incipient crises in 1878, 1890 and 1914 from developing into full-blown panics, by timely announcements and action" (p. 23). Bordo compares the two countries during the 1870–1913 periods and sees striking similarities in their business cycles: similar declines in output, price reversals, and declines in money growth. Still, the United States had four panics during this period while the United Kingdom had none. Evidence on

Germany, Sweden, and Canada supports analogous views (Bordo 1986; see also Humphrey and Kelcher 1989).

7.7.3 The Moral Hazard Issue

Since the effect of an LLR on the behavior of banks is difficult to measure, only general empirical evidence can be collected by cross-country comparisons. The Scottish case is often raised by the tenants of the Free Banking school. Still, it is worth recalling that in the Scottish free banking era, bank stockholders had unlimited liability, and this led "to take over at par the issue of failed banks to increase their own business" (Bordo 1990, 25). Of course, when this happens, the only risk is systemic risk, since any run on an individual bank could be coped with by "the market," given the interest that the other banks have in buying out one of their competitors. Switzerland is another interesting example, because it has had an experience of free banking without a record of bank runs, and even now intervention of the LLR is infrequent (Goodhart 1985).

7.8   Problems

7.8.1   Different Specifications of Preferences in the Diamond-Dybvig Model

This problem adopts a similar set of assumptions as in subsection 7.1.1. More specifically, consider a one-good, three-period economy, with a continuum of agents, each endowed with one unit of the good in period $t = 0$ and with preferences given by

$$U(C_1^i) + \rho^i U(C_2^i) \quad \text{with probability } \Pi_i \ (i = 1, 2), \tag{7.22}$$

where ρ^i is the discount rate, $(\rho^1 < \rho^2)$, and C_t^i is the consumption of agent i during period t. U is well behaved, with

$$U'(C) > 0, \quad U'(0) = +\infty, \quad U''(C) < 0.$$

The assumptions regarding technology are the same as in subsection 7.1.1: the short-run return is 1, whereas the long-run investment yields R at $t = 2$ (and only $L < 1$ if liquidated at date 1).

1. Show that in the market equilibrium, the price of the second-period good in terms of the first-period good, p, has to be $1/R$, and that $C_1^1 > C_1^2$, $C_2^1 < C_2^2$, and $C_1^1 + \frac{C_2^1}{R} = C_2^1 + \frac{C_2^2}{R}$.

2. Show that, when there is no bank run, the equilibrium with deposit contracts yields a higher return than the market equilibrium and that $C_1^1 + C_2^1/R < C_1^2 + C_2^2/R$.

3. Assume, instead, that preferences are

$$\frac{1}{\rho^i} U(C_1^i) + U(C_2^i).$$

Show that in this case $C_1^1 + C_2^1/R > C_1^2 + C_2^2/R$.

7.8.2   Information-Based Bank Runs (Adapted from Postlewaite and Vives 1987)

Consider a one-good, three-period, two-agent economy in which the gross return is $r_1(< 1)$ for an investment during the first year ($t = 0$ to $t = 1$), r_2 for an investment during the second year, and r_3 for an investment during the third year. Assume $2r_1 - 1 > 0$ and $2r_1 r_2 - 1 > 0$. The preferences can be of three types. If an agent is of type 1, her utility is $U(x_1)$. It is $U(x_1 + x_2)$ if she is of type 2, and $U(x_1 + x_2 + x_3)$ if she is of type 3. The probability that agent 1 is of type i and agent 2 is of type j is p_{ij}.

The (exogenous) banking contract allows each agent to withdraw the amount initially deposited without penalty during periods 1 and 2, but interest can be collected only if the agent waits until period 3.

1. Define a_t^i as the strategy that consists in withdrawing everything during period t. Write the matrix of payments when both agents initially deposit one unit.

2. Consider the restriction of the game to strategies a_1^i and a_2^i. What is the equilibrium if $r_1 > (2r_1 - 1)r_2$ and $1 > r_1 r_2$? Is this an efficient allocation?

3. Returning to the initial matrix, assume that $(2r_1 - 1)r_2 r_3 > 1$. Describe the equilibrium by establishing the optimal strategy for each type. Will there be any bank runs?

7.8.3   Banks' Suspension of Convertibility (Adapted from Gorton 1985)

Consider a three-period economy ($t = 0, 1, 2$) with a unique consumption good that cannot be stored but can be invested. There is a continuum of agents of total measure 1, each having one unit of the good as an initial endowment.

Agents have identical risk neutral preferences represented by $U(C_1, C_2) = C_1 + \frac{1}{1+\rho}C_2$, where C_t denotes consumption during period t.

The only available technology yields returns r_1 during period 1 and r_2 during period 2. A signal s, belonging to the interval $[\underline{s}, \bar{s}]$, characterizes the distribution of r_2. Assume that if $s_1 > s_2$, the distribution of r_2 conditionally on s_1 first order dominates the distribution of r_2 conditionally on s_2.

1. Show that the optimal consumption decision is given by

$$\begin{cases} C_1 = 1 + r_1 \text{ and } C_2 = 0 \text{ if } & 1 + \rho > E[1 + \tilde{r}_2|s] \\ C_1 = 0 \text{ and } C_2 = 1 + \tilde{r}_2 \text{ if } & 1 + \rho < E[1 + \tilde{r}_2|s], \\ \text{with undetermination if} & 1 + \rho = E[1 + \tilde{r}_2|s]. \end{cases}$$

2. Define a mutual fund contract as one in which an investment of I_0 gives a right to $I_0(1 + r_1)d_1$ during period 1 and an investment of I_1 during period 1 gives a right to $I_1(1 + \tilde{r}_2)(1 - d_1)$ during period 2, where d_1 is the fraction that is withdrawn at period 1.

Assume agents invest Q in the mutual fund equity, and that the fund is liquidated if and only if it has repurchased all the investor shares. Show that the optimal allocation is obtained.

3. A deposit contract is defined as the right to withdraw amounts d_1 and d_2 such that $d_1 \leq D(1 + r_D)$ and $d_2 = (D(1 + r_D) - d_1)(1 + r_D)$, where D is the initial deposit and r_D is the promised rate on deposits, $(r_D > \rho)$. When the bank fails to pay the amount due, its assets are distributed in proportion to the depositors' rights, so that if the bank fails during period 1,

$$d_1 = 1 + r_1, \quad 1 + r_1 < D(1 + r_D),$$

and if it fails during period 2,

$$d_2 = (1 + r_1 - d_1)(1 + r_2), \quad d_2 < D(1 + r_D - d_1)(1 + r_D).$$

Equity holders are period 2 residual claimants. The bank will choose to close only if this increases its expected net present value.

Define speculative bank runs as the ones that happen independently of s, and fundamental bank runs as the ones that arise for low values of s.

Define $\delta(\hat{d}_1, s)$ as the expected period 2 return on deposits when the other agents withdraw $\hat{d}_1$. Show that $\delta(\hat{d}_1, s)$ is increasing (resp. decreasing) in $\hat{d}_1$ if $1 + r_1 > D(1 + r_0)$.(resp. $1 + r_1 < D(1 + r_0)$). Characterize the different Nash equilibria that obtain depending on the values of $\rho(0, s)$, $\rho(D(1 + r_D), s)$, and $1 + \rho$, and show that for some of these values a speculative bank run obtains, while others result in a fundamental one.

Show that this contract does not lead to the optimal allocation.

4. Assume now that r_2 is observable by the bank's management, whereas depositors observe only s. Show that if the bank's equity holders find it profitable to pay an auditing cost c in order to make r_2 publicly observable while suspending convertibility, it is Pareto superior to do so.

7.9 Solutions

7.9.1 Different Specifications of Preferences in the Diamond-Dybvig Model

1. In a market economy an agent will choose to liquidate long-run investment I only if this yields a higher value than what she can obtain by trading the long-run investment proceeds on the market, that is, if

$L > pR.$

Assume that the equilibrium price satisfies this inequality: then the optimal level of investment is zero, since $L < 1$. But this yields a contradiction, since by investing C_2^1/R in the long-run technology each agent will be better off in autarky. Therefore liquidation plays no role; at equilibrium, the individual investment problem

$$\max_I (1 - I + pRI)$$

has to have an interior solution. This implies $p.R = 1$, with an arbitrary level of investment as usual with a linear technology. The budget constraint is therefore $C_1 + \frac{C_2}{R} = 1$. The first order conditions are

$$\frac{U'(C_2^i)}{U'(C_1^i)} = \frac{p}{\rho^i} \qquad i = 1, 2.$$

This allows expression of C_1^i as a function of C_2^i. If C_1^i is replaced by this function in the budget constraint, it is obvious that the left-hand side of this constraint is a decreasing function of C_2^i. Since $\rho^1 < \rho^2$, which implies $p/\rho^1 > p/\rho^2$, the inequality $C_2^1 < C_2^2$ obtains. Using the budget constraint yields $C_1^1 > C_1^2$ and $C_1^1 + C_2^1/R = C_1^2 + C_2^2/R$.

2. Assuming $(C_1^1, C_2^1, C_1^2, C_2^2)$ is the allocation obtained in the market equilibrium, one can establish that a slight change in this allocation improves ex-ante expected welfare. Notice, first, that the incentive compatibility constraint is fulfilled, since each agent strictly prefers her own allocation (recall that U is strictly concave). This constraint may therefore be disregarded.

Notice that $U'(C_1^i) = \lambda^i$ where λ^i is the Lagrange multiplier associated with the budget constraint when preferences are of type i.

Since $C_1^1 < C_1^2$, then $\lambda^1 < \lambda^2$, so that a transfer of income from a state of nature in which $i = 1$ to one in which $i = 2$ increases the ex-ante expected utility. But with deposit contracts there is only one global budget constraint, so that income may be transferred from $i = 1$ to $i = 2$ provided these transfers satisfy $dW^1 + dW^2/R = 0$.

Assume by way of contradiction that the allocation in a deposit contract equilibrium satisfies $\hat{C}_1^1 + \hat{C}_2^1/R < \hat{C}_1^2 + \hat{C}_2^2/R$. This would imply that the change from the market allocation to the deposit contract allocation has taken place through a transfer from $i = 2$ to $i = 1$, that is, $dW^1 > 0$ and $dW^2 < 0$. But such a transfer decreases expected utility, which yields a contradiction.

3. The last argument applies with $\lambda^1 > \lambda^2$.

7.9.2   Information-Based Bank Runs

1. The matrix of payments is as follows:

Agent 1

		a_1	a_2	a_3
Agent 2	a_1	(r_1, r_1)	$(1, (2r_1 - 1)r_2)$	$(1, (2r_1 - 1)r_2 r_3)$
	a_2	$((2r_1 - 1)r_2, 1)$	$(r_1 r_2, r_1 r_2)$	$(1, (2r_1 r_2 - 1)r_3)$
	a_3	$((2r_1 - 1)r_2 r_3, 1)$	$((2r_1 r_2 - 1)r_3, 1)$	$(r_1 r_2 r_3, r_1 r_2 r_3)$

2. The restriction to (a_1, a_2) shows a game that has the "prisoner's dilemma" structure. Strategy a_1 dominates strategy a_2. If $r_2 > 1$, the allocation is inefficient.

3. The optimal strategy will be

a_1^i \qquad if i's type is 1 or 2

a_3^i \qquad if i's type is 3

Therefore bank runs occur when one of the agents is of type 2.

7.9.3   Banks' Suspension of Convertibility

1. For a given realization of s, solve

$$\max_{0 \leq C_1 \leq 1 + r_1} C_1 + \frac{1}{1 + \rho} E\left[(1 + r_1 - C_1)(1 + \tilde{r}_2) \,|s\right],$$

which easily gives the desired result.

2. Let d_1 be the fraction of the mutual fund that is withdrawn during period 1. For a given realization of s, solve

$$\max_{0 \leq d_1 \leq 1} (1 - Q) \left\{ d_1(1 + r_1) + \frac{1}{1 + \rho} E\left[(1 + r_1)(1 + \tilde{r}_2)(1 - d_1)\right] \right\}$$

so that

$d_1 = 1$ \qquad\qquad if \quad $1 + \rho > E[1 + \tilde{r}_2 | s]$

$d_1 = 0$ \qquad\qquad if \quad $1 + \rho < E[1 + \tilde{r}_2 | s]$

d_1 undetermined \quad if \quad $1 + \rho = E[1 + \tilde{r}_2 | s]$.

The rules on the closing of the mutual fund imply that agents withdrawing $(1 - Q)(1 + r_1)$ also obtain their capital $Q(1 + r_1)$ so that their consumption is optimal.

Notice that if fees are introduced, the solution is unchanged if these fees are proportional to withdrawals or if they are redistributed to equity holders in the form of dividends.

3. The equity holders have a call option on the period 2 value of the banks' assets. Therefore, if closing the bank generates a zero profit, which happens

when $1 + r_1 < D(1 + r_D)$, the bank will never liquidate its investment, independently of the value of the signal s.

Consider the cases for which the bank does not close down during period 1.

Let $\delta(\hat{d}_1, s) = E\left[Min\left[\frac{(1+r_1-\hat{d}_1)(1+\tilde{r}_2)}{D(1+r_D)-\hat{d}_1}, 1 + r_D\right] | s\right]$.

The depositor will choose d_1 so as to solve

$$\left\{\begin{array}{l} \max_{d_1} d_1 + \frac{1}{1+\rho}\delta(\hat{d}_1, s)\left[D(1+r_D) - d_1\right] \\ 0 \le d_1 \le D(1 + r_D) \end{array}\right\}.$$

Since all agents are identical, a Nash equilibrium obtains for $d_1 = \hat{d}_1$ when there is a unique solution, so that it is a symmetrical equilibrium. First examine the symmetrical equilibria:

$$\delta(\hat{d}_1, s) = \frac{1 + r_1 - \hat{d}_1}{D(1 + r_D) - \hat{d}_1} \int_{-1}^{\hat{r}_2(\hat{d}_1)} (1 + r_2)\varphi(r_2)dr_2$$

$$+ (1 + r_D) \int_{\hat{r}_2-(\hat{d}_1)}^{\infty} \varphi(r_2)dr_2,$$

where $\varphi(r_2)$ is the generalized density function of $\tilde{r}_2$, and $\hat{r}_2(\hat{d}_1)$ is the value of r_2 for which $\frac{1+r_1-\hat{d}_1)(1+r_2)}{D(1+r_D)-\hat{d}_1} = 1 + r_D$.

Canceling out the terms in $\hat{r}_2(\hat{d}_1)$ yields

$$\frac{d\delta}{d\hat{d}_1} = \frac{1 + r_1 - D(1 + r_D)}{D(1 + r_D) - \hat{d}_1} \int_{-1}^{\hat{r}_2(\hat{d}_1)} (1 + r_2)\varphi(r_2)dr_2.$$

- If $1 + r_1 > D(1 + r_D)$, $\delta(D(1 + r_D),\ s) > \delta(0, s)$, and
  a. $d_1 = \hat{d}_1 = 0$ for $1 + \rho < \delta(0, s)$,
  b. $d_1 = \hat{d}_1 = d_1^*$ for $1 + \rho < \delta(d_1^*, s)$, and
  c. $d_1 = (1 + r_D)D$ for $1 + \rho < \delta(D(1 + r_D), s)$,

case (c) corresponds to a fundamental bank run; in case (b) the solution is undetermined, so (infinitely many) asymmetrical equilibria are obtained, provided that

$$\delta\left(\int_0^1 d_1(t)d\mu(t), s\right) = 1 + \rho.$$

- If $1 + r_1 < D(1 + r_D)$, $\delta(0, s) > \delta(1 + r_1, s)$, and
  a. $1 + \rho > \delta(0, s)$,
     $d_1 = \hat{d}_1 = 1 + r_1$, since $1 + \rho > \delta(1 + r_1, s)$.
  b. $\delta(0, s) > 1 + \rho > \delta(1 + r_1, s)$, there are three solutions:
     $d_1 = \hat{d}_1 = 0$; $\hat{d}_1$ with $\delta(d_1^*, s) = 1 + \rho$ and $d_1 = \hat{d}_1 = 1 + r_1$.

c. $1 + \rho < \delta(1 + r_1, s)$,

$d_1 = \hat{d}_1 = 0$, since then $1 + \rho < \delta(0, s)$.

Thus, in case (b) speculative bank runs occur.

The optimal allocation clearly does not obtain in equilibrium.

4. The bank's management will decide to suspend convertibility only if the second-period profit is greater than the auditing cost. This implies that the suspension of convertibility will take place only when the second-period profits are strictly positive for the r_2 that is observed. But this in turn implies that depositors obtain r_D with certainty, so they are better off under the suspension of convertibility.

Notes

1. The precise definition of a bank panic varies from one author to the other. Kemmerer himself enumerates 6 major bank panics and 15 minor ones during the period 1890 through 1908. Benston and Kaufman (1986), using another definition, found bank panics on 3 occasions: 1874, 1893, and 1908. Gorton (1988) also found panics in 1884, 1890, and 1896.

2. Miron uses this indicator to evaluate the real (as opposed to financial) effects of bank panics. However, the inverse causality cannot be dismissed: it could be argued that decreases in GNP tend to shrink the value of banks' assets, thus triggering bank panics.

3. Of course bank runs can develop into bank panics because of contagion or the domino effect.

4. This is true, for instance, if $R \to Ru'(R)$ is decreasing, which corresponds to assuming that the elasticity of substitution between periods is smaller than 1.

5. There is also a mixed-strategy equilibrium that is not considered here.

6. See Kareken (1988) and Mussa (1988).

7. By the law of large numbers, the realized proportion equals the theoretical frequency. This will change when Section 7.6 introduces aggregate liquidity risk.

8. Note that Engineer (1989) has shown that suspension of convertibility may fail to prevent a bank run if the Diamond-Dybvig (1983) model is extended to a framework with 4 periods and 3 types of agents.

9. Temzelides (1995) studies a repeated version of the Diamond-Dybvig model and models equilibrium selection (between the efficient and the "panic" equilibria) by an evolutionary process. He shows that the probability of panic decreases with the size of banks, and he studies the possibililty of contagion effects.

10. See Chapter 2.

11. Adao and Temzelides (1995) introduce Bertrand competition between banks in the Diamond-Dybvig model. They show that surprisingly, Bertrand equilibria may imply positive profits.

12. Other interesting approaches to the role of the interbank market are provided by Aghion, Bolton, and Dewatripont (1988) and Bhattacharya and Fulghieri (1994).

13. A similar question is studied in Jacklin (1993).

14. For simplicity, assume $\rho = 1$ (no discount factor).

15. See Chapter 4.

16. See also Smith (1984) for a model of the role of the LLR in the presence of adverse selection.

17. See also the references in these articles.

18. Related to the total risk of the portfolio, since only loans have an effect on the overall standard deviation of a bank's assets (see Chapter 3).

References

Adao, B., and T. Temzelides. 1995. Beliefs, competition and bank runs. Discussion paper, Research Department, Federal Reserve Bank of Philadelphia.

Aghion, P., P. Bolton, and M. Dewatripont. 1988. Interbank lending and contagious bank runs. MIT and Harvard University, Cambridge, Mass.; and Université Libre de Bruxelles. Mimeograph.

Aharony, J., and I. Swary. 1983. Contagion effects of bank failures: Evidence from capital markets. *Journal of Business* 56(3):305–22.

Alonso, I. 1991. On informationally based bank runs: The Jacklin and Bhattacharya paper revisited. University of Minnesota, Minneapolis. Mimeograph.

Anderlini, L. 1989. Theoretical modelling of banks and bank runs. In *The economics of missing markets, information and games,* edited by F. Hahn. Oxford: Oxford University Press.

Bagehot, W. 1873. Lombard Street: A description of the money market. London: H. S. King.

Benston G., R. Eisenbeis, P. Horvitz, E. Kane, and G. Kaufman. 1986. *Perspectives on safe and sound banking: Past, present and future.* Cambridge, Mass.: American Bankers Association in cooperation with MIT Press.

Benston, G., and G. Kaufman. 1986. Risks and failures in banking: Overview, history, and evaluation. In *Deregulating financial services: Public policy in flux,* edited by G. Kaufman and R. Kormandi. Mid America Institute for Public Policy Research Book Series. Cambridge, Mass.: Harper and Row.

Bhattacharya, S., and P. Fulghieri. 1994. Uncertain liquidity and interbank contracting. *Economics Letters* 44:287–94.

Bhattacharya, S., and D. Gale. 1987. Preference shocks, liquidity and Central Bank policy. In *New approaches to monetary economics,* edited by W. Barnett and K. Singleton. Cambridge: Cambridge University Press.

Bordo, M. D. 1986. Financial crises, banking crises, stock market crashes and the money supply: Some international evidence, 1887–1933. In *Financial crises and the world banking system,* edited by F. Capie and G. E. Wood. London: Macmillan.

———. 1990. The Lender of Last Resort: Alternative views and historical experience. *Federal Reserve Bank of Richmond Economic Review* 76(1):18–29.

Bryant, J. 1980. A model of reserves, bank runs, and deposit insurance. *Journal of Banking and Finance* 4:335–44.

———. 1981. Bank collapse and depression. *Journal of Money, Credit, and Banking* 13(4):454–64.

Chari, V. V., and R. Jagannathan. 1988. Banking panics, information and rational expectations equilibrium. *Journal of Finance* 43(3):749–61.

Diamond, D. W., and P. H. Dybvig. 1983. Bank runs, deposit insurance, and liquidity. *Journal of Political Economy* 91(3):401–19.

Eichengreen, B., and R. Portes. 1987. The anatomy of financial crises. In *Threats to international financial stability,* edited by R. Portes and A. Swoboda. Cambridge: Cambridge University Press.

Engineer, M. 1989. Bank runs and the suspension of deposit convertibility. *Journal of Monetary Economics* 24(3):443–54.

Freeman, S. 1988. Banking as the provision of liquidity. *Journal of Business* 61(1):45–64.

Friedman, M., and A. Schwartz. 1963. *A monetary history of the United States, 1867–1960.* Princeton, N.J.: Princeton University Press.

Goodfriend, M., and R. King. 1988. Financial deregulation monetary policy and central banking. In *Restructuring banking and financial services in America,* edited by W. Haraf and R. M. Kushmeider. AEI Studies, no. 481. Lanham, Md.: UPA.

Goodhart, C. 1987. Why do banks need a Central Bank? *Oxford Economic Papers* 39(1):75–89.

———. 1995. The central bank and the financial system. Cambridge, Mass.: MIT Press.

Gorton, G. 1985. Banks' suspension of convertibility. *Journal of Monetary Economics* 15:177–93.

Gorton, G., and G. Pennacchi. 1990. Financial intermediaries and liquidity creation. *Journal of Finance* 45(1):49–71.

Guttentag, J., and R. Herring. 1987. Emergency liquidity assistance for international banks. In *Threats to international financial stability,* edited by R. Portes and A. Swoboda. Cambridge: Cambridge University Press.

Hellwig, M. 1994. Liquidity provision, banking, and the allocation of interest rate risk. *European Economic Review* 38(7):1363–89.

Herring, R., and P. Vankudre. 1987. Growth opportunities and risk-taking by financial intermediaries. *Journal of Finance* 42(3):583–99.

Holmström, B., and J. Tirole. 1996. Private and public supply of liquidity. Working paper, IDEI, University of Toulouse.

Humphrey, D. B. 1986. Payments finality and risk of settlement failure. Chapter 8 in *Technology and the Regulation of Financial Markets,* edited by A. Saunders and L. J. White. Lexington, Mass.: Lexington Books.

Humphrey, T. 1986. The classical concept of the lender of last resort. In *Essays on inflation,* 5th ed., edited by T. Humphrey. Richmond, Va.: Federal Reserve Bank of Richmond.

Humphrey, T. M., and R. E. Keleher. 1984. The Lender of Last Resort: A historical perspective. *Cato-Journal* 4(1):275–318.

International interbank market, a descriptive study. (1983). BIS Economic Papers, no. 8, Basle: BIS.

Jacklin, C. J. 1987. Demand deposits, trading restrictions and risk sharing. In *Contractual arrangements for intertemporal trade,* edited by E. Prescott and N. Wallace. Minneapolis: University of Minnesota Press.

———. 1993. Market rate versus fixed rate demand deposits. *Journal of Monetary Economics* 32:237–58.

Jacklin, C. J., and S. Bhattacharya. 1988. Distinguishing panics and information-based bank runs: Welfare and policy implications. *Journal of Political Economy* 96(3):568–92.

Kareken, J. 1988. Federal bank regulatory policy: A description and some obervations. *Journal of Business* 59(1):3–48.

Kemmerer, E. W. 1910. *Seasonal variations in the relative demand for money and capital in the United States.* 61st Cong. 2d sess. *S.* Doc. 588.

Meltzer, A. 1986. Financial failures and financial policies. In *Deregulating financial services: Public policy in flux,* edited by G. Kaufman and R. Kormendi. Cambridge, Mass.: Harper and Row.

Miron, J. A. 1986. Financial panics, the seasonality of the nominal interest rate, and the founding of the Fed. *American Economic Review* 76(1):125–40.

Mussa, M. 1986. Safety and soundness as an objective of regulation of depository institutions: Comments on Kareken. *Journal of Business* 59(1):97–117.

Postlewaite, A., and X. Vives. 1987. Banks runs as an equilibrium phenomenon. *Journal of Political Economy* 95(3):485–91.

Saunders, A. 1987. The inter-bank market, contagion effects and international financial crises. In *Threats to international financial stability,* edited by R. Portes and A. Swoboda. Cambridge: Cambridge University Press.

Smith, B. 1984. Private information, deposit interest rates, and the "stability" of the banking system. *Journal of Monetary Economics* 14(3):294–317.

Temzelides, T. 1995. Evolution, coordination and banking panics. Discussion paper, Research Department, Federal Reserve Bank of Philadelphia.

Von Thadden, E. L. 1995. Optimal liquidity provision and dynamic incentive compatibility. Working paper, Centre for Economic Policy Research, European Science Foundation, London.

Wallace, N. 1988. Another attempt to explain an illiquid banking system: The Diamond-Dybvig model with sequential service taken seriously. *Quarterly Review of the Federal Reserve Bank of Minneapolis* 12(4):3–16.

———. 1996. Narrow banking meets the Diamond-Dybvig model. *Quarterly Review of the Federal Reserve Bank of Minneapolis* 20(1):3–13.

The management of risks, in the full acceptation of the term, can be seen as the major activity of banks, as well as other financial intermediaries such as insurance companies. Commercial banks, investment banks, and mutual funds have to control and select the risks inherent in the management of deposits, loans portfolios of securities, and off-balance-sheet contracts.

Since the risks that a bank has to manage are diverse, several classifications have been proposed, some of which are standard. Thus, economists have put forward the fundamental distinction between *microeconomic* or *idiosyncratic risks*, which can be diversified away through the law of large numbers, and *macroeconomic* or *systematic risks,* which cannot. Unlike insurance companies, which essentially deal with microeconomic risks, banks generally have to deal with both types of risks.

Another fundamental distinction, valid for any type of firm, is between *liquidity risk,* which appears when a firm is not certain to repay its creditors on time, and *solvency risk,* which appears when the total value of a firm's assets falls below the total value of its liabilities. Like any limited liability firm, banks are subject to both types of risks, but the consequences of these risks are much more dramatic for banks than for the other sectors of the economy. This has justified the implementation in most countries of complex regulation systems, studied in Chapter 9.

The classification that this chapter will use stems from the classification of banking activities offered in Chapter 1: The credit activity of banks is affected by *default risks,* which occur when a borrower is not able to repay a debt (principal or interest).[1] *Liquidity risks* occur when a bank must make unexpected cash payments. This type of risk essentially comes from the specificity of the demand deposit contract: unlike the creditors of other kinds of firms, depositors are allowed to demand their money at any time. Consequently, the deposit activity is affected by the risk of an unexpected massive withdrawal by depositors. Finally, *market risks* affect the portfolios of marketable assets (and liabilities) held by banks.

Default, liquidity, and market risks are examined successively in this chapter.

8.1 Default Risks

8.1.1 Institutional Context

Defining and measuring credit risk is equivalent to determining how the market evaluates the probability of default by a particular borrower, taking into account all the possibilities of diversification and hedging provided by financial markets. In part, the level of risk depends on the institutional arrangements to which the banks are subject, either through the interbank money market or through specialized institutions created for this purpose. This connection between the institutional framework and the different elements that determine the pricing of credit risk is particularly important in applied work.[2] Since this section is mainly concerned with the theoretical foundations of default risk, this discussion will simply list the different points that are relevant to measuring credit risk and will give a more detailed description of the institutional context and its relation to credit risk in the appendix.

Clearly the riskiness of a loan will be affected by the existence of

- collateral

- compensating balances

- endorsement

But other characteristics of the credit market will also be relevant: Do banks share information on their creditors? How is the bankruptcy process settled? When reading the next sections, the reader should keep in mind that the (random) return on a loan will depend on all these features.

Notice that in the process of international competition, as well as in a process of market integration like the one undergone by Europe, differences between these institutions or regulations across countries are fundamental not only because they may represent a barrier to entry, but also because they may tend to concentrate some banking activities in the countries that provide the more efficient institutions and regulations.

8.1.2   Evaluating the Cost of Default Risks

To understand how default risk affects the competitive pricing of loans, this discussion will begin with a simple approach that will justify the use of the risk spread (the difference between the interest rate on a risky loan and the riskless rate for the same maturity) as a measure of the credit risk of an asset. Indeed, this discussion will show how the risk spread is determined by the borrower's probability of default. It will then proceed to examine a more complete approach based on option pricing (Merton 1974).

A Simple Interpretation of Risk Spread

Assuming that default risk is diversifiable and that the bank under consideration can indeed diversify this risk away through a large population of borrowers, the only thing that matters is the probability of default. Credit scoring methods, the analogue of actuarial techniques used by insurers, allow banks to estimate a priori this probability of default based on the observable characteristics of the loan applicant.

From a financial viewpoint, the value of such a loan (subject to a diversifiable credit risk) is nothing but the expected present value of the borrower's repayments. Leaving aside interest rate risk for the moment, assume that the refinancing rate r is constant, and take e^{-r} as the one-period discount factor.[3] Consider now a risky loan, characterized by a series of promised repayments $(C_1, C_2, \ldots, C_n)$ at future dates $(t_1, t_2, \ldots, t_n)$. Assume for simplicity that if the firm defaults, the bank receives nothing. The expected cost of default risk for this loan can be measured by the difference between

$$P_0 = \sum_{k=1}^{n} C_k e^{-rt_k}, \tag{8.1}$$

the value of the loan if there were no default risk, and

$$P = \sum_{k=1}^{n} C_k p_k e^{-rt_k}, \tag{8.2}$$

the value of the risky loan, where p_k denotes the probability that the k-th repayment will not be defaulted, assuming that there are no partial repayments.

In practice, however, the most commonly used instrument for evaluating the cost of default risk is the difference (spread) between the yield to maturity R of the risky loan and the refinancing rate r. R is defined implicitly by the equation

$$P = \sum_{k=1}^{n} C_k e^{-Rt_k}, \tag{8.3}$$

and this determines the value of the spread $s = R - r$.

Bierman and Hass (1975) and Yawitz (1977) have proved the following simple result:

Result 8.1   If the firms' default follows a Poisson process of intensity λ, the spread s is independent of the characteristics of the loan. It is equal to the intensity of the Poisson process:

$$s = \lambda. \tag{8.4}$$

Proof   In a Poisson process of intensity λ, the probability of survival at date t_k is by definition

$$p_k = e^{-\lambda t_k}. \tag{8.5}$$

Combining 8.2, 8.3, and 8.5 yields

$$\sum_{k=1}^{n} C_k e^{-Rt_k} = \sum_{k=1}^{n} C_k e^{-\lambda t_k} e^{-rt_k}.$$

This equation in R has a unique solution, independent of $C_1, \ldots, C_n$:

$$R = r + \lambda.$$

Therefore:

$$s = R - r = \lambda. \qquad \blacksquare$$

Consequently, if one considers corporate debt of a certain type, the spread can be considered as the instantaneous probability of failure λ that the market assesses implicitly to the particular class of borrowers under consideration. For instance, a spread of fifty basis points indicates a failure probability of $1 - e^{-\lambda} \sim \lambda = 0.5$ percent per year.

The Option Approach to Pricing Default Risk

The simple approach just explained relies on three assumptions that are not very satisfactory: (1) the instantaneous probability of failure is constant and exogenous, (2) credit risk is completely diversifiable, and (3) in case of failure, the residual value of the firm is zero. Consider now what happens when these assumptions are relaxed.

When credit risk is not completely diversifiable, a risk premium must be introduced, and the analysis becomes more involved. However, financial markets provide insurance possibilities for banks. Therefore the risk premium quoted by banks must be in line with the ones prevailing in the securities market. This remark will allow development of a model for pricing risky debts following Merton (1974).

Consider a firm that plans to borrow a certain amount D_0 at date $t = 0$ and repay D at date $t = T$. The yield to maturity r_L is defined by

$$D = D_0 e^{r_L T}. \qquad (8.6)$$

Let $V(t)$ denote the value at date t of the firm's total assets, assumed to be marketable at no cost, and assume that the firm has no further debt outstanding. Two things can happen at date T:

1. If $D \leq V(T)$, the firm is solvent, and the bank gets D as promised.

2. If $D > V(T)$, the firm is bankrupt, its assets are liquidated, and the bank gets only $V(T)$.

The terminal payoff to the bank is thus

$$\text{Min}(D, V(T)), \qquad (8.7)$$

and the market value of the firm's equity at date T is

$$\text{Max}(0, V(T) - D). \qquad (8.8)$$

This is exactly the payoff of a call option[4] on the firm's assets with a strike price equal to D. Consequently, from a pure financial viewpoint, issuing a risky loan to a limited liability firm is similar to buying the firm's assets and selling a call option to its stockholders. Of course, this approach is somewhat simplistic, since it neglects intermediate payments and liquidation costs. Also, in most cases several loans of different maturities and seniorities coexist. But this fundamental insight will allow explicit evaluation of the cost of credit risk in some simple cases.

The only further restriction to be imposed is an assumption on the probability distribution of $V(t)$. Following Merton (1974), assume that $V(t)$ follows a geometric random walk, which is equivalent to saying that instantaneous returns on V are Gaussian, independent, and identically distributed:

$$\frac{dV}{V} = \alpha dt + \sigma dZ,$$

where α, σ are constant ($\sigma > 0$) and Z is a standard Wiener process.[5] Under this assumption, the market value C of a call option on V can be computed by the Black-Scholes formula (1973).[6] Since this discussion focuses on the (market) value D_0 of the loan, directly compute

$$D_0 = V - C,$$

and the following is obtained:

$$D_0 = V N(h_1) + D e^{-rT} N(h_2), \tag{8.9}$$

where

$$N(x) = \frac{1}{\sqrt{2\pi}} \int_{-\infty}^{x} (exp - \frac{1}{2} t^2) dt$$

is the cumulative of the standard Gaussian distribution, and

$$\begin{cases} h_1 &= \frac{1}{\sigma \sqrt{T}} \log \frac{D e^{-rT}}{V} - \frac{1}{2} \sigma \sqrt{T} \\ h_2 &= -\frac{1}{\sigma \sqrt{T}} \log \frac{D e^{-rT}}{V} - \frac{1}{2} \sigma \sqrt{T}. \end{cases}$$

Again, the interest spread s is defined as the difference between the yield to maturity r_L of the risky loan and the riskless rate r. Using formula 8.6 yields

$$s = r_L - r = -\frac{1}{T} \log \frac{D_0}{D e^{-rT}}.$$

Now, 8.9 yields

$$s = -\frac{1}{T} \log \left[\frac{N(h_1)}{d} + N(h_2) \right],$$

where $d = \frac{D e^{-rT}}{V}$ is the "quasi" debt-to-asset ratio.[7] A comparison with previous result 8.1 is easy, since one can show that $N(h_2)$ can be interpreted as the (risk-adjusted) probability of survival at T. In the previous model, the probability of survival was $p_T = e^{-\lambda T}$ and the spread was just $s = \lambda = -\frac{1}{T} \log p_T$.

Here the model is richer for three reasons:

1. The probability of failure is not exogenous; it depends in particular on the indebtedness of the firm.

2. The market pricing of risk is taken into account.

3. The liquidation value of the firm is not zero.

Merton then studies the influence of parameters d, σ, and T on s, obtaining the following properties:

Result 8.2

1. The interest spread s increases with the quasi debt-to-asset ratio d. Thus, the more indebted firms will pay higher interest rates.

2. The interest spread s increases with the volatility σ of the firm's assets. Thus, firms having riskier activities will pay higher interest rates.

3. The global risk premium sT increases with the maturity of the loan.[8] Thus, longer loans will be more costly.

All these results, proved in problem 8.6.2, confirm casual empiricism. Notice, however, that s is not necessarily increasing in T, although the global risk premium sT is.

Several restrictive assumptions limit the validity of the Merton model: deterministic refinancing rate r, no interest payments, no other outstanding loans. When stochastic interest rates are introduced (Décamps 1996), results a and c remain valid but not result b: when there is a negative correlation between r and the value V of the firm's asset, s is minimized for a positive value of σ. Intuitively, for small values of V, the firm's assets provide some insurance against fluctuations of r. More generally, Décamps shows that when interest rates are stochastic, the volatility σ ceases to be a good measure of risk for the loan. When interest payments are introduced, compound option techniques have to be used (Geske 1977), and no explicit formula is available. Finally, when several loans are simultaneously outstanding, seniority rules are fundamental. This topic has recently been the subject of interesting theoretical literature (see for example Bizer and DeMarzo 1992), but the implications on the pricing of risky loans have not been explored yet.

8.1.3 Extensions

Collateral

The previous analysis can be easily extended to secured lending (see, e.g., Schwartz and Torous 1992). In this case, the bank obtains the minimum value of

- the firms's debt.

- the collateral, net of liquidation costs, plus the fraction of the difference between the firm's debt and the value of the collateral that corresponds to the depreciation of the unsecured debt. This is true provided bankruptcy laws assign the same priority to holders of secured debt that have a residual claim as to holders of unsecured debt, as usually is the case.

In evaluating the risk of a collateralized loan, the lender will have to estimate the value of the loan at the moment when the loan arrangement is made, as well as the volatility of the stochastic process followed by the collateral's price. Use of collateral usually entails a cost that will depend on the type of collateral. In any case, a collateralized loan will always be safer, and therefore the interest rate will be lower. Recall, though, that as Chapter 4 showed, when there is moral hazard on behalf of the firm, the collateral may have a different function and lead to more efficient contracting.

Contingent Repayments

A standard debt contract is one in which the date and amounts of repayments are fixed in advance or adjusted to some level of interest rates. Although standard debt contracts are the most common type of loans, there are a number of contracts that allow for contingent repayment.[9]

Whereas it may be clear that contracts allowing for contingent repayments are more costly, the benefits of these types of contracts are clear in terms of risk sharing and limiting the cost of market imperfections (see Chapter 4).

8.2   Liquidity Risk

At the individual level, liquidity management is not fundamentally different for banks than for other firms. It can even be seen as a particular case of the general problem of managing inventories of any sort. However, for reasons that were discussed in Chapter 7, the situation is different at the macroeconomic level, since the liquidity problems of a single bank can propagate very quickly, affect other banks (externality), and give rise to what is called a "systemic" risk. This has justified the creation of three mechanisms, designed to limit the possible extension of these liquidity problems: the Lender of Last Resort, deposit insurance, and reserve requirements. These mechanisms will be studied in detail in Chapter 9.

This chapter will focus on the microeconomic level. The management of reserves is studied in subsection 8.2.1. Subsection 8.2.2 will show how the introduction of liquidity risk modifies the conclusions of the Monti-Klein model. Then subsection 8.2.3 will present another paradigm for banks' behavior based on inventory management: following Ho and Saunders (1981), a bank is assimilated to a security dealer, who determines an interest margin (bid-ask spread) between loans and deposits as a function of inventory risks.

8.2.1 Reserve Management

Consider the problem of a bank that wants to determine the quantity R of liquidities (reserves) to be held, out of a total amount D of deposits. The remaining $(D - R)$ is assumed to be invested in riskless (but illiquid) loans. Using for simplicity a static framework, suppose that the net amount of withdrawals at the end of the period is a random variable $\tilde{x}$. If the realization x of $\tilde{x}$ is greater than R, the bank has a liquidity shortage, and it has to pay a penalty $r_p(x - R)$, proportional to the shortage. A more reasonable assumption would be that the bank can borrow from the Central Bank or possibly from other banks at rate $r_p + r_D$ (where p stands for penalty and r_D is the rate on deposits), but it would imply more than one period, so this example will adopt the first approach. r_p is of course higher than the rate of return r_L on loans, which is itself higher than the interest rate r on reserves. Suppose for simplicity that deposits are costless for the bank (no interest paid, no management cost) and that the bank is risk neutral. The bank's expected profit is

$$\Pi(R) = r_L(D - R) + rR - r_p E[Max(0, \tilde{x} - R)].$$

The last term in this formula (the expected cost of liquidity shortages) is a convex function of R, which is differentiable under the assumption that the random variable $\tilde{x}$ has a continuous density $f(x)$. Let $C(R)$ denote this cost:

$$C(R) = r_p \int_R^{+\infty} (x - R) f(x) dx$$

$$C'(R) = -r_p \int_R^{+\infty} f(x) dx = -r_p \, \text{Proba}[\tilde{x} \geq R]$$

$$C''(R) = r_p f(R) \geq 0.$$

This implies that $\Pi(R)$ is a concave differentiable function of R. It is maximum when

$$\Pi'(R) = -(r_L - r) + r_p \, \text{Proba}[\tilde{x} \geq R] = 0.$$

Therefore, the optimal amount of reserves R^* is determined by the following relation:

$$\text{Proba}[\tilde{x} \geq R^*] = \frac{r_L - r}{r_p}. \tag{8.10}$$

Result 8.3 The optimal amount of reserves is the amount for which the marginal opportunity cost of holding reserves equals the expected cost of liquidity shortage. Alternatively, the optimal probability of liquidity shortage is just equal to the ratio of the liquidity premium $(r_L - r)$ to the "penalty" interest rate r_p.

For instance, if $r_L - r$ equals 3 percent and r_p equals 15 percent, the probability of liquidity shortage is 20 percent, which seems relatively important. Thus, formula 8.10 seems to overestimate a little the actual probability of liquidity shortage. Several modifications of this basic model have been suggested to increase its predictive power. For instance, if the cost of refinancing r_p increases with the amount borrowed by the bank, or if the bank is risk averse, the optimal probability of liquidity shortage will clearly decrease. Another improvement is to introduce adjustment costs and information acquisition on depositors' behavior (Baltensperger and Milde 1976, Stanhouse 1986). To increase the realism of the model, one can also introduce different kinds of deposits, and associate compulsory reserves with different coefficients, as well as penalty systems when these requirements are not met. The analysis becomes more complex but is not substantially modified.

The next subsection will show how introducing reserves management into the Monti-Klein model provides a solution to the asset–liability separation enigma mentioned in Chapter 3. With uncertainty and liquidity requirements, asset and liability decisions become interdependent.

8.2.2   Introducing Liquidity Risk in the Monti-Klein Model

One of the conclusions of the Monti-Klein model, presented in Chapter 3, was not entirely satisfactory: when there exists an infinitely elastic source of funds (money market), the optimal policy of a (monopolistic) bank will be characterized by a separation between the pricing of assets (loans) and liabilities (deposits). This seems completely in contradiction with the stylized facts of (modern) bankers' behavior, since bankers insist, on the contrary, on the necessity of global asset–liability management. Moreover, this separation result would imply, as has been seen, that any regulation on deposits has no effect on the credit market.

Prisman, Slovin, and Sushka (1986) show how introducing liquidity risk into the Monti-Klein model may alter this result. The simplest way to bring in a liquidity risk is to introduce some randomness in the volume of funds collected or distributed by the bank. Thus, the demand for loans can be stochastic, as Prisman, Slovin, and Sushka assume, or it can be the volume of deposits that is subject to random shocks, as assumed here, so as to be more in line with the last section. The (monopolistic) bank is assumed to choose the rates r_L and r_D of loans and deposits, taking into account the (downward sloping) demand function for loans:

$$L = L(r_L)$$

and the (upward sloping) supply function of deposits:

$$D = D(r_D),$$

to which a random amount $\tilde{x}$ of withdrawals will be subtracted at the end of the period. Assuming no other source of funds is available to the bank, the amount of reserves is simply

$$R = D(r_D) - L(r_L). \tag{8.11}$$

As before, the reserves are assumed to yield a return r, but in addition the bank must pay a proportional penalty r_p in case of liquidity shortage at the end of the period. The expected profit of the bank is thus

$$\Pi = r_L L(r_L) - r_D D(r_D) + rR - r_p E[Max(0, \tilde{x} - R)],$$

or, using 8.11,

$$\Pi = (r_L - r)L(r_L) + (r - r_D)D(r_D) - r_p E[Max(0, \tilde{x} - D(r_D) + L(r_L))].$$

Make the usual assumptions on L and D to ensure that Π is quasi-concave in r_L and r_D: $DD'' - 2D'^2 > 0$ and $LL'' - 2L'^2 > 0$. Under these assumptions, the maximum is characterized by the first order conditions

$$\begin{cases} \frac{\partial \Pi}{\partial r_L} &= (r_L - r)L'(r_L) + L(r_L) - r_p \operatorname{Proba}[\tilde{x} \geq R]L'(r_L) = 0 \\ \frac{\partial \Pi}{\partial r_D} &= (r - r_D)D'(r_D) - D(r_D) + r_p \operatorname{Proba}[\tilde{x} \geq R]D'(r_D) = 0. \end{cases}$$

Introducing the elasticities of the demand for loans and the supply of deposits,

$$\varepsilon_L = -\frac{r_L L'(r_L)}{L(r_L)} \qquad \varepsilon_D = \frac{r_D D'(r_D)}{D(r_D)},$$

the optimum value of r_L and r_D is

$$r_L^* = \frac{r + r_p \operatorname{Proba}[\tilde{x} \geq R]}{(1 - \frac{1}{\varepsilon_L})} \tag{8.12}$$

$$r_D^* = \frac{r + r_p \operatorname{Proba}[\tilde{x} \geq R]}{(1 + \frac{1}{\varepsilon_D})}. \tag{8.13}$$

Thus, the only difference between these formulas and those obtained in the Monti-Klein model is that in this example the cost of the bank's resource is higher than r, because it includes now the expected cost of a liquidity shortage. Since the probability of such a shortage depends on R, the difference between D and L, this introduces the desired dependence between assets and liabilities.

Prisman, Slovic, and Sushka proceed by performing an interesting comparative static analysis, the results of which are stated below:

Result 8.4

1. If the penalty rate r_p increases, the rates r_L^* and r_D^* also increase. Consequently the volume of credit L decreases and the volume of deposit D increases.

2. If the variance of $\tilde{x}$ increases (withdrawals become more uncertain), the impact on L depends on the sign of R. In the most plausible case ($R > 0$) this impact is negative: the volume of credit decreases.

These results are proved in problem 8.5.1.

8.2.3 The Bank as a Market Maker

Security traders, such as brokers and dealers in the London Stock Exchange, specialists in the New York Stock Exchange, or market makers in the Paris Bourse, now play a fundamental role in the provision of liquidity in modern financial markets. Financial economists, such as Ho and Stoll (1980) have studied the determination of the bid-ask prices as a function of the characteristics of the security, as well as the inventory policy of the trader. Ho and Saunders (1981) have had the interesting idea of adapting this modeling to banking activity, thus providing a new paradigm for banking behavior. Indeed, like the market maker, a bank can be seen as providing liquidity to the market. Like the market maker it will hold *illiquid* assets, and therefore consider the risk of an unbalanced portfolio with extreme positions either long (because it has granted more loans than desired) or short (because it has taken too many deposits).

Therefore it is worth emphasizing that this approach explains the illiquidity of banks' assets and liabilities, and therefore views a bank as different from a mutual fund.

In the Ho-Saunders approach, a bank is considered as an intermediary (market maker) on the market for funds, which sets a deposit rate r_D and a loan rate r_L (the equivalent of ask and bid prices) as a function of its inventory level and of the volatility of interest rates.

To maintain the analogy with the market maker, assume there is no credit risk and no difference in maturities between deposits and loans. To be more specific, suppose that the bank is confronted with stochastic arrivals of depositors and borrowers, modeled by Poisson processes of respective intensities λ_D and λ_L (as usual, L stands for loans and D for deposits). For simplicity, loans and deposits have the same size Q (standardization) and the same duration (no transformation). So the only thing that matters for the bank is the difference $(L - D)$, that is, its net inventory I resulting from its commercial activity. The bank has also a (fixed) portfolio γ of marketable assets and a money market (positive or negative) position M, both of which are inherited from the past and result from the need to fund loans or to invest excess liquidities. The total wealth of the bank at the end of the period is

$$\tilde{W} = \gamma(1 + \tilde{r}_\gamma) + M(1 + r) + I(1 + \tilde{r}_I), \tag{8.14}$$

where $\tilde{r}_\gamma$ (respectively $\tilde{r}_I$) is the random return on the bank portfolio (respectively on the credit activity) and r is the (deterministic) money market return. The objective of the bank is assumed to be of the mean-variance type:[10]

$$U = E(\tilde{W}) - \frac{1}{2}\rho \text{var}(\tilde{W}), \tag{8.15}$$

where ρ is a risk aversion coefficient. Using 8.14 and 8.15, compute U as a function of I and M:

$$U = U(I, M) = \gamma(1 + r_\gamma) + M(1 + r) + I(1 + r_I)$$

$$- \frac{1}{2}\rho\left[\sigma_\gamma^2 \gamma^2 + 2\sigma_{\gamma I}\gamma I + \sigma_I^2 I^2\right], \tag{8.16}$$

where

$$r_\gamma = E(\tilde{r}_\gamma), \qquad r_I = E(\tilde{r}_I), \quad \sigma_\gamma^2 = var(\tilde{r}_\gamma),$$

$$\sigma_{\gamma I} = cov(\tilde{r}_\gamma, \tilde{r}_I) \quad \text{and} \qquad \sigma_I^2 = var(\tilde{r}_I).$$

Consider now the increase in the bank's utility consecutive to the market-making activity. The mechanism is as follows: the bank sets margins a and b for deposits and loans, which means that the bank sells securities (attracts deposits) at a bid price $Q(1 + a)$ and buys them (grants loans) at an ask price $Q(1 - b)$. This means that by paying $Q(1 + a)$, the depositor will obtain at the end of the period $Q(1 + \tilde{r}_I)$. Therefore, the rate of return for depositors will be $(\frac{1+\tilde{r}_I}{1+a} - 1)$. Similarly, the rate paid by borrowers is $(\frac{1+r_{\tilde{I}}}{1-b} - 1)$. In particular, if $\tilde{r}_I$ were deterministic, these rates would be respectively

$$r_D = \frac{r_I - a}{1 + a} \quad \text{for depositors and} \tag{8.17}$$

$$r_L = \frac{r_I + b}{1 - b} \quad \text{for borrowers.} \tag{8.18}$$

When attracting an additional deposit, the bank obtains an increase of utility equal to

$$(\Delta U|\text{deposit}) = U(I - Q, M + Q(1 + a)) - U(I, M)$$

$$= Q\left\{(1 + a)(1 + r) - (1 + r_I)\right\}$$

$$- \frac{1}{2}\rho\left\{\sigma_I^2(Q^2 - 2QI) - 2\sigma_{\gamma I}\gamma Q\right\}. \tag{8.19}$$

Similarly, when granting an additional loan, the bank gets

$$(\Delta U | \text{loan}) = U(I + Q, M - Q(1 - b)) - U(I, M)$$

$$= Q\{(1 + r_I) - (1 - b)(1 + r)\}$$

$$- \frac{1}{2}\rho\left\{\sigma_I^2(Q^2 + 2QI) + 2\sigma_{\gamma I}\gamma Q\right\}. \tag{8.20}$$

When setting margins a and b, the (monopolistic) bank takes into account not only the direct effect on the quantities, but also the impact on supply and demand. More specifically, depositors and borrowers are assumed to arrive randomly, according to Poisson processes, the intensities λ_D and λ_L of which are decreasing functions, respectively, of a and b. Ho and Saunders adopt a linear symmetric specification:

$$\lambda_D = \alpha - \beta a, \quad \lambda_L = \alpha - \beta b. \tag{8.21}$$

The optimal margins a and b are the ones that maximize the (expected) increase in utility:

$$\Delta U = \lambda_D(\Delta U | \text{deposit}) + \lambda_L(\Delta U | \text{loan}).$$

The first order conditions give

$$\frac{d\lambda_D}{da}(\Delta U | \text{deposit}) + \lambda_D Q(1 + r) = 0 \tag{8.22}$$

$$\frac{d\lambda_L}{db}(\Delta U | \text{loan}) + \lambda_L Q(1 + r) = 0. \tag{8.23}$$

Using 8.21, and adding 8.22 and 8.23, yields

$$0 = -\beta[(\Delta U | \text{deposit}) + (\Delta U | \text{loan})] + (\lambda_L + \lambda_D)Q(1 + r),$$

and using $\lambda_D + \lambda_L = 2\alpha - \beta(a + b)$ yields

$$(\Delta U | \text{deposit}) + (\Delta U | \text{loan}) = Q(1 + r)\left\{2\frac{\alpha}{\beta} - s\right\},$$

where $s = a + b$ is the bid-ask spread (total margin). The optimal values of a and b are complicated expressions, involving in particular γ and I. But the optimal spread s has a simple expression, independent of γ and I. Replacing $(\Delta U | \text{deposit})$ and $(\Delta U | \text{loan})$ by their values given by equations 8.19 and 8.20 yields

$$Q(1 + r)s - \rho\sigma_I^2 Q^2 = Q(1 + r)\left\{2\frac{\alpha}{\beta} - s\right\},$$

or finally

$$s = \frac{\alpha}{\beta} + \frac{1}{2} \frac{\rho \sigma_I^2 Q}{(1+r)}. \tag{8.24}$$

Result 8.5 The total margin between loans and deposits is the sum of two terms:

• $\frac{\alpha}{\beta}$ is the "risk neutral spread" that would be chosen by a risk neutral monopoly. It depends on the elasticities of supply and demand.

• The other term is a risk premium, proportional to the risk aversion coefficient ρ to the variance of the return on the credit activity σ_I^2 (which is itself related to the volatility of interest rates) and to the size of transaction Q.

• The volume of inventories I does not affect s (but it affects a and b).

8.3   Market Risk

The modern theory of portfolio management has been developed by Sharpe (1964), Lintner (1965), and Markowitz (1952). As such, it is of course interesting for banks, which often hold large portfolios of marketable assets. More importantly, this portfolio theory has also led to another paradigm for banking behavior, essentially developed by Pyle (1971) and Hart and Jaffee (1974). The idea is to assimilate all assets and liabilities of the bank into securities of a particular sort, and to consider the whole bank itself as an enormous portfolio of these securities. In this approach, the only specificity of the bank's liabilities is that they correspond to short positions in the bank's portfolio. Portfolio theory will be discussed briefly in subsection 8.3.1. The Pyle-Hart-Jaffee approach will be presented in subsection 8.3.2, and subsection 8.3.3 will study an application to the analysis of capital requirements.

8.3.1   Modern Portfolio Theory: The Capital Asset Pricing Model

This presentation of modern portfolio theory will be extremely brief, since there are excellent references on that topic (for instance, Ingersoll 1987). The brilliant idea of Sharpe, Lintner, and Markowitz was to simplify the general problem of optimal portfolio selection by assuming that investors' preferences U depend only on the first two moments μ and σ^2 (mean and variance) of the random liquidation value of their portfolio. This can be justified by assuming that investors have quadratic Von Neumann Morgenstern preferences, or else that stochastic distributions of asset returns belong to a particular parameterized family (normal or more generally elliptical random variables).

Let W denote the initial wealth of the investor and x_i $(i = 1, \ldots, N)$ be the amount invested in the i-th risky asset. The vector $x = (x_1, \ldots, x_N)$

thus represents the risky portfolio held by the investor. The rest of her wealth $(W - \sum_{i=1}^{N} x_i)$ is invested in a riskless asset of return R_0. The random returns $(\tilde{R}_i)_i$ of risky assets have first and second moments denoted as follows:

$$E(\tilde{R}_i) = R_0 + \rho_i \qquad i = 1, \ldots, N$$

$$cov(\tilde{R}_i, \tilde{R}_j) = v_{ij} \qquad i, j = 1, \ldots, N.$$

At the end of the period, the investor's wealth is

$$\tilde{W} = [(W - \sum_{i=1}^{N} x_i) R_0 + \sum_{i=1}^{N} x_i \tilde{R}_i].$$

The first two moments of this random variable are

$$\mu = E[\tilde{W}] = W R_0 + \sum_{i=1}^{N} x_i \rho_i, \tag{8.25}$$

$$\sigma^2 = var(\tilde{W}) = (\sum_{i=1}^{N} \sum_{j=1}^{N} v_{ij} x_i x_j). \tag{8.26}$$

Under the mean variance assumption, the investor will choose x so as to maximize her utility function $U(\mu, \sigma^2)$ (where $\frac{\partial U}{\partial \mu} > 0$, $\frac{\partial U}{\partial \sigma^2} < 0$) under constraints 8.25 and 8.26. The first order conditions for a maximum are

$$\frac{\partial U}{\partial \mu} \frac{\partial \mu}{\partial x_i} + \frac{\partial U}{\partial \sigma^2} \frac{\partial \sigma^2}{\partial x_i} = 0,$$

or

$$\frac{\partial U}{\partial \mu} \cdot \rho_i + 2 \frac{\partial U}{\partial \sigma^2} \sum_{j} v_{ij} x_j = 0, \quad i = 1, \ldots, N. \tag{8.27}$$

Let $\rho = (\rho_1, \ldots, \rho_N)$ denote the vector of expected excess returns, and $V = (v_{ij})_{i,j=1,\ldots,N}$ the variance-covariance matrix of risky assets, assumed to be invertible. The first order conditions can be written in a more compact form:

$$-\lambda \rho + V x = 0,$$

where[11] $\lambda = -\frac{\partial U}{\partial \mu} / \left(2 \frac{\partial U}{\partial \sigma^2} \right)$, or

$$x = \lambda V^{-1} \rho. \tag{8.28}$$

Since V and ρ are independent of the investor, this relation implies that all investors will choose colinear risky portfolios. A more financially appealing way of expressing this result is that all investors obtain their preferred portfolio by a combination of the riskless asset and a fixed portfolio $V^{-1}\rho$, interpreted as a mutual fund. The only difference in behavior among investors is captured by the coefficient λ: a more risk averse agent will buy more of the riskless asset and less of the risky mutual fund.

An interesting part of the Capital Asset Pricing Model (CAPM), which will not be used further in this book (and therefore will not be discussed) consists in writing a general equilibrium formulation of equation 8.28. Without entering into a full description of this classical model, consider its two main implications. If the market portfolio x_M is defined as the aggregation of all individual (risky) portfolios, equation 8.28 then has two important consequences:

1. Since x_M is the sum of individual risky portfolios, which are all colinear, these individual risky portfolios may conversely be considered as all colinear to x_M. Therefore the market portfolio can be used as the mutual fund described previously.

2. The expected excess return of any asset i at equilibrium is proportional to the regression coefficient β_i of $\tilde{R}_i$ on the return $\tilde{R}_M$ of the market portfolio. Indeed, β_i is nothing but the i-th component of the vector $V x_M$, which according to 8.28 and the previous remark is proportional to ρ.

The following subsection will discuss the application of the CAPM to the modeling of banks' behavior: the Pyle-Hart-Jaffee approach.

8.3.2 The Bank as a Portfolio Manager: The Pyle (1971), Hart-Jaffee (1974) Approach

This subsection will show how mean-variance analysis can provide an adequate tool for modeling the management of market risk by commercial banks. Pyle (1971) and Hart and Jaffee (1974) have studied a new paradigm for describing the behavior of financial intermediaries. When this paradigm is compared with the one developed by Klein (1971), the main differences are that in Pyle and Hart and Jaffee the markets for assets (and liabilities) are assumed to be *competitive* and that *risk* is explicitly taken into account.[12]

As a first illustration of this new paradigm, consider the simple case of only two risky financial products L and D, to be interpreted later as loans and deposits. The bank is assimilated to a portfolio manager, who has to decide the amounts x_L and x_D to be invested in these two risky activities, the rest of his wealth being invested in reserves (riskless asset). Make no assumption a priori on the sign of x_L and x_D. The competitive behavior means that the bank takes the returns $\tilde{r}_L$, $\tilde{r}_D$, and r of these activities as given. Therefore the (random) profit of the bank is

$$\tilde{\pi} = \left[\tilde{r}_L x_L + \tilde{r}_D x_D + r(W - x_L - x_D) \right],$$

or

$$\tilde{\pi} = Wr + (\tilde{r}_L - r)x_L + (\tilde{r}_D - r)x_D.$$

Using the same notations as before, the objective function of the bank can be expressed as

$$\Phi(x) = U(E(\tilde{\pi}), \text{var}(\tilde{\pi})).$$

If x^* maximizes Φ, the first order condition implies, as before,

$$x^* = \lambda V^{-1}\rho, \tag{8.29}$$

where

$$V = \begin{pmatrix} \text{var}(\tilde{r}_L) & \text{cov}(\tilde{r}_L, \tilde{r}_D) \\ \text{cov}(\tilde{r}_L, \tilde{r}_D) & \text{var}(\tilde{r}_D) \end{pmatrix}, \quad \lambda = -\frac{\partial U}{\partial \mu} \bigg/ \left(2\frac{\partial U}{\partial \sigma^2} \right),$$

and

$$\rho = \begin{pmatrix} \bar{r}_L - r \\ \bar{r}_D - r \end{pmatrix}.$$

Thus:

Result 8.6   If $\bar{r}_D < r < \bar{r}_L$ and $\text{cov}(\tilde{r}_L, \tilde{r}_D) > 0$, then $x_L^* > 0$ and $x_D^* < 0$.

This result can be seen as an endogenous explanation for the intermediation activity of banks. If the expected excess returns on the deposit and loan activities are respectively negative and positive, and if the covariance between these returns is positive, then a competitive portfolio manager will invest a negative amount on deposits (i.e., he will issue such instruments) and a positive amount on loans. In other words, he would have loans on the asset side of the balance sheet ($L = x_L^*$) and deposits on the liability side ($D = -x_D^* > 0$). If the conclusion does not hold, it means that either $x_D^* > 0$, and the bank borrows at the riskless rate to invest in two types of loans, or $x_L^* < 0$, in which case the bank offers two types of deposits and invests the proceeds at the riskless rate.

Proof   The proof is easily derived from equation 8.29:

$$x^* = \begin{pmatrix} x_L^* \\ x_D^* \end{pmatrix} = \lambda V^{-1}\rho = \frac{\lambda}{\Delta} \begin{pmatrix} \text{var}(\tilde{r}_D) & -\text{cov}(\tilde{r}_L, \tilde{r}_D) \\ -\text{cov}(\tilde{r}_L, \tilde{r}_D) & \text{var}(\tilde{r}_L) \end{pmatrix} \begin{pmatrix} \bar{r}_L - r \\ \bar{r}_D - r \end{pmatrix},$$

where the following formula is used for inverting a 2×2 matrix:

$$\begin{pmatrix} a & c \\ b & d \end{pmatrix}^{-1} = \frac{1}{\Delta} \begin{pmatrix} d & -c \\ -b & a \end{pmatrix},$$

and $\Delta = ad - bc$ is the determinant of V.

Now λ is positive because of risk aversion $\left(\frac{\partial U}{\partial \mu} > 0, \frac{\partial U}{\partial \sigma^2} < 0\right)$, and Δ is positive because V is a positive definite matrix. Therefore:

$$x_L^* = \frac{\lambda}{\Delta}\left[\underbrace{\mathrm{var}(\tilde{r}_D)}_{>0}\underbrace{(\bar{r}_L - r)}_{>0} - \underbrace{\mathrm{cov}(\tilde{r}_L, \tilde{r}_D)}_{>0}\underbrace{(\bar{r}_D - r)}_{<0}\right],$$

and x_L^* is positive.

Similarly,

$$x_D^* = \frac{\lambda}{\Delta}\left[\underbrace{-\mathrm{cov}(\tilde{r}_L, \tilde{r}_D)}_{<0}\underbrace{(\bar{r}_L - r)}_{>0} + \underbrace{\mathrm{var}(\tilde{r}_L)}_{>0}\underbrace{(\bar{r}_D - r)}_{<0}\right],$$

and x_D^* is negative.   ∎

Notice that result 8.6 gives only a sufficient condition. The necessary condition for $x_L^* > 0$ is $\mathrm{var}(\tilde{r}_D)(\bar{r}_L - r) > \mathrm{cov}(\tilde{r}_L, \tilde{r}_D)(\bar{r}_D - r)$, and for $x_D^* < 0$ is $\mathrm{cov}(\tilde{r}_L, r_D)(\bar{r}_L - r) > \mathrm{var}(\tilde{r}_L)(\bar{r}_D - r)$. This allows financial intermediaries to exist even if $\bar{r}_D > r$ or $\bar{r}_L < r$, provided that $\mathrm{cov}(\tilde{r}_L, \tilde{r}_D) > 0$.

Another interesting outcome of the mean-variance approach is a comparative statics analysis of the bank's behavior. How are the volumes of deposits attracted and loans issued affected by changes in the expectations or variances of returns? The answer is given by the following result:

Result 8.7

1. x_L^* is an increasing function of $(\bar{r}_L - r)$ and a decreasing function of $(\bar{r}_D - r)$ and $\mathrm{var}(\tilde{r}_L)$.

2. $|x_D^*|$ is an increasing function of $(\bar{r}_L - r)$ and a decreasing function of $(\bar{r}_D - r)$ and $\mathrm{var}(\tilde{r}_D)$.

Proof   It is a direct consequence of the formula for x_L^* and x_D^* obtained in the proof of result 8.6 (remembering that $x_D^* < 0$). The only properties that are not obvious are

$$\frac{\partial x_L^*}{\partial \mathrm{var}(\tilde{r}_L)} = -\frac{x_L^*}{\Delta}\frac{\partial \Delta}{\partial \mathrm{var}(\tilde{r}_L)} < 0$$

and

$$\frac{\partial |x_D^*|}{\partial \mathrm{var}(\tilde{r}_D)} = -\frac{|x_D^*|}{\Delta}\frac{\partial \Delta}{\partial \mathrm{var}(\tilde{r}_D)} < 0. \qquad ∎$$

Hart and Jaffee (1974) have extended the analysis of Pyle to the case of an arbitrary number of assets and liabilities, also introducing additional constraints. For instance, a no-short-sales requirement can be introduced by constraining

x_i to be positive if i belongs to the asset side of the balance sheet, and negative if i belongs to the liability side (instead of endogenizing it as in Pyle 1971). Similarly, reserve requirements, liquidity ratios, and solvency ratios can be introduced as linear constraints on the different entries of the bank's balance sheet. Thus, a competitive theory of financial intermediaries is obtained in which all the posts of the balance sheet are determined in the same fashion as the portfolio of an individual investor. This approach has several problematic aspects:

- As in the CAPM, the model predicts that all banks should hold colinear (risky) portfolios. This is not consistent with the diversity of banks' balance sheets that is observed in practice.

- If the bank's capital is considered as just another liability, the wealth W of the bank becomes endogenous. No utility function can be assumed, since the identity of the bank's owners becomes irrelevant. The only restriction on the whole balance sheet of the bank (including equity) is that it is a mean-variance efficient portfolio. Then there is a fundamental undetermination on the size of banks at equilibrium: if a given balance sheet is mean-variance efficient, then any multiple of this balance sheet is also mean-variance efficient.

- Finally, if the possibility of bank failure is taken into account, the symmetry between assets and liabilities breaks. It is no longer possible to assume that the rate of return on equity demanded by investors (the stockholders or the debtholders of the bank) is independent of the assets chosen by the bank, since the latter affect the probability of failure of the bank. This question will be examined in the next subsection, in which an application of the portfolio model to the question of solvency ratios will be developed.

8.3.3   An Application of the Portfolio Model: The Impact of Capital Requirements

Since January 1993, all commercial banks in the European Union are submitted to a common solvency requirement, inspired by a similar requirement (the so-called Cooke ratio) adopted in December 1987 by the Bank of International Settlements. The portfolio model presented previously will allow an investigation of the consequences of such a regulation on the behavior of commercial banks. This section is inspired by Koehn and Santomero (1980), Kim and Santomero (1988), and Rochet (1992). The model is as follows:

- At date 0, the bank chooses the composition of its portfolio of assets and invests the amounts $x_0, \ldots, x_n$ on $(n + 1)$ securities, taking as given the random returns $\tilde{r}_i$ on these securities. Security zero is assumed to be riskless (r_0 is deterministic and normalized to zero).

- For simplicity, liabilities are fixed: deposits D and equity capital K. Deposits are remunerated at the riskless rate.

• At date 1, the bank is liquidated and stockholders receive the difference
between the value of the bank's assets and the value of deposits so that D
vanishes out of this expression:

$$\tilde{K}_1 = K + \sum_{i=1}^{n} x_i(\tilde{r}_i - r_0).$$

The bank behaves as a portfolio manager and seeks to maximize

$$\Phi(x) = Eu(\tilde{K}_1), \tag{8.30}$$

where u is a concave increasing Von Neumann–Morgenstern utility function.
Notice that the bank's owner behaves as if the bank had full liability ($\tilde{K}_1$ can
be negative). This is inconsistent with the main justification of capital requirements, namely the prevention of bank failures. This point, raised initially by
Keeley and Furlong (1990), will be discussed later. This discussion will focus
for the moment on the original formulation of Kim and Santomero, which will
show that capital requirements may severely distort the allocation of assets by
banks.

Assume, to allow application of mean-variance analysis, that the joint distribution of returns is normal, with an invertible variance-covariance matrix V.
ρ will denote the vector of expected excess returns. Under this assumption, $\tilde{K}_1$
is itself a normal random variable, of mean

$$\mu = E(\tilde{K}_1) = K+ <x, \rho>.$$

(where $<a, b>$ denotes the scalar product of vectors a and b), and variance

$$\sigma^2 = var(\tilde{K}_1) = <x, Vx>.$$

Therefore,

$$\Phi(x) = U(K+ <x, \rho>, <x, Vx>),$$

where by definition

$$U(\mu, \sigma^2) = \frac{1}{\sqrt{2\pi}} \int_{-\infty}^{+\infty} u(\mu + t\sigma) \exp -\frac{t^2}{2} dt.$$

**The Behavior of a "Full Liability" Bank in the Absence of a Solvency
Regulation**

The behavior of a "full liability" bank in the absence of a solvency regulation
is characterized by the solution of

$$(\mathscr{P}_1) \begin{cases} \text{Max} \Phi(x) \\ x \in \mathbb{R}^n. \end{cases}$$

The solution of this program, x_1^* is such that

$$x_1^* = \lambda_1 V^{-1} \rho,$$

where

$$\lambda_1 = -\frac{\partial U}{\partial \mu} \Big/ \left(2 \frac{\partial U}{\partial \sigma^2} \right) > 0.$$

As already noted, this formulation is inconsistent with previous assumptions, since the bank does not take into account its limited liability clause. However, failure occurs when $\tilde{K}_1 < 0$. The probability of this event is easily computed, since $\tilde{K}_1$ follows a Gaussian distribution of mean μ and variance σ^2. Therefore, $\frac{\tilde{K}_1 - \mu}{\sigma}$ follows a normalized Gaussian distribution of cumulative function $N(\cdot)$, and

$$\text{Proba} \left[\tilde{K}_1 < 0 \right] = \text{Proba} \left[\frac{\tilde{K}_1 - \mu}{\sigma} < -\frac{\mu}{\sigma} \right] = N \left(-\frac{\mu}{\sigma} \right).$$

Thus, the probability of failure of a bank choosing an asset portfolio x^* and having initial net worth K is

$$\text{Proba} \left[\tilde{K}_1 < 0 \right] = N \left[-\frac{K + <x^*, \rho>}{(<x^*, Vx^*>)^{1/2}} \right].$$

A solvency ratio is usually computed as the ratio of the level of capital divided by a weighted sum of assets $\sum_{i=1}^{n} \alpha_i x_i^*$ (weights α_i are assumed to reflect the relative riskiness of assets; in particular, it is natural to take $\alpha_0 = 0$):

$$CR = \frac{K}{<\alpha, x^*>}.$$

The solvency regulation imposes an upper bound on this ratio. The rationale for it is that if banks behave as described by program $\mathcal{P}_1$, then their probability of failure will be a decreasing function of the capital ratio. This is established in the following result:

Result 8.8   In the absence of a solvency regulation, and if banks do not take into account the limited liability clause, the probability of banks' failure is a decreasing function of their capital ratio, independent of the nonnegative weights used in the computation of the ratio.

Proof   Because of the mean-variance property, all banks choose colinear portfolios. Let $x_1^*(K)$ denote the portfolio chosen by a bank having net worth K:

$$x_1^*(K) = \sigma(K) x_M,$$

where x_M is defined as the portfolio colinear to $V^{-1}\rho$ such that its return has a unitary variance. $\sigma(K)$ is a nonnegative constant, equal to the standard deviation of the return of $x_1^*(K)$. Using a similar notation, $\mu(K)$ will represent the expectation of $\tilde{K}_1$:

$$\mu(K) = K + <x_1^*(K), \rho> = K + \sigma(K) <x_M, \rho>.$$

As a consequence,

$$\text{Proba}(\tilde{K}_1 < 0) = N\left(-\frac{\mu(K)}{\sigma(K)}\right) = N\left(- <x_M, \rho> - \frac{K}{\sigma(K)}\right),$$

whereas

$$CR(K) = \frac{K}{<x_M, \alpha> \sigma(K)}.$$

Therefore,

$$\text{Proba}(\tilde{K}_1 < 0) = N(- <x_M, \rho> - <x_M, \alpha> CR(K)).$$

Since $<x_M, \rho>$ is positive, the probability of failure is a decreasing function of $CR(K)$. ∎

The Behavior of a Full Liability Bank After Introduction of a Solvency Regulation

Since a capital ratio is a good indicator of the failure risk of a bank, it may seem reasonable to impose a lower bound on this ratio to limit the risk of failure. However, introducing such a ratio may alter the asset allocation of the bank, since its behavior is now characterized by a new program (in the case of a full liability bank):

$$(\mathcal{P}_2) \begin{cases} \text{Max}\,\Phi(x) \\ <\alpha, x> \le K, \end{cases}$$

where, without loss of generality, the minimum capital ratio is normalized to 1:

$$CR = \frac{K}{<\alpha, x>} \ge 1 \Leftrightarrow <\alpha, x> \le K.$$

If ν denotes the Lagrange multiplier associated with this constraint, the first order condition of $\mathcal{P}_2$ becomes

$$\nabla\Phi(x_2^*) = \frac{\partial U}{\partial \mu}\rho + 2\frac{\partial U}{\partial \sigma^2}Vx_2^* = \nu\alpha.$$

Therefore,

$$x_2^* = V^{-1}\left[\lambda_2\rho + \nu_2\alpha\right],$$

where

$$\lambda_2 = -\frac{\partial U}{\partial \mu} \bigg/ \left(2 \frac{\partial U}{\partial \sigma^2}\right) \qquad \text{and} \qquad v_2 = v \bigg/ \left(2 \frac{\partial U}{\partial \sigma^2}\right).$$

Thus, the following result has been proved:

Result 8.9   If α is not colinear to ρ and if the solvency constraint is binding, the bank will choose an inefficient portfolio: x_2^* will not be colinear to $V^{-1}\rho$.

Therefore, in general (if α is not colinear to ρ), introducing a solvency regulation will entail an inefficient asset allocation by banks. The total volume of their risky portfolio will decrease, but its composition will be distorted in the direction of more risky assets. Kim and Santomero (1988) have even shown an example in which the probability of failure *increases* after the capital ratio is introduced. The explanation is that the adverse structure effect (recomposition of the risky portfolio) dominates the direct volume effect.

However, there is a simple way (in theory) to suppress this adverse recomposition effect:

Result 8.10   If the weights α_i used in the capital ratio are proportional to the systematic risks β_i of the risky assets, the solvency regulation becomes efficient: all banks choose efficient portfolios, and their probability of failure decreases.

Proof   If α is colinear to β (or to ρ, since the CAPM implies that vectors β and ρ are themselves colinear), the first order condition of $\mathcal{P}_2$ becomes

$$x_2^* = (\lambda_2 + v_2) V^{-1}\rho.$$

Therefore, x_2^* is mean-variance efficient. Moreover, the probability of failure is a decreasing function of CR (as in $\mathcal{P}_1$). This implies that imposing a capital ratio (with correct weights, that is, proportional to the market evaluation of risk given by the β_i's) is instrumental for limiting the failure risk of banks.   ∎

To conclude this discussion of the portfolio model applied to banks' solvency ratios, return to the criticism of Keeley and Furlong (1990). What happens when the limited liability option is correctly taken into account by the bank? Rochet (1992) has studied this question. He shows the mean-variance approach can still be used, but that the indirect utility function of the bank has a different expression, $U_{LL}(\mu, \sigma^2)$. The bank's decision problem becomes

$$(\mathcal{P}_3) \begin{cases} \max \psi(x) \\ <\alpha, x> \le K, \end{cases}$$

where

$$\psi(x) = U_{LL}(K + <\mu, x>, <x, Vx>),$$

and

$$U_{LL}(\mu, \sigma^2) = \frac{1}{\sqrt{2\pi}} \int_{-\frac{\mu}{\sigma}}^{+\infty} u(\mu + t\sigma) \exp -\frac{t^2}{2} dt.$$

U_{LL} is the indirect utility function under limited liability. Rochet shows that U_{LL} is not always decreasing in σ^2: for low levels of K, the bank chooses a portfolio with maximal risk and minimum diversification. As a result, a solvency regulation (even with "correct" weights) is not sufficient for taking care of moral hazard. Rochet suggests introducing an additional regulation, namely a minimum level of capital, independent of the size of the banks' assets.

8.4   Appendix : Institutional Aspects of Credit Risk

8.4.1   Interest Rate and Rate of Return

In the United States it is a common practice, especially for short-term loans, to require borrowers to maintain a deposit at the lending bank, the amount of which is related to the loan that has been granted. This practice of *compensating balances* is unusual in Europe, although it exists for some specific types of loans, such as *account receivables discounting.*[13]

Alternatively, a bank may set an upper limit for the funds that are available to the firm, but define the "loan" as the part that has been disposed of (so that the amount that is lent varies from day to day). This is quite common in Europe, and the repayment is computed on the basis of a fee on the nondisposed part of the loan, and a rate on the loan itself. Thus, on this kind of loan the rate of interest may not be directly comparable among countries.

8.4.2   Collateral

Loans may be collateralized by a specific asset or else unsecured, in which case the assets of the firm guarantee the repayment of the debt and can be seized in case of bankruptcy. Again, there is a difference between the United States and Europe, since in the United States short-term loans tend to be unsecured, whereas in Europe they tend to be collateralized or endorsed by a third party. Deeds that are commonly used as collateral are

- real property, automobiles, and goods that can be mortgaged;
- equipment, crops, and inventories;
- accounts receivable; and
- securities and saving accounts, as well as mutual funds and life insurance.

The bank determines the maximum amount of the loan in proportion with the collateral. This may be a consequence of the bank's policy, but the bank may also be bound to do so because of regulation. The higher the volatility of the collateral's value and the lower its marketability, the smaller the amount of the loan. Thus, for instance, a bank may lend up to 90 percent of the value of high-grade municipal bonds but only 75 percent of the value of major common stocks, and much less on inventories.

In valuing the collateral, the bank may prefer to use the services of an independent agency. This may even be compulsory for mortgage loans if the bank wants to resort to some particular types of security issue, backed by its portfolio of mortgage loans. Regulation may also impose limits on the lending capacity. Thus, in the United States, real estate loans must be secured by a mortgage, deed, trust, or leasehold agreement on the real estate, with conditions such that a loan must not exceed two-thirds of the property's appraised value for unimproved real estate, or 90 percent if it is improved by a building.

Once the property is used as collateral, the borrower is assumed not to dispose of it. There is a cost for this to be a credible commitment, which may be quite different from one type of collateral to another and will become part of the total cost of the operation. Thus, the cost of warehouse financing of inventories is particularly high because it includes the cost of storage by a third party. Even so, warehouse financing may be at risk because the firm may change the (nonobservable) quality of goods, and more generally because of fraud.

The cost of the process of arranging a loan with collateral and payment is a determinant of the level of efficiency of the financial system. Technical progress may therefore be important. For example, in France it is estimated that the development of standardized computer techniques has divided the cost of account receivables discounting by five (Burgard 1988). In Spain, the amount lent through this channel has been constantly shrinking and replaced by short-term credit.

8.4.3   Endorsement and Insurance

If a loan is endorsed by a third party, in case of default of the borrower the third party is committed to repay the borrower's debt. From the point of view of the lender, the existence of an endorsement is akin to collateral, since in case of bankruptcy the lender has an additional recourse. If the loan is endorsed by a financial institution, it will inherit the rating of the institution itself. The mechanism of endorsement by a government agency (which can appear as a market distortion) is introduced when the activity financed by the loan is thought to be generating externalities. In many countries, housing finance and export finance loans are secured by specialized institutions. In the United States, the Federal National Mortgage Association (FNMA) and Government National Mortgage Association (GNMA) have played this role for housing loans, whereas the Foreign Credit Insurance Association (an association of insurance companies in cooperation with the Export-Import Bank of the United States) offers policies protecting U.S. exporters against the risk of nonpayment by foreign debtors. It is difficult to ascertain whether the fees charged by these institutions are close to market values, but a standard argument is that, absent subsidies, the market could do as well in providing insurance. Therefore, this guarantee is seen as an indirect way to subsidize U.S. exporters.

8.4.4   Loan Covenants

Since the loan is backed not only by the firm's assets but also by the future stream of cash flows, the credit contract may contain covenants limiting the possible actions of the firm (see the section on moral hazard in Chapter 4). Affirmative covenants stipulate responsibilities of the borrower to submit financial statements and maintain adequate insurance for the firm's assets. Negative covenants impose restrictions on the firm's actions. Particularly important in valuing the firm's debt (and stock) is the fact that the firm may commit not to issue new debt, or the new debt may be subordinated to an existing one. A weaker form could be to restrict the issue of new debt with higher priority unless all existing debt is upgraded so as to have an equal priority (this clause, called "pari passu," has been used in the market for eurocredits). This excludes the use of some of the firm's assets as collateral for new debt, which would create an externality to the existing creditors. A similar strategy on the part of the firm could be to sell its assets in order to obtain new funds. To prevent this strategy, covenants on the disposition of the firm's assets are introduced in the debt contract. Other covenants may restrict dividend payment (or any other type of payment to equity holders) if some ratio (liquidity or leverage) has not reached a critical level, and in the same way covenants may limit purchases of major assets or merger activity. These covenants rely on accounting data and make intensive use of prescribed values for ratios that can be easily monitored.[14]

8.4.5   Information Costs

When making the decision to grant a credit, banks use information on both the potential borrower and the characteristics of the firms that operate in the same industry (for business loans) or the characteristics of comparable individuals (for personal loans). The risks on a specific firm or individual are valued according to statistical techniques. These data are a public good that may be supplied by the market or by a regulatory institution. The recent decrease in the cost of processing information, due to cheaper and more efficient computer technology, has improved the quality of this information. Banks may agree to share information or not (an issue addressed by Jappelli and Pagano (1993) for personal loans). In some countries lenders pool their information on house-holding, by creating "credit bureaus" in the United States and Canada, "credit reference agencies" in the United Kingdom and Australia, and "central credit registers" in Belgium and France. In other countries, such as Greece, Italy, and Spain, there is so far no information sharing.

8.4.6 Accounting

Although a default on a loan always drastically affects its (potential) market value, the book value may or may not be altered, depending on the bank's obligations regarding the provisions to be made as a result of the default.

Regulations differ across countries about both the definition and the interpretation of a reported default on a loan. In the United States, the current method is to rank loans by descending probability of a substantial loss—substandard, doubtful, and loss (with respective weights of 20 percent, 50 percent, and 100 percent)—that will be charged against the reserves deducted from income during each period for that purpose, thus diminishing the book value of equity. Still, all or part of the loan may be recovered, and in particular it may be re-structured if the time pattern of the revenues that were intended to repay the loan has changed. Since in case of default there is frequently a penalty clause that applies, a default may, occasionally, be a source of additional profit.

8.4.7 Bankruptcy

Although most theoretical models see bankruptcy as a state in which creditors simply take over the firm and choose the strategy that allows them to get a higher repayment, the bankruptcy process is in reality far more complex. The legal context is usually different from one country to the other, because the level of protection of the different parties involved in the bankruptcy process (the State, workers, suppliers, shareholders, and creditors) is different. These differences in bankruptcy legislation may explain why in some countries there is a higher risk spread between public and private debt. Hence, for instance, the higher U.S. spread relative to that in Europe may reflect a stronger power of the stockholders in bargaining over the reorganization plan. The empirical results obtained by Franks and Torous (1994) show that between 1983 and 1990, an estimated $878 million that was expected to go to secured creditors (mostly banks) accrued in fact to junior creditors and shareholders. Consequently the elements that determine what each type of claimholder receives in case of bankruptcy is an important part of the debt contract. But this does not mean that the bankruptcy laws completely determine what each party obtains in each state of nature. Usually, there is a residual uncertainty (see the section on incomplete contracts in Chapter 4), which seems to be due to the willingness of authorities to give the firm the best chances to survive. But by so doing, they also give more power to the management and the stockholders, whereas theoretically the firm's creditors could easily take over and impose their will.

A bankruptcy is a negotiation process, and as such has to be represented, from a theoretical standpoint, as a game in which moral hazard and adverse selection are present, and in which legislation sets the reservation values of the players. The process begins when the firm is insolvent, a term that has a precise legal meaning: either the firm is unable to face repayment of a claim or else its equity reaches a zero value. Then the creditors or the firm itself will trigger bankruptcy, and a bargaining process begins between shareholders and creditors, with the firm's management being possibly involved as a third party. The issues to be negotiated include (1) whether the firm must be liquidated or will continue as a going concern, and in the latter case whether a rundown or a reorganization of some of the firms' activities has to be proposed, and (2) how the parties involved will share the proceeds may depend on the behavior of other parties (e.g., suppliers). If there is no agreement, a third party may be called in (a trustee or an administrator) to act as a referee. It is important to recall that other parties (such as workers, suppliers, and possibly customers) are directly or indirectly involved in the outcome of the bankruptcy process, so their attitude has an effect on the firm's expected cash flows in case of reorganization.

Although this section will not attempt to describe differences in bankruptcy legislation, it is interesting to illustrate how these differences will affect the value of the bank's claim on the bankrupt firm. As a first distinction, it is important to know whether the bank's debt is secured. If the bank debt is secured, and if the proceeds of the collateral sale are inferior to the firm's debt, the bank becomes an unsecured creditor for the amount of the difference.

Even if the bank holds a secured claim, the secured asset may be more or less well protected. In the United Kingdom, for instance, the appointment of a receiver gives the bank all the necessary protection, so the firm cannot modify the secured asset quality. In other bankruptcy legislation this is not so.

The bankruptcy legislation for unsecured loans may specify some obligations for the bank during the period prior to bankruptcy. Thus, for instance, if the bank has actively participated in the management of the bankrupt firm, it may lose its right to be on an equal level with the other creditors and become only a residual claimant.

Yet, the main difference across bankruptcy legislation concerns the choice that is made between creditors' protection and the objective of keeping the firm alive, motivated by the externalities created by a bankruptcy (such as layoffs and losses for suppliers). The stockholders being in general favorable to continuation, the law may give them additional power that may be more or less favorable to creditors. In the United States, filing for Chapter 11 bankruptcy allows the current management to become the debtor in charge, and therefore to take responsibility for the firms' current operations. This is important because the probability of generating a coherent project for the bankrupt firm increases, but the benefits of such a reorganization may accrue only to the stockholders.[15] In the United States the bankruptcy law also implies that no interests are paid during the period of reorganization, which may last several years. In exchange, the bank may be able to continue its lending to the firm, with good securities and high interest rates.

Finally, some residual legal uncertainty has to be considered, because a *change in bankruptcy laws* (which may occur at any time) affects all the contracts that have not yet expired.

8.4.8   Fraud

Some of the provisions that are made in the loan contract are based on bona fide reporting of the firms' behavior through accounting. When the firm or its management does not fulfil this requirement and uses fraudulent strategies, the bank will only be able to prosecute. The frequency of fraudulent behavior, its statistical importance, and its distribution among types of firms and industries will, obviously, be reflected in the estimated risk and the pricing of loans.

8.5   Problems

8.5.1   The Model of Prisman, Slovin, and Sushka (1986)

Recall that the expected profit of the bank studied in subsection 8.2.2 is given by

$$\Pi(r_L, r_D) = \Pi_0(r_L, r_D) - C(R, \theta),$$

where

$$\Pi_0(r_L, r_D) = (r_L - r)L(r_L) + (r - r_D)D(r_D)$$

is the (gross) profit obtained in the Monti-Klein model (assuming $D' > 0$ and $L' < 0$),

$$R = D(r_D) - L(r_L)$$

is the level of reserves, and

$$C(R, \theta) = r_p E[\text{Max}(0, \tilde{x} - R)]$$

is the expected cost of liquidity shortages. Here θ represents any parameter that will influence this cost: it can be r_p, the penalty rate, or the variance of $\tilde{x}$. The first order conditions, which determine the optimal values r_L^* and r_D^*, are thus

$$\begin{cases} \frac{\partial \Pi}{\partial r_L}(r_L, r_D) = \frac{\partial \Pi_0}{\partial r_L}(r_L, r_D) + \frac{\partial C}{\partial R}(R, \theta)L'(r_L) = 0 & (8.31) \\[2mm] \frac{\partial \Pi}{\partial r_D}(r_L, r_D) = \frac{\partial \Pi_0}{\partial r_D}(r_L, r_D) - \frac{\partial C}{\partial R}(R, \theta)D'(r_D) = 0. & (8.32) \end{cases}$$

Question 1 can be skipped by readers familiar with the techniques of convex analysis.

1. Compute the matrix of the second order derivatives of Π at (r_L^*, r_D^*) and show that it is indeed definite negative under the following assumptions:

$$DD'' - 2D'^2 < 0, \, LL'' - 2L'^2 < 0.$$

2. By applying the implicit function theorem to equations 8.31 and 8.32 and using the inequalities given in 1, show that $\frac{dr_L^*}{d\theta}$ and $\frac{dr_D^*}{d\theta}$ both have the same sign as $\left(-\frac{\partial^2 C}{\partial R \partial \theta}\right)$. In other words, all changes that decrease the marginal cost of reserves also increase r_L^* and r_D^* (trick: use $\frac{\partial^2 \Pi}{\partial r_D^2}L' + \frac{\partial^2 \Pi}{\partial r_D \partial r_L} = (r - r_D - \frac{\partial C}{\partial R})D''L' - 2D'L'$ and the first order conditions).

3. Prove the first part of result 8.4 by showing that $\frac{\partial C}{\partial R}$ increases with r_p.

4. Suppose that $\tilde{x}$ equals $\sigma \tilde{x}_0$, where $\tilde{x}_0$ has zero mean and unit variance. Show that $\frac{\partial C}{\partial R}$ increases with σ (where $\sigma > 0$) if and only if the optimal level of reserves is positive. Deduce the second part of result 8.4, namely: $\frac{dL}{d\sigma} < 0$ if $R > 0$.

8.5.2 The Risk Structure of Interest Rates (Adapted from Merton 1974)

Recall that the market value of a risky debt in the Merton model studied in subsection 8.1.2 is given by

$$D_0 = VN(h_1) + De^{-rT}N(h_2) \tag{8.33}$$

with

$$\begin{cases} h_1 = \frac{1}{\sigma\sqrt{T}}\log d - \frac{1}{2}\sigma\sqrt{T} \\[2mm] h_2 = -h_1 - \sigma\sqrt{T} \end{cases}$$

and $d = \frac{De^{-rT}}{V}$ is the nominal debt-to-asset ratio.

1. Show that 8.33 can be rewritten as

$$\frac{D_0}{De^{-rT}} = \min_x \left\{ \frac{N(x)}{d} + N(-x - \sigma\sqrt{T}) \right\}. \tag{8.34}$$

2. The interest spread H is defined by

$$H = -\frac{1}{T}\log\frac{D_0}{De^{-rT}}.$$

By applying the envelope principle to equation 8.34, show the following

- H increases with d.
- H increases with σ.
- HT increases with T.

8.5.3   Using the CAPM for Loan Pricing

A bank computes the nominal interest rate r_L that it charges on a certain type of loan by the following formula:

$$\frac{(1-\delta)(1+r_L) - \gamma_L - (1-\alpha)(1+r)}{\alpha} = 1 + r + \pi,$$

where

- δ is the proportion of defaulting loans, assuming the proceeds of a defaulting loan are zero.
- γ_L is the management cost per unit of loan.
- r is the interbank rate, taken as the riskless rate.
- π is the risk premium demanded by stockholders.
- α is the capital coefficient required for this type of loan.

1. Compute the expected return on a loan and show that the above pricing formula is closely related to the CAPM approach.

2. Assuming that the bank has a monopoly power on the loans side but faces a competitive market on its liabilities side, compute what should be the modified pricing formula, for given δ and β, as a function of the elasticity of the demand for loans.

3. How should the formula be modified if there is a tax on profits at a rate τ?

8.6   Solutions

8.6.1   The Model of Prisman, Slovin, and Sushka

1. Compute the second order derivatives of Π:

$$\frac{\partial^2 \Pi}{\partial r_L^2} = \frac{\partial^2 \Pi_0}{\partial r_L^2} + \frac{\partial C}{\partial R} L'' - \frac{\partial^2 C}{\partial R^2} L'^2,$$

$$\frac{\partial^2 \Pi}{\partial r_L \partial r_D} = \frac{\partial^2 C}{\partial R^2} L' D',$$

$$\frac{\partial^2 \Pi}{\partial r_D^2} = \frac{\partial^2 \Pi_0}{\partial r_D^2} - \frac{\partial C}{\partial R} D'' - \frac{\partial^2 C}{\partial R^2} D'^2.$$

Using the first order conditions, at the optimum

$$\frac{\partial C}{\partial R}(R, \theta) = -\frac{1}{L'}\frac{\partial \Pi_0}{\partial r_L}(r_L^*, r_D^*) = \frac{1}{D'}\frac{\partial \Pi_0}{\partial r_D}(r_L^*, r_D^*).$$

Thus,

$$\frac{\partial^2 \Pi}{\partial r_L^2} = \left(\frac{\partial^2 \Pi_0}{\partial r_L^2} - \frac{L''}{L'}\frac{\partial \Pi_0}{\partial r_L}\right) - \frac{\partial^2 C}{\partial R^2}L'^2,$$

$$\frac{\partial^2 \Pi}{\partial r_D^2} = \left(\frac{\partial^2 \Pi_0}{\partial r_D^2} - \frac{D''}{D'}\frac{\partial \Pi_0}{\partial r_D}\right) - \frac{\partial^2 C}{\partial R^2}D'^2.$$

But now a simple computation yields

$$\begin{cases} \frac{\partial^2 \Pi_0}{\partial r_L^2} - \frac{L''}{L'}\frac{\partial \Pi_0}{\partial r_L} & = & 2L' - \frac{L''L}{L'} \\ \frac{\partial^2 \Pi_0}{\partial r_D^2} - \frac{D''}{D'}\frac{\partial \Pi_0}{\partial r_D} & = & -2D' + \frac{D''D}{D'}. \end{cases}$$

By assumption, these quantities, denoted respectively by α and β, are negative. Since C is convex in R, then $\frac{\partial^2 \Pi}{\partial r_L^2}$ and $\frac{\partial^2 \Pi}{\partial r_D^2}$ are also negative. It remains to show that the determinant of the second order derivative of Π is positive:

$$H = \frac{\partial^2 \Pi}{\partial r_L^2}\frac{\partial^2 \Pi}{\partial r_D^2} - \left(\frac{\partial^2 \Pi}{\partial r_L \partial r_D}\right)^2.$$

$$= \left(\alpha - \frac{\partial^2 C}{\partial R^2}L'^2\right)\left(\beta - \frac{\partial^2 C}{\partial R^2}D'^2\right) - \left(\frac{\partial^2 C}{\partial R^2}\right)^2 L'^2 D'^2.$$

$$H = \alpha\beta - \beta\frac{\partial^2 C}{\partial R^2}L'^2 - \alpha\frac{\partial^2 C}{\partial R^2}D'^2.$$

Since α and β are negative, H is positive.

2. A total differentiation of 8.31 and 8.32 with respect to θ yields

$$\begin{cases} \frac{\partial^2 \Pi}{\partial r_L^2}\frac{dr_L}{d\theta} + \frac{\partial^2 \Pi}{\partial r_L \partial r_D}\frac{dr_D}{d\theta} & = & -\frac{\partial^2 C}{\partial R \partial \theta}L' \\ \frac{\partial^2 \Pi}{\partial r_L \partial r_D}\frac{dr_L}{d\theta} + \frac{\partial^2 \Pi}{\partial r_D^2}\frac{dr_D}{d\theta} & = & \frac{\partial^2 C}{\partial R \partial \theta}D', \end{cases}$$

from which can be deduced

$$\frac{dr_L}{d\theta} = \frac{1}{H}\frac{\partial^2 C}{\partial R \partial \theta}\left[-\frac{\partial^2 \Pi}{\partial r_D^2}L' - \frac{\partial^2 \Pi}{\partial r_D \partial r_L}D'\right],$$

$$\frac{dr_D}{d\theta} = \frac{1}{H}\frac{\partial^2 C}{\partial R \partial \theta}\left[\frac{\partial^2 \Pi}{\partial r_L^2}D' + \frac{\partial^2 \Pi}{\partial r_L \partial r_D}L'\right].$$

Since H, the Hessian determinant computed previously, is positive, it remains to show that the terms between the brackets are negative:

$$\frac{\partial^2 \Pi}{\partial r_D^2} L' + \frac{\partial^2 \Pi}{\partial r_D \partial r_L} D' = \left(r - r_D - \frac{\partial C}{\partial R} \right) D'' L' - 2 D' L'.$$

Using the first order condition again:

$$r - r_D - \frac{\partial C}{\partial R} = \frac{D}{D'},$$

the following is obtained:

$$\frac{\partial^2 \Pi}{\partial r_D^2} L' + \frac{\partial^2 \Pi}{\partial r_D \partial r_L} D' = L' \left[\frac{D'' D}{D'} - 2D' \right] > 0.$$

Similarly,

$$-\frac{\partial^2 \Pi}{\partial r_L \partial r_D} L' - \frac{\partial^2 \Pi}{\partial r_L^2} D' = -\left(r_L - r + \frac{\partial C}{\partial R} \right) L'' D' - 2 L' D'$$

$$= D' \left[\frac{L'' L}{L'} - 2L' \right] > 0.$$

3, 4. $\frac{\partial C}{\partial R} = -r_p \, \mathrm{Proba}[\tilde{x} \geq R] = -r_p \, \mathrm{Proba}\left[\tilde{x}_0 \geq \frac{R}{\sigma} \right].$

This obviously decreases with r_p; therefore result 3 is proven. Moreover, $\frac{\partial C}{\partial R}$ decreases with σ if and only if $R > 0$. When $R > 0$, then $\frac{dr_L}{d\sigma} > 0$ and therefore $\frac{dL}{d\sigma} < 0$. ∎

8.6.2 The Risk Structure of Interest Rates

1. Let $\varphi(x)$ denote the term between brackets in 8.34:

$$\varphi(x) = \frac{N(x)}{d} + N(-x - \sigma \sqrt{T}).$$

A straightforward computation shows that φ has a unique minimum for $x = h_1$, which establishes result 1 by comparison with 8.33.

2. It is immediate from 8.34 that $\frac{D_0}{De^{-rt}}$ is a decreasing function of d and σ, as a minimum of decreasing functions of d and σ. Therefore the interest spread H is also decreasing in d and σ. The dependence in T is more complex. According to the envelope theorem,

$$\frac{\partial}{\partial T} \left[\frac{D_0}{De^{-rT}} \right] = -\frac{\sigma}{2\sqrt{T}} N'(h_2) < 0.$$

Therefore, HT is indeed an increasing function of T. However, the dependence in T is not clear-cut. ∎

8.6.3   Using the CAPM for Loan Pricing

1. The gross expected return on a loan is

$$E(1 + \tilde{\rho}) = (1 - \delta)(1 + r_L) - \gamma_L.$$

The proposed pricing formula is equivalent therefore to

$$E(\tilde{\rho}) - r = \alpha\pi.$$

The CAPM approach requires

$$E(\tilde{\rho}) - r = \beta\pi.$$

Hence, the two formulas are equivalent provided that

$$\beta = \alpha.$$

2. The monopolist bank's program is

$$\max_{r_L}[(1 - \delta)(1 + r_L) - \{\gamma_L + (1 - \alpha)(1 + r) + \alpha(1 + r + \pi)\}]L(r_L).$$

The first order condition implies

$$\frac{(1 - \delta)(1 + (1 - 1/\epsilon_L)r_L) - \gamma_L - (1 - \alpha)(1 + r)}{\alpha} = 1 + r + \pi,$$

where $\epsilon_L = -\frac{r_L L'(r_L)}{L(r_L)}$ is the elasticity of the demand for loans. (It is assumed that the second order condition is satisfied.)

3. Simply replace $r + \pi$ by $(r + \pi)/(1 - \tau)$.

Notes

1. In addition, *transformation risks* occur because banks' assets typically have a longer maturity than banks' liabilities: banks transform "short" deposits into "long" loans.

2. See, for example, Altman (1983), or, more specifically, the classic textbook of Hempel and Simonson (1991).

3. The exponential discount factor e^{-r} is used here because it simplifies the formulas.

4. For the definition, properties, and pricing formulas of a call option, see Ingersoll (1987) or Huang and Litzenberger (1988).

5. A standard Wiener process is a Gaussian process with continuous trajectories such that $E(Z(t)) = 0$, $E[Z(t)Z(s)] = \min(t, s)$.

6. See also Ingersoll (1987).

7. The "correct" evaluation of the debt-to-asset ratio $\left(\frac{D_0}{V}\right)$ is endogenous, and cannot be taken as a parameter.

8. Notice that interpreting sT as a global risk premium (because $e^{r_L T} - e^{rT} \sim sT$) is valid only when T is small.

9. Examples of this type of contract can be found in the financing of the English Channel tunnel, where the amount of repayment depended on the revenues of the project. Also, contingent repayments have been included in mortgage loans to limit the so-called tilt effect that arises when the limit of 25 percent of income usually imposed to determine the amount of repayment on a loan is attained, while in an inflationary context it will only be an important restriction during the first year of the loan's life. Price Level Adjustment Mortgages (PLAMs) make repayment contingent on a price or wage index. Shared Appreciation Mortgages (SAMs) make it contingent on the appreciation in the value of the mortgaged property.

10. Recall that this is equivalent to maximizing a constant absolute risk aversion (CARA) or exponential utility function when the returns are normally distributed.

11. The negative sign in the definition of λ is introduced for convenience: λ should be positive.

12. However, liquidity risk is disregarded so as to emphasize the credit and interest rate risk the bank assumes.

13. A firm obtains a loan, using as collateral the invoices it has on its clients that are due at a future date, corresponding usually to the maturity of the loan.

14. See Smith and Warner (1979a, 1979b) for an excellent analysis of covenants.

15. Notice, though, that if this is correctly anticipated by creditors, they will require higher interest rates so that ex ante it also implies a higher cost for the firm.

References

Altman, E. I. 1983. *Corporate financial distress: A complete guide to predicting, avoiding and dealing with bankruptcy risks.* New York: John Wiley and Sons.

Baltensperger, E., and H. Milde 1976. Predictability of reserve demand, information costs and portfolio behavior of commercial banks. *Journal of Finance* 31(3):835–43.

Bierman, H., and J. Hass. 1975. An analytic model of bond risk differentials. *Journal of Financial and Quantitative Analysis* 10(5):757–73.

Bizer, D., and P. DeMarzo. 1992. Sequential banking. *Journal of Political Economy* 100(1):41–61.

Black, F., and M. Scholes. 1973. The pricing of options and corporate liabilities. *Journal of Political Economy* 81(3):637–54.

Burgard, J. J. 1988. *La Banque en France.* Paris: Presses de la Fondation Nationale des Sciences Politiques.

Décamps, J. P. Forthcoming. Integrating the risk and term structure of interest rates. *European Journal of Finance.*

Franks, J., and W. Torous. 1994. A comparison of financial recontracting in distressed exchanges and Chapter 11 reorganizations. *Journal of Financial Economics* 35(3):349–70.

Geske, R. 1977. The valuation of corporation liabilities as compound options. *Journal of Financial and Quantitative Analysis* 12(4):541–52.

Hart, O., and D. Jaffee. 1974. On the application of portfolio theory of depository financial intermediaries. *Review of Economic Studies* 41(1):129–47.

Hempel, G. H., and D. G. Simonson. 1991. *Bank financial management: Strategies and techniques for a changing industry.* New York: Wiley.

Ho, T., and A. Saunders. 1981. The determinants of bank interest margins: Theory and empirical evidence. *Journal of Financial and Quantitative Analysis* 16(4):581–600.

Ho, T., and H. Stoll. 1980. On dealer markets under competition. *Journal of Finance* 35(2):259–67.

Huang, C. F., and R. Litzenberg. 1988. *Foundations for financial economics.* Amsterdam: North-Holland.

Ingersoll, J. E., Jr. 1987. *Theory of financial decision making.* Totowa, N.J.: Rowan and Littlefield.

Jappelli, T., and M. Pagano. 1993. Information sharing in credit markets. *Journal of Finance* 48(5):1693–1718.

Keeley, M., and F. Furlong. 1990. A reexamination of mean-variance analysis of bank capital regulation. *Journal of Banking and Finance* 14(1):69–84.

Kim, D., and A. Santomero. 1988. Risk in banking and capital regulation. *Journal of Finance* 43(5):1219–33.

Klein, M. 1971. A theory of the banking firm. *Journal of Money, Credit, and Banking* 3:205–18.

Koehn, M., and A. Santomero. 1980. Regulation of bank capital and portfolio risk. *Journal of Finance* 35(5):1235–44.

Lintner, J. 1965. The valuation of risk assets and the selection of risky investments in stock portfolios and capital budgets. *Review of Economics and Statistics* 47:13–37.

Markowitz, H. 1952. Portfolio selection. *Journal of Finance* 7(1):77–91.

Merton, R. 1974. On the pricing of corporate debt: The risk structure of interest rates. *Journal of Finance* 29(2):449–76.

Prisman, E., M. Slovin, and M. Sushka. 1986. A general model of the banking firm under conditions of monopoly, uncertainty and recourse. *Journal of Monetary Economics* 17(2):293–304.

Pyle, D. 1971. On the theory of financial intermediation. *Journal of Finance* 26(3):737–47.

Rochet, J. C. 1992. Capital requirements and the behaviour of commercial banks. *European Economic Review* 36(5):1137–70.

Schwartz, E. S., and W. N. Torous. 1992. Prepayment, default, and the valuation of mortgage pass-through securities. *Journal of Business* 65(2):221–39.

Sharpe, W. 1964. Capital asset prices: A theory of market equilibrium under conditions of risk. *Journal of Finance* 19:425–42.

Smith, C., and J. Warner. 1979a. Bankruptcy, secured debt, and optimal capital structure: Comment. *Journal of Finance* 34(1):247–51.

———. 1979b. On financial contracting: An analysis of bond covenants. *Journal of Financial Economics* 7(2):117–61.

Stanhouse, B. 1986. Commercial bank portfolio behavior and endogenous uncertainty. *Journal of Finance* 41(5):1103–14.

Yawitz, J. 1977. An analytical model of interest rate differentials and different default recoveries. *Journal of Financial and Quantitative Analysis* 12(3):481–90.

Banking regulation now exists in virtually every country with a well-developed banking system. It is of capital importance because of its effect both on the behavior of banks' managers and on the specific characteristics of the banking industry. In fact, it is practically impossible to study the theory of banking without referring to banking regulation. This is why the preceding chapters have already studied the effects of several aspects of banks' regulation.

Bank regulation has a long history: the production of (private) money has always been taxed, the seigniorage or monopoly premium on coins being the property of the government. Contemporary banking regulation contemplates more complex problems, since the set of regulatory instruments has become richer and the regulators have set more ambitious macroeconomic and prudential objectives. Since the scope of this book is restricted to microeconomic banking theory, this discussion will address exclusively issues related to the safety and soundness of the banking system.[1]

9.1   Regulation Theory and Banking Theory

We could think of addressing banking regulation prima facie as an application of a general theory of public regulation to the specific problems of banking. But in fact this would be misleading. It is worth devoting some effort to understanding first why banking regulation raises some questions that are not addressed within the general theory of public regulations. Although some instruments and models of the theory of regulation can be adapted to cope with issues in banking regulation, there are exceptions. The discussion then will examine the similarities and differences between the general theory of regulation and banking regulation from three perspectives: their justifications, their scope and the regulatory instruments.

9.1.1   The Justification of Regulation

In general, public regulation is justified by market failures that can come from (1) the presence of market power, (2) the importance of externalities, or (3) asymmetric information between buyers and sellers.

However, the "official" justification for banking regulation (see the detailed discussion in subsection 9.2.3) is the necessity of providing a "safety net" for banks to protect depositors from the risk of failure of their bank.[2] (An interesting discussion is proveded by Kareken 1986.) Clearly, this is closely related to justification 2; banks are regulated because bank failures generate negative externalities on their customers (mostly their depositors). The failure of any type of firm also generates externalities, however, whereas prudential regulations are essentially limited to banks, insurance companies, and other financial intermediaries. Subsection 9.2.3 will show that this specificity of bank failures can be explained by asymmetric information problems (point 3 of the earlier classification). Therefore, although the justifications of banking regulations can be related to the same fundamental market failures classified by the general theory of public regulation, they are so intertwined that a specific analysis is called for.

Adopting the view that prudential regulations should be imposed on banks may create at least two types of distortions:

• Creating a safety net may sometimes generate excessive risk taking on behalf of banks' managers, and therefore call for additional regulations. This question is studied in detail in Sections 9.3 and 9.4.

• As argued by Bhattacharya and Thakor (1993), if regulation does not fully exhaust all the surplus created, the government may feel empowered to regulate banks for reasons other than safety and soundness. This may take the form of an implicit tax, as in the case of reserve requirements, or an obligation for the bank to subsidize some of its products.

In any case, banking regulation is costly, both directly (salaries of supervisors, administrative costs for banks) and indirectly (through the distortions it generates). Also, it may generate rents for banks. Therefore, if regulators are self-interested (see Boot and Thakor 1993), they may be "captured" by the banking industry.

For all these reasons, advocates of free banking prefer an imperfectly competitive market to an imperfectly regulated banking sector. Their ideas will be discussed in Section 9.3.

9.1.2   The Scope of Banking Regulation

General regulation theory is concerned with the design of the optimal regulatory rules.[3] It is therefore mainly *normative*. However, only a minor part of the literature on banking regulation follows this "regulation design" approach. The main strand takes a *positive* approach—"regulation analysis." Its aim is to analyze the consequences of a given regulation that either exists or is under study by the regulatory authorities. Regarding, for instance, capital adequacy requirements, those following this approach would ask questions such as, Will this regulation succeed in attaining its objectives (reduction of the bank failure risk)? Will it induce more risk taking by banks? Will it change the equilibrium rates in the credit market?

9.1.3   Regulatory Instruments

Traditionally, regulation theory draws a line between the regulation of structure and the regulation of conduct. The former establishes which firms are qualified to develop a certain type of activity; the latter concerns the permitted behavior of firms in their chosen activities (see, e.g., Kay and Vickers 1988). Both are relevant for the study of banking regulation: the Glass-Steagall Act would be an example of a structure regulation, whereas capital or reserve requirements would be a typical conduct regulation. Still, the application of the general theory of regulation may well stop here. Assuming that the ultimate objectives of bank regulation are to ensure the development of a safety net for depositors and to promote sound investment policies on behalf of the banks, then the instruments of banking regulation must be specific to the banking sector.[4]

Safety and soundness regulatory instruments in use in the banking industry could be classified into six broad types:

1. Deposit interest rate ceilings

2. Entry, branching, network, and merger restrictions

3. Portfolio restrictions, including (besides the Glass-Steagall type of regulation) reserve requirements and even, as an extreme case, narrow banking

4. Deposit insurance

5. Capital requirements

6. Regulatory monitoring (including not only closure policy but also the use of market values versus book values)

Except for entry and merger restrictions, these regulatory instruments are typical of the banking industry. The absence of other, classical instruments could be explained by the constraints that limit regulatory actions.[5]

To conclude, banking regulation appears to involve diverse issues, all of them worth devoting effort to, but so heterogeneous that no model can encompass the main issues. Also, it is important to view this area as being in full evolution, where many issues remain unsolved (see Bhattacharya, Boot, and Thakor 1995 for an assessment).[6]

Section 9.2 will discuss the pros and cons of free banking, and in particular the existence of a Central Bank. A Central Bank is usually assigned two functions: the control of inflation and the maintenance of a safe banking sector (with, in particular, a smoothly operating payment system).[7] As explained by Capie, Goodhart, and Schnadt (1994), the tenants of the free banking school "claim that the existence of a central bank is necessary for neither (function), and maybe inimical to both" (p. 87). This chapter will discuss their arguments: using the title of an article by Goodhart (1987), Section 9.2 will examine the question, Why do banks need a Central Bank?

Then the discussion will turn to study the six main regulatory instruments listed previously. Since the issues of deposit interest rate ceilings and entry, branching, and network restrictions have already been addressed in Chapter 3, this discussion will consider the four remaining points. Section 9.3 will briefly discuss portfolio restrictions. Then Section 9.4 will examine deposit insurance, and Section 9.5 will study capital requirements. Finally, Section 9.6 will discuss regulatory monitoring, focusing particularly on bank closure.

9.2   Why Do Banks Need a Central Bank?

Even though a Central Bank is present today in virtually every country, and the oldest of them (the Bank of England) has recently celebrated its tercentennial anniversary, some economists consistently argue against the existence of a Central Bank, and in favor of free banking. This section will examine the pros and cons of free banking in three domains: the monopoly of money issuance (subsection 9.2.1), the fragility of banks (subsection 9.2.2), and the protection of depositors (subsection 9.2.3).

9.2.1   The Monopoly of Money Issuance

The usual argument for justifying the government monopoly in money issuance is that the private issuance of means of payment could easily generate fraud, counterfeiting, and adverse selection problems à la Akerlof (1970). A good summary of these arguments can be found in Friedman (1960). However, a growing body of literature provides new arguments for the contrary positions of the free banking school. Hayek (1978) and Fama (1980) argue that there is no point in putting money creation under the exclusive control of the government. This is supported by empirical studies of the Scottish (White 1984) and U.S. (Rolnick and Weber 1983) free banking eras. These studies conclude that free banking systems can perform reasonably well.[8]

During the U.S. free banking era (1838 through 1863), U.S. banks issued distinct private monies, called bank notes. These bank notes were perpetual, non-interest-bearing debt claims that could be redeemed on demand (at par) in species. However, these bank notes were subject to the risk of failure of the issuer, and redemption also typically implied the cost of traveling to the issuing bank. Therefore, as pointed out by Friedman (1960), these deposit contracts were particularly difficult to enforce and fraud was peculiarly difficult to prevent. One main concern was the possible emergence of "wildcat banks" that overissued their currency, making convertibility at par impossible. Friedman sees this behavior as a major critique of private money issuance.[9] Another argument against private money issuance is the simple fact that transactions costs are increased when as many as three thousand distinct bank notes circulate in a given geographical area (as was the case in the United States and Canada in this period, when these notes were traded in a specialized exchange in Philadelphia).

Working on an interesting data set giving the complete set of bank note prices from 1839 to 1859, Gorton (1993) studies the informational efficiency of the Philadelphia bank note market. In other words, Gorton tries to assess whether the risk of these notes was correctly priced by the market. Using a simple contingent-claims framework, Gorton shows that each of these bank notes was equivalent to a risky debt with a maturity equal to the travel time from Philadelphia to the site of the issuing bank, and he uses a variant of the Black and Scholes (1973) option formula to price them. His conclusions are that wildcat banking was not really prevalent, because market participants managed to discipline banks by incorporating into prices a correct evaluation of the banks' risks. Similarly, Sargent and Wallace (1982) develop a model in which laissez-faire banking leads to a Pareto-optimal equilibrium allocation, whereas prohibiting banks from issuing notes would lead to an inefficient equilibrium.

Williamson (1992) constructs an overlapping generations model with adverse selection in which, on the contrary, laissez-faire banking is dominated by regulated banking. In Williamson's model, agents have private information about the quality of the physical capital (fruit trees) they own. They also face liquidity shocks à la Diamond and Dybvig (1983). In a free banking system, agents can issue private money backed by their physical capital. However, there is a "lemons" problem à la Akerlof. Two types of equilibrium can exist: one in which Gresham's law holds (in the sense that only bad money circulates), the other in which there is fraud: good money circulates together with bad money.[10] In this case, the value of assets is inversely related to their velocity of circulation. On the contrary, if private money is prohibited, there is a unique stationary equilibrium that Pareto dominates the other ones. The reason is that this prohibition destroys the adverse selection problems present in the laissez-faire banking system.

9.2.2   The Fragility of Banks

The history of banking shows that bank panics are as old as the fractional reserve system. In other words, as soon as banks started to finance illiquid loans through demand deposits, most recessions were accompanied by losses of confidence by the public in the banking system, often leading to bank panics. Soon, banks privately developed cooperative systems for protecting their collective reputation. These systems were later taken on and transformed by Central Banks when governments decided to impose control on the banking systems of most developed countries. However, several free banking episodes (such as in Scotland and the United States) showed that completely unregulated banking industries would be conceivable, since the banks managed to generate privately some of the services an actual bank would provide.

For example, Calomiris (1993) compares the panics in the United States during the U.S. National Banking Era (1863 through 1913) and the banking collapse of the 1930s. He argues that, during the National Banking Era, few banks actually failed, and panics were limited by temporary suspensions of convertibility during which bank notes circulated as a substitute for currency. This did not happen in the 1930s, which may explain the large number of bank failures that occurred then. Calomiris argues that the risk of runs can be reduced dramatically when banks are allowed to form large networks (like in the Scottish free banking era) and to enter into voluntary coinsurance and other cooperative arrangements with other banks (like the "Suffolk system," studied, for example, in Calomiris and Kahn (1996)).[11]

Chapter 7 already explained the role of banks in providing liquidity insurance to households, as modeled by the Bryant (1980) and Diamond and Dybvig (1983) paradigm.[12] It also explained the "unique" role played by banks in screening and monitoring borrowers who cannot obtain direct finance from financial markets. As Chapter 7 showed, it is the combination of these two functions that generates the fragility of banks. As Klausner and White (1993) argue, it is the nature of these "core" bank services to depositors and borrowers that explains the financial structure of banks (liquid liabilities and illiquid assets), which in turn explains the vulnerability of banks to runs. A possibility for eliminating this vulnerability is the narrow banking (or 100 percent reserves) proposal (advocated, for example, by Friedman 1960, Tobin 1965, and Litan 1987), under which the two core activities of banks would be strictly separated: demand deposits would be invested in Treasury securities, whereas loans would be financed by noncheckable liabilities. Goodhart (1987) argues on the one hand that "the concept of a 100% segregated reserve against checkable deposits would . . . reverse the evolution of banking" (79), but on the other hand that "monetary payments' services could be provided more safely by collective investment funds" (80) than by traditional banks. Gorton and Pennacchi (1993) examine how money market funds provide payment services and finance companies provide, separately, asset services. Although both types of firms could in principle experience panics (money market funds offer in great majority fixed share prices, whereas finance companies issue an important amount of short-term callable bonds), Gorton and Pennachi show that, so far, money market funds do not seem to be that vulnerable. However, Goodhart (1987) argues that even narrow banks would "still require the assistance of Central Banks" because "the really important distinction between banks and other financial institutions resides in the characteristics of their asset portfolio" (90). To some extent, securitization can be seen as an attempt to get rid of this "specialness" of banks' assets.[13]

An important argument against narrow banking was expressed by Black (1975) and was later reformulated by Fama (1985) as follows: "The ongoing history of a borrower as a depositor provides information that allows a bank to identify the risks of loans to depositors and to monitor the loans at lower cost than other lenders. . . . Two facts tend to support these arguments. First, banks usually require that borrowers maintain deposits (often called compensating balances). Second, banks are the dominant suppliers of short-term inside debt. The inside debt or private placements offered by insurance and finance companies (which do not have the monitoring information provided by ongoing deposit histories) are usually much longer-terms than bank loans" (38). Nakamura (1993) tests this conjecture on a large data set of U.S. banks and finds that, at least for small banks, scope economies exist between deposits and loans. However, this does not seem to be the case for large banks, which mainly lend to large firms. An explanation may be that large firms deal with multiple banks, which decreases the value of the information held by each of these banks.

Finally, it is often argued that a crucial role of banking authorities is to prevent systemic risk, namely the risk that the failure of a particular bank would spread to other banks (or other firms) linked to the failing bank by financial contracts (interbank loans or deposits). Few theoretical models of systemic risk are available so far, one exception being Rochet and Tirole (1996), which models the trade-off of the pervasive attitude of Central Banks to rely on peer monitoring by commercial banks and its necessary counterpart, namely the risk of failure propagation.

9.2.3   The Protection of Depositors

In a free banking world, bank failures may be very costly, especially to the financiers of the failing bank (such as depositors, stockholders, and other banks) and, to a lesser extent, to borrowers who had previously developed a close relationship with the failing bank. Moreover, a bank failure may spread to other banks (interbank lending accounts for a significant proportion of banks' balance sheets) and similarly endanger the solvency of nonfinancial firms. Also, a bank failure may temporarily harm the payments system, since the finality of the payments managed by the failing bank just before its failure may be reconsidered. Therefore, the "official" justifications of banks' solvency regulations (given by regulators themselves), namely protection of the public (essentially depositors) and safety of the payments system, appear prima facie as quite reasonable.

However, two simple counter-arguments can be found. First, there is no *qualitative* difference between the failure of a bank and that of a nonfinancial firm: all the negative externalities caused by bank failure are also present when a nonfinancial firm fails. Solvency regulations exist essentially for financial intermediaries and are absent in nonfinancial industries. Then, to quote the title of a famous article by Fama (1985), "What's different about banks?" Second, unless dishonest behavior is suspected on the part of banks' managers, they should not have any interest in provoking the failure of their own bank.

How is it justified that the staff of the regulatory authority (who has a priori less competence, less inside information, and fewer incentives than a bank's manager) should decide on the solvency ratio of a commercial bank?

A partial answer to the first question has already been discussed: the specificity of banks (and more generally of financial intermediaries) is that their *creditors* are also their *customers.* Contrarily to nonfinancial firms, the debt of which is held in majority by "professional investors" (i.e., banks, venture capitalists, or "informed" private investors), the debt of banks (and insurance companies) is held in large part by uninformed, dispersed small agents (mostly households) who are not in a position to monitor the banks' activities. It is true that large corporations are also financed by the public: stocks and bonds issued by large companies are indeed widely diffused. However, there are two differences: *these securities are not used as a means of payment* (which moderates the free rider problem involved in bank monitoring), and *the debt-to-asset ratio is substantially higher* for financial intermediaries than for nonfinancial firms. Therefore the free rider problem involved in the monitoring of widely held firms seems to be quantitatively much more serious in the case of banks and insurance companies.

As for the second question (why shouldn't banks' managers themselves choose the "optimal" solvency ratio?), the answer is given by the important remark (initially from Jensen and Meckling 1976) that there are *conflicts of interest* inside firms, between managers, stockholders, and bondholders. Consider for instance the case of a bank, the capital of which is held by a small number of equity holders (insiders) who manage the bank themselves. As shown by Jensen and Meckling, these owner-managers will tend to choose an investment policy that is more risky than what depositors would like. Since these depositors are not in a position to control the banks' activities (or to bargain with the owners), their interests must be defended by some institution (leading to another form of delegated monitoring than in Section 2.4). This institution can be either a public regulator (that is given the mission of maximizing the utility of depositors) or a deposit insurance company (the objective of which is to minimize the expected costs of insuring depositors).

Another important case of conflict of interest is that of a large bank, the capital of which is widely held. In that case the most important conflict is between the bank's managers and the outside financiers (depositors and stockholders). It is more difficult then to understand why the financial structure (debt-to-asset ratio) of the bank matters, since it is a priori unrelated to the relevant dimension, namely managerial incentives.

This puzzle can be solved by introducing the incomplete contract paradigm (explored in Section 4.5). If no contract can be written (and enforced) that specifies the actions of the manager, the only way to discipline this manager is to threaten him with external intervention.

Dewatripont and Tirole (1993) have developed a general theory of corporate structure along these lines. Their most spectacular result is that debt and equity are precisely the adequate instruments for inducing optimal managerial performance. The intuition for their result is that debt and equity generate a separation of tastes and tasks among financiers. Indeed, equity gives a payoff function that is convex with respect to the liquidation value of the firm (because of limited liability). Therefore equity holders tend to favor risky decisions by the manager: it is thus appropriate to give them the control rights when the firm performs well. On the contrary, debtholders have a concave payoff function: they tend to be more risk averse. It is thus appropriate to give them the control rights when the firm performs badly (bankruptcy). This model can be adapted to the framework of bank regulation, as in Dewatripont and Tirole (1994), which is examined in subsection 9.5.3.

9.3 Portfolio Restrictions

Activities permitted under the regulation of commercial banks differ between the U.S. and Europe concerning securities operations. In the United States, the Glass-Steagall Act of 1933 forbade commercial banks to hold corporate equity, leaving the underwriting of securities to investment banks. In Europe, commercial banks are *universal* and therefore are allowed to hold demand deposits while dealing with corporate equity. A recent debate in the United States has questioned the Glass-Steagall regulation and opened a discussion on the cost–benefit effects of the separation of commercial and investment banking.[14] The question therefore is, Is it efficient for the banking industry to establish a distinction between commercial banks (which are allowed to hold demand deposits) and investment banks (which are allowed to hold corporate equity)?

The main arguments in favor of separating commercial and investment banking are (1) that the holding of equity by banks may increase their risk exposure and (2) that there is a potential conflict of interest. The first argument is obvious for all the banks that are "rationed" on the level of risk they want to take, but it does not affect all the banks. The potential conflict of interest is due to the fact that banks having lent to firms in financial distress may be willing to underwrite these firms' poor securities to pay off the loans they hold.

Theoretical research has not provided a generally accepted model to analyze whether the increase in the bank's riskiness and the potential conflict of interest costs are compensated by the economics of scope and the informational economies the bank is able to obtain. Rajan (1992), for example, finds a trade-off between the two. On the other hand, concerning the effect of separation on the bank risk exposure, John, John, and Saunders (1994) show that holding equity may diminish some of the perverse effects of debt financing and therefore decrease the total amount of portfolio risk of the bank. The crucial point is that standard unsecured debt contracts give an incentive to invest in inefficient risky projects, because if the project is successful the firm wins, and if it is not the bank bears the losses. Using a model close to that of Bernanke and Gertler (1990) (see subsection 6.3.2), the authors establish that if the level of investment is high, an increase in equity will induce the firms' managers to choose the investment project more efficiently, and this will lower the total portfolio risk of the bank.

9.4 Deposit Insurance

To avoid bank panics and their social costs, governments have established deposit insurance schemes.[15] Under such schemes the bank pays a premium to a deposit insurance company, such as the Federal Deposit Insurance Corporation (FDIC) in the United States, and in exchange its depositors have their deposits insured up to a fixed limit in case the bank fails.

In the United States, deposit insurance mechanisms were developed by the Fed as a response to the Great Depression bank panics. They were later adopted by most developed countries with different modalities: insurance may be compulsory or simply voluntary, it may be implemented by one or by several funds, it may cover only principal or principal plus interest, and the limits may differ widely (from $100,000 in the United States to the equivalent of $15,000 in Spain). Before implementing deposit insurance some European countries had *implicit deposit insurance* systems based on direct government intervention to pay depositors, sharing the losses with the country's other main banks.

In most cases, deposit insurance schemes are public, although some economists have advocated recourse to private insurance systems. Such a system has in fact been recently reintroduced in some U.S. states with mixed success (see Mishkin 1992, 377). The potential advantage of private systems is that competition between companies provides incentives for information extraction and accurate pricing. There are also important drawbacks: because of systemic risks, private insurance systems lack credibility unless they are backed by the government, which in turn casts doubt on the incentives of private companies to look for an accurate pricing of deposit insurance. Also, since Central Bank interventions and closures of commercial banks are public decisions, private insurance schemes can function only if the government establishes explicit contingent closure policies, which is a difficult task (see Benston et al. 1986).

Chapter 7 showed how deposit insurance could provide a solution to bank runs (Diamond and Dybvig 1983). This section will examine several other aspects of deposit insurance: the moral hazard issue (subsection 9.4.1), risk-based pricing (subsection 9.4.2), and incomplete information problems (subsection 9.4.3).

9.4.1 The Moral Hazard Issue

Before developing the well-known arguments related to the moral hazard consequences of deposit insurance, this subsection will briefly describe the simple model that will be used here. It is a static model with only two dates. At $t = 0$ the deposit insurance premium is paid by the bank. At $t = 1$ the bank is liquidated, and depositors are compensated whenever the bank's assets are insufficient. For simplicity, the riskless rate (and the deposit rate) is normalized to zero. The balance sheets of the bank are thus:

Assets		Liabilities		Assets		Liabilities	
Loans	L	Deposits	D	Loan Repayments	$\tilde{L}$	Deposits	D
Insurance Premium	P	Equity	F	Insurance Payment	$\tilde{S}$	Liquidation Value	$\tilde{V}$
		$t = 0$				$t = 1$	

At date 1, the stockholders receive the liquidation value of the bank:

$$\tilde{V} = \tilde{L} - D + \tilde{S}, \tag{9.1}$$

where $\tilde{S}$ is the payment received from deposit insurance:

$$\tilde{S} = \max(0, D - \tilde{L}). \tag{9.2}$$

Using the balance sheet at date 0 to replace D, $\tilde{V}$ can also been written as

$$\tilde{V} = F + (\tilde{L} - L) + [\max(0, D - \tilde{L}) - P]. \tag{9.3}$$

Thus the value of equity will be the sum of its initial value, the increase in the value of loans, and the net subsidy (positive or negative) from the deposit insurance.

Suppose, for instance, that $\tilde{L}$ can take only two values: X with probability θ (success) and 0 with probability $(1 - \theta)$ (failure). The expected profit for the bank's stockholders will be

$$\pi \overset{\text{def}}{=} E(\tilde{V}) - F = (\theta X - L) + ((1 - \theta)D - P), \tag{9.4}$$

where the first term represents the Net Present Value (NPV) of the loans and the second term is the net subsidy from the deposit insurance system. If deposit insurance is fairly priced, this term is nil ($P = (1 - \theta)D$), and the strong form of the Modigliani-Miller result obtains: the market value of a firm, $E(\tilde{V}) + D$, is independent of its liability structure.

The moral hazard problem is easily captured from formula 9.4. Suppose that P is fixed and that banks are free to determine the characteristics (θ, X) of the projects they finance in a given feasible set. Then, within a class of projects with the same NPV $(\theta X - L = \text{constant})$, the banks will choose those with the lowest probability of success θ (or the highest risk). This comes from the fact that the premium rate $\frac{P}{D}$ is given, and does not depend on the risk taken by the bank. Such a "flat" rate deposit insurance pricing was in place in the United States until December 1991, when Congress legislated a new system involving risk-related insurance premiums. The following subsection will show how such pricing rules can be designed theoretically, and whether they provide a solution to the moral hazard problem.

9.4.2   Risk-Related Insurance Premiums

As can be seen from formula 9.2, the deposit insurance payment $\tilde{S}$ is identical to a put option on a bank's assets $\tilde{L}$ at a strike price D.[16] This was originally observed by Merton (1977), who proposed using the arbitrage pricing method for finding the appropriate pricing policy for deposit insurance. This method requires the existence of complete (and perfect) financial markets, on which the deposit insurance (or option) contract can be duplicated by a portfolio of tradable securities. In the absence of arbitrage opportunities, the price of such a contract can be computed as its expected NPV under some "risk-adjusted" or "martingale" probability measure (which incorporates market corrections for risk). Suppose, for instance, that the value of the bank's assets at date t follows a geometric random walk:

$$\frac{d\tilde{L}}{\tilde{L}} = \mu dt + \sigma dZ, \tag{9.5}$$

where $Z(t)$ is a standard Brownian motion. If the riskless rate r and deposit rate r_D (measured in continuous terms) are constant, and if T denotes the time between two examination dates, the Black-Scholes formula (1973) applies and the no-arbitrage (or actuarial) price of deposit insurance is given by

$$P^* = De^{(r_D - r)T} N(h_2) - LN(h_1), \tag{9.6}$$

where $N(\cdot)$ is the standard Gaussian cumulative distribution function (c.d.f.) and

$$h_1 = \frac{1}{\sigma\sqrt{T}} \log \frac{De^{(r_D - r)T}}{L} - \frac{1}{2}\sigma\sqrt{T} \tag{9.7}$$

$$h_2 = h_1 + \sigma\sqrt{T}. \tag{9.8}$$

Homogeneity of these formulas allows for focusing on the (actuarial) premium rate $\frac{P^*}{D}$, as a function of the deposit-to-asset ratio $\frac{D}{L}$ and the volatility of assets σ. Classical properties of the Black-Scholes formula imply the following (unsurprising) result.

Result 9.1   The actuarial rate $\frac{P^*}{D}$ of deposit insurance is an increasing function of the deposit-to-asset ratio $\frac{D}{L}$ and of the volatility σ of the bank's assets (Merton 1977).

Marcus and Shaked (1984) and Ronn and Verma (1986) have tried to estimate the difference between these theoretical premiums P^* and those actually paid by U.S. banks, in an attempt to evaluate the importance of implicit subsidies to the banking industry. Buser, Chen, and Kane (1981) argue that the implicit subsidy gives a price to banks' charters. On the other hand, Result 9.1 has been extended to take into account audit costs (Merton 1978), liquidation costs (Mullins and Pyle 1991), and interest rate risk (McCullough 1981, Kerfriden and Rochet 1993).

Another extension of Merton's option pricing model for pricing deposit insurance is put forth by Pennacchi (1987), who analyzes the impact on bank insurance pricing and bank failure resolution. In particular, Pennacchi contrasts the consequences of a purchase and assumption transaction with a policy of making direct payments to depositors. In the latter case, even if deposit insurance is fairly priced, banks will tend to take excessive risks. In the former case however, sufficient monopoly rents (charter values) would induce banks to prefer to increase their capital.

If the authorities can close the bank *before* the end of the contract, deposit insurance becomes analogous to a *callable put option*, and dynamic considerations have to be introduced. Acharya and Dreyfus (1988) develop a model along these lines. At each date the authorities receive a report X on the true value of the bank's assets. Using this information, the optimal closure policy is determined (simultaneously with the price of deposit insurance) as the minimum cost policy for the deposit insurer. Acharya and Dreyfus show that the insurer will optimally close the bank whenever

1. the net increase in the insurer (discounted) liability exceeds the immediate cost of reorganizing the bank, or

2. the bank's current asset value is too low for the insurer to be able to charge an actuarially fair premium.

In a competitive banking industry, bank closure will always happen with a positive probability. Thus Acharya and Dreyfus's results imply a more involved formula for the market value of deposit insurance. They do not alter the nature of the result: if the deposit insurance company is able to observe the bank's risk characteristics (D/V and σ), then it is theoretically possible to price deposit insurance in an actuarially fair way. However, this is more complex under asymmetric information.

9.4.3   Is Fairly Priced Deposit Insurance Possible?

The title of this subsection is taken from a recent article by Chan, Greenbaum, and Thakor (1992), who show that when asymmetric information is present, fairly priced deposit insurance may not be feasible. A first issue is timing: even if the portfolio decisions of banks are perfectly observable, there is a time lag between these decisions and the subsequent premium adjustments by the regulator or the insurer. Therefore, if the bank is seriously undercapitalized, its managers may decide to "gamble for resurrection" during this time lag even if they know that later they may have to pay for it. Also, increasing insurance premiums may increase this incentive to gamble for resurrection, because the bank's stockholders know that they will not be liable in case the bank fails.

A second issue, examined in more detail by Chan, Greenbaum, and Thakor, is adverse selection. Consider the simple model developed in subsection 9.4.1 and suppose that θ, the probability of repayment of the bank's loan, is private information of the bank. Fairly priced deposit insurance can nevertheless be possible if there exists a (nonlinear) premium schedule $P(D)$ such that

$$P[D(\theta)] = (1 - \theta)D(\theta)$$

(premiums equal expected losses),

where $D(\theta)$ is the profit maximizing level of deposits for a bank of "characteristic" θ. Namely: $D(\theta)$ realizes $Max_D \Pi(D, \theta)$, where by definition

$$\Pi(D, \theta) = (\theta X - L) + (1 - \theta)D - P[D(\theta)].$$

The first order condition of this problem is

$$\frac{\partial \Pi}{\partial D}(D(\theta), \theta) = 0 = (1 - \theta) - P'[D(\theta)].$$

Differentiating the fair pricing condition yields

$$P'[D(\theta)]D'(\theta) = (1 - \theta)D'(\theta) - D(\theta).$$

Multiplying the first equation by $D'(\theta)$ and comparing it to the second equation gives $D(\theta) \equiv 0$, which is, of course, absurd. Chan, Greenbaum, and Thakor conclude that fairly priced deposit insurance is not viable, because of asymmetric information. Freixas and Rochet (1995) show that, in a more general case, fairly priced deposit insurance may in fact be viable under asymmetric information, but that it will never be completely desirable from a general welfare viewpoint. The reason is that cross-subsidies between banks are Pareto improving in an adverse selection context. However, these cross-subsidies may also lead to an artificial survival of inefficient banks, thus generating a trade-off between static and dynamic efficiency.

Bond and Crocker (1993) study the consequences of linking deposit insurance premiums to the capitalization of banks, in an interesting model based on the costly state verification paradigm of Townsend (1979) and Gale and Hellwig (1985). In this model, inspired also by Diamond (1984), banks attract the funds of risk averse depositors and invest them in industrial projects. These are small banks, managed by their owners (the bankers) and prevented from diversification by organization costs (as in Cerasi and Daltung 1994). The return $\tilde{x}$ on a bank portfolio is observable only by its manager, except if depositors pay an audit cost. The optimal deposit contract is therefore a standard debt contract (transposed to the deposit side): depositors receive $\min(\tilde{x}, R)$, where R is the nominal rate of deposits, and pay the audit cost when $\tilde{x} < R$. Bond and Crocker start by analyzing the competitive equilibrium of the banking sector in the absence of deposit insurance. Banks determine the capital level K^* and the deposit rate R^* that maximize the depositors' expected utility under the constraint that banks break even. Banking capital is useful in this context, because it provides partial insurance to risk averse depositors against fluctuations in banks' portfolio returns. Bond and Crocker then show that introducing actuarial deposit insurance provides banks with an additional tool for insuring depositors. They find that complete deposit insurance would be suboptimal in this context, since it suppresses the incentive of depositors to require that banks self-protect through capitalization. Finally, Bond and Crocker study the optimal deposit insurance plan, in which insurance premiums paid by banks depend on the banks' capitalization.

9.4.4   The Effects of Deposit Insurance on the Banking Industry

The positive approach to banking regulation is concerned with the effects of regulation on equilibrium in the deposit and credit markets. The complexities of this approach stem from the fact that for regulation to be justified (i.e., for free banking not to be optimal), an imperfection of capital markets must be introduced. Since there is no general consensus in the literature on which imperfection is the crucial one, there are multiple models, which also differ as to the way regulation is introduced. This discussion therefore will not try to survey the different approaches to modeling the effects of banking regulation, but instead will focus on some contributions that illustrate the main types of results that can be obtained.

The simplest way to model the effects of regulation is, of course, to disregard the imperfections of the financial markets. This approach has been used to analyze the effect of flat deposit insurance (i.e., insurance for which the premium is just proportional to the volume of deposits and thus does not depend on the level of risk of the bank's assets). As already explained in subsection 9.4.1, flat deposit insurance gives the banks an incentive to take too much risk. But the consequences on the equilibrium level of deposit and loan margins are not obvious. The analysis of these effects has been the subject of two articles by Suarez (1993a, 1993b). Assuming risk neutrality and limited liability of banks, Suarez shows that the banks' portfolio problem has solutions of the bang-bang type, which are quite intuitive: high margins on deposits will lead the banks to assume a lower risk. Still, even if the margin on loans is negative, the banks may be interested in lending (provided they have sufficient leverage through deposits), simply because they obtain a subsidy via deposit insurance. Similar bang-bang results could be obtained in a dynamic equilibrium in which the banks' level of risk taking has an effect on the probability of bankruptcy (the present value of future profits forgone) but increases the value of the banks' claim on the deposit insurance company. If future profits are low, the banks will choose to take a maximum amount of risk; if instead the banks have some market power, they will take less risk (Suarez 1993b).

Gennote and Pyle (1991) also consider the effect of deposit guarantees, although they focus on the banks' portfolio of loans. They show that deposit guarantees will lead to inefficient investment and that increases in bank capital requirements could not compensate for the increase in risk (see subsection 9.5.1 for other results contained in the same article).

Among the few articles that explicitly introduce a capital market imperfection that makes free banking inefficient are two articles by Matutes and Vives (1996a, 1996b). In the first paper they use Hotelling's (1929) model of horizontal differentiation and obtain situations of market failure, in which free banking is not viable. In this context, they show that deposit insurance is desirable first because it prevents market collapse, and second because it allows an increase in the market size by restoring the confidence of depositors. However, as a result of deposit insurance, the banks will compete more fiercely, which increases the expected cost of failure. In Matutes and Vives (1996b), a model of imperfect competition in the presence of a social cost of failure is considered, and flat deposit insurance regulation results in excessive risk taking. One of the implications of this model is that deposit rate regulation may be desirable.

9.5   Solvency Regulations

9.5.1   The Portfolio Approach

The portfolio approach, developed originally by Kahane (1977) and Kareken and Wallace (1978), and examined later by Crouhy and Galai (1986), Kim and Santomero (1988), and Koehn and Santomero (1980), is parallel to the literature presented in subsection 9.4.2. The main idea is that if banks behave as portfolio managers when they choose the composition of their portfolio of assets and liabilities, then it is important to use risk-related weights for the computation of the capital-to-asset ratio. Like Crouhy and Galai (1986), Kareken and Wallace use a complete markets framework and show that in that context, capital regulations are dominated by risk-related insurance premiums as an instrument for solving the moral hazard problem. Of course, as has been repeatedly argued in this book, the complete market setting is not really appropriate for modeling banks.

As a proxy for incomplete markets, Kim and Santomero introduce risk aversion in the bank's objective function.[17] This is legitimate in the case of a small bank, owned and managed by the same agent, who cannot completely diversify his risk. Using a mean-variance model, Kim and Santomero compare the bank's portfolio choice before and after a solvency regulation is imposed. They show that in general, the solvency regulation will entail a recomposition of the risky part of the bank's portfolio in such a way that its risk is increased. As a consequence, even if the global size of this risky portfolio decreases (because of the solvency regulation), the probability of the bank's failure may *increase* after the solvency regulation has been imposed, which is rather ironic (this had already been pointed out by Kahane). Kim and Santomero, and later Rochet (1992a), show that this distortion in the banks' asset allocation disappears when regulators use "correct" (i.e., market-based) measures of risk in the computation of the solvency ratio.

Keeley and Furlong (1990) and Rochet criticize the Kim-Santomero approach for inconsistency, in the sense that the limited liability option is not introduced in the bank's objective function. Rochet shows that when this option is properly accounted for, the efficiency of solvency regulations is jeopardized even more. Even when market-based risk weights are used, it may be necessary to require an additional regulation in the form of an additional minimum capital requirement for banks (in absolute terms), independent of their size.

Gennotte and Pyle (1991) revisit the analysis of the impact of capital regulations on bank risk by assuming that banks can invest in projects that have a positive NPV. As has already been argued, if all banks' assets have zero present value (because, for instance, these assets are traded on perfect capital markets), not only do banks have no social value, but also the only reason their portfolio decisions may be relevant is that they enjoy rents (which may come from underpriced deposit insurance or from imposed restrictions on competition). This is a caricatural vision of banking. On the other hand, in Gennotte and Pyle, banks have a social utility because they screen and monitor industrial projects that could not be directly financed by capital markets. By investing v in a project of risk characteristic σ, a bank generates an NPV denoted $J(\sigma, v)$. If banks could completely self-finance, they would optimally choose the size

v^* and the risk characteristic σ^* that jointly maximize $J(\sigma, v)$. Since in fact they finance themselves in part by attracting insured deposits D, they benefit from the option value associated with limited liability. Therefore the bank's objective function is distorted in the direction of excessive risk taking.

Finally, it is worth mentioning that the macroeconomic implications of solvency regulation has begun to be explored (see Blum and Hellwig 1995).

9.5.2   The Incentive Approach

As was emphasized previously, it is natural to assume that banks have better information regarding their own risks and returns than the regulator does. Modeling this issue with techniques similar to those developed by Laffont and Tirole (1986, 1993) has led to a new approach to solvency regulations, initiated by Giammarino, Lewis, and Sappington (1993); Rochet (1992b); Bensaid, Pagès, and Rochet (1993); and Freixas and Gabillon (1996).

In this approach, solvency regulations are modeled as a principal agent problem between a public insurance system (operated, say, by the Central Bank) and a private bank. The latter is run by managers who carry out risky projects (loans) and invests in a safe asset (reserves). Both activities are financed by cash collected from depositors and by capital raised among outside shareholders. When there is no conflict of interest between shareholders and the managers of the bank, the regulator simply attempts to minimize the expected loss of deposit insurance under the individual rationality constraint of both managers and shareholders. Since insurance is costly (overhead, deadweight loss of taxation, etc.), the cost of public funds will in the end determine the optimal trade-off faced by the regulator between the cost of banking capital and that of insuring depositors. The main results obtained by Giammarino, Lewis, and Sappington and by Bensaid, Pagès, and Rochet as follows:

• Functional separation between deposit and loan activities is in general inefficient. In this setup, the proper allocation of capital is consistent with some risk transformation, and this always implies some positive probability of failure. In this respect, free and narrow banking appear as special cases of optimal regulation when the cost of public funds is respectively zero or infinite.

• The optimal incentive scheme may be decentralized through a solvency requirement that induces banks to internalize the cost of the deposit insurance system. The appropriate regulation imposes the capital-to-asset ratio which, at the margin, leaves unaffected the expected cost of deposit insurance.

• Efficient regulation should be risk adjusted. Under the 1988 international Basle agreement, assets are essentially risk weighted according to the institutional nature of the borrower.[18] Here another dimension of risk adjustment is stressed, according to the size of the bank's portfolio: the risk brought about by a marginal increase in loans of any credit category should be larger than the average risk of that category. Hence, the marginal capital-to-asset ratio is set above the average ratio. This may be achieved through a system of lump-sum deductibles, under which equity is not strictly proportional to the assets outstanding.

• Finally, the capital-to-asset ratio should be contingent on the quality of banks' assets, measured for instance by ratings performed by independent agencies.

The social costs of an insured failure is a matter of concern that could justify regulation of the banks' capital ratios. Still, when deposits have a utility, or when capital is costly, the trade-off between capital requirements and the cost of bank failure must be considered. In a perfect information setting, this could be determined simply as a marginal condition. But this issue becomes particularly relevant in an adverse selection setting in which mechanism design theory can be used to obtain the optimal regulatory scheme. Freixas and Gabillon (1996) consider mechanisms that combine the amount of risk-free assets (reserves) a bank is bound to hold, the amount of capital it is required to have, and the deposit insurance premium it has to pay. The banks are assumed to have private information on the initial value of their portfolio of loans, but this value follows the Merton formula for pricing the claims on the deposit insurance company. Using this framework, Freixas and Gabillon characterize the optimal mechanism, that is, the one that maximizes social surplus when deposits and loans have a social value, and when there is a social cost of bankruptcy, constraining the mechanisms to be incentive compatible and respecting an individual rationality constraint for the banks. The result they obtain is that, if loans have a positive NPV, banks will never hold reserves, and the deposit insurance premium will have to be decreasing with the bank's capital.

9.5.3   The Incomplete Contract Approach

It is clear that the majority of large modern banks is owned by a large number of small investors. The previous approach, which has assumed that banks were owned and managed by the same agent (the banker) does not fit this empirical evidence. In reality, bank managers own (at most) a small fraction of their bank's capital. Therefore it may be reasonable to concentrate on the incentive scheme of these managers rather than on that of the stockholders. It is then more difficult to understand why banks' solvency (i.e., the financial structure of banks) matters, since there is no obvious relation between this financial structure and the performance of managers. In particular, if complete contracts can be written between the owners of the bank and its managers, the Modigliani-Miller theorem applies and the financial structure is irrelevant.

Therefore the only possibility for reintroducing the relevance of banks' solvency in this context is to consider that contracts are incomplete in the sense that some decisions cannot be prespecified. Therefore the allocation of the control rights on the bank becomes important. It is the financial structure of the firm (here the solvency regulation of the bank) that determines the allocation of these control rights among claimholders, and in particular when and how these claimholders can intervene in management. The approach that will be followed now (taken from Dewatripont and Tirole 1994) is an application to the banking sector of a general theory of the financial structure of firms (also due to Dewatripont and Tirole 1993), and directly connected to Aghion and Bolton's (1992) general approach to bankruptcy as a mechanism for transferring control rights between claimholders. See also Tirole (1994) for a survey of the main issues this approach may be used to explain.

This discussion will not go into the details of this general theory, but will briefly describe the main features of the model used by Dewatripont and Tirole in applying their theory to the banking sector. This model is very simple, with three dates:

1. At date 0, the initial balance sheet of the bank is given: deposits D_0 and equity E_0 are used to finance loans $L_0 = D_0 + E_0$. The manager can improve the quality of these loans by exerting some effort, which costs K. The problem will be to provide the manager with the incentives to exert this effort, which always will be assumed here to be the efficient solution. The manager's incentives will be closely related to the allocation of control rights between the regulator (who represents the depositors) and the stockholders.

2. At date 1, a first repayment v is obtained from the loans, and a signal u is observed about their future liquidation value η at date 2: u and v are independent, but both are related to the level of effort. Suppose that v is reinvested at a riskless rate normalized to zero: the final (overall) performance of the bank (the liquidation value of its assets) will therefore be $v + \eta$. After observing u and v, the controlling party (who could be the board of directors on behalf of the stockholders, or the regulator, representing the depositors) decides if the bank will continue to operate (action C for "continuing") or if it will be reorganized (action S for "stopping"). This action determines the distribution of η, conditionally on u: it is denoted $H_A(\eta|u)$, where $A \in \{C, S\}$.

3. Then at date 2, the liquidation value $v + \eta$ is observed.

The crucial point is that the action A is noncontractible; therefore the determination of the controlling party at $t = 1$ will be fundamental. This is the role of the solvency regulation. For simplicity, it is assumed that monetary incentives cannot be given to the manager. Incentives for managerial effort can be given only indirectly through the threat of reorganizing the bank, in which case the manager will be fired and will lose the private benefit B attached to running the bank.

Since u and v are independent, the optimal action under complete information depends only on u. The expected profit $D(u)$ from continuing (instead of stopping) at $t = 1$ (conditionally on u) is easily computed:

$$D(u) \stackrel{\text{def}}{=} E[\eta | u, C] - E[\eta | u, S],$$

which is equal to

$$D(u) = \int_0^{+\infty} \eta \, dH_C(\eta | u) - \int_0^{+\infty} \eta \, dH_S(\eta | u),$$

or, after integrating by parts,

$$D(u) = \int_0^{+\infty} \{H_S(\eta | u) - H_C(\eta | u)\} d\eta.$$

Continuing is optimal under complete information if and only if $D(u)$ is nonnegative. To fix ideas, Dewatripont and Tirole assume that $D(\cdot)$ is increasing, so that the first best rule can be described as follows: *continue when $u \geq \hat{u}$; stop when $u < \hat{u}$*. The threshold $\hat{u}$ is defined by

$$D(\hat{u}) = 0.$$

From now on, assume that the effort level of the manager (which can take only two values: $e = \underline{e}$ (insufficient) or $e = \bar{e}$ (correct)) is not observable by others. However u and v are positively correlated with e: higher realizations of u (or v) indicate a greater likelihood that $e = \bar{e}$. If $f(u|e)$ and $g(v|e)$ denote the conditional densities of u and v, this means that $\frac{f(\cdot | \bar{e})}{f(\cdot | \underline{e})}$ and $\frac{g(\cdot | \bar{e})}{g(\cdot | \underline{e})}$ are both increasing functions. Let $x(u, v)$ denote the probability of continuing when (u, v) is observed. The second best decision rule is obtained by maximizing the expected (incremental) profit from continuing $\int\int x(u, v) D(u) f(u|\bar{e}) g(v|\bar{e}) du\, dv$ under the incentive compatibility constraint:

$$B \int\int x(u, v)\{f(u|\bar{e})g(v|\bar{e}) - f(u|\underline{e})g(v|\underline{e})\} du\, dv \geq K,$$

which means that the expected loss from shirking is higher than the cost of effort. The Lagrangian of this problem is simply

$$L = \int\int x(u, v)\{(D(u) + \mu B) f(u|\bar{e}) g(v|\bar{e}) - \mu B f(u|\underline{e}) g(u|\underline{e})\} du\, dv - \mu K,$$

where μ is the multiplier associated with the incentive constraint. Pointwise maximization of L with respect to $x(u, v) \in [0, 1]$ gives the second best decision rule:

$$\begin{cases} x(u,v) & = 1 \quad \text{if} \quad D(u) + \mu B \geq \mu B \frac{f(u|\underline{e})g(v|\underline{e})}{f(u|\overline{e})g(v|\overline{e})} \\ & = 0 \quad \text{otherwise} . \end{cases}$$

In other words, continuing is optimal under incomplete information if and only if

$$\frac{f(u|\overline{e})}{f(u|\underline{e})} \left\{ 1 + \frac{D(u)}{\mu B} \right\} \geq \frac{g(v|\underline{e})}{g(v|\overline{e})}. \tag{9.9}$$

Let $u^*(v)$ be defined as the value of u such that condition 9.9 is satisfied with equality, for a given value of v. Because the left side of 9.9 is increasing in u, continuing will be optimal if and only if $u \geq u^*(v)$. Moreover, the right side of 9.9 is decreasing in v; therefore the function $u^*(\cdot)$ is itself decreasing.

Let $\hat{v}$ be defined implicitly by

$$u^*(\hat{v}) = \hat{u}.$$

Figure 9.1 (taken from Dewatripont and Tirole 1994, 66) illustrates the differences between the first best and the second best decision rules. The shaded areas correspond to the two regions of ex-post inefficiency: for v larger than $\hat{v}$, there are values of $u(u \in [u^*(v), \hat{u}])$ for which the bank is allowed to continue, although ex-post efficiency would imply closing it (inefficient passivity). Conversely, for v smaller than $\hat{v}$, there are values of $u(u \in [\hat{u}, u^*(v)])$ for which the bank is stopped, although ex-post efficiency would imply continuing (inefficient interference).

The crucial step in the Dewatripont-Tirole theory of financial structure is to show that a convenient combination of debt and equity can provide outsiders with the appropriate incentives to implement this ex-post inefficient decision rule. As is well known, the payoff of equity is a convex function of the profit of the bank, which implies that equity holders tend to favor risky decisions. Symmetrically, the payoff of a deposit is a concave function of the profit of the bank, which implies that depositors tend to favor less risky decisions. Therefore, under the reasonable assumption that closing the bank is less risky than continuing, stockholders (resp. depositors) will have a tendency to excessive passivity (resp. interference). It is then not surprising (considering Figure 9.1) that stockholders (resp. depositors) should be given the control rights of the bank when the first-period performance is good, $v \geq \hat{v}$ (resp. when this performance is bad, $v < \hat{v}$). Exact implementation of the second best optimal decision rule can then be obtained by several alternative means: composite claims, net worth adjustments, or voluntary recapitalization (see Dewatripont and Tirole 1994, 81–84, for details).

Notice that, as already remarked, this theory is very general: it can be applied as well to managerial corporations (with bondholders or creditors replacing depositors). The main specificity of banks is that their creditors (depositors)

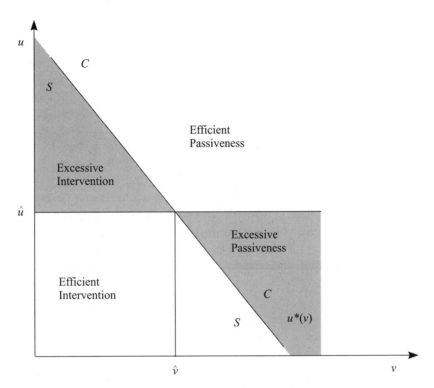

Figure 9.1
Best and Second Best Decision Rules

are small and uninformed. Thus the depositors are not in a position to monitor the bank's manager: the role of the regulator is to represent their interest and act on their behalf. Therefore the solvency regulation of banks brings in a rule specifying under what conditions the stockholders remain in control for the bank, and under what conditions it is the regulator who represents the interest of depositors. A detailed discussion of the practice of solvency regulation (in light of this theory) is given by Dewatripont and Tirole.

9.6   The Resolution of Bank Failures

In a Modigliani-Miller environment, in which the liability structure of a bank is irrelevant, bank closures would occur only when they are efficient (i.e., when the risk-adjusted NPV of continuation is negative). But when depositors are insured (and deposit insurance premiums cannot be adjusted in real time to the investment decisions of the banks), moral hazard appears: bankers have incentives to take too much risk, and in particular to keep operating (at the expense of the deposit insurance fund) in situations in which liquidation would be efficient. The reason is that limited liability gives the bank owners the equivalent of a call option on the bank's assets. This option appreciates when the volatility of these assets increases, and keeps a positive value even when the NPV of continuation is negative.

In such a context, banking regulations can be efficient only when they include closure policies that prevent such behavior (sometimes described as "gambling for resurrection"). More generally, regulation must address the question of resolution of banks' distress, which matters, for instance, when a profitable bank has liquidity problems. This section will begin with a discussion of the instruments and policies that can be used for the resolution of banks' distress. It will then examine the two alternative philosophies for dealing with bank closure: adopting rigid rules that determine banks' closure as a function of "objective" information, or promoting discretion, that is, delegating the decision to some organization (typically a regulatory body) that should be provided with adequate incentives to do its job properly.[19]

9.6.1   Resolving Banks' Distress: Instruments and Policies

In a recent article, Goodhart and Schoenmaker (1993) present an interesting data set surveying 104 bank failures in 24 countries between 1970 and 1992.[20] They classify the resolution methods used by the banking authorities for dealing with these failures into four categories: (1) a rescue package (which may include emergency aid by the Central Bank and a recapitalization by the stockholders), (2) a takeover by other banks (under the "purchase and assumption" regime), (3) the creation of a special regime administered by the government or the deposit insurance fund (in case of chain failures, such as the savings and loan debacle in the United States, or the recent banking crises in Scandinavia and Japan), and (4) liquidation of the financial institution. Among the lessons drawn by Goodhart and Schoenmaker are the following three conclusions:

1. Bank failures are not uncommon, nor are they limited to a few countries.

2. Authorities have been reluctant to see such failures end in straightforward liquidation (only 31 out of 104 instances).

3. Separation of authority between monetary and supervisory agencies is less likely to lead to involvement by tax payers or by other commercial banks in the form of financing rescues (the "survivors pay" rule).

If recapitalization is not possible or not desirable, the deposit insurance company takes over the bank. It then has the option of either *liquidating* the bank (payoff and liquidation), in which case uninsured depositors will not receive full payment, or keeping it in operation and selling it as a going concern (under the purchase and assumption procedure).[21] In this latter case, the deposit insurance company can obtain a higher price by auctioning off the bank (because bidders will value the bank's goodwill), but it will also be bound to make a full payment to all uninsured depositors (and even to all other depositors if a no-preference clause is present). Note that bank regulation usually allows the regulator to dismiss a bank's manager, but this occurs unfrequently.

The banking authorities also must choose the procedure to be used for solving a bank's distress. In particular, they can adopt rigid rules that condition closure upon verifiable criteria, or delegate the decision to the monetary authorities (the Central Bank) or to the deposit insurance fund. The preferences of these two institutions are of course different, and delegation may result in excessive passivity (forbearance) or excessive intervention. The following subsections will examine the contributions of Repullo (1993) and Mailath and Mester (1994), who model these issues in a game theoretical model in an incomplete contract setup. Repullo studies the delegation problem: Who should decide on banks' closure? Mailath and Mester study the credibility problem for the closure decision and its consequences on the choice of assets by banks.

9.6.2   Who Should Decide on Banks' Closure?

Repullo (1993) analyzes the problem of optimal delegation of bank closure decisions in a model inspired by that of Dewatripont and Tirole (1994) studied in subsection 9.5.3. This closure decision can depend on two variables: a verifiable signal v (assumed to give withdrawals on the bank's deposits at the interim date) and a nonverifiable signal u (interpreted as giving information on the bank's future profitability). Since u is nonverifiable, the allocation of control (between the Central Bank and the insurance company) can depend only on v. Of course, once this control has been allocated, the controlling party can base its decision on u. In fact, it will make the decision that maximizes its own preferences. The main result of Repullo is that, if the Central Bank is a junior creditor with respect to depositors, it is optimal to allocate control to the Central Bank when withdrawals are small, and to the insurance fund when they are large. The following discussion will examine the details of the model.

Depositors are modeled as in Chapter 7: each of them invests 1 at $t = 0$ and decides to withdraw v at $t = 1$, and $1 - v$ at $t = 2$ (the interest rate is normalized to zero). The bank's investments return $\tilde{R}$ at $t = 2$, but can also be liquidated for an amount L (with $\frac{1}{2} < L < 1$) at $t = 1$. In addition, a signal u on future returns is publicly observed at $t = 1$. From an ex-ante viewpoint, both u and v are random. Without loss of generality, assume $E[\tilde{R}|u] = u$. Therefore, the first best closure rule (the value maximizing decision) is: close the bank if and only if $u < L$.

Since u is not verifiable, this policy is not implementable (at least directly), and the only thing that can be done by the banking authorities is to delegate the closure decision either to the Central Bank or to the deposit insurance fund. These two cases will be examined successively.

Closure Decided by the Central Bank

Repullo assumes that the Central Bank is a junior claimant.[22] If the (commercial) bank is liquidated, the Central Bank loses $1 - L$. If not, the Central Bank has to lend v to the commercial bank; the return on that loan is v if the bank is solvent, and $\max(R - (1 - v), 0)$ if not. Therefore the net loss to the Central Bank is

$$\begin{cases} l = 0 & \text{if} \quad R > 1 \\ l = 1 - R & \text{if} \quad 1 - v < R < 1 \\ l = v & \text{if} \quad R < 1 - v. \end{cases}$$

The Central Bank will close the commercial bank if and only if $E[l|u] > 1 - L$.[23]

Closure Decided by the Deposit Insurance Fund

If the closure is decided by the deposit insurance fund, the decision will depend only on u, since, independently of v, the deposit insurance fund will have to pay on aggregate $\max(0, 1 - R)$ to the depositors.

Closure will be implemented if and only if $E[\max(0, 1 - R)|u] > 1 - L$. Since the expected losses $E[\max(0, 1 - R)|u]$ are superior to $E[1 - r|u]$, the deposit insurance fund will tend to be tougher than what the first best rule would require.

It is easy to see that the continuation loss for the Central Bank is always (weakly) smaller than that of the deposit insurance fund. Therefore the Central Bank will tend to be more lenient than the deposit insurance fund.

Optimal Allocation of Control

The main result obtained by Repullo is the following:

Result 9.2 The optimal allocation of the decision to close banks is to grant this power to the Central Bank when withdrawals are small ($v < \hat{v}$) and to the deposit insurance fund when they are large ($v > \hat{v}$).

A Positive Analysis of Bank Closure

One of the main problems a regulator must face is the bad incentives of nearly insolvent banks to invest in excessively risky assets. In a perfect world,[24] a regulator would be able to close a bank whenever its assets were too risky. Nevertheless, the closure threat is not necessarily credible.

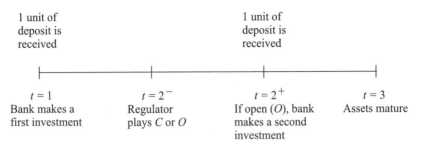

Figure 9.2
Structure of the Regulatory Game

Mailath and Mester (1994) model this question using a dynamic game, and look for the perfect Nash equilibria of this game. More specifically, they consider a two-period model in an incomplete contract setting in which the banks and the regulator cannot commit to a particular future action. The banks receive one unit of deposits and choose first at $t = 1$ the risk level of their assets, which can be either safe (S) or risky (R). Next, at $t = 2$ the regulator decides, knowing the risk level of the bank assets, whether it is better to close down the bank (C) or to leave it open (O). If the bank remains open it plays again at time $t = 2$, choosing once more either a risky or a safe new investment, out of the additional unit of deposits it receives. Then at $t = 3$ all assets mature (so that one asset has maturity 2 and the other maturity 1) and returns are realized. Figure 9.2 illustrates the timing of the bank and the regulator decisions.

Interest rates are normalized to zero, and the net return on the bank (private) safe asset is assumed to be equal to r with certainty, with $r > 0$. This is a rent justified by the bank know-how, and no arbitrage is possible. The risky project returns $(1 + \rho)$ with probability p and zero otherwise. Assume that it has a negative NPV: $p(\rho + 1) < r + 1$, although if successful it offers ex post a larger return $\rho > r$. In addition, assume that $r < 1$, so the bank cannot repay its depositors if one of its projects fails.

This discussion will focus on the cases in which, if unregulated, the banks would choose a sequence of strategies for times 1 and 2 that is either (R, R) or (R, S) (which is equivalent here to (S, R)). If the bank were to choose (S, S), regulation would be redundant.

Case 1 is defined as an environment in which (absent regulation) (R, S) is strictly preferred to (R, R), and case 2 indicates a case in which (R, R) is weakly preferred to (R, S).

Computing the bank's expected profits derived from the two strategies (under limited liability), (R, S) is strictly preferred to (R, R) if and only if

$$p(\rho + r) > 2p^2\rho, \tag{9.10}$$

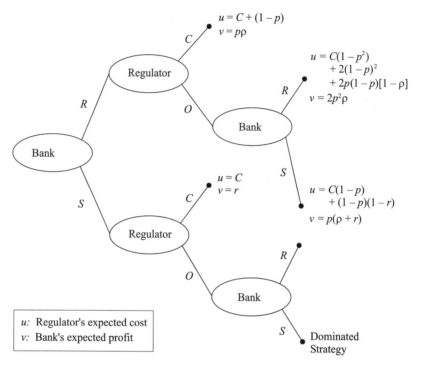

$u = C + (1 - p)$
$v = p\rho$

$u = C(1 - p^2)$
$+ 2(1 - p)^2$
$+ 2p(1 - p)[1 - \rho]$
$v = 2p^2\rho$

$u = C$
$v = r$

$u = C(1 - p)$
$+ (1 - p)(1 - r)$
$v = p(\rho + r)$

u: Regulator's expected cost
v: Bank's expected profit

Dominated
Strategy

Figure 9.3
The Regulatory Game in Mailath and Mester (1994)

so that case 1 is defined by 9.10, which simplifies as

$$r > (2p - 1)\rho. \tag{9.11}$$

If the regulator wants to close the bank, she must incur a fixed cost C. This cost is the same if the bank is closed at time $t = 2$ or if it is liquidated after its failure at time $t = 3$.

With these notations, the game can be represented as in Figure 9.3. The regulator is also assumed to repay fully the depositors of the failed bank (see Mailath and Mester 1994 for an analysis of the alternative objective function).

Consider first case 1. At time 2, the regulator observes either R or S. If the bank is not closed, it will choose the other type of assets, S or R. If the bank plays S, the regulator knows it will choose R next, so if the cost C is not too high $(pC < (1 - p)(1 - r))$, it will be optimal to close the bank. But if the bank plays R first, then the regulator will never close the bank, because the bank will have larger resources at the end of period 3 by remaining open. Hence the solution to the game will always be to play (R, S) for the bank and to leave it open (O) for the regulator. This can be regarded as forbearance, since a risky bank is left open. Regulation is ineffective. If anything, it changes the bank decision from (S, R) to the equivalent one (R, S).

Consider now case 2. Again the regulator will observe R or S, and if the bank is left open it will always play R. The total expected cost of bank closure to the regulator (expected repayment to depositors plus closure cost) is

$$(1 - p) + C.$$

If the bank remains open, the expected cost to the regulator is

$$2(1 - p)^2 + 2(1 - p)p[1 - \rho] + C(1 - p^2).$$

Consequently, the regulator prefers to close the bank if and only if

$$0 > -(1 - p) + 2p(1 - p)\rho + Cp^2, \tag{9.12}$$

that is,

$$C < \frac{(1 - p)(1 - 2p\rho)}{p^2}. \tag{9.13}$$

In case 2 the regulator will close the bank only if condition 9.13 is fulfilled. Any threat to close a bank that has chosen R at time $t = 1$ would be otherwise ineffective because it would be noncredible.

This implies that in case 2, if 9.13 is *not* satisfied (if closure costs are large, if the probability p or ρ is high, or simply if $p > \frac{1}{2}$), the bank will play (R, R) and the regulator will play (O), and again she will be unable to enforce the efficient choice of assets. If instead 9.13 is satisfied, then the bank must choose between playing R and facing liquidation (which gives it an expected profit $p\rho$) or playing S. But then the regulator knows the bank will play R at time 2.

The cost of closure would be C, and the cost to leave the bank open would be $(1 - p)(C + (1 - r))$. Thus, in case 2 the regulator, having observed S, will close the bank if and only if

$$\left(\frac{1 - p}{p}\right)(1 - r) > C. \tag{9.14}$$

If 9.14 is satisfied, then the bank knows it will be closed and therefore will prefer to choose R at time $t = 1$, provided $p\rho > r$.

Figure 9.4 describes for each value of the parameters (p, c) the structure of the solution.

Forbearance need not indicate that a regulator is lenient, but only that she cannot commit ex ante to be tough, either because closure is costly or because she knows that the cost of closing the bank will be lower in the future period (case 1). The threat of closure may be effective for some parameter values

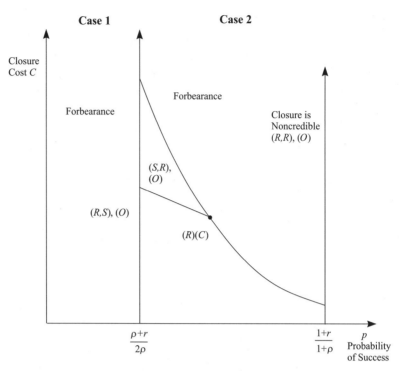

Figure 9.4
The Equilibrium of the Regulatory Game

(satisfying 9.13 but not 9.14) that will induce the bank to switch from (R, R) to (S, R).

9.6.3 Can Banks Be "Too Big to Fail"?

Recent examples of bailouts of large insolvent banks by governments (such as Continental Illinois in the United States) have persuaded the public (and probably also some bank executives) that some banks are "too big to fail." In other words, the economic and political consequences of the failure of a large bank may be so big that governments are forced to bail them out, which obviously generates moral hazard, since the managers of these large banks can thus take excessive risks. Obviously, Central Banks would never admit ex ante that they adhere to this view. They have tried to put forward a less clear-cut policy of "constructive ambiguity," which is supposed to maintain some uncertainty about the criteria actually used for deciding whether to bail out a failing bank. Rochet and Tirole (1996) try to lay some theoretical foundations for this doctrine in a model in which the Central Bank wants to promote peer monitoring among commercial banks. They show that a situation in which a bank is too big to fail can arise only if this peer monitoring takes place after the liquidity shocks have occurred, and also that the size of the failing bank cannot be the main criterion (except maybe for political reasons) for deciding on a bailout. What is more important is the amplitude of its financial connections (essentially through interbank loans) with other banks.

9.7   Complements

Besanko and Thakor (1992) use a spatial differentiation model à la Salop (1979) to model the implications of banking deregulation, and more specifically of relaxing entry barriers. Borrowers and depositors are uniformly located on a circle, and choose the bank that offers them the best combination of interest rate and proximity. Since there is no interbank market in this model, banks must use equity to match the (possible) gap between loans and deposits. It is assumed that banks' shareholders are risk neutral and therefore try to maximize expected profit. Because of transportation costs, banks extract surplus from borrowers and lenders, and bank charters have a positive value.[25] Besanko and Thakor study the decision made by banks at equilibrium. They show that increasing the number of banks implies increasing the deposit rate and decreasing the loan rate, but also decreasing the equity/debt ratio. When a capital requirement is introduced, it has the effect of decreasing interest rates on both deposits and loans, which means that borrowers benefit from the capital requirement, whereas depositors are hurt.

Campbell, Chan, and Marino (1992) formalize the notion of susbstitutability between capital requirements and monitoring in controlling the behavior of bank managers. This control can be exerted directly by regulators or indirectly by giving adequate incentives to stockholders to do so. An interesting aspect of their paper is that they also explicitly study the incentives of depositors to monitor their banks. Kane (1990) has convincingly argued that the adverse incentives of regulators were one of the main explanations for the problems of U.S. depository institutions in the 1980s. In particular, if regulators have long-run career concerns, they have an interest in delaying the disclosure of difficulties encountered by the institutions under their supervision. Campbell, Chan, and Marino consider three versions of their model:

1. Monitoring of banks' assets is impossible, and the regulator uses capital requirements to prevent excessive risk taking by the bank.

2. Monitoring is feasible, and the regulator is benevolent. There is substitutability between bank capital and monitoring effort. At the optimum, capital requirements are less stringent and simultaneously the banks take less risk.

3. Monitoring is still feasible, but the regulator is self-interested. The crucial limitation to the incentive scheme that the depositors have to design for the

monitor is the limited liability of the monitor. In that case, the penalty that can be inflicted on a shirking monitor is limited; this induces distortions on the levels of capital and monitoring that were obtained in version 2. As expected, more capital will be needed and less monitoring effort will be required.

Boot and Greenbaum (1993) analyze the interaction of reputation and financial structure on the risk-taking and monitoring behavior of commercial banks. They distinguish three sources of finance for banks: (1) inside equity; (2) insured deposits; and (3) outside finance, raised on capital markets (such as outside equity, wholesale deposits, or subordinated debt). Since the cost of outside finance is related to the bank's reputation, the bank has an incentive to avoid risk and increase monitoring to improve its reputation, thus improving efficiency. These reputational benefits are therefore a substitute for the rents that banks may obtain from imposed restrictions on entry or competition in the banking sector. Boot and Greenbaum show that these reputational benefits are negligible when the bank invests in safe assets, but important when the bank's assets are risky. Given that efficiency improves with reputational benefits, they see this as a new support for the narrow banking proposal of investing all insured deposits into safe assets, whereas uninsured deposits (and more generally outside finance collected on capital markets) can be invested in risky assets. Thus their results are in line with the general perception that outside (short-term) uninsured finance improves market discipline, an idea that is also developed by Rey and Stiglitz (1994).

Finally, Smith (1984) explores the structure of banking competition in a Diamond-Dybvig environment. He considers several banks that compete for deposits by offering first- and second-period interest rates. When information is perfect, the optimal contract is obtained. But when there are two types of depositors, each of them characterized by a different probability of withdrawing early, under adverse selection a classical inexistence problem first pointed out by Rothschild and Stiglitz (1976) may be faced. (See Chapter 5 for a similar development by Bester 1985.) The inexistence of equilibrium is due to the fact that the equilibrium contracts, either separating or pooling, are destroyed by the existence of positive profit contracts that are addressed specifically to a segment of depositors. Smith interprets this inexistence of equilibrium as an instability of the deposit market (a point that she does not develop explicitly in a dynamic model) and argues that regulating the deposit rate is the appropriate response.

Notes

1. Some of the models analyzed in Chapter 6 have direct implications for macroeconomic policy.

2. One can also argue that some borrowers may be hurt by the failure of their bank, if they have developed close ties with it that allow them to obtain favorable conditions for credit.

3. As already remarked, there is a competing school of thought that sees regulation as the result of opportunistic behavior of politicians, and considers that regulators are captured by the industry they officially supervise in the interest of the general public.

4. Traditional regulatory instruments such as the auctioning of rights (as for television bandwidth) or use of quality standards are not directly relevant to banking regulation.

5. Laffont and Tirole (1993) distinguish (1) *informational constraints*, which limit regulation because the relevant information is held by the firm; (2) *transactional constraints*, which limit the possibility of writing contingent contracts; and (3) *administrative and political constraints*, which impose limits on the scope of regulation as well as on the available instruments.

6. Bhattacharya, Boot, and Thakor (1995) establish a list of the five main unsolved issues:

   a. Are demand deposits important for investors' welfare?

   b. Is the safety net of deposit insurance necessary?

   c. What should be the goal of financial regulation?

   d. What role (if any) should the government play in coping with liquidity shocks?

   e. What portfolio restrictions should be imposed on banks?

7. See Capie, Goodhart, and Schnadt (1994) for a comparison of the objectives assigned to Central Banks in various countries. See also Goodhart 1988.

8. It is interesting to notice, though, that 16 out of the 19 Scottish banks of that time were unlimited liability banks (Calomiris 1993).

9. However, several authors (see, for instance, Rolnick and Weber 1983, 1984) argue that free banking failures and losses were caused not by systematic wildcat banking, but by recessions. See also Glasner (1989) and Selgin (1988).

10. See problem 2.6.2.

11. Other economists adopt similar views. For example, Dowd (1992) challenges the view that fractional reserve banking is inherently liable to runs and crises, and Kaufman (1994) argues that the likelihood of contagion in a properly established system and the size of externalities in case of banking failures are not greater in banking than in other industries.

12. A more recent contribution by Holmström and Tirole (1996) offers a new rationale for the superiority of banks over financial markets in the provision of liquidity insurance. Their model focuses on the liquidity needs of firms. They show that, when moral hazard is present, financial markets are dominated by banks in the provision of liquidity insurance. A variant of this model is used by Rochet and Tirole (1996) to model interbank lending.

13. An interesting account of the present development of securitization is given in Boot (1995): "So far, securitization barely exists in Europe. In the US securitization has spread rapidly in the last decade but almost exclusively for car loans, mortgages and credit-card receivables. The standardization and modest size of these credits allows diversification of idiosyncrating risks upon pooling . . . What does this imply for the larger, more customized and heterogeneous commercial loans? These tend to be more information sensitive. Their quality is therefore more dependent on the rigor of initial screening and subsequent monitoring. Hence, the pooling of commercial loans does less to dissipate their information sensitivity, attenuating the benefits of securitization."

14. Part of this debate has dealt with historical data to establish whether the data support the arguments. White (1984) has shown that the riskiness of the commercial banks in the 1920s did not depend on their being engaged in securities operations. Kroszner and Rajan (1994) examined the conflict of interest argument prior to the Act and obtained no evidence of such behavior by commercial banks. See also Litan (1987).

15. In the United States, deposit insurance schemes were privately developed prior to the creation of the Fed.

16. A put option on a security entitles its owner to sell the security at a future date at a prescribed price. For details, see Ingersoll (1987).

17. The articles discussed in this paragraph and the next have already been presented in detail in Chapter 8, as an application of the portfolio model to banking.

18. The subsequent regulation of market risks (including exchange rate, interest rate, or other off-balance asset risks) is ignored; see the Basle Proposal on Banking Supervision (Dermine 1993).

19. Of course, this question of "rules versus discretion" has a much broader relevance in economics. For example, Fischer (1994) provides an interesting discussion of rules versus discretion in the determination of monetary policy.

20. The main purpose of this article is to study whether the two main functions of Central Banks, namely monetary policy and banking supervision, should be separately provided by distinct agencies.

21. This discussion will not describe exhaustively all the procedures that can be used for solving banks' failures. The reader interested in a more complete approach to these institutional aspects is referred to Bovenzi and Muldoon (1990).

22. This is in opposition to Bagehot's view of Central Banking (see Section 7.7).

23. Another way to see this is to compare L to the continuation value for the Central Bank:

$$V_{CB} = 1 - E[l|u].$$

24. To be precise, this means a world in which a perfect commitment of the regulator is possible.

25. Notice, though, that even with free entry, this charter value would have to be positive to compensate for entry costs.

References

Acharya, S., and J. F. Dreyfus. 1988. Optimal bank reorganization policies and the pricing of federal deposit insurance. *Journal of Finance* 44(5): 1313–34.

Aghion, P., and P. Bolton. 1992. An incomplete contract approach to financial contracting. *Review of Economic Studies* 59: 473–94.

Akerlof, G. 1970. The market for lemons: Quality uncertainty and the market mechanism. *Quarterly Journal of Economics* 84(3):488–500.

Bensaid, B., H. Pagès, and J. C. Rochet. 1993. Efficient regulation of banks' solvency. IDEI, Toulouse. Mimeograph.

Benston, G., R. Eisenbeis, P. Horvitz, E. Kane, and G. Kaufman. 1986. *Perspectives on safe and sound banking, past, present and future.* Cambridge: MIT Press.

Bernanke, F., and M. Gertler. 1990. Financial fragility and economic performance. *Quarterly Journal of Economics* 105(1): 87–114.

Besanko, D., and A. V. Thakor. 1992. Banking deregulation: Allocational consequences of relaxing entry barriers. *Journal of Banking and Finance* 16:909–32.

Bester, H. 1985. Screening vs rationing in credit markets with imperfect information. *American Economic Review* 75(4):850–55.

Bhattacharya, S., A. Boot, and A. Thakor. 1995. The economics of bank regulation. Working paper no. 516, CEMFI, Madrid.

Bhattacharya, S., and A. Thakor. 1993. Contemporary banking theory. *Journal of Financial Intermediation* 3:2–50.

Black, F. 1975. Bank funds management in an efficient market. *Journal of Financial Economics* 2:323–39.

Black, F., and M. Scholes. 1973. The pricing of options and corporate liabilities. *Journal of Political Economy* 81:637–59.

Blum, J., and M. Hellwig. 1995. The macroeconomic implications of capital adequacy requirements for banks. *European Economic Review* 39(3–4):739–49.

Bond, E., and K. Crocker. 1993. Bank capitalization, deposit insurance, and risk categorization. *Journal of Risk and Insurance* 60(3):547–69.

Boot, A. 1995. Challenges to competitive banking. Discussion paper, University of Amsterdam.

Boot, A., and S. Greenbaum. 1993. Bank regulation, reputation, and rents: Theory and policy implications. In *Capital markets and financial intermediation,* edited by C. Mayer and X. Vives. Cambridge: Cambridge University Press.

Boot, A., and A. Thakor. 1993. Self-interested bank regulation. *American Economic Review* 83(2):206–12.

Bovenzi, J. F., and M. E. Muldoon. 1990. Failure-resolution methods and policy considerations. *FDIC Banking Review* 3(1):1–11.

Bryant, J. 1980. A model of reserves, bank runs, and deposit insurance. *Journal of Banking and Finance* 4:335–44.

Buser, S., A. Chen, and E. Kane. 1981. Federal deposit insurance, regulatory policy and optimal bank capital. *Journal of Finance* 36:51–60.

Calomiris, C. 1993. Regulation, industrial structure, and instability in US banking: An historical perspective. In *Structural change in banking,* edited by M. Klausner and L. White. New York: New York University.

Calomiris, C., and C. Kahn. 1996. The efficiency of self-regulated payment systems: Learning from the Suffolk system. *Journal of Money, Credit, and Banking* 28(4):766–97.

Campbell, T. S., Y. S. Chan, and A. M. Marino. 1992. An incentive-based theory of bank regulation. *Journal of Financial Intermediation* 2:255–76.

Capie, F., C. Goodhart, and N. Schnadt. 1994. The development of central banking. In *The future of central banking, the Tercentenary Symposium of the Bank of England,* edited by F. Capie, C. Goodhart, S. Fischer, and N. Schnadt. Cambridge: Cambridge University Press.

Cerasi, V., and S. Daltung. 1994. The optimal size of a bank: Costs and benefits of diversification. Discussion paper, Financial Markets Group, London School of Economics.

Chan, Y. S., S. I. Greenbaum, and A. V. Thakor. 1992. Is fairly priced deposit insurance possible? *Journal of Finance* 47:227–45.

Crouhy, M., and D. Galai. 1986. An economic assessment of capital requirements in the banking industry. *Journal of Banking and Finance* 10:231–41.

————. 1991. A contingent claim analysis of a regulated depository institution. *Journal of Banking and Finance* 15:73–90.

Dermine, J. 1993. The evaluation of interest rate risk: Some warnings about the Basle proposal. Working paper, no. 93/40/Fin, INSEAD, Fontainbleau.

Dewatripont, M., and J. Tirole. 1993. Efficient governance structure: Implications for banking regulation. In *Capital markets and financial intermediation,* edited by C. Mayer and X. Vives. Cambridge: Cambridge University Press.

————. 1994. *The prudential regulation of banks.* Cambridge, Mass.: MIT Press.

Diamond, D. 1984. Financial intermediation and delegated monitoring. *Review of Economic Studies* 51(3):393–414.

Diamond, D., and P. Dybvig. 1983. Bank runs, deposit insurance, and liquidity. *Journal of Political Economy* 91(3):401–19.

Dowd, K. 1992. The experience of free banking. London: Routledge.

Fama, E. 1980. Banking in the theory of finance. *Journal of Monetary Economics* 6(1):39–57.

————. 1985. What's different about banks? *Journal of Monetary Economics* 15:29–40.

Fischer, S. 1994. Modern central banking. In *The future of central banking, the Tercentenary Symposium of the Bank of England,* edited by F. Capie, C. Goodhart, S. Fischer, and N. Schnadt. Cambridge: Cambridge University Press.

Freixas, X., and E. Gabillon. 1996. Optimal regulation of a fully insured deposit banking system. Finance and Banking Discussion Paper Series no. 16, and Economics Working Papers Series no. 175, Universitat Pompeu Fabra, Barcelona.

Freixas, X., and J. C. Rochet. 1995. Fairly priced deposit insurance: Is it possible? Yes. Is it desirable? No. Finance and banking discussion paper, no. 4, Universitat Pompeu Fabra, Barcelona.

Friedman, M. 1960. A program for monetary stability. New York: Fordham University Press.

Gale, D., and M. Hellwig. 1985. Incentive compatible debt contracts: The one-period problem. *Review of Economic Studies* L11:647–63.

Gennote, G., and D. Pyle. 1991. Capital controls and bank risk. *Journal of Banking and Finance* 15(4-5):805–24.

Giammarino, R. M., T. R. Lewis, and D. Sappington. 1993. An incentive approach to banking regulation. *The Journal of Finance* 48:1523–42.

Glasner, D. 1989. *Free banking and monetary reform.* Cambridge: Cambridge University Press.

Goodhart, C. 1987. Why do banks need a central bank? *Oxford Economic Papers* 39:75–89.

———. 1988. *The evolution of central banks.* Cambridge: Cambridge University Press.

Goodhart, C., and D. Schoenmaker. 1993. Institutional separation between supervisory and monetary agencies. In *Prudential Regulation, Supervision and Monetary Policy,* edited by F. Bruni. Milano: Universita Bocconi.

Gorton, G. 1993. Bank regulation, reputation and rents: Theory and policy implications: Discussion. In *Capital markets and financial intermediation,* edited by C. Mayer and X. Vives. Cambridge: Cambridge University Press.

Gorton, G., and G. Pennacchi. 1993. Money market funds and finance companies: Are they the banks of the future? In *Structural change in banking,* edited by M. Klausner and L. White. New York: New York University.

Hayek, F. 1978. *The denationalisation of money.* London: Institute for Economic Affairs.

Holmström, B., and J. Tirole. 1996. Modelling aggregate liquidity. *American Economic Review, Papers and Proceedings* 86(2):187–91.

Hotelling, H. 1929. Stability in competition. *Economic Journal* 39:41–5.

Ingersoll, J. E., Jr. 1987. *Theory of financial decision making.* Totowa, N.J.: Rowan and Littlefield.

Jensen, M., and W. R. Meckling. 1976. Theory of the firm, managerial behaviour, agency costs and ownership structure. *Journal of Financial Economics* 3:305–60.

John, K., T. John, and A. Saunders. 1994. *Journal of Banking and Finance* 18(2):307–23.

Kahane, Y. 1977. Capital adequacy and the regulation of financial intermediaries. *Journal of Banking and Finance* 1:207–18.

Kane, E. 1990. Principal agent problems in S&L salvage. *Journal of Finance* 45(3):755–64.

Kareken, J. H. 1986. Federal bank regulatory policy: A description and some observations. *Journal of Business* 59:3–48.

Kareken, J. H., and N. Wallace. 1978. Deposit insurance and bank regulation: A partial equilibrium exposition. *Journal of Business* 51:413–38.

Kaufman, G. G. 1994. Bank contagion: A review of the theory and the evidence. *Journal of Financial Services Research* 8(2):123–50.

Kay, J., and J. Vickers. 1988. Regulatory reform in Britain. *Economic Policy* 7:286–343.

Keeley, M. C., and F. T. Furlong. 1990. A reexamination of mean-variance analysis of bank capital regulation. *Journal of Banking and Finance* 14:69–84.

Kerfriden, C., and J. C. Rochet. 1993. Actuarial pricing of deposit insurance. *Geneva Papers on Risk and Insurance Theory* 18(2):111–30.

Kim, D., and A. M. Santomero. 1988. Risk in banking and capital regulation. *Journal of Finance* 43:1219–33.

Klausner, M., and L. White. 1993. Bank regulatory reform and bank structure. In *Structural change in banking,* edited by M. Klausner and L. White. New York: New York University.

Koehn, M., and A. Santomero. 1980. Regulation of bank capital and portfolio risk. *Journal of Finance* 35:1235–44.

Kroszner, R. S., and G. R. Rajan. 1994. Is the Glass-Steagall Act justified? A study of the US Experience with universal banking before 1933. *American Economic Review* 84(4):810–32.

Laffont, J. J., and J. Tirole. 1986. Using cost observations to regulate firms. *Journal of Political Economy* 94:614–41.

———. 1993. *A theory of incentives in procurement and regulation.* Cambridge: MIT Press.

Litan, R. E. 1987. *What should banks do?* Washington, D.C.: The Brookings Institution.

Mailath, G., and L. Mester. 1994. A positive analysis of bank closure. *Journal of Financial Intermediation* 3(3):272–99.

Marcus, A., and I. Shaked. 1984. The valuation of the FDIC deposit insurance using option-pricing estimates. *Journal of Money, Credit and Banking* 16:446–60.

Matutes, C., and X. Vives. 1996a. Competition for deposits, fragility, and insurance. *Journal of Financial Intermediation* 5(2):184–216.

———. 1996b. Imperfect competition, risk taking, and regulation in banking. Institut d'Anàlisi Economica, CSIC, Universitat Autonoma de Barcelona. Mimeograph.

McCullough, H. 1981. Interest rate risk and capital adequacy for traditional banks and financial intermediaries. In *Risk and capital adequacy in commercial banks,* edited by S.J. Maisel. Chicago: University of Chicago Press.

Merton, R. 1977. An analytic derivation of the cost of deposit insurance and loan guarantees. *Journal of Banking and Finance* 1:3–11.

———. 1978. On the cost of deposit insurance when there are surveillance costs. *Journal of Business* 51:439–52.

Mishkin, F. 1992. *The economics of money, banking and financial markets.* London: Scott, Foresman.

Mullins, H., and D. Pyle. 1991. Risk based bank capital. University of California, Berkeley. Mimeograph.

Nakamura, C. 1993. Commercial bank information implications for the structure of banking. In *Structure change in banking,* edited by M. Klausner and L. White. New York: New York University.

Pennacchi, G. 1987. Alternative forms of deposit insurance, pricing and bank incentive issues. *Journal of Banking and Finance* 11:291–312.

Rajan, R. 1992. Insiders and outsiders: The choice between informed and arm's-length debt. *Journal of Finance* 47(4):1367–400.

Repullo, R. 1993. Who should decide on bank closures? An incomplete contract model. Working paper, CEMFI, Madrid.

Rey, P., and J. Stiglitz. 1994. Short-term contracts as a monitoring device. Discussion paper no. 9446, INSEE, Paris.

Rochet, J. C. 1992a. Capital requirements and the behaviour of commercial banks. *European Economic Review* 36:1137–78.

———. 1992b. Towards a theory of optimal banking regulation. *Cahiers Economiques et Monétaires de la Banque de France* 40:275–84.

Rochet, J. C., and J. Tirole. 1996. Interbank lending and systemic risk. *Journal of Money, Credit and Banking* 28(4):733–62.

Rolnick, A., and W. Weber. 1983. New evidence on the free banking era. *American Economic Review* 73:1080–91.

———. 1984. The causes of free bank failures. *Journal of Monetary Economics* 14:267–91.

Ronn, E. I., and A. K. Verma. 1986. Pricing risk-adjusted deposit insurance: An option-based model. *Journal of Finance* 41:871–95.

Rothschild, M., and J. Stiglitz. 1976. Equilibrium in competitive insurance markets: An essay on the economics of imperfect informations. *Quarterly Journal of Economics* 90(4):630–49.

Salop, S. 1979. Monopolistic competition with outside goods. *Bell Journal of Economics* 10(1): 141–56.

Sargent, T., and N. Wallace. 1982. The real bills doctrine vs the quantity theory: A reconsideration. *Journal of Political Economy* 90:1212–36.

Selgin, G. 1988. *The theory of free banking.* Totowa, N.J.: Rowan and Littlefield.

Smith, V. 1984. *The rationale of central banking and the free banking alternative.* Indianapolis: Liberty Press.

Suarez, J. 1993a. Banking regulation in an equilibrium model. Discussion paper no. 9308, CEMFI, Madrid.

———. 1993b. Closure rules, market power and risk-taking in a dynamic model of bank behaviour. Discussion paper, Universidad Carlos III, Madrid.

Tirole, J. 1994. On banking and intermediation. *European Economic Review* 38(3–4):469–87.

Tobin, J. 1986. Financial innovation and deregulation in perspective. In *Financial innovation and monetary policy: Asia and the West Proceedings of the Second International Conference held by the Institute for Monetary and Economic Studies of the Bank of Japan,* edited by Y. Suzuki and H. Yomo. Tokyo: University of Tokyo Press. Distributed by Columbia University Press, New York.

Townsend, R. 1979. Optimal contracts and competitive markets with costly state verification. *Journal of Economic Theory* 21:265–93.

White, L. 1984. *Free banking in Britain: Theory, experience and debate 1800–1845.* Cambridge: Cambridge University Press.

Williamson, S. 1992. Pricing free bank notes. Discussion paper, Wharton School, Philadelphia.

Index